Slavery and the Democratic Conscience

EARLY AMERICAN STUDIES

Series editors:
Daniel K. Richter, Kathleen M. Brown,
Max Cavitch, and David Waldstreicher

Exploring neglected aspects of our colonial,
revolutionary, and early national history and culture,
Early American Studies reinterprets familiar themes
and events in fresh ways. Interdisciplinary in character,
and with a special emphasis on the period from about
1600 to 1850, the series is published in partnership with
the McNeil Center for Early American Studies.

A complete list of books in the series
is available from the publisher.

SLAVERY
AND THE
DEMOCRATIC
CONSCIENCE

Political Life in Jeffersonian America

Padraig Riley

PENN

UNIVERSITY OF PENNSYLVANIA PRESS

PHILADELPHIA

Published by
University of Pennsylvania Press
Philadelphia, Pennsylvania 19104-4112
www.upenn.edu/pennpress

Printed in the United States of America on acid-free paper
1 3 5 7 9 10 8 6 4 2

Library of Congress Cataloging-in-Publication Data
Riley, Padraig, author.
Slavery and the democratic conscience : political life in
Jeffersonian America / Padraig Riley.
    pages   cm — (Early American studies)
    Includes bibliographical references and index.
ISBN 978-0-8122-4749-7 (alk. paper)
    1. Slavery—Political aspects—United States—History. 2.
Republican Party (U.S. : 1792–1828)—History. 3. Federal Party
(U.S.)—History. 4. Political parties—United States—History. 5.
United States—Politics and government—1789–1809. 6. United
States—Politics and government—1809–1817. 7. United States—
Politics and government—1817–1825. 8. Jefferson, Thomas, 1743–
1826. I. Title. II. Series: Early American studies.
E446.R55   2016
306.3'620973—dc23   2015017224

To Boo

CONTENTS

North of Jefferson

The Problem

Historians and the wider public continue to be fascinated by Thomas Jefferson, who seems to embody a fundamental American contradiction. An advocate of republican government, principal author of the Declaration of Independence, and given at times to ideological musings that bordered on the anarchic, Jefferson also owned hundreds of slaves, had a long-term affair with his bondwoman Sally Hemings, and, like most slaveholders, considered the birth of slave children "an addition to capital."[1] Driven by hagiography, criticism, and, more often than not, the passion engendered by his many contradictions, scholars continue to study Jefferson's life and voluminous correspondence, hoping to discover some fundamental truth about the American political order, about the vexed relationship between liberty, power, and race that runs throughout the history of the United States.

But for all the attention devoted to Thomas Jefferson, there has been surprisingly less analysis of the problem of slavery within the Democratic-Republican party, the political coalition that elected Jefferson president of the United States in 1800. Jeffersonian democracy, far more so than Jefferson's personality, shaped the long-term relationship between freedom and slavery in American history. As a political movement, it brought together northerners and southerners, gentry elites and men on the rise, evangelicals and freethinkers, cosmopolitans and nationalists, and, most crucially of all, democrats and slaveholders. The Democratic-Republican coalition united the vanguard of democratization in the northern states and the most adamant representatives of southern mastery. Men who believed the United States should be a beacon of democracy for a world enslaved by aristocratic power became the political allies of men who believed the United States was obliged to protect a master's right to enslave. This diverse composition was torn at times by sectional and ideological conflict, but it consistently found unity in American nationalism and the political aspirations of white men. And that unity proved essential to the preservation of slavery in a democratizing polity.

This book studies a diverse set of white men who helped build Jeffersonian democracy in the North from the late 1790s to the early 1820s. As a group, these northerners present a very different intellectual problem from that posed by a slaveholder who believed in universal human freedom yet could not free his slaves. They force us to think about how slavery was tolerated not by the minority of masters in the early American electorate, but by the majority of non-slaveholders, whose relationships to slavery were often far less direct. To trace these relationships is to examine the pervasiveness of slavery, a complex institution that affected masters, non-slaveholders, and slaves alike. Masters and slaves understood slavery as governed first and foremost by individual control and domination; such power was necessary to maintain property rights in slaves. But the masters themselves were governed by a national polity in which non-slaveholders predominated. Slavery thus required some degree of toleration, if not consent, by non-slaveholders. Beyond the individualized dominion of masters, slavery required individual acts of accommodation on the part of the masterless majority, daily decisions to accept life in the midst of the extreme authority necessary to enslave. Without such accommodation, the slaveholding republic of the United States could not have survived as long as it did.[2]

And yet such accommodation could never be taken for granted, for the very ideological commitments that brought Jeffersonians together threatened to drive them apart. This was especially true at the national level, despite the protections of slaveholder property rights and power in the U.S. Constitution. Had the Democratic-Republican coalition simply been a racial compact between white men, all of whom agreed that perpetuating slavery served their political, social, and economic interests, it would have been far more reliable from the perspective of slaveholders. Instead, ties to slavery were often more subtle, formed out of universalist ideals and aspirations as much as narrow prejudice and self-interest. Northerners embraced the Democratic-Republican coalition for two primary and often intertwined reasons: to advance democracy and build the American nation-state. Throughout the early republic, democracy and nationalism bound whites to a slave society, as northern Republicans looked to southern masters like Jefferson to lead them to political freedom. This ideological encounter with slavery inevitably warped democratic ideals. Accommodation of slaveholder power subdued antislavery argument and promoted disregard for African Americans as legitimate political subjects. Institutional and ideological pressures to reconcile with Jeffersonian slaveholders constrained democratic universalism, as race and national belonging began to take precedence over more cosmopolitan ethical and political commitments.

But the democratic reconciliation with slavery always remained uneasy. Northern Republicans frequently challenged southern power at the national level, and they occasionally made universalist claims in defense of free African Americans, even as the northern polity became more restricted by race. Slaveholders, meanwhile, consistently demanded autonomous control over the regulation of slavery. These demands were produced by the nature of slaveholder power, not simply by a general desire to limit the power of the new federal government over the states. And they were rarely acceded to by all northerners. In practical terms, the accord between slavery and American democracy was clearly successful, as both institutions expanded dramatically throughout the early national period. But in ideological terms, it remained tenuous, because slaveholder power could never fully be incorporated into a democratic ethos.

This book reexamines the rise of early national democratic ideology in the context of slavery, tracing northern responses to slaveholder power as they shifted back and forth between accommodation and dissent. While I include some figures from the northern political elite, relative equals to southern gentry like Jefferson, the majority of characters in this book come from the "middling" ranks of early national American society—tradesmen and farmers who rose to political prominence through the Republican coalition, newspaper editors, a Baptist minister, and a number of European immigrants and democratic radicals.[3] These white men were the principal agents and beneficiaries of Jeffersonian democracy, and their words and actions constitute the main sources used in this book.[4]

The predominance of white men in the narrative reflects their predominance in the Democratic-Republican coalition and in the United States government, but it also obscures the more complex world of early national politics. As a number of historians have shown, women played an active role in early national political life. They also engaged in wider ideological debates over slavery in civil society. Likewise, free African-Americans had an important impact on northern politics and particularly on the politics of slavery, even in places where they were barred from the polls by various mechanisms.

Yet formal democratic politics—voting and office-holding—were confined to
men and, over time, to white men especially. While there are good studies
that document how race and gender shaped the rise of American democracy,
this book focuses instead on the impact of slavery which, as I argue throughout, had a determinative influence on the politics of race in the northern
states.[5] Taking white male democrats on their own terms, through the political institutions and political culture that they developed, I focus my analysis
on how their responses to slavery shaped democracy in the North and at the
national level.

I focus primarily on ideology and political argument in Congress, in
newspapers and pamphlets, and in political celebrations. But I also pay close
attention to the individual political actors whose thoughts and words com-
pose the primary evidence in this study, in order to capture the subjective
dimension of early national political life. Jeffersonians believed that to be a
democrat was to think for oneself: to form independent political opinions
and exercise autonomous judgment. Mobilizing individuals was therefore a
task not for customary authorities but for self-conscious political actors, men
who employed ideology to build connections between individual subjects
and partisan and state institutions. Opponents sometimes castigated Jeffersonian ideologues as schemers with purely instrumental ends, but to true believers, political argument had a higher purpose—to liberate men from
arbitrary rule so that they could think and vote on their own behalf. Democracy thus depended on individual conscience as much as political
institutions.

What was true for democracy was true for slavery, since these two institutions were inseparable in the Democratic-Republican party and in Jeffersonian America. Slavery affected democratic thought and practice from the
outset, and it posed an ideological problem that democratic subjects had to
address. Contending with slavery was an almost daily act for anyone who
read the main Jeffersonian paper from Washington, the *National Intelligencer*,
as fugitive advertisements and slave sales consistently lined its pages. It was
an even more pressing issue for northerners who traveled to Washington
after 1800, since slavery was a viable institution in the new national capital
and southern slaveholders predominated in the federal government. This
book emphasizes that all of these individual encounters with slavery mattered deeply to the development of democratic politics and political culture
in the United States. In a far more pervasive and deeper way than Jefferson's
by turns agonized and racist musings in *Notes on the State of Virginia*, it was

countless individual acts of conscience—decisions to accept, ignore, challenge, and attack slavery—that defined the relationship between bondage and freedom in the early United States.

That relationship, this book argues, was ultimately ambivalent. On the one hand, northern democrats made significant concessions to slavery, both ideological and institutional. That allowed slaveholders considerable freedom under the United States government, which they used to protect and expand human bondage. On the other hand, when faced with blunt manifestations of slaveholder power, northern Jeffersonians tended to oppose their southern colleagues. At times, they also defended the rights of free African Americans. In practical terms, this dialectic between accommodation and conflict was decided in favor of slaveholders, who were by any measure more powerful and more secure in the 1820s than they were in the 1790s. Taking the long view, however, Jeffersonian democracy did reveal a potential threat to the institution of slavery: the possibility that a majority of American citizens would refuse to tolerate the coercion necessary to maintain it. That threat existed not because the founding documents or fathers of the United States somehow possessed an inherent antislavery idealism, but because enslaved people, free blacks, abolitionists, slaveholders, and nonslaveholding whites, in various ways and with various motives, forced the problem of slavery into national political life.[6] By the end of the Jeffersonian period, slaveholders had secured considerable power in the national government, while the rise of white supremacy and racial exclusion in the North constrained abolitionism and free African American agency. On the other hand, by 1820 slaveholding had become an irrepressible problem in national democratic politics. That would not change until slavery was abolished.

Historiography

Analyzing the democratic relationship to slavery requires paying attention to local, national, and transatlantic political developments, much as Jeffersonians themselves did in the newspapers that were the foundation of the early national public sphere. There are good, detailed studies of Jeffersonian democracy in the North, but their state level or regional focus entails a lack of attention to slavery, which began to decline across the northern states in the early nineteenth century. Until quite recently, national studies of early American democracy have either overlooked slavery or taken the northern United

States as indicative of a wider American reality. Thus the constant caveat, "in the North at least," in the work of Gordon Wood, who has done the most to popularize a vision of early national politics built around the contest between deference and democracy. Collectively, these versions of early national politics imply that slavery never became a substantive problem for the Republican coalition and that it therefore had little bearing on the formative years of democratic ideology and political culture.[7]

In many ways, this is an argument Jefferson would have endorsed. He famously called the Missouri Crisis of 1819–1821 a "fire bell in the night," implying that the early national period had been free from serious conflict over slavery before then. But historians have long known this was not the case. Antislavery historians writing before and after the Civil War stressed the political impact of the "slave power" from the Constitution onward. Slavery and sectional difference were less present but still potent in Henry Adams's brilliant synthesis of the early republic, published in the 1880s. In the early twentieth century, however, the influential scholarship of Charles Beard established a new narrative for the early republic. Beard insisted that Jeffersonian democracy was driven by conflict between agrarian and financial interests, much along the lines he had laid out in his *Economic Interpretation of the Constitution of the United States.* Identifying a shared hostility to finance capital between southern slaveholders and northern farmers, Beard minimized the impact of slavery on early national politics.[8] The contemporaneous reinterpretation of the Civil War and Reconstruction by William Dunning and his students likewise suppressed an earlier antislavery historiography. These two traditions merged in the work of popular historian, Democratic partisan, and Indiana racist Claude G. Bowers, who wrote best-selling narratives of the early republic, Jacksonian democracy and "the tragic era" of Reconstruction.[9]

African American historians and intellectuals contested these stories of the United States, which left little room for black people, past or present, and suppressed the influence of slavery on national political life. W. E. B. Du Bois's Harvard dissertation on the international slave trade documented the influence of slavery on domestic politics and foreign policy, while his *Black Reconstruction in America* opposed the mainstream interpretations of the Dunning school.[10] Finally, in the mid-twentieth century, following in the wake of new histories of slavery by John Hope Franklin, Kenneth Stampp, and others, scholars began to bring the problem of slavery back into studies of the early republic. Inspired by abolitionist historians and the Civil Rights movement, Staughton Lynd criticized Beard and insisted on the political importance of slavery in a series of essays in the 1960s. In the 1970s, David Brion Davis and political scientist Donald Robinson wrote detailed histories of slavery as an ideological and political problem after the American Revolution. In the late 1980s, Robin Blackburn's comparative work offered a hemispheric context for thinking about the relationship between the rise of a democratic nation-state and the expansion of slavery in the early United States.[11] Yet these books did not have a major impact on early American political history as a whole, which is somewhat surprising given the intellectual power of Davis's and Blackburn's work. Political historians instead focused on the problem of "republicanism," rather than slavery, for much of the 1970s and 1980s.[12] Throughout the twentieth century, dominant historical interpretations of early national political life have treated slavery as a marginal institution.

This state of affairs now seems to have changed, perhaps in a permanent way. In recent years, a large number of historians have returned to the political history of slavery and abolition in the early national period. Institutional historians have examined slavery's deep impact on the structures of American governance from the Revolution to the early republic;[13] historians of political culture have shown the intricate ways slavery affected early American political ideology;[14] and political historians and historians of abolitionism have documented intense debate over slavery in the early republic, in conflicts over territorial expansion, fugitive slaves, antislavery petitions to the Congress, diplomacy with Saint-Domingue, and the treatment of free African Americans in the North.[15] The intensity of early national conflict did not match the Missouri debates, or the subsequent antebellum struggle over slavery. But in many ways it helped set the terms for those later debates, not least by shaping a democratic political order in which slavery was deeply entrenched.

Yet the problem of slavery for Jeffersonian democracy remains relatively unexplored. Studies of the Federalist party, the minority opposition after 1800, have collectively drawn a subtle portrait of a northern and conservative antislavery voice that was especially strong in New England.[16] In contrast, analysis of the northern Jeffersonian relationship to slavery tends to be less complex, with historians generally taking one of two positions: either Jeffersonians opposed slavery on democratic grounds, or else they accepted slavery as the price of a white man's democracy, anticipating the racialized republic of the Jacksonian period.[17] Neither position captures the true dilemma of Jeffersonian politics, which tied slavery to democracy in a number of far more intricate ways, relying as much on egalitarian idealism as on racial exclusion. The reconciliation between democratization and enslavement was uneasy and never straightforward, but in pragmatic terms it was quite successful. Slavery and democracy expanded together, bound in an alliance that proved difficult to untangle.

Narrative

The Democratic-Republican coalition took form in the 1790s in order to oppose the Federalist coalition that had emerged under the presidency of George Washington. Ideological divisions over the nature and power of the new federal government were already present in the First Congress, which sat in New York, and escalated when the national capital moved to Philadelphia in 1790. The diplomatic and ideological repercussions of the French Revolution further heightened partisan conflict, and by the mid-1790s Republicans and Federalists were fighting each other from Georgia to Massachusetts and had begun to coordinate local and national struggles. Republicans were stronger in the South than in the North in the 1790s, as the presidential election of 1796 demonstrated: Jefferson won all the southern states save Maryland and Delaware. But during the Adams administration, the Republican opposition gained power in the North in response to the 1798 Alien and Sedition Acts, which sought to suppress democratic agitators in the North and exclude immigrant radicals from the United States. In this predominantly northern struggle, southern Republicans proved key allies. In the election of 1800, the bisectional Democratic-Republican coalition recorded one of the signal triumphs in American political history. Without the organization of the mass democratic parties of the antebellum period, Republicans swept Federalists from office in the presidency and in both houses of Congress, inaugurating two decades of national dominance by Jeffersonian democracy.

The "Revolution of 1800" (as Jefferson called it) is often represented as a victory for democracy, which it no doubt was for many Republican partisans. It was also a victory for slaveholders. In the southern states, the Republicans were already the dominant party in 1800, and southern Federalism, outside Maryland and Delaware, had all but collapsed by Jefferson's second term. The three-fifths clause in the U.S. Constitution, which gave additional electoral weight to the South based on the slave population, augmented the national power of southern Republicans. Southern preponderance was most obvious in the fact that Republicans elected Virginia slaveholders to the presidency for six terms in a row: Thomas Jefferson (1801–1808), James Madison (1809–1816), and James Monroe (1817–1824). Beyond the presidency, slaveholders held sway in the early Jeffersonian Congresses, where they defended the rights of masters to govern their slaves, and the institution of slavery, as they saw fit. A coalition that promoted democracy in the North also protected the prerogatives of slaveholders in the South.

The heyday of Jeffersonian democracy coincided with a pivotal period in the history of American slavery. From the 1790s to the 1820s, masters began to aggressively push the peculiar institution to the West, as they exploited enslaved labor to produce short-staple cotton for the British market. The slave population of the South surged from roughly 700,000 to 1.5 million between 1790 and 1820, and the United States entered the antebellum period poised to become the dominant slaveholding society in the Western Hemisphere. Jeffersonians played a critical role in this process. Aggressive foreign and military policies helped cement territorial sovereignty over the new states of Mississippi, Alabama, and Louisiana. The defense of slaveholder property rights by southern Jeffersonians facilitated the rise of a massive domestic trade in enslaved people after 1808. By 1820, Republican victories at the state and national levels had confirmed the triumph of democracy for white men in the North. Meanwhile, slaveholder power in the Republican coalition, in conjunction with southwestern expansion, cotton production, and the domestic slave trade, ensured the dominance of slavery in the antebellum South.[18]

This book integrates the two main developments of Jeffersonian America by trying to understand how white northerners, in the midst of their democratic transformation, came to terms with the growing power of slavery. The northern Republican response to slavery varied from individual to individual and, in many cases, an individual's response to slavery varied across time, shifting from opposition to accommodation—and then, in more cases than one, back to opposition. The strength of Jeffersonian political culture lay less in its ability to impose any one uniform response to the problem of slavery than in its ability to contain contradictory sentiments about the institution in a wider culture of democratic nationalism.

Jeffersonian democracy thus followed a crooked path, but not a haphazard one. The political intensity of the 1790s created powerful pressures and incentives for northerners to join southern masters in the fight against

Federalism, and that entailed some accommodation of slaveholder power.
The first two chapters explore this process in two different locations, Federalist New England and Jeffersonian Philadelphia, where negotiating the problem of slavery was an inevitable condition of democratic politics.

In New England, Federalists contested Republican claims to be persecuted democrats by arguing that Jeffersonian political power depended directly on the institution of slavery. This forced Republicans to publicly come
to terms with their ties to the South. They did so by insisting on their own
political oppression, aggrandized throughout the Jeffersonian press. The experience of northern freedom served as collateral in an ideological alliance
that brought democracy to New England while entrenching slavery in the
South.

Similar transactions defined the nature of Jeffersonian democracy in Philadelphia, but the terrain was very different. Philadelphia, was in many ways
the most heterogeneous and egalitarian place in the early United States, home
to a large free black community, an influential antislavery organization, and
articulate immigrant radicals who imported European struggles against aristocracy into the United States. Philadelphia was a crossroads where democracy collided with slavery and cosmopolitanism collided with race. Chapter 2
examines these intersections from the perspective of three Irish American
immigrants, John Binns, Thomas Branagan, and William Duane. All three believed that America should serve, as Tom Paine had argued, as an "asylum of
freedom" and an exemplar of democratic rule. They reframed personal and
transatlantic struggles for liberation in terms of American nationalism, lending the illusion of universality to the recently invented United States. At the
same time, all three men came to some sort of accommodation with slavery, a
coercive institution bent on denying asylum to enslaved people.

In New England and Pennsylvania, the rise of the Republican coalition
demanded some accommodation of slavery. Jeffersonian success, however,
also produced new sources of sectional discord. Chapters 3 and 4 examine
sectional conflicts over slavery in the Republican coalition, which often
turned on the relationship between slaveholder power and democratic governance. The relative ideological accord between slavery and democracy developed by white men in the North repeatedly broke down when it came to the
institutional politics of slavery at the national level.

As Chapter 3 demonstrates, from the 1790s onward, conflict over slavery
was no longer resolved by brokering between regional elites. Instead, slavery
was entangled in partisan struggles between Federalists and Republicans,

and thus in the national politics of democracy. When northern Jeffersonians came to Washington after 1800, they encountered some of the most powerful slaveholders in the nation, who were often far more adamant in the defense of slavery than Thomas Jefferson. On issue after issue, from fugitive slave rendition, to the end of the international slave trade, to the expansion of slavery to the West, southerners confronted northern Republicans and fought to control slavery on their own terms. Effectively, they demanded that democracy check its advance where slavery was concerned. On that question, slaveholders alone should rule. As northern Republicans repeatedly encountered the antidemocratic posture of slaveholders, they turned to dissidence, disillusion, and in some cases revocation of the Jeffersonian alliance.

Slavery was hardly the only issue that fueled northern discontent with the Democratic-Republican coalition. Republican attempts to respond to the diplomatic crises of the Napoleonic wars by restricting American commerce alienated many men in the North, catalyzing sectionalism and regional envy of southern power. Once northerners began to think in sectional terms, it was difficult to prevent them from attacking the political power of slavery in the federal government. Chapter 4 outlines the emergence of northern sectionalist thought in the Democratic-Republican coalition, from the early Jeffersonian years to the onset of the War of 1812. Tracing debates over Jeffersonian foreign policy and northern resentment of Virginia rule, the chapter concludes with an analysis of the Clintonian campaigns of 1808 and 1812, when George and then DeWitt Clinton challenged James Madison for the presidency. In 1812, DeWitt Clinton came close to defeating Madison and undoing Virginia's hold on the presidency, while some of Clinton's supporters broke with the ideological structure of Jeffersonian democracy created in the 1790s.

Yet in the midst of internal dissent and renewed Federalist attacks, Jeffersonian democracy demonstrated a remarkable resilience. The Democratic-Republican coalition's true strength became apparent in the critical year of 1812. Faced with domestic and diplomatic challenges, Jeffersonians managed to maintain their preponderance in national politics and redefine American nationalism on Republican terms. Northerners played a critical role in this process, as Chapter 5 argues. Pennsylvania Republicans resolutely supported declaration of war against Great Britain on June 18, 1812 and they likewise backed the reelection of James Madison later that fall. Despite military and political setbacks during the war, martial nationalism became a new and potent ideological bond between Republicans North and South. Chapter 5 follows the ideological war of 1812, in which immigrant radicals once again played a pivotal role. Republicans redefined the United States as an aggrieved democracy, struggling against internal and external enemies. Nationalism suppressed the problem of slavery, as Federalists and enslaved people who challenged bondage during the war were cast as allies of Britain and opponents of the United States.

Once again, however, national ideological unity broke down over the practical politics of slavery. The final chapter of this book traces the congressional conflict of 1819–1821 over the expansion of slavery to the new state of Missouri. In contrast to Republican nationalism during the War of 1812, the Missouri Crisis appears much as Jefferson described it, as an alarming interruption in national political life. But the Missouri Crisis was also the culmination of a long Jeffersonian argument about the power of slavery in the United States. A debate that began over the expansion of slavery to the West became a referendum on Jeffersonian democracy, American nationalism, and slaveholder power.

The Missouri Crisis presented northern Republicans with a dilemma at once ideological and historical. Northern Republicans tried to use Jeffersonian nationalism to restrict slavery expansion by arguing that the founding ideals of the United States were opposed to slaveholder power. But they faced a contending nationalist argument that stressed the protection of slavery as the price of Union and celebrated the expansion of American sovereignty under Republican rule. That counterargument was persuasive in good part because northern Jeffersonians had often accommodated slaveholder power in the past. Republican advocates of restriction were defeated, in other words, by their own ideological commitments, which had tolerated a major expansion of American slavery during two decades of Jeffersonian rule. During the Missouri Crisis, northerners took a stronger stance against slavery than they ever had before. But they did so in a political context where nationalism, the American nation-state, and the economic power of slaveholders were far stronger than they had been previously. Thus in addition to the difficulty of confronting slaveholder power, northern Jeffersonians faced the more complicated task of confronting their contradictory history as democrats in a slaveholding republic.

The Missouri Crisis had no decisive conclusion in northern political thought, and it left a divided legacy for the antebellum era. Antislavery northerners left the Missouri Crisis bitter at southern defenses of slaveholder power, but also confident in their commitments to the American nation and the core democratic principles of Jeffersonian politics. Other northerners, in contrast, responded to the Missouri Crisis and especially its final phase, which focused on the rights of free African Americans, by endorsing a racist consensus in which the political union of the United States and the political rights of white men required the subordination of black Americans, free and enslaved. As the Missouri Crisis concluded, moreover, New York's Martin Van Buren began early attempts to revive the Jeffersonian coalition, thus setting in motion a renewed North-South partnership that would flourish by the late 1820s, with the rise of Jacksonian democracy.[19]

While this book ends as antebellum politics begins, it also looks beyond the Jacksonian era to a longer, deeper, and ongoing story about the relationship between democratic freedom, oppression, and power in the United States. Ultimately, it explores a problem raised in a starker form by antebellum abolitionists and especially by escaped slaves who joined the antislavery struggle: why did nonslaveholders tolerate the existence of slavery? And how could they be persuaded to oppose to it? As Frederick Douglass told a British audience in March of 1847, "the northern states claim to be exempt from all responsibility in the matter of the slaveholding of America . . . but this is a mere subterfuge." In fact, northerners buttressed slaveholder power by supporting the United States Constitution, while their "deep prejudice against the coloured man" constricted African American freedom. Upon returning to the United States a few months later, Douglass bitterly noted:

> I have no love for America, as such; I have no patriotism. I have no country. What country have I? The institutions of this country do not know me, do not recognize me as a man. I am not thought of, or spoken of, except as a piece of property belonging to some Christian slaveholder, and all the religious and political institutions of this country, alike pronounce me a slave and a chattel.

As Douglass was well aware, abolishing slavery would require overturning that state of affairs, so that a slave could become a man. There was far more at stake in that transformation than a physical contest with mastery. Abolition would require non-slaveholders to reject the legitimacy of slaveholder power and to accept the legitimacy of Frederick Douglass and other African Americans as equal political subjects. That effectively meant reconstructing a democratic culture that had been built through the toleration of slaveholding authority.[20]

It would take a concerted and complex struggle by antislavery politicians, abolitionists, enslaved people, and white northerners to dislodge slaveholder power from the center of national political life and to destroy slavery during the American Civil War. Yet in many ways, after the war, as after multiple crises over slavery in the past, the institutional and ideological constraints of Jeffersonian democracy returned in new forms, as racist violence and racial union displaced black emancipation. The postbellum Democratic party, a descendant of the Jeffersonian coalition, maintained an alliance between northern freedom and southern oppression well into the twentieth century.[21] In order to liberate individuals and build democracy, northern Jeffersonians embraced slaveholders and accommodated bondage. The toleration of coercive, antidemocratic authority has been a dominant aspect of American political culture ever since.

CHAPTER 1

The Emancipation of New England

In a letter to Elbridge Gerry of Massachusetts in 1801, Thomas Jefferson reached out in sympathy to an oppressed compatriot. "Your part of the Union tho' as absolutely republican as ours," said Jefferson, "had drunk deeper of the delusion [of Federalism], & is therefore slower in recovering from it. The aegis of government, & the temples of religion & of justice, have all been prostituted there to toll us back to the times when we burnt witches. But your people will rise again." Characteristically, Jefferson's exaggerated metaphor had an element of truth: after the election of 1800, in which Jefferson became president and his Democratic-Republican party took control of Congress, New England became a bastion of Federalist resistance.[1] Republicans quickly came to predominate in the middle states and the South, but they remained a minority in New England, where they confronted the proud remnant of the Federalist party. New England Republicans thus faced a difficult electoral and ideological challenge. In Connecticut, Republicans did not gain significant congressional power until 1819, and Federalists likewise controlled state politics until 1817. Massachusetts was competitive throughout the Jeffersonian era, as were Rhode Island, New Hampshire, and Vermont, but Republicans never achieved the widespread success in New England that they did in the mid-Atlantic states and the South. Thus, in many ways, the political contests of the 1790s continued in New England throughout the Jeffersonian era, as Republicans intent on democratizing the political order confronted Federalists who sought to maintain existing social and political hierarchies.

The Jeffersonian fight against Federalism induced paroxysms of hyperbole on both sides, but it did have considerable substance. Outside Rhode Island, suffrage in New England was fairly widespread in the early nineteenth century, but few regional elites endorsed the idea of "democracy," whether as institution or culture. There were established churches in Massachusetts,

New Hampshire, and Connecticut long after 1800, and in the latter state, Federalists protected their hegemony through the notorious stand-up law, compelling citizens to vote in public in order to buttress the paternalist power of local elites. While Connecticut was most hostile to Republicans, Massachusetts Federalists held out the longest, defeating a determined opposition in 1820 to retain crucial conservative features in the state constitution. In addition, Federalists cultivated an antidemocratic political culture in newspapers, pamphlets, and orations, scorning the naïve idealism of men who assumed that "the people" were inherently good and prepared to govern in their own best interest.[2] In response, Republicans championed political freedom for ordinary white men, while a Jeffersonian vanguard defended democracy as an ideal system of government.

These New England struggles had national significance: in the months before the election of 1800, Republican newspapers North and South documented the perfidy of Federalists in the "Eastern states," and such rhetoric continued well after Jefferson's election. Jefferson appointed three New Englanders to major executive positions in his first term, and he reached out to religious and political dissidents from the region.[3] New England Republicans believed Jefferson would lead them toward a bountiful political future of self-government and religious freedom. New England Federalists, in contrast, contested the very premises of the Republican coalition. Instead of a party of liberation, said Federalists, the Republicans were a party of slavery, dominated by the masters of the South. Acerbic and at times cynical, such comments rested on an obvious truth: the Democratic-Republican party was the dominant political organization in the slaveholding states, and during the twenty-four years of the Virginia dynasty, Republicans North and South helped slaveholders win and maintain national political power. Federalists thus forced New England Republicans to confront the contradiction at the heart of their political coalition, which fought simultaneously to expand democracy in the North and protect the power of slavery in the South.

New England politics, then, were far more complex than the Jeffersonian narrative of virtuous Republicans struggling against a Federalist elite. Although Federalists openly condemned democracy, they were also severe critics of southern slaveholders, while New England Jeffersonians, who condemned the Federalist elite, made common cause with slaveholders to liberate themselves from Federalist rule. Doing so often required a complex ideological adaptation, since a number of Jeffersonians had opposed slavery early in their careers, and some maintained that opposition well after 1800. In the 1780s and 1790s, many budding Jeffersonians in the Northeast described slaveholding as a despotism fundamentally unfit for America; after 1800, these same men defended Republicans from Federalist charges that the Jeffersonian coalition was run by and on the behalf of slaveholders. In response to Federalist criticism, Republicans emphasized their own oppression at the hands of the New England elite, often claiming they were the true slaves, virtuous democrats yearning to be free.

The fact that white men could describe their relative oppression as enslavement reflected the well-established usage of slavery as a metaphor in Anglo-American political thought. Jeffersonian politics in many ways restaged the alchemy of the Revolution, in which white men denounced their political slavery to England in a manner that often obscured or lent direct support to the presence of chattel slavery in the colonies.[4] New England Republicans likewise protested their enslavement by Federalist masters by transforming antislavery argument in order to come to terms with chattel bondage. In the early national era these arguments circulated in a much denser, democratizing public sphere and in a nation-state that had explicitly incorporated slavery in its formation.

Yet there was no inherent ideological accord between slavery and democracy. While the American Revolution had encouraged white men to see themselves as slaves, it also rendered African slavery an ideological problem in new ways, subject to criticism in the rebellious colonies and in England.[5] The United States Constitution of 1787 granted slaveholders considerable institutional security, but it also incorporated slavery into a complex new political order, one that came to include partisan political competition, an expansive public sphere, and radical egalitarian ideologies. As slavery and democracy expanded throughout the early national period, they came into conflict in multiple arenas: at the national level, in the northern states, in print culture, and in the minds of the new citizens of the United States.

In other words, slavery became a democratic problem in the early republic. Toleration of its ongoing growth and power thus required a democratic solution. In the 1790s, numerous northern Republicans had called slavery into question. While they did not threaten to overturn the Constitution, they did express antislavery arguments that challenged southern power, and they lived in states where slavery was subject to ideological and political attack. New England especially represented a potential threat to slavery, as the institution had declined rapidly across the region by 1800.[6] However, as the Democratic-Republican relationship between North and

South intensified in the late 1790s and early 1800s, New England Republicans focused not on slavery but on the power of Federalism in their states and in their lives. In doing so, they helped to build an ideological accommodation with southern slaveholders that was as important as the institutional protections of bondage in the Constitution. Although less precise than the three-fifths bonus, these ideological negotiations between democratic subjectivity and slaveholder power were essential to the formation of the Jeffersonian coalition.

With the rise of Jefferson, democratic sentiment, instead of challenging slavery, often worked to support it: while New England men were liberated from Federalist rule, most southern slaves met the opposite fate at the hands of their Republican masters. Over time, these bonds between freedom and slavery would be reinforced by race, but early New England Jeffersonians did not found their alliance with the South on terms of white supremacy. Instead, they made their case in much more universal language, binding the egalitarian aspirations of ordinary white men to a political coalition that protected slavery at the national level.

The Air in America Is Too Pure for Slavery

By 1800, New England had old and deep ties to slavery. New England wealth grew in syncopation with the rise of Atlantic slavery, as New England merchants exploited the carrying trade to the Caribbean, and Rhode Islanders dominated North American participation in the African slave trade. Revolutionary era abolitionism remained limited by this history of slavery. While the institution had only a marginal presence in the region by 1800, gradual emancipation clauses in Connecticut and Rhode Island ensured that there would be slaves in both states until the 1840s. Throughout New England, free people of color faced official and informal discrimination. Yet beginning in the late eighteenth century, some New Englanders had begun to contest slavery in the region and in the new United States. An outlier in the colonial era due to the relative scarcity of chattel bondage, New England produced determined secular and religious opponents of slavery in the new United States. Antislavery critics fought to end slavery within the region and to challenge its power in the national government.[7]

Some of these early opponents of slavery would later become important members of the New England Republican coalition. Levi Lincoln of

Worcester, Massachusetts, for example, defended the freedom of Quock Walker in the 1781 case of *Jennison v. Caldwell*, long assumed to mark the beginning of the end of slavery in his home state. During Jefferson's presidency, he was a key regional ally. Anticipating the growing strength of New England Republicans in September 1800, Jefferson told James Madison that Lincoln was "undoubtedly the ablest & most respectable man in the Eastern states."[8]

While historians have written about Lincoln's antislavery argument on behalf of Walker and his later partisan arguments on behalf of Jefferson, they have done little to think about these two moments of his career in relationship to each other. In part, this reflects the long distance in time—close to twenty years—between Lincoln's defense of Walker and his defense of the slaveholding Republican Jefferson. But there was far less ideological distance between those two moments in Lincoln's career, as other New England Jeffersonians demonstrate. Antislavery argument was intertwined with early Democratic-Republican ideology in New England, as Jeffersonians turned to universalist conceptions of human freedom both to denounce slavery and to justify their own case for emancipation from Federalist rule. At least some white men expressed the logical conclusions of their beliefs in self-government, freedom of conscience, human equality, and opposition to tyranny. Slavery contradicted those principles; therefore, it was wrong and should end. But as Federalist-Republican antagonism intensified in the 1790s, tightening bonds between emergent Jeffersonians North and South, New England Republican thought turned inward, and political sentiments that once embraced a strong opposition to slavery were refigured in support of liberating white men from Federalist control. Their emancipator was Thomas Jefferson, who acted the part quite effectively. Alliance with Jefferson meant alliance with the dominant contingent of southern slaveholders in national politics, who likewise embraced the Democratic-Republican cause. Freedom in New England became harnessed to slavery in the South, which inevitably warped Republican antislavery argument.

The Quock Walker case arose in Worcester County, Massachusetts, in 1781 when Walker, an African American, left his reputed master Nathaniel Jennison to work for Seth and John Caldwell. Jennison first attempted to retain Walker by force, and then sued the Caldwells for enticing away his servant, winning his case in the Worcester Court of Common Pleas. On appeal to the Superior Court, Lincoln argued for the Caldwells and presented an impassioned argument against the institution of slavery. Jennison's claim had no merit, said Lincoln, because Walker was free, and therefore not subject to any man's will. Lincoln pointed to the Massachusetts Constitution of 1780, which claimed "all men are born free and equal," but he also invoked natural and divine law to argue that all men shared a foundational equality. We "are born in the same manner, our bones clothed with the same kind of flesh, live and die in the same manner." The legality or illegality of slavery was almost beside the point—if any "law of man" established slavery, said Lincoln, it contradicted the law of God, and the latter injunction took precedence. Better to sacrifice your bodies in disobeying a corrupt human law, Lincoln told the jury, than to disregard the will of God and sacrifice "your own souls." Lincoln also modified an argument associated with the 1772 *Somerset* case, declaring "the air in America was too pure for a slave to breathe in."[9] While Lord Mansfield's decision in *Somerset* did not end slavery in England, it did destabilize the security of slavery throughout the British Empire and later influenced American antislavery legal strategy.[10] In attempting to establish Walker's freedom, Lincoln expressed far-reaching arguments that theoretically undermined slavery throughout the emerging United States. In his mind, divine and natural law, and the very nature of the American polity, opposed any positive law establishing slavery. In a separate decision in 1783, Massachusetts Superior Court Justice William Cushing would argue that the state constitution of 1780 did as well. Lincoln won his case in 1781, and a variety of similar legal actions, alongside informal challenges to bondage by African Americans, undermined slavery throughout Massachusetts.[11]

Twenty years later, Lincoln emerged as a powerful regional member of the Democratic-Republican coalition. Elected to Congress in 1800 as a Republican, Lincoln quickly gained the confidence and approbation of Thomas Jefferson, who appointed him attorney general. Lincoln resigned after one term, but continued to advise the president about the state of politics in New England and make recommendations about federal patronage. A paper he helped found in Worcester, Massachusetts, the *National Aegis*, became an important regional voice of Republicanism, and Lincoln returned to political office in 1807, as the Republican lieutenant governor and then, on the death of James Sullivan, governor of Massachusetts. In 1810, Jefferson and Madison hoped he would accept an appointment as a Supreme Court justice, and friends in Washington wrote to persuade him of widespread Republican support for his nomination, particularly from southern members of Congress. Those southern members were presumably unaware of Lincoln's role in the Quock Walker case; had he become a justice and acted on the principles articulated in *Jennison v. Caldwell*, he might have attempted to end slavery in the United States.[12]

In the end Lincoln declined the nomination on account of age and partial blindness. Yet southern congressmen were likely right to place their faith in Lincoln. By 1810, his years of service to the Republican cause outweighed his antislavery past, and he had never publicly reasserted his bold claim from 1781 that "the air in America was too pure for a slave to breathe in." As is it turned out, the early national air was pure enough for slavery. All the northern states provided some degree of comity to slaveholders when they entered the federal union, agreeing to the rendition of fugitives and passing sojourner laws protecting southern slave property, in what Paul Finkelman has termed a "rejection of Somerset." In 1788, Massachusetts refused to allow nonresident African Americans to stay in the state longer than two months, preventing the state from becoming a haven for free and fugitive slaves. The Supreme Judicial Court acknowledged that masters outside Massachusetts had retained a property right to enslaved persons who fled or traveled to the state. Such legal and institutional changes made slavery an inherent part of the American polity, as the institution became more stable under the Constitution.[13] Yet the relative security of slave property under the Constitution depended on writing slavery into the structure of the federal government, ensuring that as national political and ideological bonds developed after 1787, slavery would remain subject to sectional and partisan debate.

Slavery became a pressing issue for New England Republicans after 1800, because their political coalition had strong ties to the South, while their political convictions challenged traditional social and institutional hierarchies. Multiple Republicans followed Lincoln's path from early criticism of slavery to embrace of the Jeffersonian cause in the 1790s and 1800s as allies of the slaveholding South. However, unlike Lincoln, many of these men did not so much forget their antislavery arguments as transform them, in order to make peace with their southern colleagues and their own political and ethical convictions.

Freedom Against Slavery

The northern Democratic-Republican coalition was socially and ideologically diverse: Levi Lincoln was a free-thinker and a Unitarian, while his fellow Jeffersonian John Leland was an evangelical Baptist minister who became a leading Republican in western Massachusetts. In terms of social status, Lincoln was similar to many Federalist leaders: he attended Harvard, practiced law, stood firmly on the side of creditors during Shays' Rebellion, and even married the daughter of a prominent local Federalist. He was representative of the gentlemen outsiders who emerged as leading Republicans throughout Massachusetts, like the Crowinshields of Salem, Elbridge Gerry of Marblehead, and Henry Dearborn of the District of Maine.[14] Leland, in contrast, born to a middling family in Grafton, Massachusetts, in 1754, had a limited education, never attended college, and spent his early career as an itinerant in Virginia. He was skeptical of lawyers and proud to note that few Baptist ministers in Virginia had "received the *diploma* of MA," as it proved their "work has been of God and not of man." He was far more representative of the new class of men Jeffersonian politics brought into power, relative unknowns who rose to prominence in the midst of a democratizing, anti-deferential political culture. Yet Lincoln and Leland had two important ideological connections: they both believed in the Republican cause and opposed Federalist rule in Massachusetts, and they were public opponents of slavery early in their careers.[15]

Leland's opposition to slavery apparently originated during his years in Virginia. After a conversion experience in 1774, Leland became a Baptist minister and spent fifteen years as an itinerant in Virginia, from 1776 to 1791. He and his fellow Baptists worked to proselytize for their faith and disestablish the Anglican Church; their evangelism, in addition to the support of gentry leaders like James Madison, led to passage of the Statute for Religious Freedom in 1786. Leland became a political supporter of Madison's during the Virginia debates over ratification of the Constitution and endorsed his election to the House in 1789; Madison in turn promised that he would defend religious liberty in the federal government. Their experiences no doubt later predisposed Leland toward the Democratic-Republicans. In an 1801 sermon on freedom of religion, Leland called Jefferson his "hero." Ultimately, however, his ideological alliance with Jefferson developed in the very different political context of New England, where established churches retained power into the nineteenth century. Virginia introduced him to the evils of slavery, while Connecticut and Massachusetts introduced him to the evils of Federalism. In his confrontation with the New England elite, Leland found new sources of accord with Virginia Republicans and developed a new ideological relationship to southern slavery.[16]

Returning to New England in 1791, Leland immediately spoke out against the persistence of religious establishment, focusing first on the state of Connecticut. The title of a pamphlet he published that year gives a fair indication of his sentiments: *The Rights of Conscience Inalienable, and therefore Religious Opinions not Cognizable by Law: Or, the high-flying Churchman, Stript of his legal Robe, Appears a Yaho[o]*. The pamphlet contained a crucial definition of "conscience": "the word signifies *common science,* a court of judicature which the Almighty has erected in every human breast: a *censor morum* over all his conduct. Conscience will ever judge right, when it is rightly informed, and speak the truth when it understands it." According to Leland, conscience had never been surrendered to regulation by the state, and therefore religious establishments were ethically wrong. A few months later he brought this argument to Massachusetts, eventually settling in what would become Cheshire, Massachusetts, in 1792. Leland was thus part of a long line of thinkers whom Staughton Lynd termed "dissenting radicals," men for whom freedom of conscience was the paramount natural right. Leland's radical sense of religious individualism made him a firm advocate of the separation of church and state. While he was more extreme than many Baptists, he developed a strong following in Cheshire as he attacked Federalist tyranny over the individual conscience.[17]

In Leland's Republican oratory, the Jeffersonians represented the cause of political and religious freedom. The new president, Leland claimed in 1801, was "the *Man of the People,* the defender of the rights of man and the rights of conscience." Yet Leland, like Lincoln and other New England Republicans, was also opposed to slavery, a sentiment presumably discordant with the emergent national Republican coalition and its deep roots in the Jeffersonian South. As Leland explained in a retrospective chronicle of his southern itinerancy published in 1790, his time in Virginia had left him disgusted with "the whole scene of slavery." The institution afflicted his conscience and contradicted deeply held political ideals, because it embodied such abusive power. In 1789, he authored a resolution for the Baptist General Committee in Virginia that described slavery as "a violent deprivation of the rights of nature and inconsistent with a republican government." In a 1791 letter to some of his Virginia congregants, he repeated that claim and added that slavery was likewise "destructive of every humane and benevolent passion of the soul, and subversive to that liberty absolutely necessary to ennoble the human mind." He simply could not "endure to see one man strip and whip another, as free by nature as himself." In essence, slavery was a violation of subjective freedom. Like many evangelicals, Leland believed that enslaved people could experience "a work of grace in their hearts"; "liberty of conscience," he argued, "in matters of religion, is the right of slaves, beyond contradiction." Yet many slaveholders, claimed Leland, openly violated the natural right of slaves to worship, often beating them for attending religious meetings. Like Jefferson, Leland attributed the abusiveness of masters to the institution of slavery, which instilled "pride, haughtiness, domination, cruelty, deceit and indolence" in slaveholders. He likewise tempered his antislavery views: he emphasized the moral burdens borne by truly Christian masters and he called on slaves, in his letter to Virginia Baptists, to obey their masters, be "patient in your hardships" and look to Heaven for redemption. He condemned slavery, but believed emancipation impracticable, since slaves were treated as property. The government of Virginia could hardly afford to purchase all of the state's slaves, while emancipation without compensation would be unjust. And, like Jefferson, he worried that a post-emancipation society would be consumed by violent black retribution and interracial sexual union, whether through marriage or "forcible debauches." Yet unlike Jefferson, Leland also criticized such racist paranoia, noting that white men would surely object to similar arguments were they enslaved in Africa. In a radical moment, Leland wondered "whether men had not better lose all their property, than deprive an individual of his birth-right blessing—freedom. If a political system is such, that common justice cannot be administered without innovation, the sooner such a system is destroyed, the better for the people."[18]

Such antislavery thoughts were not uncommon among New England Republicans in the 1790s. Connecticut's Abraham Bishop, arguably the most important Jeffersonian ideologue in the region, went even farther, challenging not only slavery but also racism in a series of articles from 1791 published under the title "The Rights of Black Men" and widely reprinted. Comparing the American Revolution to the slave uprising in Saint-Domingue that had begun that year in August, he celebrated their shared principles, while elevating the struggle of the slave rebels, who sought to destroy real, not metaphorical, slavery. Bishop denounced theories of racial difference and minimized the political stakes of the American Revolution:

If freedom depends upon colour, we have only to seek for the whitest man in the world, that we may find the freest, and for the blackest, that we may find the greatest slave. But the enlightened mind of

Americans will not receive such ideas. We believe that Freedom is the natural right of all rational beings, and we know that the Blacks have never voluntarily resigned that freedom. Then is not their cause as just as ours? We fought with bravery, and prayed earnestly for success upon our righteous cause, when we drew the sword, and shed the blood of Englishmen—for what!—Not to gain Freedom; for we were never Slaves; but to rid ourselves of taxes, imposed without our consent, and from the growing evils of usurpation.[19]

The "enlightened mind of Americans" had failed to live up to its principles. In the United States, Bishop argued, the power of slavery consistently overpowered the promise of freedom: "the blacks are still enslaved within the United States," he complained bitterly, "the Indians are driven into the society of savage beasts, and we glory in the equal rights of men, provided that *we white men can enjoy the whole of them.*" Bishop's uniqueness lay in that last ironic note, a forward-looking criticism of white male democracy and racial exclusion. He believed that race should determine political status. That presumably provided grounds not only to support the rebels of Saint-Domingue, but to support equal citizenship for all throughout the United States.[20]

In this respect, Bishop reflected a radical side of transatlantic republican politics. In Saint-Domingue, slave rebels pushed free men of color and eventually representatives from Revolutionary France to embrace an anti-slavery agenda. In August 1793, after a desperate battle over the summer to retain control of Cap Français and the Northern Province of Saint-Domingue, French commissioner Léger Félicité Sonthonax declared the end of slavery in the Northern Province. That decision was soon echoed throughout the island, and in February 1794, the National Convention in Paris abolished slavery "throughout the territory of the Republic." Although such proclamations were the result of contingency as much as idealism, and depended on the constant struggle of enslaved people in Saint-Domingue, they suggested the broad egalitarian potential of radical republican politics. During his brief tenure as minister to the United States, "Citizen" Edmond-Charles Genet, despite his favorable reception by slaveholders in the American South, lent support to Sonthonax's decision and was openly hostile to white refugees from Saint-Domingue in the United States. Although many of the Democratic-Republican societies that arose in the wake of Genet's mission overlooked the slave rebellion in Saint-Domingue, multiple Republican papers in the North, like the *Boston Argus*, which published

Bishop's essays, attacked both slavery and racism from a radical cosmopolitan perspective.[21]

While few of his contemporaries went as far as Bishop and supported revolution by the enslaved, his combination of antislavery argument and democratic politics was not atypical. Many Jeffersonians believed, like John Leland, that slavery was "inconsistent with republican government." Matthew Lyon of Vermont, who became infamous for spitting in the face of Connecticut Federalist Roger Griswold on the floor of Congress in February 1798, became a national icon of Jeffersonian democracy in New England later that fall as a martyr of the Federalist Sedition Act. In the midst of his egalitarian invectives in Congress, he found time to defend the right of petition on behalf of antislavery groups. John Bacon, a Presbyterian minister turned farmer turned Anti-Federalist turned Republican from Stockbridge, Massachusetts, was more akin to Bishop. He too articulated an early antiracist position, by opposing a clause in the 1780 state constitution that would have barred "Negroes, Indians, and Mulattoes" from the franchise outright. During his single term in Congress in 1801–1803, he argued bluntly for national recognition of African American citizenship. Multiple individual cases suggest that Democratic-Republicans refused to condone slavery because it embodied what Jeffersonians hated most: power and oppression.[22]

In New England, such sentiments were supplemented by a regional pride in being untainted by slavery. According to Massachusetts flagship Republican paper the *Independent Chronicle*, "the people of New England are the only people on earth, who ever deserved to be considered as really and exclusively <u>FREE</u>," since "in <u>Massachusetts</u> no man can be a slave, by the constitution." As Joanne Melish has argued, such "disowning" of slavery entailed historical amnesia about the prevalence of slavery in the past and racial exclusion of nominally free African Americans in the present.[23] In addition to barring African Americans from outside Massachusetts from taking up permanent residence in the state, for example, Massachusetts outlawed interracial marriage and began to implement segregation in many areas of public life. Yet Massachusetts citizens had also opposed slavery in national politics. During the Constitutional Convention, Elbridge Gerry, later to become a Jeffersonian stalwart, attacked the three-fifths clause, and refused to sign the document in part because of its protections of slavery. Similar skepticism arose during the ratifying debates in Massachusetts, where members of the convention and ordinary citizens objected to the three-fifths clause and the slave trade clause. In contrast to the ratification debates in Virginia, Anti-Federalists in Massachusetts were suspicious of the new federal government not because it seemed liable to threaten slavery, but because it gave the institution so much support.[24]

New England Federalists, more so than Republicans, revised and reissued objections to the three-fifths clause in the early Jeffersonian years. Yet Republicans were hardly acquiescent on the subject of slavery. In principle, their ideological commitments were far more dangerous to slavery than Federalist thought. A Jeffersonian vanguard, influenced by the American and French Revolutions and transatlantic radicalism, began to articulate a far-reaching argument for the political transformation not just of the United States, but of the world. In their minds, hatred of aristocracy and monarchy amounted to far more than a technical argument about how the American government should be organized. Anti-aristocratic thought instead expressed a universal condemnation of all forms of political hierarchy, a plea for the oppressed of the world. Writing from Philadelphia in December 1797, Massachusetts Republican congressman Joseph Bradley Varnum exemplified this anti-aristocratic ethos in a letter to his son. "While the innate principles of Justice, humanity, the Love of rational Liberty and of Mankind, Expand the virtuous heart with affectionate concern," he wrote,

> for the many millions of the human race, who have for a long time, been suffering under the rod of Tyranny, Oppression, War and bloodshed, in different parts of the World; the vicious hereditary Monarchs, and Aristocrats, with their selfish views and diabolical intrigues, wantonly invert the power which the people have put into their hands for the best of purposes, into an unjust usurpation of those rights, which every human being is entitled to the enjoyment of without molestation. Instead of being a blessing to society, they become the greatest curse, that can be experienced in life; like the Voracious animal, they devour all that falls in their way; while millions are pining & languishing with hunger, their unrelenting hearts riot and grow fat on the labors of the distressed; they are the fomenters of all the Distressing wars which pervade the nations of the Earth; they wish to bring all men to be subservient to their views and obeisant to their Commands; when this is refused, they invidiously destroy the disobedient with unrelenting fury. I hope and trust, that the people of these states,

will avoid that rock on which many Nations have foundered; and accept a system of equal justice for the General good of mankind.[25]

Varnum articulated two key concepts that shaped northern democratic thought: a belief in human equality (in Varnum's letter, on the basis of natural rights) and opposition to unjust political authority. Both ideas impelled Jeffersonians to think beyond the bounds of the new American nation and its constituent states and, in theory, both ideas challenged the political authority required to maintain slavery.

Anti-aristocratic universalism deeply influenced Jeffersonians in New England and throughout the North. In describing his political ambitions to Connecticut Republican Ephraim Kirby, the young printer Samuel Morse emphasized his "wish for the welfare of man, and a universal love for the human race." At political celebrations, Republican toasts frequently looked beyond national horizons to celebrate a worldwide struggle for liberty. Honoring Jefferson's inauguration in March 1801, Republicans in Torringford, Connecticut, offered the following tribute: "Democracy: May it bestride the universe and the whole human race become fellow citizens."[26]

Such universalist sentiments at times included open opposition to slavery. In July 1800, Boston's *Independent Chronicle* reprinted a poem by the Liverpool writer Edward Rushton in order to commemorate the Fourth of July. The poem closes by exhorting Americans to attack slavery, in honor of the rights of man and their revolution against authority.

O perceive what your prowess procur'd
And reflect that your rights are the rights of MANKIND;
That to ALL they were bounteously given
And that he who in chains would his FELLOW MAN bind,
Uplifts his proud arm against HEAVEN.

How can you, who have felt the oppressor's hard hand,
Who for freedom all perils did brave—
How can you enjoy ease, while one foot of your land
Is disgrac'd by the toil of a *Slave*?
O rouse then, in spite of a merciless few,
And pronounce this immortal decree—
That "whate'er be man's tenets, his fortune, his HUE,
HE IS MAN—and shall therefore be free!"[27]

Rushton took the universalist claims of transatlantic republicanism to their logical conclusion: American slavery was unjust and all men, regardless of color, should be free. The editors of the *Chronicle* apparently agreed.

Joseph Bradley Varnum likely would have read Rushton's lines with approbation. On January 30, 1797, his distaste for oppression led him to speak on behalf of four black petitioners to Congress, men who had been manumitted by their Quaker masters in North Carolina, but whose manumission was retroactively abrogated by the state legislature, along with over a hundred other enslaved people who had likewise been set free. Their petition, brought to the House by a Pennsylvania Republican, described a series of harrowing journeys to temporary freedom in Philadelphia, fleeing from slave catchers first in North Carolina and then in Virginia. All left behind family members, some of whom had also been freed and then coerced back into slavery. The petitioners particularly objected to the Fugitive Slave Act of 1793, which left them and other nominally free African Americans in the North vulnerable to kidnapping.

Southern slaveholders, Republican and Federalist alike, objected to the petition in varying degrees of outrage. Thomas Blount of North Carolina deemed the petitioners legally slaves, and therefore powerless to address the House; William Loughton Smith thought the petition should be sealed up and sent back, to express the House's disdain; James Madison politely offered to let the petition lie on the table while just as politely insisting that nothing at all could be done to address the petitioners' grievances.

Northerners, Republican and Federalist alike, spoke in favor of the petitioners, and Varnum joined cause with the leading antislavery Federalist in the House, George Thatcher of Massachusetts. Varnum believed the men had a right to petition the government and he believed that the Fugitive Slave Act promoted the rights of slaveholders and allowed for kidnapping. He hoped that Congress would "take all possible care that freemen should not be slaves." Varnum lost this debate, as the House voted 50-33 to reject the petition, but he demonstrated that New England Republicans were willing to challenge the power of slavery when they believed that it violated fundamental political commitments. As Varnum explained, very much in harmony with John Leland, "to be deprived of liberty was more important than to be deprived of property."[28]

The case of the North Carolina freedmen, petitioning from Philadelphia, demonstrates that northern antislavery sentiment could move from theoretical objection to practical challenge to southern interests. Antislavery sentiment could also challenge northern practices of racial exclusion, since contests over slavery often brought up the problem of racial discrimination before the law. "Color and complexion," said the black petitioners, should not exclude individuals from "common humanity"; Varnum argued that color should not be automatically identified with slave status, as the fugitive law seemed liable to do. Such antislavery arguments merged with Republican anti-aristocratic and egalitarian thought, as multiple cases from the 1790s demonstrate. But as the partisan conflict of the 1790s intensified during John Adams's presidency, Republicans in New England and throughout the North began to focus on the oppression—the slavery, many said—that they suffered at the hands of Federalist elites. They looked to the emerging Republican coalition, and often to Thomas Jefferson himself, to free them from Federalist oppression. In doing so, they made apparent the capacity of egalitarian thought not only to deny equal justice on the basis of race, but also to make considerable allowance for the hierarchical and violent authority wielded by slaveholders. The unitary world envisioned by Varnum, in which aristocrats preyed on the weak, fractured in the American context, where slaveholders appealed to republican argument to win national power, and New Englanders appealed to slaveholders to defeat Federalism. Instead of opposing transatlantic republicanism because of its potential threat to slaveholding (as did South Carolina Federalists), the Jeffersonian coalition embraced anti-aristocratic republican thought while tempering its antislavery content. As Varnum and his colleagues clamored for equal justice in alliance with Jefferson and Virginia, southern slaves experienced tightening of the bonds of control.

Abraham Bishop's Phi Beta Kappa Address

Antislavery feeling in New England was widespread and diverse before 1800. But as Republicans like Bishop and Lincoln joined the cause of Jefferson, Federalist "tyranny" in New England became a far more important problem than slavery. Republicans North and South drew closer together as they tried to elect Thomas Jefferson president in 1800 and overturn the administration of John Adams. Northerners were particularly outraged by the Alien and Sedition Acts of 1798, which sought to repress the more outspoken members of the Republican coalition. By 1800, Matthew Lyon had been jailed for sedition, as had Vermont's Anthony Haswell and Connecticut's Charles Holt (both Haswell and Holt would later publish works by John Leland). In Connecticut, the Congregational Church remained established, and the congressional delegation was dominated by Federalists. To Republicans inside and outside New England, the state symbolized the extent of Federalist power.

It was in this context that Abraham Bishop composed his best-known oration and pamphlet, *Connecticut Republicanism: An Oration, on the Extent and Power of Political Delusion*. Reprinted throughout the nation, the speech became a defining document of New England Republican thought. The occasion of the speech itself demonstrated how Bishop, once a gentleman in good standing with Federalists like David Daggett and Noah Webster, revoked his ties to the New Haven elite in order to pursue the democratization of Connecticut—and power and fame as a Republican along the way. Chosen by the Phi Beta Kappa society at Yale to give its annual lecture in September 1800, Bishop wrote a blistering political indictment of Connecticut Federalism that closed with an exhortation to elect Thomas Jefferson president. When he gave the advance copy of the speech to the Phi Beta Kappa society, it decided at the last minute to revoke the invitation, immediately publicizing the decision in handbills that claimed the society was apolitical. Undeterred, Bishop gave the speech at the White Haven meetinghouse in New Haven, to a crowd estimated at 1,500 people. He opened by rejecting "literary" speeches, classical languages, and intellectual theorizing. Instead, Bishop, a Yale alumnus, allied himself with the anti-elitist intellectual culture of Republicans like John Leland. He would serve a "plain dish" full of his chosen topic, "THE EXTENT AND POWER OF POLITICAL DELUSION."[29]

Thus began a relentless assault on Federalism in state and nation. Bishop attacked Alexander Hamilton's funding system, Federalist naval expenditures, banks, excessive commercial wealth, the New England clergy, and the lack of democracy in Connecticut. The indictment was meant to inspire, not simply harangue. Bishop wanted ordinary people to think freely and seize political power for themselves. He wished them to be free of delusion—to be free of the various arts that the "wise, rich, and mighty men of the world" (dating back to Satan, the primeval deluder) used to manipulate and control "the laboring and subordinate people of the world." Here he chose a theme that resonated with Republicans throughout New England. John Leland sought to defend freedom of conscience, while the Republican printer Samuel Morse told Ephraim Kirby in July of 1800 that he had been subject to "illiberal abuse . . . because I dare to think for myself." As another Republican

sympathizer Philo Murray put it in September 1801, describing the rise of
Connecticut Republicanism, "People have begun to dare to think." Autonomous thought was both the highest aim of individual subjects and the
means—the very medium, as Jeffrey Pasley has shown in the case of Morse
and other Republican printers—of political contestation. Jeffersonians like
Bishop sought not simply to inform the state but to take it over. Mobilizing
public opinion, they aimed to bring ordinary men to their senses, and then to
the polls.[30]

Thus by the end of his address, Bishop turned to open electioneering,
calling on Republicans to "be awake" on the upcoming Election Day, which
was "more important than any day of your revolution. Now republicanism
dies or lives forever." A vote for Jefferson was a vote for "redemption" from
the "great and little tyrants" who dominated men's lives. As was true of Varnum, Bishop's anti-aristocratic message, although focused on a male electorate in Connecticut, expanded to indict hierarchical forms of political power
throughout the world. "Nearly the whole of Africa and a considerable part of
Asia, are subject to the delusions of Europe," Bishop told his audience. "Slaves
in immense troops must sweat under a scorching sun to bear or follow the
palanquin of a lordly master: slaves by ship loads must be dragged from their
homes to serve imperious tyrants." This passage remained general enough
not to point a direct finger at the Republican slaveholders who were likewise
stumping for Jefferson in the South, but it demonstrated that Bishop's hatred
of oppression, which had informed his defense of the slave rebels of Saint-
Domingue in the early 1790s, retained a degree of universalism. The evils of
Federalism were the evils of the deluders the world over, including the "imperious tyrants" who enslaved captive Africans.[31]

Yet Republican thought moved in a parallel direction at the same time.
Instead of extending outward, in a universalizing condemnation of illicit
power, it began with slavery and moved inward, employing bondage as a
metaphor to define the Republican condition in New England. As Bishop
warned in 1800, Federalist measures threatened to "launch this country from
liberty to slavery, from a republican to a monarchical government." Writing a
year later in response to Federalist criticism, Bishop declared self-righteously
that he would no longer truckle to the Connecticut elite. "I am no slave to
clergy or merchants," he declared, before symbolically renouncing his Phi
Beta Kappa membership. Henceforth, he would be a member of "the great
community of unprivileged men, to whose emancipation from the tyranny of
the 'friends of order' and from the arts of political delusion I shall always

chearfully devote those talents, which were never made for *literary* societies." Bishop's renunciation came in an appendix to a pamphlet in which slavery served as the central metaphor for the experience of white male Jeffersonians in Connecticut. While Bishop meant to indict Federalist economic as well as political power, the "slavery" he felt most deeply was ideological. "If you wish to reduce any man or number of men to complete slavery, the surest mode is first to enslave the mind," he wrote in an 1802 pamphlet protesting religious establishment in Connecticut. Republicans sought what Bishop promised his New Haven audience that September evening in 1800: freedom of the self; freedom to think and choose based on one's own conscience, unencumbered by delusion or deference. Free minds would make free men.[32]

Liberation on those terms was a delicate act, however, and the slavery metaphor, an inevitable hyperbole, pointed to the liabilities of Republican ideology when it came to confronting actual chattel slavery in the American South and in the emerging Jeffersonian coalition. In seeking freedom from Federalist oppression, Bishop and his fellow partisans elevated slaveholders as their champions, transforming Jefferson in particular into a secular messiah of liberty. Their quest for autonomy became the very currency of political alliance with the slaveholding South. Federalists would not let them forget that fact, as they spent the early 1800s denouncing the slaveholding foundations of the Jeffersonian coalition. This forced Republicans to come to some sort of terms with the fact that their freedom had become intertwined with the distant oppression of others. In this respect, as in others, Abraham Bishop was in the vanguard of American political modernity.[33]

Federalist Antislavery and Republican Nationalism

While some New England Federalists had openly opposed slavery in the 1790s, the Jeffersonian "revolution" of 1800 encouraged them to take a much stronger sectional stance. After 1800, southern Federalism quickly declined. Meanwhile, Republicans made inroads in the Federalist heartland of New England, gaining congressional seats in Massachusetts and Rhode Island in the election of 1800. In the Federalist citadel of Connecticut, Republicans could not win a congressional seat until after the War of 1812, but they made limited gains at the state level before then, winning 40 percent of the seats in the state House of Representatives in 1804. In the face of this rising Republican tide, Federalists grew tired of hearing themselves denounced as tyrants and compared to slaveholders. Many shared the sentiments of Delaware Federalist James Bayard, who found it hard to understand how he and his colleagues could be indicted as aristocrats. That charge, he told Congress in 1798, was far more applicable to southern Republicans, who had "been born in a land of slavery, whose cradles had been rocked by slaves, and who had been habituated from infancy to trample on the rights of man." New England Federalists felt similarly, and spent the months after the election of 1800 decrying the slaveholding roots of Republican electoral success, thus ensuring that local Republicans could not simply ignore slavery. Federalist criticism forced them to reckon with two obvious facts that contradicted their emerging democratic vision: the oppression of slaves and the excessive power wielded by slaveholders.[34]

Federalist antislavery escalated in earnest after Jefferson's election in 1800, particularly in New England. Multiple papers complained that Jefferson never won the votes of a majority of free men in America, but instead owed his election to the three-fifths clause of the Constitution. As the *New-England Palladium* explained, the clause "operates exclusively in favour of the southern division of the Union," to the disadvantage of the North; worse yet, it was institutionalized hypocrisy, since the purported "men of the people" in the Republican party would "ride into the TEMPLE OF LIBERTY, upon the shoulders of slaves."[35] New England Federalists labeled Jefferson a "Negro President," because he obtained political support from the subject population of the South, in a transparent attempt to mobilize northern support by appealing to antislavery sentiment. In 1802, some papers went farther, and published claims by James Thompson Callender and others that Jefferson slept with his female slave, Sally Hemings. This led to choice remarks throughout the Federalist press, such as Thomas Green Fessenden's "Great Men will never lack Supporters / Who manufacture their own voters." A young John Quincy Adams joined the fray as well, ironically exhorting "Dear Thomas" to "deem it no disgrace with slaves to mend thy breed / nor let the wench's smutty face deter thee from thy deed."[36]

The Federalist treatment of "Black Sal" appealed to racial prejudice and demonstrated a lack of humanitarian concern for the enslaved. Many historians consider Federalist antislavery argument a utilitarian political tactic at best. Federalists were happy to editorialize in support of slavery if it suited their cause, warning southerners of the dangers of republicanism and "French" influence on their slaves during the election of 1800. Not all Federalists fit this pattern, however. Many leading Federalists supported manumission societies in the North, and Federalists took strong anti-southern positions in national level debates over slavery. Overall, Federalists were less inclined toward racism than Republicans, as they believed in an organically ordered society in which "respectable" African Americans could find a legitimate place, and in which deference, rather than race, governed social difference. Furthermore, after 1800, they had less and less reason to reach out to the South at all, because Republican success in the region was so far-reaching. In the last Federalist Congress (1799–1801), Federalists held 23 southern seats in the House; in the first Jeffersonian Congress, the 7th, which sat in 1801–1803, they held 12; in the 8th of 1803–1805 they held 9; and by the 9th of 1805–1807, there were only 4 southern Federalists remaining in the House. Their rapidly diminishing southern wing left the Federalists more or less free to denounce the "slaveholding Lords" as they saw fit.[37]

Republicans responded to Federalist criticism through self-aggrandizement and nationalism. In pamphlets, orations, and toasts, they emphasized their own oppression at the hands of New England elites, while building a Jeffersonian patriotism that cast Federalism as the bitter voice of regional resentment. In a June 1802 letter to Jefferson, Levi Lincoln described New England as "that difficult part of the country, of which I am an inhabitant." As Lincoln and Jefferson tried to bring the region into a national Republican consensus, they traded malicious descriptions of Federalism back and forth: Jefferson was sure that extreme Federalists "wish to sap the republic by fraud, if they cannot destroy it by force, & to erect an English monarchy in its place"; Lincoln, who at first believed that moderate Federalists might join with Republicans in a spirit of patriotic accord, became convinced that Jefferson's government would "never be countenanced" by Federalists and that Republicans "had to depend solely on themselves." Jefferson promised Lincoln in October 1802 that he would "sink federalism into an abyss from which there will be no resurrection." Their strategy was both institutional and ideological: Lincoln helped Jefferson make patronage decisions about New England federal offices, to ensure they went to sympathetic Republicans, and he helped found a newspaper in his hometown of Worcester to counteract the local Federalist press. The *National Aegis* debuted in December 1801, preceded by a prospectus that promised "to expose the fallacy of pretended federalism; to increase the energy of republican principle." In conjunction with a series of letters from "A Farmer" that Lincoln began to publish in the fall of 1801, the *Aegis* worked to instill Republican nationalism throughout New England, by celebrating Jefferson and Republican values and marginalizing Federalist dissent as borderline treason.[38]

Republished as a pamphlet in 1802, Lincoln's "Farmer's letters" indicted
Federalists for slandering the president and insulting "the majesty of the people." He was particularly upset at their fusion of religion and politics, claiming that Federalists had "prostituted" their "altars" in order to foment dissent;
their political attacks, he decided, were "virtually, treason." The *New-England
Palladium*, source of many of the charges against Jefferson and the three-
fifths clause, was his principal target. He considered the "tenor of the obnoxious *paper*" a fair indication "of propensity to insurrection" and argued that
even subscribers to the paper should be held accountable for the seditious
material they consumed. Obsessed with the political abuses of New England
Congregationalists, Lincoln did not answer in detail Federalist attacks on
Virginia slavery, but he did turn to the subject once, with predictable tones of
nationalist affront. Federalist ideologues who attempted to place "prejudices"
between "the Farmer, and his readers, the northern and the southern States,
Republicans and *Republicans*, the people and their administration," said Lincoln, betrayed the legacy of the American Revolution, when the "inhabitants
of the South, these Virginian slave holders, with a swell of magnanimity, run
to the North, and hurried about our Capital, to rescue the endangered, or to
perish in the attempt."[39] Intended as a sarcastic rebuff of Federalist attacks on
the three-fifths clause and Republican sincerity, Lincoln's phrase also suggests the difficulty of celebrating national unity when it came to slavery: in
order to defend those "Virginian slaveholders," he had to name them as such,
and exhort New Englanders to celebrate their salvation at the hands of southern masters.

Jeffersonian nationalism was not always so awkward, but it was per-
sistently defiant. The *National Aegis* likewise responded to charges that Jefferson was a sectional president, elected by the "votes" of black slaves, by
invoking the virtues of national union. "The Monitor," writing in March of
1802, argued that the underlying objective of Federalist sectionalism was "to
divide the northern from the southern States, and on the ruins of such division, to erect a Monarchical Government." And yet, he exclaimed, those
monarchists "are the men who are reviling the present administration; comparing the President to a Nero, and calling him a Negro President! Was he
not chosen under the same Constitution that Washington and Adams were,
and does not the same base reflection rest on them as it does on Mr. Jefferson? Shameful disgrace to our national character !!!" The disgrace, to be clear,
was not the three-fifths clause, but the fact that anyone would use the clause
to criticize Jefferson. A month earlier, "A Traveler" made the same point. He

acknowledged the popularity of Federalist charges that Jefferson was elected by the three-fifths clause, but, like Lincoln, decried such criticism as the suggestion of treason, as a betrayal of the Constitution and the nation. The unstated counterpart to that message was critical to Jeffersonian success in the North: being an American meant not talking about the political power of slavery.[40]

Federalists were hardly deterred. Though some members in Congress worried that they might be overwhelmed by a Republican tide and "go home without their heads," Federalist dissidents only escalated their attacks on slavery and southern power.[41] In 1804, they proposed a constitutional amendment abolishing the three-fifths clause, attempting to strike a blow at both the political power of the South and the political conscience of the North. Known as the Ely amendment, for its sponsor in the Massachusetts Senate, William Ely, the proposal gained little traction, but it once again placed Jeffersonians on the defensive, as Federalists exposed the institutional contradictions of Jeffersonian democracy. John Quincy Adams, one of two Federalist senators from Massachusetts, joined the attack as "Publius Valerius" in the fall of 1804, hoping to influence the presidential contest in Massachusetts. Relatively silent on slavery in the Senate, Adams was vociferous in print, denouncing the three-fifths clause for creating "a privileged order of slave-holding Lords, and a race of men degraded to a lower station, merely because they are not slave-holders."[42]

Massachusetts Republicans responded with a familiar mixture of nationalism and accusation: In their minds, Ely's proposal was yet another byproduct of disaffected, antidemocratic resentment by sectional elites. Barnabas Bidwell, soon to begin a short-lived national political career as a Jeffersonian, reminded the Massachusetts Senate of the once powerful bonds between his own state and Virginia. Those bonds were a staple trope for New England Republicans, who constantly retold the story of the Revolution, when Virginia came to the aid of Massachusetts. Rather than sons of the Revolution, Federalists were portrayed as its traitors. Virginians, in contrast, from the Revolution to the ascendancy of Jefferson, were the guarantors of New England freedom. As Elbridge Gerry explained to Thomas Jefferson in 1803, the three "antirepublican" states of New England "had great merit in establishing their independence but owe the preservation of it to the southern states." Until the rise of "*Federalism*," said the *Independent Chronicle*, "*Massachusetts* and *Virginia* were happily united and harmonious in their politics." Throughout early 1805, the *Chronicle* reprinted criticisms of the Ely amendment from multiple state legislatures, as part of a campaign to paint Federalists as national pariahs. Republicans from the Pennsylvania House claimed that the sectional obstacles in the way of union—of both the "physical" and "moral" kind—required "a reciprocal spirit of conciliation and compromise, in the formation of a general government." To trifle with that spirit, they claimed, might send the whole national edifice crashing to the ground. Similar comments followed from the legislatures of South Carolina, Kentucky, and Maryland. The national chorus defined the three-fifths clause as the necessary price of Union. According to the *Chronicle*, it was a price worth paying.[43]

Such arguments aggravated John Quincy Adams to no end. In his mind, the three-fifths clause was unjust, and anyone who advocated against the Ely amendment on grounds of "patriotism" or "union" prostrated themselves with the "fear of giving offense by the exercise of an indisputable right." To feel such fears was to act the slave; to instill them was to employ the "language of a negro driver on a plantation, to the wretches who tremble under his lash." Adams doubted that such cowardly motives could truly exist "in the heart of a New England farmer."[44] In the midst of this bombast, he had a point: New England Jeffersonians consistently attacked Federalist elitism and hierarchy, while claiming the right and power of ordinary citizens to make political decisions in their own interest and on their own terms. But when it came to the three-fifths clause they advocated either outright suppression of political debate or, at best, leaving the issue to their southern colleagues to resolve. Such arguments effectively mirrored the southern response to antislavery argument at the national level. When Joseph Bradley Varnum and other Republicans spoke on behalf of African American petitioners and against the Fugitive Slave Act in 1797, southern slaveholders responded by demanding that the subject be rejected altogether. "This is a kind of property on which the House has no power to legislate," explained South Carolina's William Loughton Smith; "it was not a proper subject for Legislative attention."[45] Acceding to such autocratic claims should have galled any true democrat, implied John Quincy Adams, who was distressed as much by self-censorship among New England Republicans as by southern Republican dependence on the three-fifths clause.

But the political landscape was even more convoluted than he made it out to be. While New England Jeffersonians celebrated democracy and suppressed the problem of slavery, Federalists, who were quick to indict the political inequality created by the three-fifths clause, were also eager to scorn the degradations of democracy. In addition to denouncing the "Negro

President," the *New England Palladium* instructed its readers about the dangers of "universal suffrage." In March of 1801, "Farmer Johnson" proposed that the vote be restricted to men "who hold a good character and a reasonable share of property," lest "the bad men" (who were generally men without property) elect "bad candidates" to office. "Democracy," the paper explained that October, "says to the destitute mob, protect the rights of man, which are two, the one vengeance and the other pillage." In the fall of 1802, the *Palladium* insisted that a political system based on the "uncontrouled power of the multitude," would lead to "the slavery of all, even of that of the blind multitude." Such openly antidemocratic professions only justified the Republican image of Federalists as unrepentant aristocrats.[46]

To Jefferson and his supporters, Federalist disdain for democracy simply reflected the perversity of New England elites, and a number of historians have remained squarely in the Jeffersonian tradition. Yet many Federalists developed a complex interpretation of American politics, one rooted in a transatlantic, conservative critique of the violent potential of unchecked popular sovereignty. This conservatism had its repressive side, as was obvious from the Alien and Sedition laws or the suppression of the Whiskey Rebellion and Fries's Rebellion in 1790s Pennsylvania; on the whole, however, Federalist "tyranny" was mild compared to either the Jacobin Terror or British political repression, on brutal display in Ireland in 1798. It was likewise far less violent than Virginia's response to Gabriel's failed slave rebellion in Richmond in the summer of 1800. In the end, Federalist conservatism was not driven, as Jeffersonians argued, by the simple desire to control. Many Federalists were skeptical of the human character and the human capacity for good, and they consequently favored an organic social hierarchy, tied to traditional sources of authority and order. Connecticut's Noah Webster, for example, believed that only old men should vote and hold office because the majority of men were "ignorant, or what is worse, governed by prejudices & authority." In contrast, Connecticut Republican Samuel Morse believed that "the human mind is capable of improvement, the human heart susceptible of much amendment, and human happiness of great extension." To Federalists, such optimism for human progress was foolhardy at best. Republican claims that democracy and reason would liberate mankind were contradicted by the violence of the French Revolution and the slaveholding South. Yet Federalists rarely made these points in isolation from far more simplistic antidemocratic arguments, in which they derided the capacity of ordinary people to govern. This did not aid their electoral prospects and it limited the impact of their criticism of Republican hypocrisy on the slavery question. Confronted with Federalist outrage, Jeffersonians consistently refocused political debate on the purportedly true source of inequality in America: New England elitism.[47]

Doing so, as in the debate over the Ely Amendment, sidelined Federalist challenges to slavery. This had obvious practical benefits for Republicans. The ideological virtues of "union" and the Republican cause were frequently supplemented by the virtues of patronage and political favors. Levi Lincoln, for example, along with prominent Republicans like Gideon Granger, Henry Dearborn, William Eustis, and Elbridge Gerry, joined the Jefferson and Madison administrations in Washington; Republicans like Abraham Bishop and Ephraim Kirby were rewarded with federal patronage. As Jeffrey Pasley has argued, less genteel Republicans, like the Connecticut printers Charles Holt and Samuel Morse, did not fare as well when it came to political rewards.[48] Democratization had obvious institutional limits tied to class and status, even among white male Republicans. Yet on the whole, national success helped sustain the Republican movement locally. New England Jeffersonians gained power at home after 1800 by employing the political capital of the nationally dominant Republican party. Jeffersonian nationalism helped Republicans remain competitive in Massachusetts from Jefferson's election until the War of 1812: They held the governorship outright in four of thirteen elections, and garnered a majority of the Massachusetts delegation to the House of Representatives in two elections before the war. Republicans fared well in Vermont, Rhode Island, and New Hampshire as well. They had a harder road in Connecticut, but after the War of 1812 they eventually defeated the reigning Federalists.[49] The alliance between men like Lincoln, John Leland, and Abraham Bishop and men like Jefferson and Madison was thus in many ways pragmatic. And as long as the power of Federalist aristocrats over their own lives seemed more ominous to northern Jeffersonians than the power of southern slaveholders over their slaves, joining the Virginians at the national level made eminent sense. Raising the issue of slavery would only destabilize an effective political coalition, so the subject was best left in silence.

The Big Cheese

Yet Jeffersonian political behavior constantly exceeded instrumental explanation, as the now often told story of John Leland and the "Mammoth Cheese" indicates. For many ordinary people, Jeffersonian politics offered a new understanding of one's self and national political culture, rather than direct institutional benefits in the form of patronage. John Leland's hometown of Cheshire, Massachusetts, settled by Rhode Island Baptists, was apparently overwhelmed with Republican enthusiasm. The town voted 181-0 for Jeffersonian electors in the presidential election of 1804.[50] In the election 1800, the Massachusetts legislature, controlled by Federalists, cast all of the state's electoral votes for John Adams rather than allow the presidential contest to be fought out in separate electoral districts. Cheshire Republicans managed to find a way to demonstrate their loyalty to Jefferson nonetheless. Likely spurred by Leland, the town decided to commemorate Jefferson's rise to the presidency by producing a giant cheese. Requiring a cheese vat six feet in diameter and the milk of 900 cows, the cheese had preposterous proportions: the finished product weighed in at 1,235 pounds. Even before it was completed, the so-called "mammoth cheese" became a topic of national discussion. Federalists mocked the proposed endeavor, while Republican papers from Rhode Island to Pennsylvania reported on its production and anticipated its arrival at Washington in early 1802.[51]

Leland did not disappoint. Starting in November 1801, he traveled overland to the Hudson River, then by boat to New York, where the cheese was briefly on display, then by ship to Baltimore, and finally by wagon to Washington, where he delivered the cheese to the president on January 1, 1802. Jefferson called the cheese "an ebullition of the passion of republicanism in a state where it has been under heavy persecution." On the day of its delivery, he cemented his ties to New England Baptists by writing a letter to the Danbury Association in Connecticut, where he employed his now famous metaphor of a "wall of separation between church and state," lending his charisma to the dissenters' fight for religious disestablishment.[52] Federalists in Washington were far less fond of Leland's cheese. Manasseh Cutler, with a flourish of disdain, referred to it as "this monument of human weakness and folly." He was even less impressed by Leland's preaching abilities when the "Mammoth Priest" gave a sermon in the House of Representatives a few days later. William Plumer, the New Hampshire senator, had the chance to sample the cheese two years later while dining with Jefferson, and remarked simply that it "is very far from being good." Samuel Taggart of Massachusetts was served some of the cheese a week before Plumer and described it as "wretched enough." Similarly arch comments echoed in Washington throughout the cheese's career.[53]

The people of Cheshire had inscribed on the cheese the motto that Benjamin Franklin had proposed for the seal of the United States, a succinct expression of their evangelical political radicalism: "Rebellion to Tyrants is Obedience to God." In an address from his townsmen read by Leland at the presentation of the cheese, religion and politics were similarly combined. "We believe the supreme Ruler of the Universe," said Leland, "has raised up a Jefferson at this critical day, to defend *Republicanism* and to baffle the arts of *Aristocracy.*" Leland then went on to note that "The Cheese was produced by the personal labor of *Freeborn Farmers*, with the voluntary and cheerful aid of their wives and daughters, without the assistance of a single slave." As the historian Jeffrey Pasley has suggested, we may today be surprised by such language, "given the modern view of Jefferson as an avatar of slavery."[54] But one might have expected contemporaries to be somewhat surprised at the language too, since, avatar or not, Jefferson surely partook of the fruits of slave labor. In Washington, Jefferson preferred to employ "white servants" rather than his own slaves, and his chef was a Frenchman, Honoré Julien. Yet he did have both slaves and free blacks in his presidential household, including Edith Fossett, whom he brought to Washington to be trained under Julien. She became Jefferson's cook at Monticello after his retirement, and she remained enslaved until his death, at which point she was sold along with her children to settle Jefferson's many debts. Fortunately, her husband, freed by Jefferson's will, later managed to purchase Edith and the rest of their family.[55] While Jefferson did not have much compunction about the political status of those who produced his food, one might have expected Leland to be aware of the irony in offering a glorified free-labor cheese to a slaveholder, since his own writings demonstrate an intimate knowledge of the everyday despotism inherent in slaveholding. What is surprising when one reads his address is not that we moderns view Jefferson and the southern Republicans as so closely bound to slavery, but that Leland did not.

Leland did not overlook Jefferson's attachment to slavery simply because it served his interest to do so. Instead of discarding his criticism of slavery as he embraced Jefferson and the Democratic-Republican cause, Leland harnessed it to a critique of New England Federalism and religious oppression. He truly believed that Jefferson had a providential role in American history, and that an aristocracy, in the form of the Federalist party, controlled the government of Massachusetts and oppressed Republicans and evangelicals alike. To Leland, the subjection of conscience in New England was not only analogous but somehow equivalent to the subjection of African American slaves. In a Fourth of July oration at Cheshire in 1802, Leland lamented that "a great number of thousands of people, within the United States, are still held in lasting slavery," forced to "drag the galling chain of vassalage under their despotic masters." He then made a remarkable transition from the South to New England: "As personal slavery exists chiefly in the southern states," he explained, "so religious slavery abounds exclusively in three or four of the New England states. Here the rights of conscience are made articles of merchandise, and men, who differ in opinion from the majority of a town, have to buy them." These were patently different forms of oppression, but in essence, Leland argued, "tyranny is always the same." He closed with a prayer that both tyrannies would be abolished together, in some far off "halcyon day . . . when the chains of personal slavery, and the manacles of religious despotism may be broken asunder, and freedom and religion pervade the whole earth."[56] In theory, Leland's vision of universal freedom was both compelling and coherent. But in terms of the Jeffersonian alliance, it had some major problems: Leland relied on the Democratic-Republicans to bring religious liberty to New England, while southern Republicans relied on the same coalition to represent their interests, including the protection of slavery, at the national level. The institutional context of Jeffersonian democracy, in other words, made Leland's "halcyon day" incredibly unlikely.

In contrast, the ideological context of Jeffersonian democracy made such contradictory relationships between northern liberation and southern slavery not only possible but necessary. Slavery as metaphor allowed Leland to substitute his evangelical brethren for southern bondspersons, which in turn displaced slavery as fact. Thus a slaveholder like Jefferson could become the folk hero of a band of anti-aristocratic Baptists who objected to despotism in all of its forms and took pride in their free labor cheese. Jefferson encouraged these identifications and substitutions through his patronage of men like Leland. Although he never imagined Leland as a social and intellectual equal, receiving a giant cheese required more than condescension. Jefferson gave Leland $200 for the cheese and, more importantly, welcomed him in Washington as a man with political standing. Leland, in turn, gave crucial substance to Jeffersonian ideology, in a way that Jefferson himself, a quintessential Virginia slaveholder, could never have done. Leland fought for the basic objectives of political liberty and reform at the heart of the Jeffersonian message. He lived the democratic life that Jefferson, at his best, envisioned himself defending. That Leland saw Jefferson as a providential hero leading a party of the oppressed, and not as a master leading a party of slaveholders, only solidified their ideological bonds. Leland's celebration of Jefferson did far more than parry Federalist recriminations of the "Negro President." It helped Leland and other northern Republicans reconcile hostility toward slavery with political ties to southern masters. Imagining Jefferson as an emancipator served obvious partisan ends, but it also helped Leland believe that his aspirations for freedom were untainted by slavery. The Cheshire Republicans could celebrate their free-labor cheese and dream of liberty without acknowledging their institutional dependence on southern bondage through the Jeffersonian coalition. The giant cheese eventually moldered away, but the alliance between northern freedom and southern slavery that Leland helped form lasted well into the antebellum period.

The Rebellion of the White Slaves

Abraham Bishop had defined a vanguard position in 1791, when he defended the slave rebellion in Saint-Domingue in 1791 and attacked the racial cast of American politics. In many ways, he defined a similarly innovative position in 1801 when he called for a new antislavery movement in New England, led by "societies for the emancipation of white slaves." In 1791, Bishop had denied that the American British revolutionaries had ever been enslaved, disputing the comparison between imperial rule and bondage. But in Jeffersonian Connecticut white Americans had become slaves, to an insidious group of masters among the Federalist party.

This argument crystallized at a daylong celebration of Jefferson's inauguration in Wallingford, Connecticut, on March 11, 1801. Advertised as a "day of Thanksgiving" to celebrate Jefferson's election, the Wallingford event brought together the many strands of Connecticut Republicanism and "an immense concourse of people" that included at least 1,000 Republicans (according to the Republican paper *The American Mercury*). In the morning, Gideon Granger read the Declaration of Independence and the Unitarian minister Stanley Griswold gave a sermon, after which the celebrants drank several toasts. In the evening, Abraham Bishop gave an oration at Wallingford's North Meeting House, festooned for the occasion with "the names of *Jefferson* and *Burr* in large capitals over the door." The night ended "with a brilliant exhibition of Fireworks."[57]

In his speech, Bishop delivered a blunt indictment of Federalist rule. Returning to the themes of *Connecticut Republicanism*, Bishop identified

Federalists as the latest incarnation of the "friends of order"—the few who attempted to rule the many and suppress the message of human equality, from the days of Jesus Christ to the time of Jefferson. The "friends of order" maintained political and economic inequality by force but especially by ideology: by "enslaving the minds of men." Connecticut Federalists pursued this object by controlling the press, through localist paternal power, and especially through the union of church and state. But their time had finally come, for "the American and French revolutions were doubtless intended to improve the moral and political condition of man by redeeming the people from the tyranny of the friends of order. All our victories, all our defeats have been so many pledges for the eventual triumph of the rights of man." In Bishop's eyes, Jeffersonian Republicanism was an anti-elitist political movement that would liberate New Englanders from Federalist authority.[58]

"Slavery" as a political metaphor appeared throughout Bishop's speech, in attacks on the power wielded by the "friends of order." A preface to the published version of the speech, however, indicated that Bishop was specifically thinking of southern slavery when considering the predicament of New England Republicans. These men were "white slaves," he claimed, who had it far worse than their southern counterparts:

When a Southern slave breaks his fetters of bondage and declares for liberty, a hue and cry is raised, the daring culprit is apprehended and death is his portion. When a Northern slave declares for the emancipation of himself and his white brethren, all the masters are in an uproar, the pursuit is close, all means are fair and the daring wretch is doomed to all the vengeance of his oppressors.

But a Southern slave has only one master; a northern one has many, yea, he has a master to every power and faculty, to every thought and opinion on every subject. It is not necessary to the character of a slave that he have a chain about his leg, or a rope about his neck. Invisible slavery is more dreadful, extensive and intolerable than visible slavery, because in the first case the masters will often deny its existence.

Like Leland, Bishop did not attempt to ignore slavery in the South. Instead he incorporated slavery into a political vision that emphasized the oppression of northern white men. In doing so, he reconciled his liberation with slaveholder power, through a self-aggrandizing celebration of New England

freedom. "THE REIGN OF TERROR is no more," Bishop told his Wallingford audience, "and we are allowed, on this festive day, to render thanks for
our emancipation. . . . Slaves in every part of the world are bursting their
chains and proving that 'man in his soul abhors tyranny.'" [59] Toasts offered at
the Wallingford celebration and elsewhere echoed Bishop's salute to emancipation from tyranny. "Republican Printers," said the Wallingford Republicans: "of all men the most hated and persecuted, because of all men the most
dangerous to Tyrants." In Torringford, Connecticut, Jeffersonians toasted
"The people of the United States: May the despotic chains from which they
are emancipated, teach them to form into a phalanx impenetrable to the
shafts of monarchical or aristocratical delusion."[60] Republicans would defend
their liberated minds.

But in many respects, these episodes of emancipation best revealed the
compromises that Jeffersonians made with slavery and slaveholder power.
While they continued to represent their cause in terms of egalitarian universalism, the Republican political alliance caused such principles to founder, as
black slaves and white democrats met different fates in the Jeffersonian
United States. In Virginia, when slaves attempted to burst their chains during
Gabriel's Rebellion in August of 1800, they were met by state violence, as the
masters maintained their power by killing slaves who abhorred their condition. In Connecticut a few months later, such conflicting details disappeared
in the grandiosity of Bishop's rhetoric and its narrow focus on northern white
men. Whereas cosmopolitan radicalism in the 1790s caused Bishop to turn
outward, including slavery under a broad critique of unjust power, Jeffersonian politics invited a turning inward, as distant oppression became a metaphor for the self. Emphasizing their bondage in Federalist Connecticut,
Bishop and his Republican comrades came to uneasy terms with slavery in
Jeffersonian America.

New England Republicans accommodated the institutional power of
slavery in a similar way, by insisting on their own relative oppression. Discussing the three-fifths clause in 1803, Bishop again returned to the language
of white slavery: "The Southern States modestly claimed a representation
only on 3 fifths of their black slaves, but the northern states insisted on esti-
mating the whole number of their *white slaves*." A year prior, he had lamented
"the condition of tens of thousands of our brethren, who have no more voice
in our councils than the black slaves in the Indies; men of full age and capacity, industrious, intelligent, useful members of society, who happened not to
have property enough to entitle them to a vote." In response to Federalist

attacks on the institutional power of slavery in the Jeffersonian coalition, Bishop pointed to the political slavery of northern whites, suffering under property qualifications for the franchise. Such comparisons may have been intended to prove Federalists hypocrites, but the metaphorical substitution of white bondsman for black also obscured the political power of Jeffersonian slaveholders. The coercive minority of southern masters became lost in the midst of Republican clamoring for emancipation and democracy.[61]

Leland and Bishop were not alone in thinking themselves enslaved by Federalism. The *Independent Chronicle*, the leading Republican paper in New England, likewise substituted northern Jeffersonian for southern slave, albeit in a much more mundane way. Like the *National Aegis*, the *Chronicle* parried Federalist criticism of the three-fifths clause, Virginia slaveholders, and Jefferson's personal relationship to mastery and despotism. It pointed to Jefferson's antislavery principles, on record in the *Notes on the State of Virginia*, and observed that the Virginia House of Burgesses had opposed slave importation (while conveniently overlooking the racist passages in the *Notes* and Virginia's self-interest in curtailing the international trade). As to the three-fifths clause, the *Chronicle* insisted, like the *National Aegis*, that it was an essential part of the Constitution, a compromise Massachusetts had always supported. Moreover, the *Chronicle* argued, Virginians did not in fact derive additional political power from their slave population. Because of the large state-small state bargain, Virginia actually sacrificed federal representation in the interest of Union. Returning to charges that Jefferson was elected by the three-fifths clause, the *Chronicle* claimed the truly "subject" votes in the election of 1800 were those of Massachusetts, since the Federalist legislature had refused to allow the people to determine the electoral vote.[62]

In other words, the Massachusetts Republicans were the real slaves, to Federalists who controlled their votes, just as Virginian slaveholders, presumably, controlled the votes of their bondsmen. The logic here was far more convoluted than in Bishop and Leland's comparisons, since the three-fifths clause did not deny anyone the right to vote—it simply gave additional power to slaveholders. But the *Chronicle* was undeterred, exclaiming in a later piece, "Let the *Centinel* then say that Mr. Jefferson has been chosen by slaves! If the true republicans of the United States are slaves, what is the other party?" Regardless of Federalist efforts, the paper continued, "the friends of Mr. Jefferson are not yet slaves; and under a merciful and protecting Deity, are not likely to become so." The article likely referred to complaints in the *Columbian Centinel*, similar to those in the *New-England Palladium*, that Jefferson's election depended on the three-fifths clause. As the *Centinel* put it in December 1800, "the wise and good of other countries . . . will regret that any policy shall impose on the United States a Chief Magistrate elected by the *influence of Negro slaves.*" In response, the *Chronicle* simply substituted northern Republicans as the referent for "slaves," and turned Federalist criticism of the South into slander of Jeffersonian New England. Then the paper righteously protested this Federalist abuse. As sophistry, this may not inspire, but unconsciously, such a substitution expressed the essence of the Jeffersonian coalition. Jefferson's friends in the North became the true slaves, a people fighting for freedom from oppression by aristocrats, religious zealots, nativist prejudice, and Anglophiles, while southern slaveholders became iconic leaders of northerners fighting for political and social equality.[63]

Abraham Bishop said it best. "Nothing could have prevented a monarchy here but the accession of Jefferson and Burr to the presidency," he told his Wallingford audience in 1801. In terms of the wider Republican coalition, this meant that the very men who, as a class, forestalled emancipation in the South, freed the northern slaves from the shackles of aristocratic tyranny. Bishop claimed forthrightly, "if the white slaves should rise in mass, they would be too much for their masters." The image was meant to provoke, but Bishop was not joking: in his mind, Jeffersonian democracy was a slave rebellion.[64]

These comparisons and substitutions seem irrational and exaggerated in retrospect, and to most Federalists, they appeared so at the time. But most New England Republicans were true believers, despite constant Federalist harping that the Republican emancipators were in fact slaveholding lords. Northern Republicans were perhaps misguided but they were not insincere. Men like Bishop and Leland believed ardently in the Republican cause, and they also believed that slavery was wrong. In contrast to most Republican commentary on the three-fifths clause, they did not try to suppress discussion of slavery or minimize southern bondage; nor did they condone the institution by appeals to race. But in substituting northern political inequality for southern slavery, they helped create a complex political alliance that in turn made it difficult to achieve antislavery objectives in national politics. For some Republicans, mere political calculation made this knot difficult to unravel, since there was no political organization more devoted to ridding New England of Federalism than Jefferson's Democratic-Republicans. But for others, ideological and emotional bonds were decisive: if one really had felt liberated by the rise of Jeffersonian democracy—hardly an implausible emotion in early nineteenth century Massachusetts or Connecticut—then the temptation to magnify one's own oppression in order to come to terms with slavery in the South must have been all the more powerful.

New England Jeffersonians, like Republicans throughout the North, helped provide American slaveholders, a distinct minority in a democratizing polity, what they needed most: tacit majority consent. They did so not by linking arms in racial fellowship, but rather by transforming themselves into slaves, and slaveholders into their emancipators. They won their freedom from Federalism, as Jefferson had promised Elbridge Gerry, but freedom on those terms proved hard to escape.

CHAPTER 2

Philadelphia, Crossroads of Democracy

Writing in Philadelphia's *Aurora General Advertiser* in 1804, Thomas Paine defined the political novelty of Jeffersonian America. According to Paine, popular sovereignty and political equality made the United States home to a new type of man. Once they left Europe and its "hereditary potentates" behind, men began to consider "government and public affairs as part of their own concern," and thereby "found themselves in possession of a new character, the character of sovereignty."[1] Alongside the freedom to govern one's self, however, there was a very different type of sovereignty in America, as Paine knew well—the sovereignty of the master over the slave. Slaveholding power did not inspire all men to see government as "part of their own concern," as it was inherently antidemocratic. But in Jeffersonian political culture, these two forms of sovereignty were closely bound to each other, as the autonomy of new men helped sustain a nation-state that perpetuated bondage.

More than any other location in the early republic, Philadelphia expressed the conflicting strands of early national democracy. Tensions between North and South, Europe and the United States, black and white, cosmopolitanism and nationalism were woven throughout the city in a complex and combustible mix. Following the path of Tom Paine, English and Irish radicals flocked to the United States in the 1790s in response to British political repression, only to encounter the nativist and anti-Jacobin sentiments of the Federalist party. In Philadelphia and Pennsylvania, such men acquired national significance in the partisan struggles that created and sustained Jeffersonian democracy. These migrants gave an international cast to the rise of American democracy, since they connected their fight against Federalism to the French Revolution, the struggle for Irish autonomy, and a global ideological war against aristocracy. They also fought, by their very presence, to achieve Paine's vision of America as an "asylum for liberty." Northern Jeffersonians, immigrant and native alike, were the strongest supporters of liberalizing citizenship laws in the early nation. They embodied, in their lives and experiences, some of the most egalitarian ambitions of the Jeffersonian coalition.

In the midst of such cosmopolitan ardor, the state of Pennsylvania also had an important practical role in the Jeffersonian coalition. It was by far the most crucial ally to the South and the Republican cause. Jefferson wrote multiple letters about Pennsylvania in the lead-up to the election of 1800, explaining to confidantes that Pennsylvania "nearly holds the balance between the North & South"; that through "harmonizing by it's public authorities with those to the South," Pennsylvania "would command respect to the Federal constitution."[2] The 1799 election of Republican Thomas McKean as governor of Pennsylvania was seen as a bellwether for Republican success in the presidential contest the following year. As it turned out, Pennsylvania almost did not cast an electoral ballot in the election of 1800, since Federalists maintained enough power in the state senate to block a popular vote of the state's electors. But Jefferson was right about Pennsylvania's role in the Republican coalition. A relatively united South allied to one of the larger northern states, New York or Pennsylvania, could control national politics (or, in Jefferson's more subtle rendering, "command respect to the Federal constitution"). New York joined southern Republicans in 1800 to bring Jefferson to the presidency, but it quickly proved unreliable, in part because of factional competition among the state's Republicans, and in part because New Yorkers quickly moved to challenge Virginia for predominance in the federal government. After the election of 1800, by contrast, Pennsylvania proved to be the most reliable northern state in the Democratic-Republican column: it supported every Democratic-Republican presidential candidate and then every Democratic presidential candidate until the election of 1840. Other than Martin Van Buren in 1836, all these candidates were southern slaveholders. This record of capable support earned the state its moniker, "the keystone in the democratic arch," a label that, for some southerners, reflected the state's tractability as much as its position in the Union. Thus Henry Clay, in the midst of the Missouri Crisis, asked that the state remember itself as "the unambitious Pennsylvania, the keystone in the federal arch," and cease stoking sectional discord.[3] From Clay's perspective, among Pennsylvania's chief virtues was its ability to keep quiet on the problem of slavery.

Yet when it came to political conflict over slavery, Pennsylvania had not exactly been unambitious. In 1780, the state instituted gradual emancipation, and Jeffersonian Philadelphia was home to the Pennsylvania Abolition

Society, the most powerful antislavery group in the early republic, as well as a significant and politically active free black community. Southerners were well aware of Pennsylvania's antislavery tendencies, since the first major congressional crisis over slavery was sparked by antislavery petitions Pennsylvanians sent to the House. Southerners who came to Philadelphia in the 1790s, when the city served as the national capital, were wary of antislavery and free black residents; George Washington made sure to keep his slaves shuttling back and forth to Mount Vernon when he served as president, anxious that they would seek their freedom under Pennsylvania law. This reflected a common problem for slaveholders who traveled to or lived in proximity to Pennsylvania. Despite obtaining a fugitive slave law in 1793 that aided masters in recapturing their human property, slaveholders from Maryland and Virginia complained that their slaves frequently escaped to Pennsylvania, and they soon petitioned the federal government for stricter fugitive laws. Even though Pennsylvania accommodated sojourning slaveholders in state law, masters worried that Pennsylvanians, white as well as black, might refuse to tolerate the force and authority necessary to maintain power over their slaves.[4]

From the perspective of African Americans like Philadelphia's James Forten, however, freedom in the white-dominated society of early national Pennsylvania was deeply compromised. Most Pennsylvania whites were not willing to accept African Americans as social and political equals, barring them informally from the polls, juries, militia companies, and political celebrations. Gradual emancipation itself kept blacks born before 1780 enslaved and others indentured for over twenty years, an outright denial of equal standing. Moreover, in the years after 1780, many African Americans who by rights should have become free were illegally sent to the southern states or kidnapped into slavery. Similar developments shaped the post-abolition world of New York and New Jersey as well, but not until 1799 and 1804 respectively, when those states passed gradual emancipation laws. In 1800, there were still more than 20,000 slaves in New York and 12,000 in New Jersey (compared to roughly 1,700 in Pennsylvania), and New Jersey masters frequently published runaway ads in Philadelphia papers. The unfinished state of mid-Atlantic abolition meant that antislavery efforts in Pennsylvania were constantly embattled in the local politics of race and emancipation.[5]

Philadelphia was a crossroads where multiple strands of early national politics intersected, overlapped, and collided: antislavery agitation, immigrant radicalism, slaveholder power, and democracy. Looking beyond the local struggles over race and abolition in the city that have been well documented by historians, this chapter examines the Jeffersonian encounter with slavery in terms of national and transnational ideological struggles over democracy. The major focus throughout is on three Irish American insurgents—William Duane, Thomas Branagan, and John Binns—whose lives exemplify the crucial connections between slavery, nationalism, transatlantic democracy, and race in early national Philadelphia. Taking this wider perspective suggests a more complicated genealogy for the emergence of white male democracy in the North. As Jeffersonians sought a language to explain themselves and their bonds to southern power, they increasingly turned to race, which allowed them to redefine democracy in ways that made solidarity with slaveholders seem more legitimate. Whiteness, in other words, was as much about making cognitive and ideological allowances for the extreme authority of slaveholding, as it was a method for excluding free African Americans from equal political standing.[6]

But race was always an unstable category, reflecting the complicated origins of the Jeffersonian alliance. The relationship between slaveholders and democrats was not built on open claims of white supremacy, but rather in a long political fight to democratize the American polity. Throughout the 1790s, cosmopolitan democrats sought to redefine American nationality and citizenship along egalitarian lines. Embracing the United States from the outside, such men had little respect for the claims of tradition or nativity. Yet they also confronted American slavery from an external perspective. It was not an institution that immigrants could take for granted, since they did not have historic ties to the American nation-state. Instead, they had to choose citizenship in the slaveholding republic of the United States. In doing so, immigrant radicals presented the conflict between cosmopolitan democracy and chattel slavery, a defining contradiction of the age of revolution, in one of its starkest forms. Ultimately, nation, race, and democracy fused in a complex and volatile arrangement in Pennsylvania, as immigrants claimed the slaveholding republic as their own, and as the world's best hope for democratic government.

George Washington, Slaveholding Tyrant

The relationship between transatlantic radicalism and Pennsylvania democracy began during the American Revolution, as exemplified by Thomas Paine, who defined a cosmopolitan argument for American independence in

Common Sense and supported the radically republican Pennsylvania Constitution of 1776.[7] The career of William Duane, who became the most important Jeffersonian editor in the United States during the election of 1800, reflected the ongoing ties between anglophone radicalism and American democracy in the early national period. Born in the North American colonies to Irish emigrant parents in 1760, Duane spent his early years on the New York frontier, near Lake Champlain.[8] He returned to Ireland with his mother in 1771, then moved to England in the early 1780s, and then, in 1787, to Calcutta, where he edited two newspapers, the *Bengal Journal* and the *World*. By 1794, his support for the French Revolution and disgruntled officers in the army of the East India Company put Duane at odds with colonial elites, who forcibly banished him from Bengal. In a parting editorial, Duane proudly claimed American citizenship and told his fellow "Englishmen" that he planned to return to America, where he hoped to find his countrymen enjoying true liberty: "I trust in God I shall find them free, that I may forget that slavery exists anywhere." That proved to be an impossible ambition, in the short term because he was confined to a ship (aptly named the *William Pitt*) bound for England.[9]

Duane arrived in England in 1795, where he worked briefly with the London Corresponding Society (LCS), a group of political radicals and reformers who sought to democratize British politics and society. In the context of war between Britain and revolutionary France, LCS members were targets for government repression, as Duane's counterpart John Binns learned firsthand. Duane emigrated to the United States in 1796, evading Prime Minister William Pitt's crackdown on the LCS. In America, he continued to pay close attention to British and European politics. He especially supported the United Irishmen, a group of radicals, including John Binns, who fought for an independent Irish republic. His transatlantic politics were shared by Philadelphia Jeffersonians, as the toasts at a December 1799 political celebration suggest: Republicans drank to the cause of democracy in Pennsylvania and the character of Thomas Jefferson as well as to the "rights of man," the downfall of the "despots of Europe," and "The United Irishmen, rebellion against tyrants is the law of God."[10]

In the United States, Duane soon found himself at the center of national political conflict. He began to work for Benjamin Franklin Bache at Philadelphia's *Aurora General Advertiser*, the most prominent Republican paper in the 1790s. Bache, Benjamin Franklin's grandson, imported European political radicalism into the United States. He published Paine's work throughout the 1790s, and repeatedly instigated conflict with the Federalist party. After Bache died of yellow fever in 1798, Duane continued to publish the *Aurora* on behalf of his widow, Margaret Bache. He later took over the paper on his account and married Margaret. With financial assistance from prominent Republicans, the *Aurora* became the most important Jeffersonian paper in the election of 1800, and Duane retained fairly close ties to Jefferson for the rest of his career. Duane's life in the United States mirrored those of other British and Irish immigrants like Binns, Joseph Priestley, Thomas Cooper, and Thomas Addis Emmet, who achieved political standing in the United States and infused democratic politics with cosmopolitan radicalism.[11]

As in New England, early democratic politics in Pennsylvania frequently embraced open opposition to slavery. Soon after arriving in the United States, Duane penned a blistering attack on George Washington and his 1796 farewell address to the American people. Addressing the president directly, through a public letter, Duane indicted Washington for numerous faults, from his partiality to Britain to his endorsement of Hamilton to the warnings against partisanship in the farewell address, which Duane described as "the loathings of a sick mind." Duane saw himself as a patriot in defense of the new American nation, unafraid to criticize the hero of the Revolution. He warned his readers that republics had often faltered because of excessive "confidence placed in the virtues and talents of individuals"; he therefore sought "to expose the PERSONAL IDOLATRY into which we have been heedlessly running." At the end of his letter, Duane ruthlessly assessed Washington's character. He claimed that Washington's repressive political behavior reflected his moral failures, and entertained doubts about the sincerity of his patriotism during the Revolution. Most damning of all, Washington was a slaveholder. Duane argued that future generations would look back on Washington as a hypocrite and tyrant. They would "discover," said Duane,

> that the great champion of American Freedom the rival of Timoleon and Cincinnatus, twenty years after the establishment of the Republic, was possessed of FIVE HUNDRED of the HUMAN SPECIES IN SLAVERY, enjoying the FRUITS OF THEIR LABOUR WITHOUT REMUNERATION, OR EVEN THE CONSOLATIONS OF RELIGIOUS INSTRUCTION—that he retained the barbarous usages of the feudal system, and kept men in LIVERY—and that he still affected to be the friend of the Christian Religion, of civil Liberty, and moral equality—and to be withal a disinterested, virtuous, liberal and unassuming man.[12]

To Duane, slaveholding was fundamentally antidemocratic.

His denunciations of Washington were echoed across the Atlantic by the Liverpool radical Edward Rushton, who published in 1797 a letter he had written Washington the previous year. A supporter of the French Revolution, Rushton marveled at the contradiction of Washington, "a man who, notwithstanding his hatred of oppression, and his ardent love of liberty, holds at this moment hundreds of fellow-beings in a state of abject bondage."[13] Indictments of American hypocrisy on the slavery question were not confined to conservative critics of the American and French Revolutions. Transatlantic republicans likewise attacked slavery and pointed to the gap between American political rhetoric, which celebrated freedom, and the American political economy, which depended on bondage. But in the context of the 1790s, egalitarian attacks on slavery became entangled in partisan conflict and the emergence of Jeffersonian democracy. Thus Duane sought to turn his antislavery condemnation of Washington to partisan ends. Any advocate of democracy opposed to aristocratic rule, he implied, should oppose slavery and George Washington, and support the emerging Democratic-Republican coalition.

Antislavery Republicans

Duane was hardly alone in combining opposition to Federalism with opposition to slavery. The more genteel Republican Albert Gallatin, a Swiss immigrant, had become a member of the Pennsylvania Abolition Society in 1793, and supported a resolution in the Pennsylvania legislature to abolish slavery in the state, as the institution was "inconsistent with every principle of humanity, justice, and right." Gallatin briefly served as a U.S. senator in the winter of 1793–1794, until Federalists ejected him on the grounds that he had not been a citizen of the United States the required nine years. In 1795, he returned to Congress as a member of the House of Representatives, where he argued on behalf of antislavery causes. He presented a Quaker antislavery petition to the House in November 1797, and fought southern Federalists to have it read and sent to committee; he likewise defended, albeit in a more circumspect way, the right of free blacks from Philadelphia to petition the House in 1800.[14]

In defense of the Quaker petitioners, Gallatin told southern members of Congress that "all men are free when they set their foot within the State" (of

Pennsylvania), the only exception being slaves of southern congressmen. That was a considerable overstatement, since the Fugitive Slave Act of 1793 allowed masters to recapture enslaved people who escaped into Pennsylvania, while state law permitted slaveholders to reside for up to six months in Pennsylvania, slaves in tow. Congressmen, as Gallatin noted, were immune even from the six-month limit, a clear sign of Pennsylvania's willingness to accommodate the slaveholders of the American federal government. On the other hand, Gallatin, one of the more important Republicans in the House, had no qualms about uttering such openly antislavery sentiments in Congress. His southern Federalist colleagues took him seriously and were fairly incensed by his idealization of an antislavery Pennsylvania. In their eyes, at least, northern Republican hostility to slavery was far from superficial.[15]

Gallatin's colleague John Swanwick, a Republican merchant from Philadelphia, also supported the November 1797 Quaker petition. Back in December 1796, Swanwick had argued for federal intervention to prevent kidnapping of free African Americans. He provoked a debate with South Carolina Federalist William Loughton Smith, in the course of which Swanwick claimed that free African Americans "ought to be protected in their freedom, not only by the State Legislatures but by the General Government." In January 1797, Swanwick presented a petition from North Carolina freemen (at the time, residents of Philadelphia), protesting the abrogation of their manumissions in North Carolina and the racist operation of the fugitive slave law. Like Republican Joseph Bradley Varnum of Massachusetts, Swanwick believed free African Americans had the right to petition the government, for "if men were aggrieved, and conceive they have the claim to attention, petitioning was their sacred right, and that right should never suffer innovation." For most southerners, granting legitimacy to black petitioners was dangerous in and of itself, since it implied some recognition of African American political standing. In the case of the North Carolina freemen, accepting the petition also implied that Congress might investigate southern slavery. The status of slaves from North Carolina, southerners argued, was the proper concern of North Carolina, not the federal government. Northern petitioners and their congressional advocates threatened to instigate a struggle over the control of slavery, one which southern slaveholders wanted by all means to suppress.[16]

They consistently failed to do so. Slaveholders successfully blocked northern antislavery proposals, but they could not control the legislative discussion of slavery. When they attempted to suppress discussion, they often demonstrated an antidemocratic authority that further agitated antislavery northerners. In response to Gallatin's Quaker petition in November 1797, John Rutledge, Jr., complained that Philadelphia Quakers "attempt to seduce the servants of gentlemen travelling to the seat of Government" and that their petition attempted to incite a slave rebellion. Instead of referring the petition to a committee, he was "for its laying on the table, or under the table, that they might not only have done with the business for to-day, but finally." Rutledge, in other words, agreed with fellow South Carolina Federalist William Loughton Smith, who told Congress in January 1797 that slavery was "a kind of property on which the House has no power to legislate." Some historians interpret such claims to exclusive authority over slavery, the indispensable axiom of slaveholder political thought, as arguments for the state-level regulation of the peculiar institution. But many northern Republicans in Congress saw them differently, as attempts to resist democratic governance of an institution dependent on coercive power. Such transparent claims to power in national politics only supported Duane's portrayal of slaveholders as irredeemable enemies of liberty.[17]

Congressional conflict would eventually tear at the sectional bonds of the Jeffersonian coalition, but in the early years of Republican enthusiasm many northerners managed to maintain antislavery principles alongside support for Thomas Jefferson, who was no less a master than George Washington. In Congress, this was made possible in part by the fact that southern Federalists were the most voluble defenders of slavery. They were likewise exceedingly hostile to immigrant Republicans like Gallatin. In March 1798, Gallatin, along with Joseph Bradley Varnum, supported Massachusetts Federalist George Thatcher's plan to restrict expansion of slavery in the new Mississippi Territory. It was very much a minority position, as only twelve members of the House ended up backing Thatcher's visionary plan. Gallatin, in other words, much like Duane, was not afraid to speak out against slavery, and he likely felt an extra motivation when attacking arch-Federalists like the South Carolinians John Rutledge, Jr., and Robert Goodloe Harper. An opponent of Thatcher's motion in March 1798, Harper would soon be denouncing immigrants like Gallatin in debates over the Federalist Naturalization Act of 1798. In May 1798, Harper told Congress that citizenship should be confined to those born in the United States, and "that none but persons born in this country should be permitted to take a part in the Government."[18]

In contrast to men like Rutledge and Harper, it was hard for Thomas Jefferson not to appear liberal-minded. Nor was it difficult for northern Republicans, into the early 1800s, to maintain antislavery arguments alongside devotion to Jefferson. James Sloan, a Quaker who lived across the Delaware River from Philadelphia in Gloucester County, New Jersey, was a defiant Republican and Jefferson adulator: "Instead of a haughty Monarchist," he told fellow Republicans in 1801, after Jefferson's election, "we are now blest with a meek and amiable Democrat in the presidential chair." He was likewise a confirmed opponent of slavery: he was a member of a local abolition society, and after arriving in Congress in 1803, he fought consistently against slavery at the federal level, at one point proposing the emancipation of all the slaves in Washington, D.C.[19] Sloan was often joined in his antislavery attacks by two long-serving Pennsylvania representatives, William Findley and John Smilie. All three men embodied the democratizing impulse of Jeffersonian politics. Findley, in many ways the unspoken hero of the work of historian Gordon Wood, immigrated from Ireland in 1763 and began his American life as a weaver. Smilie had immigrated from Ireland in 1741, almost starving to death en route. He survived to become a prosperous farmer, and then spent a long career representing western Pennsylvania in Congress. These men owed their prominence, and their sense of political belonging, to the success of Jeffersonian democracy at the state and national levels.[20]

That success was subject to constant Federalist rebuke, as the case of James Sloan indicates. He often marketed his goods (including, presumably, hogs and cattle) in Philadelphia, leading Federalists to lampoon him as a common tradesman unfit for political power. In 1806, a Federalist paper mocked "Jemmy Sloan, who has been so often seen with his apron, his steel, and his cleaver, in the Philadelphia shambles, grease and blood to the eyes." His colleague in the House, Massachusetts Federalist Samuel Taggart, called him "emphatically the small end of small things," and could not understand how men like Sloan were elected to office. Taggart took solace in a frequently used metaphor for the rise of Jeffersonian democracy: "the faster the pot boils the sooner it will throw off the scum."[21] The pot was democracy, and Sloan was the scum. Such vitriol reflected the democratizing effect of Jeffersonian politics, which brought men like Sloan into political power.

In Taggart's New England, antagonism between Federalists and Republican often served to deflect attention from the national politics of slavery. But in Congress, Republican commitments to democracy and equality often led to conflicts over slavery with southern Federalist masters. In January 1800, Smilie, like Gallatin, defended the right of Absalom Jones and other free blacks from Philadelphia to petition the federal government, in the face of pronounced southern hostility. The Philadelphia petitioners requested reconsideration of the Fugitive Slave Act of 1793, an end to the international slave trade and, most alarming of all to slaveholders, "measures as shall in due course emancipate the whole of their brethren." Southerners immediately moved to reject the petition and suppress any discussion of slavery. John Rutledge, Jr., scorned the petition as an expression of "this new-fangled French philosophy of liberty and equality," and deemed its contents "unconstitutional to discuss." The young Virginia Republican John Randolph, serving his first term in Congress, "wish[ed] that the conduct of the House would have been so indignant as to have passed it over without discussion." But John Smilie wanted to discuss the petition, for he believed parts of it fell under the purview of the House; more important, he contended that free blacks in the North were "a part of the human species, equally capable of suffering and enjoying with others, and equally objects of attention, and therefore they had a claim to be heard." Smilie admitted that the House could not grant all the petitioners' requests—by which he meant their plea for a plan of national gradual emancipation—and he later voted with the overwhelming majority of the House (85-1) to affirm this point and appease slaveholders like Rutledge. Yet his defense of the right of petition, like Gallatin's and John Swanwick's, should not be taken lightly, since it suggested that in resistance to southern arguments for absolute control over slavery, northerners might acknowledge the political standing of free African Americans and their "claim to be heard."[22]

Smilie's appeal to the rights of the "human species" indicated the importance of cosmopolitan and universalist conceptions of political freedom among northern Republicans. These beliefs, Rutledge acknowledged, could challenge slavery by inciting sympathy for the enslaved or by granting free African Americans in the North a limited degree of political standing. In a related way, egalitarian sentiments could challenge slavery by inciting antipathy for slaveholders. Although by no means economic levelers, many northern Jeffersonians opposed elite privilege, in part because so many Federalists treated upstart Republicans as men who did not deserve to govern. Pennsylvania's Republican governor from 1808 to 1817, Simon Snyder, had once been a tanner. Pennsylvania representative and then senator Jonathan Roberts's father was engaged in politics, but Roberts began his own career as an apprentice wheelwright. Duane scrambled for money throughout his career, constantly imploring subscribers to the Aurora to pay their bills, and requesting patronage from gentlemen Republicans in positions of power. Such men were not accustomed to luxury; they made a virtue of their middling backgrounds, and, like the more genteel Abraham Bishop in Connecticut, they were often indignant at the wealth and power of "the great, the wise, the rich and mighty men of the world." Such attitudes, often generated by disputes with northern Federalists, could also engender hostility to slaveholders, as in Duane's attack on George Washington. As Pennsylvania Republican John B. C. Lucas (originally Jean-Baptiste, a republican immigrant from France) argued in Congress in 1804, slavery was an institution run by and for "the rich part of the community."[23]

Thus, as in New England, Pennsylvania Jeffersonians demonstrated a wide range of antislavery sentiment. Of course, as Democratic-Republicans, all these men were allied to powerful slaveholders in the southern states. And as in New England, instead of rejecting that alliance, they found ways to embrace it. Immigrant Jeffersonians elevated the Jeffersonian alliance beyond partisanship, as they fought for political inclusion in the United States. In response to Federalist nativism, immigrants leagued with Republican slaveholders to protect their political future in America. Through this relationship, cosmopolitan conceptions of American citizenship and a democratic public sphere became closely tied to what William Duane had defined, in 1796, as their antithesis: American slavery.

Slaves in the Bowels: Thomas Branagan

The Irish immigrant Thomas Branagan enacted the most poignant rendering of this ideological encounter, in a series of eccentric works that defined the intersection of egalitarianism, slavery, race, and conscience. A Jefferson acolyte, but not formally a Republican, Branagan began his American career relatively penniless. He appears to have come from means in Dublin, but he was disinherited for abandoning Catholicism, and arrived in Philadelphia without capital and with few connections. Before coming to the United States, Branagan, according to his autobiography, had participated in both the transatlantic slave trade and Caribbean slavery. As a young man in 1790, he joined a slave ship operating out of Liverpool and traveled to Africa and then the Caribbean to help buy and sell African slaves. He remained in the Caribbean for the next eight years, working as a seaman, a privateer, and finally as an overseer in Antigua. At some point he had a conversion experience and embraced a form of evangelical Christianity, likely Methodism; while an overseer, he experienced a more profound conversion to antislavery principle. "Impressed with a sense of the villainy and barbarity of keeping human beings in such deplorable conditions as I often saw the slaves reduced to," Branagan abandoned his position, returned to Dublin long enough to be disinherited, and then made for the United States. He would eventually come to call himself a "Penitential Tyrant," a man driven by remorse for his past participation in the evil of slavery.[24]

Branagan expressed a different side of northern democratic culture than William Duane: he was far less interested in secular politics, and on some issues, he was closer to New England Federalists than Jeffersonian Republicans. While he shared Duane's anti-elitism and his ardor for Thomas Jefferson, Branagan ultimately believed in divine justice far more than secular redemption. God, not natural law or reason, judged the good and evil in men and provided the foundation for human solidarity and individual morality. Like many evangelicals, Branagan stressed an individual connection to God, rooted in "conscience," but antislavery arguments radicalized his sense of religious individualism. He echoed antislavery figures from Pennsylvania's past, like the Quaker Benjamin Lay, and pointed to future abolitionist appeals to a "higher law": "it is better for me to hearken to, and obey the voice of conscience, (when under the influence of scripture and reason,)," said Branagan in 1807, "than the requisitions or prohibitions of men."[25] As was true of Jeffersonians throughout the North, Branagan understood democracy in terms of the freedom of the individual subject to think and act autonomously. But liberation from religious or political authority was less important to Branagan than coming to terms with human interdependence, and especially the relationship between one's self and suffering others. As Branagan put it in verse, humans, inspired by Jesus Christ (the "guest of celestial race"),

> Feel sympathetic love for all our race,
> And circle mankind in one kind embrace;
> Our greatest grief is to see human wo,
> Yet can't relieve, or stop the tears that flow.[26]

Branagan's individual was caught in an empathic web of connections to others, oppressed and oppressors alike. One's conscience was the arbiter of these relationships, the place where the pain of the suffering and the power of despotism were felt most keenly, and where the work of opposition began.[27]

Like many middling Jeffersonians, Branagan challenged the power of traditional elites to control access to knowledge. He had little faith in classical learning, and had no desire to comprehend Greek or Latin—although he did base much of his literary work on imitations of Homer and Virgil. "What in the name of common sense," Branagan wondered, "is the use of using language that one reader in one thousand cannot understand, and which has no other tendency but to notify the reader, who is not a latinest, and notify him that his author is one."[28] This populist and peculiar writer did not achieve much in the way of literary merit, but more than any other white Pennsylvanian, he gave voice to the powerful connections and contradictions between democratic subjectivity, slaveholder power, and race in the early national North.

From 1804 to 1805, Branagan published four long works indicting the international slave trade and the power of slavery in the United States. The first, *A Preliminary Essay on the Oppression of the Exiled Sons of Africa*, introduced his cause and attempted to raise subscription funds for two poetic works, *Avenia* and *The Penitential Tyrant*, both published in 1805, that dramatized the evil of the slave trade and slavery. Branagan apparently caught the attention of New York Quaker and antislavery publisher Samuel Wood, who helped release *Avenia* in 1805 and printed an extended edition of *The Penitential Tyrant* in 1807.[29] Finally, Branagan also published his *Serious Remonstrances Addressed to the Citizens of the Northern States* in 1805, a pamphlet that sought to incite northerners to confront the problem of American slavery. *Serious Remonstrances* also marked a departure from his other work, characterized by a deep empathy for the enslaved, as Branagan now embraced a racist paranoia and proposed to colonize all persons of African descent outside the United States. Thus in a compressed period, Branagan expressed a wide range of responses to slavery and African Americans: egalitarian disgust for slaveholders; empathy for the enslaved; and racist fear of black equality. The tensions between these positions were never reconciled in Branagan's work. *Serious Remonstrances*, contrary to some interpretations of Branagan, was not a conclusive sign of his departure from the empathic politics of his earlier work, as Branagan republished *Tyrant* in 1807 and *Avenia* in 1810 and continued to publish antislavery writings in the antebellum period.[30] The two Branagans, empathic and racist, were very much contemporaneous, just as egalitarian thought in the early national North was torn between indictment and accommodation of American slavery.

In many ways, Branagan defined a vanguard antislavery position for his time, combining Christian ethics, democratic sentiment, and empathy for the oppressed. He believed that all humans were fundamentally equal, and that slavery was unjust according to Christian principle; that slaveholders were despots who threatened the rights of all individuals, not only their own slaves; and, finally, that every individual had a compassionate interest in ending slavery, whether or not they owned slaves themselves. In a complex restatement of the Golden Rule, Branagan understood society as an interdependent web of humans, all spiritually equal, which made the oppression of any one human an ethical problem for all others. One should feel not only pity for the enslaved, he argued, but also guilt for tolerating the violent authority of slaveholders. Political belonging, insofar as it formalized these social ties, escalated the gravity of one's responsibility for actions committed by the state and fellow citizens. Every free American, in other words, was culpable for the crime of slavery.

The frontispiece to the 1807 edition of *The Penitential Tyrant* dramatized this argument. Branagan used an engraving by David Edwin which had served as the frontispiece for a previous edition of *Tyrant* as well as the 1805 edition of *Avenia*. It depicted a man gesturing to the Goddess of Liberty, who sat beneath a pillar adorned with the motto of the state of Pennsylvania, "Liberty, Virtue, and Independence." In the background were "African slaves, landed on the shores of America." An accompanying description emphasized the contrast between "Practical Slavery and Professional Liberty" in the United States. As they attacked American hypocrisy, Branagan and his publisher Samuel Wood emphasized the guilt of the average citizen as much as that of the slaveholder. "Sons of Columbia, hear this truth in time," said the description, "he who allows oppression shares the crime." An introduction written by Wood offered a maxim that indicted the American political order and those who supported it: as "slavery and tyranny are completely inseparable . . . no man who holds a slave ought to be intrusted with a post, either great or small, among a free people."[31] In a democracy like the United States, one's own life, however remote from the scene of a plantation, bore some responsibility for the tyranny of slaveholding.

Branagan's sense of racial equality was fairly straightforward—all humans were racially the same, he argued in his *Preliminary Essay*, and contending otherwise "subverts the whole fabric of revealed religion." He mocked scientific speculations that diversity of physical appearance indicated diversity of species.[32] *Avenia*, arguably his most ambitious production, rendered this sense of human equality in poetic form, by presenting a gory epic of the African slave trade, told from the perspective of the title character, an African princess, and her friends and relations. Much of the poem recounts a brutal battle on the African coast between slave trading "Christians," as Branagan sarcastically called Europeans, and virtuous Africans. Modeled on the *Iliad*,

Figure 1. Frontispiece from Thomas Branagan, *The Penitential Tyrant, or Slave Trader Reformed* (New York: Samuel Wood, 1807). Courtesy of the Library Company of Philadelphia.

DESCRIPTION

OF

The Frontispiece.

IT is intended as a contrast between Practical Slavery and Professional Liberty, and suggests to the citizens of the American States the following important distich:

" Sons of Columbia, hear this truth in time,
He who allows oppression shares the crime."

The temple of Liberty, with the motto of the Commonwealth of Pennsylvania, which would as well become her sister states, is displayed; the Goddess, in a melancholy attitude, is seated under the Pillar of our Independence, bearing in her hand the Sword of Justice surmounted by the Cap of Liberty, while one foot rests on the Cornucopiæ, and the Ensigns of America appear at her side. She is looking majestically sad on the African Slaves, landed on the shores of America, who are brought into view, in order to demonstrate the hypocrisy and villainy of professing to be votaries of liberty, while, at the same time, we encourage, or countenance, the most ignoble slavery.

Figure 2. Description of frontispiece from Thomas Branagan, *The Penitential Tyrant.*

the poem indulges in depictions of violence—characters are burned alive, have spears thrown through their heads, and are struck by lightning in an act of divine retribution. The narrative has a simple moral lesson: the so-called Christians are violent men and hypocrites, while the Africans are heroic individuals who represent the true spirit of Christianity. Branagan remained within the model of the "virtuous slave," as identified by François Furstenberg, in which white representations of slave resistance typically end not with liberty for the enslaved but rather with tragic death.[33] Having proved their capacity for freedom by resisting enslavement, all the Africans in *Avenia* eventually die. The Christians win the battle on the African coast and bring captive slaves to the Caribbean, where Avenia, after being raped by her master, decides to kill herself in a noble and predictably ghastly plunge from a cliff, looking back toward her African homeland. Because violent claims of black autonomy were safely contained by literary demise, Branagan and his readers did not have to imagine how slaves who demonstrated the capacity for freedom would achieve it in fact.

Yet Branagan's work had a disruptive potential, and it often broke down the boundaries of the "virtuous slave" narrative. He relished describing the deaths of Christians at the hands of Africans, clearly endorsing African resistance and, by extension, slave resistance in the Americas. He named one of his African heroes Louverture, after Toussaint Louverture of the Haitian Revolution; his counterpart among the Christian enslavers was Leclerc, the name of the French general who tried to reconquer Saint-Domingue for Napoleon in 1802. Both men die in the course of the poem, but meet different fates. Leclerc is electrocuted by God's retributive lightning bolt, while Louverture, killed by Christian treachery, ascends into heaven, to take a seat alongside other virtuous men, including George Washington, John Wesley, George Whitfield, Branagan's infant son (who died in 1802), and Jesus Christ. That mental picture of the afterlife encapsulates Branagan's idiosyncratic political imagination. Like most moments in *Avenia*, the scene is elaborately overworked, and it salvages Christianity even as it indicts "Christian" slave traders. Christian faith remains the fundamental determinant of goodness and truth, judging Europeans and Africans alike. Yet the scene also exemplifies Branagan's more complex political motivation, which runs throughout much of his early work: to advocate empathetic identification with the victims of slavery.[34]

In *The Penitential Tyrant*, his second poetic endeavor, Branagan argued for a human universalism based on empathetic recognition. Inspired by God, humans should "feel our brother's grief, our brother's wo; / Feel sympathetic love for all our race, / And circle man in one kind embrace." For Branagan, sympathy was rooted not in pity for the weak, but rather in empathetic acknowledgment of another's suffering. In an essay appended to the 1807 edition of the poem, Branagan asked white Americans to put themselves in the position of the slave. Imagine, Branagan asked his readers, that a French army had invaded New York, captured 10,000 white Americans (including one's family members) and enslaved them in the West Indies. The thought experiment sought to provoke white Americans to regard African slaves as their "brothers and sisters indeed, children of the same primeval parents, but dispersed over the face of the earth by the accumulation of intermediate generations." African slaves were not alienated from the American body politic, but rather equal members of the human family. Their slavery was as morally revolting as the slavery of one's own kin.[35]

Many northern Jeffersonians, like Duane, understood slavery as an institution that embodied unjust power. They perceived the authority and wealth of a man like George Washington from an ideological distance and deemed slavery wrong because slaveholders behaved like aristocrats. Although Branagan made similar arguments, he constantly asked his readers to think of slavery from the perspective of the slave and thus to understand slaveholder power in terms of the suffering it caused. This shift in perspective enabled Branagan to interrogate how non-slaveholders participated in such suffering. Whereas Duane's attack on Washington emphasized his and like-minded democrats' distance from slavery, Branagan emphasized his and his readers' proximity to the institution and their complicity in sustaining it. For example, like other early antislavery radicals, he opposed the use of sugar, because it was tainted by slavery. He implored his readers (especially those "desirous of vindicating the propriety of using the produce of slavery") to put themselves,

> for one moment, in the same condition in which the poor unhappy slaves now are; and view, from the West-Indies, the votaries of liberty and religion, in America, drinking out of their jovial bowls, or China tea cups, the produce of thy labour, thy sweat, and thy blood—and then, and not till then, let thy conscience answer, is it right or wrong? is it just or unjust? is it pleasing or not to that impartial holy Being who is no respecter of persons?[36]

The passage illuminates the importance of empathy in Branagan's work, and the critical role of conscience as the seat of ethical judgment—the intersection in the mind between one's own life, the lives of the oppressed, and abstract principles of equality and justice.

Branagan put his vision of human solidarity into practice during his time in Philadelphia, as he formed relationships with elite African Americans in the city, who helped support his literary efforts. Readers of the *Preliminary Essay* were asked to contribute funds for *Avenia* by way of Richard Allen, Absalom Jones, and James Forten, three of the most prominent black men in Philadelphia; Allen had paid for the printing of Branagan's first work, perhaps believing Branagan an ally in the antislavery cause. Yet when Branagan spoke directly to white northerners, he spurned Allen's generosity by endorsing racial exclusion in Pennsylvania. In his *Serious Remonstrances . . . to the Citizens of the Northern States*, also published in 1805, Branagan set out to explain the dangers of slavery to the North. He indicted the abusive power of the masters over their slaves, and their institutional power under the three-fifths clause of the Constitution. But he also contended that the northern states had to end slavery because the institution foisted free and runaway blacks onto them—or rather, into them, as their very "bowels" were filled with "three hundred thousand well informed and aspiring Negroes." The metaphor indicated Branagan's convoluted thought: "bowels" in this case referred to either the stomach or simply the interior of the body; the incorporation of "Negroes" promised internal explosion. But in the early nineteenth century, "bowels" also referred to the seat of sympathy, or sympathy itself. As Branagan would ask in one of his later essays, "Can we be so unreasonable as to suppose, that God will hear the prayers of the person who shutteth up his bowels of compassion against his brother?"[37] Yet Branagan had trouble maintaining the two main senses of "bowels" alongside each other. Pennsylvania was beset by an internal enemy, and Branagan, who had befriended slaves in Antigua and glorified Africans in *Avenia*, now argued "that the Northern States would have flourished far more, if there was not a negro in the Union."[38] He turned to a series of racist phobias to explain why these free and "aspiring Negroes" were a danger to northern whites: black men might be elected to Congress (or even the presidency); they would marry white women; they would sexually violate young white girls; they would compete with whites for jobs. The result would be the creation of a mongrel nation, filled with degraded interracial children. The solution was removal of all African Americans, free as well as slave, to a colony somewhere in the new Louisiana Territory, where blacks could rule themselves—as well as, Branagan added, in a faint nod to his earlier arguments for human solidarity, any whites who chose to remove with them.[39]

How to reconcile the two Branagans? One was an idiosyncratic antislavery radical; the other, in many ways, was in the vanguard of northern racism. One Branagan argued for human equality and formed ties to men like James Forten; the other claimed that free black men were merely "up-start gentlemen" on the lookout for white wives. Such men contributed nothing to the United States; their race and their history of enslavement, not their standing or character, determined whether they could belong to the American polity.[40]

In the work of historian Gary Nash, Branagan reflects the rise of racism in Pennsylvania. Throughout the early national period, many whites who had once opposed slavery embraced racial exclusion. In Philadelphia, this played out in the most practical of ways, as whites forcibly excluded blacks from July Fourth celebrations in the city, enacting the racial limits of their vision of democracy. In 1813, a Jeffersonian Republican named Jacob Mitchell proposed legislation in the Pennsylvania state legislature that would both bar all black in-migration and compel all current black residents to carry a certificate proving their free status. Philadelphia petitioners also demanded that in case of certain crimes, black men and women should be indentured for a term of years to compensate their victims. James Forten fought to keep Mitchell's proposal from becoming law, appealing to white Pennsylvanians to honor the universalism of the founding principles of the United States and their own state, and protect equality before the law for all citizens, black and white. Mitchell's bill did not pass, but in many ways the tide was turning against Forten. In the early 1820s, Philadelphia Federalist Samuel Breck was liberal enough to meet Forten in the street and shake his hand ("knowing his respectability," said Breck, though he mistook his name); Forten informed Breck that he had brought fifteen of his white journeymen to the polls to vote for Breck in a recent congressional election. Yet Forten himself did not vote, as Breck noted that black citizens "never presume to approach the hustings" at election time, since they were kept from the polls—as well as juries and militia musters—by "custom, prejudice or design." These informal practices foreshadowed later attempts to formally exclude African Americans from the franchise and define full political citizenship as the exclusive prerogative of white men.[41]

Thomas Branagan experienced this democratic culture in formation, and did not appear to question it: in his mind, embracing democracy in Philadelphia entailed embracing racism. He intended *Serious Remonstrances* to be a popular work, written for the "the honest farmer and industrious mechanic"; the essay was filled with denunciations of the idle rich in the North and the slaveholding elite in the South. He adopted a Paineite vision of the United

States, but one now deeply modified by race: "America," he believed, "was appropriated by the Lord of the universe to be an asylum for the oppressed, the injured sons of Europe." Maintaining that vision required colonization of free blacks, lest the "injured sons of Europe," on arrival in the United States, be compelled "to associate with negroes, take them for companions, and what is much worse, be thrown out of work and precluded from getting employ to keep vacancies for blacks."[42] In other words, American citizenship was meant for white men.

Historians of whiteness have argued that white supremacy enabled immigrants in the antebellum period, especially the Irish, to separate themselves from slaves and free blacks and claim belonging as Americans in the face of nativist xenophobia. White supremacy also helped secure the consent of nonslaveholders to the coercive power that masters wielded over enslaved people.[43] Focusing primarily on Jacksonian democracy, accounts of whiteness have underscored the prevalence of race and racial exclusion in American political culture. But such accounts do not fully capture the political and ideological transactions that led democratic radicals like William Duane and Thomas Branagan to embrace slaveholders as political allies in the early national period. Transnational republicans arriving in the United States found that they had to "associate," not only with black men and women, but with slaveholders, who were a dominant presence in the early Republican coalition. Immigrant radicals did not immediately condone political alliance with slaveholders on the terms of white supremacy. Instead, they recast universal democratic principles in terms of American nationalism and partisan politics. Doing so entailed some toleration of slaveholder power, especially for immigrants who became significant members of the Jeffersonian coalition. That political encounter with slavery ultimately rendered democratic radicalism more amenable to white supremacy, as repeated accommodation of coercive power impaired egalitarian commitments.

Immigrant Radicals and American Nationalism

In the 1790s, Federalists attempted to undermine and constrain Republican agitators like Duane through the Naturalization Act and the Alien and Sedition Acts, a series of laws that directly targeted immigrants. If Branagan did not want European immigrants to "associate with negroes," Federalists did not want immigrants to associate with the United States. The Naturalization

Act of 1798 imposed a fourteen-year waiting period for citizenship, and compelled all immigrants to register themselves forty-eight hours after entering the country; the Alien Enemies Act gave the president the power to deport citizens of any country with whom the United States was at war; the more far-reaching Alien Friends Act gave the president the power to deport any alien deemed "dangerous to the peace and safety of the United States"; and the Sedition Act criminalized "false, scandalous, or malicious" statements made against the president, Congress, or the federal government.[44]

The *Aurora General Advertiser* was a principal target of the Sedition Act, as Federalists had long opposed Benjamin Franklin Bache; when Duane assumed the editorship after Bache's death, he quickly became a target for repression as well. Pennsylvania Federalists first attempted to corral him through the charge of seditious riot, issued against Duane and three other men, including United Irishman Dr. James Reynolds, for a fracas that occurred outside a Philadelphia Catholic church, when the four attempted to obtain signatures for a memorial in protest of the Alien Friends Act. In defense of Duane, Republican Alexander Dallas argued that the charges were politically motivated, and a Philadelphia jury acquitted him. But Federalists continued to pursue Duane, and attempted to charge him twice with seditious libel, and once on a manufactured charge of contempt of the Senate of the United States. Secretary of State Timothy Pickering and President John Adams considered deeming Duane an alien and deporting him from the United States. More crude methods were employed by McPherson's Blues, a Federalist militia company. Taking objection to Duane's portrayal of their role in the suppression of Fries rebellion, a tax rebellion in eastern Pennsylvania, members of the militia company invaded Duane's office on May 15, 1799, dragged him into the street, and beat him mercilessly. As Duane's biographer Kim Phillips relates, Federalist editor John Ward Fenno commended the attack, noting that Duane had once insulted George Washington and that he "was not an American, but a foreigner, and not merely a foreigner, but an United Irishman." Meanwhile, other northern Republicans, like Vermont's Matthew Lyon and Duane's Pennsylvania comrade Thomas Cooper, were sent to jail for violations of the Sedition Act. To militant Federalists, immigrant radicals threatened the security of the United States and therefore had to be repressed.[45]

Federalist repression backfired, however, as Republican printers continued to publish their papers and elevated Sedition Act victims as martyrs for democratic freedom. Cooper published essays in the *Aurora* dated from the

Philadelphia prison where he was held, while Lyon ran for and won reelection to Congress from jail. Equally important, the Alien and Sedition Acts were critical in forming ideological and political bonds beyond northern and southern Republicans. When Republicans like Duane supported Jefferson in the election of 1800, they were seeking freedom from political repression in the form of the Sedition Act, and they were fighting to reverse the nativist limits to American citizenship imposed by the Naturalization Act. They argued for an open society, in which a free press protected and expanded democratic freedom and European immigrants could claim citizenship and belonging in the United States. "The press is the engine which every tyrant fears," said Duane's *Aurora* in 1806; "put out the press, and there is an end to democracy." John Binns, an Irish republican who arrived in the United States in 1801, and eventually became a rival of Duane's, put this principle on the masthead of his paper, underneath an image of a printing press: *The Democratic Press* was "the tyrant's foe, the people's friend." The fight against the Sedition Act was, in many ways, a struggle over language, as Duane and later Binns used their newspapers to celebrate "democracy," a word and idea Federalists disparaged as unchecked, illegitimate popular rule. As Duane would write to Jefferson many years later, the rise of Jeffersonian democracy was as much a "revolution in speech" as a revolution in government. The Republicans won on both counts, driving the Federalists from power and building democracy in the United States, as practice and idea.[46]

Immigrant radicals like Duane and Binns likewise responded to Federalist nativism by championing cosmopolitanism and ethnic diversity. Duane claimed that he was born in colonial New York and that he was therefore an American citizen, but Federalists disputed that claim, and eventually won a court ruling that deemed Duane an alien and a British subject. He became a naturalized citizen in 1802.[47] As much as he liked to imagine himself a free-born American, Duane also delighted in celebrating his checkered ethnic and national past. Nativism did not automatically create incentives to claim a blanket white identity, as immigrant radicals instead argued for the political and cultural value of ethnic diversity. "It continues to distress the *tories*," wrote Duane, "that a half Irish, half Indian, making for a while a whole American British subject—should be found so fond of the Declaration of Independence—it is downright *rebellion* against the Lord's anointed!"[48]

The conflict between nativism and ethnic heterogeneity persisted well after the triumph of the Democratic-Republicans in 1800. In Jeffersonian Pennsylvania, elite Republicans were skeptical of Duane's attachment to

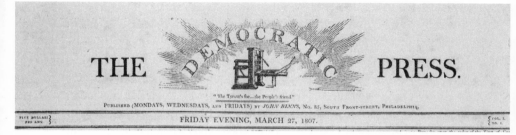

Figure 3. Masthead of John Binns's *Democratic Press*, March 27, 1807.
Courtesy of the American Antiquarian Society.

European immigrants and opposed Philadelphia's Tammany Society because it accepted aliens as members. When Duane ran for a seat in the Pennsylvania state Senate in 1807, he was attacked by Federalist editors, in particular George Helmbold, who edited the satirical paper *The Tickler* under the moniker "Toby Scratch'em." Helmbold, son of a German immigrant, had once published a German-language paper and even written for the *Aurora*, but had come to embrace a nativist worldview. He promised that *The Tickler* "shall invariably be purely American—excluding all foreign partialities or prejudices." He deemed Duane "a literary adventurer" whose "abilities are comprised in the single faculty of abusing" and mocked immigrants as "Imported Patriots." Such men were "the scum of Europe," said Helmbold, modifying Shakespeare's Richard III, "rascals, runaways / whom their o'er cloyed country vomits forth." Particular scorn was reserved for the Irish, whose speech, appearance, and intellect were subject to constant ridicule. *The Tickler's* intemperance reflected an ongoing battle for control of the American political system and American political culture. Although Federalists managed to keep Duane from the state Senate, they were losing the larger struggle to keep the *Aurora* editor and his supporters out of the United States.[49]

Duane and other radical Jeffersonians saw their fight for democracy in international terms. Duane consistently identified himself as Irish, and openly declared his ideological sympathy for the United Irishmen, as part of a wider program of resistance to the British government. He organized Irish immigrants in Philadelphia to help support the Democratic-Republican party, inaugurating a long relationship between urban democratic political organizations and the immigrant vote.[50] Meanwhile, Federalists like Connecticut's Uriah Tracy warned that Duane and the United Irishmen were bringing revolution to American soil. In many respects Tracy was correct, as the case of John Binns makes clear. Duane had only briefly spent time in England during the heyday of Paineite radicalism in the 1790s; he had returned from India to England in July 1795, but remained for only ten months before leaving for the United States. Binns, in contrast, lived through the height of William Pitt's repression of British political dissent. Both he and Duane took part in a London Corresponding Society (LCS) meeting of over 100,000 men near Copenhagen House on October 26, 1795; a few days after the meeting, King George III was attacked by a mob while riding in his carriage. Binns, for one, thought it might have been beneficial had the king been "trampled to death," as his demise might have led to the establishment of a republic in England. The attack on the king was linked to the meeting near Copenhagen House and the LCS, leading to the passage of the Two Acts on November 13, 1795, which gave the British government broad powers to outlaw "seditious practices" that threatened the king, as well as "seditious assemblies." Duane, still in London at this point, chaired an even larger meeting to protest the Two Acts on November 12, 1795, where he defended the right of petition and free assembly. Despite widespread public protest, the acts were approved the following day. Had Duane remained in England, he no doubt would have soon found himself at odds with William Pitt, the prime minister who led the suppression on the LCS. But in May 1796, Duane fled for the United States.[51]

Binns, in contrast, remained in England and repeatedly came into conflict with the British state. In March 1796, he was arrested for delivering "seditious and inflammatory lectures" in Birmingham. He was acquitted, only to be arrested again in February 1798, along with four other Irishmen, on the charge of treason. Binns had attempted to find passage to France for United Irish leader Arthur O'Connor so that he could join the French army to plan for an invasion of Ireland. Once again, Binns was ultimately found innocent, but James Coigley, a Catholic priest who had been caught along with him, and who had on his person a letter discussing potential French support for revolution in Ireland, England, and Scotland, was not so fortunate. He was found guilty of treason and executed June 7, 1798. In the summer and fall of 1798, the British ruthlessly suppressed multiple uprisings in Ireland and defeated two French invasion forces, which effectively put an end to the United Irishmen's vision of an independent Irish Republic.[52]

Binns, meanwhile, was arrested again in March 1799 and detained in prison until 1801, under a suspension of the Habeas Corpus Act. When he was finally freed, he emigrated to the United States. Thus Binns arrived in

Pennsylvania, even more so than Duane, with a visceral sense of the oppressive power of the British state. After landing in Baltimore in the late summer of 1801, he found his way to Northumberland, Pennsylvania, where he became close friends with Joseph Priestley, the more famous Birmingham radical who had come to the United States in 1794, as well as Thomas Cooper, who had arrived from Manchester in 1794 as well, after joining Paine's attack on Edmund Burke. This triumvirate had counterparts all throughout the northern states, from Duane in Philadelphia to the Irishman Thomas Addis Emmet in New York (whose brother, Robert Emmet, was executed for treason after a final United Irish uprising in Dublin in 1803). Such men, who had fled British tyranny to find political asylum in the United States, often found new political influence in the Democratic-Republican party as well. Their politics were inherently transatlantic, both because they understood the American nation from the perspective of past British abuse, and because Federalists in the United States saw these foreign radicals as an inherent danger to American sovereignty.

Irish Americans thus became vocal supporters of what historian James Kettner eloquently termed "volitional allegiance," the fairly radical notion that one's political affiliation should result from conscious choice, rather than nativity or longstanding residence. After Jefferson's election, the new Republican Congress repealed the Federalist Naturalization Act of 1798, shortening the waiting period for citizenship from fourteen to five years. Republicans in the northern states pushed for even more lenient provisions, while portraying the United States as a haven for the oppressed democrats of the world. Binns, who called himself an "Irishman by birth, American by choice, and a United Irishman from principle," is a powerful example of this emergent democratic political culture. He became an American, he relates in his autobiography, not upon taking a formal oath of citizenship, but when, days after landing in the country, he saw a Pennsylvania militia company at drill, under a banner bearing the state's motto, "Virtue, Liberty, and Independence." "It was then," Binns recalled, "under the broad expanse of heaven, without the adoption of any form of words, I took my first oath of allegiance and fidelity to the United States; an oath which, according to my best judgment, I have faithfully kept, at all times, in all places, and under all circumstances, in peace and war."[53]

The United States provided refuge for Binns, who, like Duane and Paine before him, envisioned the American nation as fulfilling a secular providence, offering an "asylum of freedom" to the world's oppressed. Shortly after his inauguration, Jefferson endorsed this cosmopolitan image in a flattering letter to Joseph Priestley in which he expressed his "heartfelt satisfaction that, in the first moment of my public action, I can hail you with welcome to our land, tender you the homage of it's respect & esteem, cover you under the protection of those laws which were made for the wise & good like you." He also promised to "disclaim the legitimacy of that libel on legislation," the Alien Friends Act.[54] Jefferson offered Priestley a home, a place where he would be protected by the law as an equal. Such protection would reverse Federalist policy; it was also in essence the complete reversal of the position of the slave, who was in theory permanently alienated from equal standing in the political community and could not make the volitional choice, like Binns, to be a free American.

Historian Gordon Wood cites the Priestley letter as evidence that Jefferson was "the fount of American democracy," the source of "American ideas and ideals that have persisted to this day." But in many ways, it was the immigrant radicals who were the fount of democracy, as they fought with Federalists to obtain political standing in the United States. Conflicts between Federalists and Republicans over citizenship and democracy were far more than domestic squabbles, as they ultimately allowed immigrants to gain political standing in the United States, where they fought to establish democratic ideals that were transatlantic in origin. Federalists were not entirely mistaken, then, when they warned that such foreigners would revolutionize the American republic. Yet at the same time, the rise of the Democratic-Republican coalition led to a retrenchment of some of the more radical cosmopolitan arguments of the 1790s. As Duane and Binns claimed their place as Americans, they redefined an internationalist agenda for democratic reform in nationalist terms. Much like Paine before them, they helped build the case for American exceptionalism. Binns, for example, in the first issue of his *Democratic Press*, identified his lifelong struggle against political tyranny with the United States, whose "extensive, federative, democratic republic is, indeed, and in truth, the only hope of the world." The American nation now enclosed the universal principles of democratic radicalism, and Binns promised that he would "regard every attempt to dismember its territory, or violate the principles of its government, not only as a Treason against the Government and People of the United States, but as a Treason, of the deepest dye, against the whole human race."[55]

Judged on these terms, the fight between immigrant radicals and the Federalist party appears a straightforward conflict between democratic idealism and conservative reaction. But in the context of the Republican movement as a whole, the struggles of men like Duane and Binns were far more complicated, insofar as they worked to bind northern democrats to the slaveholding South. Although they did not join them in jail cells, many southern Republicans embraced the democratic martyrs of the North. Stevens Thomson Mason, a Republican senator from Virginia, traveled to Vermont with funds collected from prominent Virginians to pay Matthew Lyon's Sedition Act fine, and he was duly outraged at Thomas Cooper's conviction. Irishman John Daly Burk fled from New York to Virginia to avoid having to leave the United States and remained there for much of the rest of his life. Mason provided refuge for James Thompson Callender, who had fled from Philadelphia to Virginia in fear of the Adams administration in 1798. When Callender was tried by Judge Samuel Chase in Richmond, making him the only "southern" victim of the Sedition Act, Virginia Republicans again came to his defense, raising funds on his behalf and contributing legal talent to his defense. Callender proved a turncoat, and by 1802 he had disowned Jefferson and exposed the president's relationship to Sally Hemings. But many Republican victims of Federalist repression were grateful for the patronage of southern Republicans, and some later took up residence in the South. Lyon toured Virginia in support of Jefferson in 1800 and Burk subsequently wrote a celebratory history of the state, which he dedicated to Jefferson. Like Burk, Lyon later moved to the South, eventually settling in Kentucky. In Vermont, Lyon and his son published a paper known as *The Scourge of Aristocracy*; after moving to Kentucky, he soon became a slaveholder. Defending the three-fifths clause in Congress in 1803, he claimed that it represented a sacrifice by southerners, who "gave up two-fifths of their slaves" in order to compromise with the North. "The blacks who are slaves," Lyon went on to observe, "are much more useful and beneficial to the community and to the nation, according to their number, than those that are free." Thomas Cooper, who had published an early attack on the slave trade in the 1780s, maintained strong connections to the South after his prosecution for sedition: he eventually moved to South Carolina, where he became an instructor of the planter elite at South Carolina College and an early exponent of states' rights.[56]

These episodes point to a more widespread ideological accommodation with slavery in the early Democratic-Republican party. In claiming their place in America through an alliance with Virginia Republicans, Duane and other radicals tempered their criticism of slaveholders. Immigrant radicals infused American nationalism with transatlantic republican idealism, but at the same time, the political context of the American nation-state worked to constrain their cosmopolitan principles. For Republicans like John Binns, defending the United States as the representative of the entire "human race" marked a crooked path toward accommodation with American slaveholders and toleration of human bondage.

Republican Masters Versus Rebellious Slaves

Jeffersonian politics was formed by multiple bonds between the subjective experience of freedom and the reality of the American political system, where slavery was powerful and protected. Democrats in Pennsylvania in the early 1800s had a clear sense of what it meant to be politically free: it meant participating in a government based on popular sovereignty, in which individual citizens had the power to influence political decisions. William Duane believed that all humans had equal rights to political freedom, and that freedom was best protected by democracy. "Democracy upholds, as Christianity upholds," said the *Aurora* in 1806, "that all men are equal." Democracy was likewise the only practical defense against political oppression: "the only foundation of free and virtuous Government." Theoretically then, the *Aurora* supported the simple idealism of a Republican toast from 1799: to defend the rights of man "until all oppressed nations are emancipated from tyranny." Such principles seemed, logically, to pose a serious danger to any institution based on coercive authority, including slavery. Duane had made the connection himself on more than one occasion, and he insisted in 1805 that the *Aurora* had always been an advocate "for the freedom of the Africans."[57]

Practically, however, democracy in the United States was a much more complicated affair, as the institutional power of slaveholders in the federal government and the Republican coalition proved a powerful check on northern antislavery sentiment. As Duane's son William John remembered, his father taught him "to entertain an hereditary dislike of all privileged classes."[58] But William Duane's anti-elitism wavered when it came to slavery. As Duane was well aware, the political strength of the Republican party lay in the southern states, and Jefferson was the most important political icon for the Republican movement. Given these political ties, Duane attempted to accommodate slavery and slaveholders in his larger political worldview. In doing so, he at times turned to the language and ideology of race, instigating white paranoia of black Americans. However, while white solidarity served as a key method of accommodation for Duane, it was never his primary motivation. Instead, he wanted to ensure that the Democratic-Republican party won and maintained institutional power, in order to advance his ideological agenda of achieving democracy in America and abroad. Instead of consciously embracing whiteness and white supremacy as political values, Duane embraced slaveholders as allies in a project of democratization. Choosing to tolerate the antidemocratic, coercive authority of slavery, Duane and other Jeffersonians helped lay the foundations for a more openly white supremacist politics in the future.

The record in the *Aurora* of Duane's engagement with race and slavery demonstrates the complicated ideological and ethical negotiations at the heart of Jeffersonian democracy. In the months before the election of 1800, Duane did not suppress antislavery content in the *Aurora*; instead he sought to bolster Thomas Jefferson's antislavery image. He frequently republished a now famous passage from the *Notes on Virginia*, where Jefferson, after describing the evil effects of slavery on the manners of white people, declares, "I tremble for my country when I think that God is just; that his justice can not sleep forever." Imagining that God would side with the enslaved in a rebellion, Jefferson took solace in the fact that "the spirit of the master is abating, that of the slave rising from the dust, his condition mollifying, the way I hope preparing, under the auspices of heaven, for a total emancipation." Judged by that quote, Jefferson appeared to be both deeply religious and opposed to slavery. Duane did not reprint Jefferson's extended racist musings from the *Notes*, but he did address them. An article on September 22, 1800, criticized attempts to turn the "friends of the blacks in the city of Philadelphia" against Jefferson on account of his reputedly racist statements. Jefferson had a long antislavery record, said the *Aurora*, and his statements about black inferiority were, as he himself said, suspicions only, put forth with the spirit of "a circumspect philosopher, and a philanthropist." Two days later, the *Aurora* claimed more grandly that Jefferson's entire life "has been marked by measures calculated to procure the emancipation of the blacks." Similar defenses of Jefferson's character persisted after his election. In the fall of 1803, Duane claimed that the United States was "in a constant course of banishing negro slavery, for Thomas Jefferson proposed measures for the relief of the blacks in 1776, before the laws for the gradual abolition of slavery in New Jersey and Pennsylvania, and the principles of Thomas Jefferson remain the same."[59]

Duane's comments point to the significance of partisan politics in the construction of an antislavery Jefferson. In comparison, Liverpool's Edward

Rushton, who joined Duane in excoriating George Washington as a slave-holder, did not believe that Jefferson had profound antislavery convictions. Rushton read the *Notes on Virginia* differently than Duane, and emphasized Jefferson's racism rather than his prophecies about emancipation. He simply found Jefferson less sincere than Washington, because instead of confronting the problem of slavery, Jefferson adopted the "subterfuge" of claiming that "the negroes are an inferior order of beings."[60] Not entangled in American partisan conflict, Rushton did not discriminate between Federalist and Republican slaveholders.

In addition to portraying Jefferson as an antislavery herald, Duane described Virginia as a state dedicated to freedom. The *Aurora* claimed that gradual abolition in Pennsylvania had been inspired by plans first developed in Virginia; that Virginia was "distinguished for men of genius and energetic republicanism"; that the state was the source of religious liberty; that "she," as a Republican celebration put it in December 1799, was the "twin sister" of Pennsylvania, "distinguished for her talents and love and liberty. May her example be emulated throughout the United States." The contrast to Virginia was always New England, and particularly Connecticut, which was ruled by an "aristocracy" of Federalists. John Adams was an enemy of democracy and religious freedom; Thomas Jefferson was their champion. These ideological constructions were entirely partisan, and perhaps purely instrumental in intention. But they had a complex effect: Instead of being portrayed as a land ruled by the coercive authority of slavery, Virginia—and, by extension, gentry slaveholders like Jefferson—appeared in the *Aurora* as the source of antislavery principle and political liberty.[61]

These various descriptions of Jefferson and Virginia were not simply rebuttals of Federalist criticism. They also served to incorporate slaveholders as legitimate partners in a project of democratization. Thus in January 1800, Duane transformed the young congressman and slaveholder John Randolph into a republican hero. Careful readers of the *Aurora* might have noticed that Randolph's glorification followed shortly after he spoke against the antislavery petition of Absalom Jones and other free African Americans from Philadelphia. However, during this last congressional session in Philadelphia before Congress departed for Washington, Duane emphasized Randolph's oppression, not Jones's, at the hands of the federal government. On January 9, just a week after he called on the House to reject Jones's petition, Randolph gave a rousing speech in opposition to a standing army in the United States. Some American soldiers took offense, and at a local theater that evening, two marine officers hectored Randolph in his box and grabbed his collar; they later knocked into him on the stairs. Randolph turned the incident into political theater through a histrionic letter to President John Adams, in which he complained that "the independence of the Legislature has been attacked, the majesty of the people . . . insulted." He demanded that Adams seek "to deter others from any future attempt to introduce the reign of terror into our country." Adams sent Randolph's letter to the House, provoking an investigation of the incident and a lengthy debate, which soon made its way into the Jeffersonian press. Duane and his fellow Republican editor James Carey lauded Randolph as a Virginian patriot, "too ready at the hazard of life and fortune to do [his] duty, to fear the frowns of power." Americans would have to decide, said Duane, whether the assault on Randolph was "fit for a country where all men are equal . . . whether it is worthy of freemen!" And thus a slaveholder became a republican rebel and a symbol of American equality.[62]

As Duane incorporated slaveholders into his democratic vision, he also excluded slaves, particularly those who challenged bondage. In contrast to his depiction of Randolph as a champion of freedom, Duane portrayed Gabriel's Rebellion, a thwarted Virginia slave uprising in August 1800, as a misguided accident caused by Federalist policy. Gabriel, enslaved by Thomas Henry Prosser of Henrico County, Virginia, was engaged in a far more serious contest for liberty than Randolph or Duane. While historians disagree significantly about Gabriel's motivations, it is clear that Gabriel and dozens of other slaves living around Richmond, the state capital, developed a dramatic plan for revolt in the summer of 1800. In company with other enslaved men, Gabriel planned to enter Richmond, start a fire to distract the white population, seize weapons from the state armory, and take the Governor of Virginia, James Monroe, hostage. Some of the rebels claimed that they planned to kill all white men, others that they might spare those whites perceived as friendly to their cause, including Frenchmen, poor whites, Quakers, and Methodists. In the end, the rebellion never occurred. Gabriel and most of his coconspirators were betrayed on the afternoon of the appointed date for the uprising, August 30. They still might have managed to commence the rebellion, but a rainstorm that evening flooded a key bridge crossing on the way into Richmond. Authorities began to arrest suspected slaves on September 1. Gabriel at first managed to escape, but he was soon captured, tried, and hanged to death, as were twenty-six other rebels.[63]

The rebellion became national news in September, forcing Republicans to respond to Gabriel's attack on slavery in the midst of the presidential election of 1800. John Randolph, who at this point was still dating his letters by reference to the Declaration of Independence, expressed grudging respect for Gabriel and his comrades. The slave rebels, Randolph told his friend Joseph Nicholson, "have exhibited a spirit, which, if it becomes general, must deluge the southern country in blood. They manifested a sense of their rights, a contempt of danger, & a thirst for revenge which portend the most unhappy consequences." Federalists in Virginia and elsewhere contended that the rebellion was an example of the dangerous influence of "French principles of Liberty and Equality" in order to attack Virginia Republicans like Randolph, Monroe, and Thomas Jefferson. These claims had a degree of substance because some of the rebels reported that they had been influenced by two Frenchmen. But they were mostly an electioneering tactic by which Federalists hoped to sway southern voters away from the Democratic-Republicans in the upcoming election.[64]

Duane might have responded to these Federalist attacks by pointing out that the Republican coalition was fairly strong throughout the South and led by slaveholders at the national level and thus had little interest in promoting slave rebellion. But Duane chose to respond quite differently, by describing Gabriel's Rebellion as the unfortunate outcome of Federalist policy. In a September 24 article with the curious title "Negro Slavery, Versus Alien Laws," Duane argued that slavery had been "inflicted" on the South by British imperial policy, and augmented in recent years by incorrigible citizens from the "Eastern States" who pursued slave trading. Meanwhile, Duane continued, Adams and the Federalists had effectively checked the one thing that could end slavery in the South—the "encrease of the white population"—through the alien laws. Federalist nativism, slave rebellion, and British power were linked in Duane's mind as threats to the republic. National salvation lay in embracing more people like Duane, white immigrants fleeing tyranny. They would secure the republic against slaves who sought to overthrow their masters.[65]

Thus Duane, like Jefferson in the Notes on Virginia, envisioned a demographic end to slavery, through the gradual replacement of the black population by white immigrants. His vision of whiteness was far more heterogeneous than Jefferson's, but it likewise functioned to postpone confrontation with slavery's growing power. Under Republican leadership, Duane believed, blacks would diffuse throughout the United States, while whites would immigrate in much greater numbers, eventually replacing slavery (and presumably black people) altogether. This accorded well with contemporary thought on slavery in the upper South, where the relative abundance of slaves led some masters to argue for "diffusion," a strategy that postponed emancipation until the concentration of black people had declined through their dispersal—so as to avoid the internecine race war prophesized by Jefferson and others. Of course, since that decline occurred primarily through the forced migration and sale of slaves out of the upper South, diffusion was effectively a passive way to endorse the expansion of slavery. The concept functioned similarly for Duane, who would later describe the rise of cotton production and southwestern expansion as antislavery measures: the acquisition of Louisiana put the United States "in a fair way of dispersing our present coloured population over such a vast surface, and of finally eradicating slavery altogether," claimed the *Aurora* in fall of 1803. The previous February, "A Friend to Agriculture" argued that cotton production "will occasion the happy diffusion of a certain dangerous description of our laboring inhabitants over a greater extent of country, so as to be mixed with and checked by the white people." And there would be more white people to check those "dangerous" inhabitants, according to the *Aurora*, because cotton manufacturing (which would be based in the South) would "have the highly desirable tendency of attracting and condensing white population in those states." These fantasies allowed Duane a way to imagine that the South would soon be free of slavery and reflect his own democratic sentiments. And that in turn allowed him to make peace with southern slaveholders in the Republican coalition.[66]

Duane likewise used Gabriel's Rebellion as an occasion to justify Jefferson's antislavery reputation. Ultimately, he claimed, the rebellion would lead to a better future for the South, as the nation would soon adopt "the effectual stoppage of the African trade" and "measures for a gradual emancipation of the offspring of those who now exist in slavery, upon the same plan long since suggested by Dr. *Franklin*, and which Mr. *Jefferson* endeavored without effect to accomplish." Gabriel's rebellion would lead not to "bloodshed nor massacre by military execution or the gibbet," but rather to the election of Thomas Jefferson, whose lifelong commitment to emancipation was known to all.[67] Duane's fantasy turned out to mean little as far as Gabriel was concerned. Captured on September 23, he was executed on October 10, 1800. And Duane's optimism about a Jeffersonian antislavery future also proved to be mistaken. Jefferson's presidency did not lead to gradual emancipation but instead facilitated the critical expansion of American slavery. To only see Duane's projections in terms of their errors, however, obscures their ideological significance. For white men like Duane, Jeffersonian democracy entailed the ability to fantasize about the emancipatory promise of the United States. When Gabriel attempted to act on dreams of freedom in Virginia, he was met with state violence and death. In contrast, by imagining an antislavery nation led by Thomas Jefferson, Duane confirmed his standing as a Democratic-Republican and as an American. In other words, fantasizing about emancipation in America allowed Duane to come to terms with slavery and the denial of autonomy to men like Gabriel.

The Slaveholding Asylum

Whiteness was essential to Duane's response to Gabriel's Rebellion, as he attempted to define a position at once opposed to Federalism, opposed to slavery, and accommodating to Jeffersonian slaveholders. His attack on Federalist nativism emphasized a major Republican principle from the 1790s, one that was critical to Pennsylvania Jeffersonians: to ensure that the United States, as Thomas Branagan put it, remained "an asylum for the oppressed, the injured sons of Europe."[68] Virginia Republicans had supported Duane and his fellow editors when they fought the Alien and Sedition Acts in the 1790s; Duane's argument that those laws had somehow also caused Gabriel's Rebellion (and that European immigration would solve the problem of slavery) expressed that complicated alliance. But in tying his anti-nativism to a political movement that embraced slaveholder power, Duane moved away from the radical universalism and heterogeneity of his "half Irish, half Indian" self toward a more open embrace of whiteness as a political and social category.

The ties between whiteness and immigration were very much taken for granted, as was clear in congressional conflicts over the Federalist Naturalization Act in the early 1800s. In those debates, Republican advocates of European immigration consistently retained language excluding nonwhite immigrants from the United States. In April 1802, Republicans repealed the hated Federalist naturalization policy from 1798 by adopting a new law that stated that applicants for citizenship had to reside in the United States for five years (as opposed to fourteen), and had to declare their intention to become citizens three years prior to being admitted as such. Yet Republicans did not change the policy, in place since 1790, that limited naturalization to "any alien, being a free white person," effectively barring free nonwhite immigrants from citizenship in the United States. In early 1803, Republicans pushed for an additional provision to the 1802 act to allow immigrants who had been in the

country between 1798 and 1802, but had not declared their intention to become citizens due to fear of Federalist reprisals, to do so retroactively. They
would thus have an easier and quicker path to citizenship under the 1802 act,
so long as they met the five-year residence provision.[69] Republicans brought
petitions to Congress from Pennsylvania Irishmen that boldly attacked the
late Adams administration as an enemy to liberty, and trumpeted Ireland's
long history of resistance to "slavery" at the hands of Britain. The candor of
these petitions alienated Federalists and moderate Republicans alike, who rejected them due to their "intemperate language." In response, pro-immigrant
Republicans submitted similar petitions with the offending language struck
out and fought for the rights of the "Pennsylvania Aliens." John Smilie defended his fellow Irishmen, who had every right to complain about their
"dreadful" situation in 1798 and 1799; such men, he contended, were ideal
candidates for citizenship, because they had "rendered themselves obnoxious
to tyrants." In contrast to rebellious slaves, white immigrants could claim political belonging in the United States through their resistance to unjust authority. In doing so, they formed attachments to a nation-state that protected
slavery. In 1804, Smilie and his supporters finally won their desired provision,
but they once again retained the racial restrictions on naturalization, which
would last throughout the nineteenth century.[70]

Whiteness cemented the bonds between European immigrants and the
United States, but those bonds were based on deeper political transactions, in
which immigrants became free Americans in part through tolerating slavery.
The Naturalization Act of 1802 incorporated language from the 1795 Naturalization Act that required immigrants to renounce their former political
ties (as well as any "title or order of nobility") and declare their willingness
to support the Constitution of the United States. When one Thomas Bradley
petitioned to become a citizen before a Philadelphia court on June 4, 1812, he
had to declare "on his solemn oath before the said court, that he would support the Constitution of the United States, and that he did absolutely and
entirely renounce and abjure all allegiance and fidelity to every foreign
prince, potentate, state and sovereignty whatever and particularly to the
King of the United Kingdom of Great Britain and Ireland, of whom he was
before a subject." Effectively, becoming an American meant declaring one's
support for the institutional protections of slavery in the Constitution. The
process of immigration required immigrants to render themselves obnoxious to European tyrants while rendering themselves amenable to American
slaveholders.[71]

If becoming an American required the toleration of slaveholder author-ity, for many white Republicans it also entailed rejecting resistance to that authority by enslaved people. Whiteness played an important role here, but as the result of a complex ideological process in which Republicans sup-pressed black claims to autonomy and political standing. The slave rebellion in Saint-Domingue, for example, a possible inspiration for Gabriel's Rebel-lion in Virginia, led many northern Republicans to recast national belonging and political freedom in racially exclusive terms. Federalists, according to Duane, had conspired with Britain "to establish an independent empire of blacks in the island of *St. Domingo*" and thereby provoked Gabriel's Rebel-lion: "while our administration was encouraging to revolt and treating with Toussaint in the West Indies, what could be expected from the unfortunate blacks in our states from the example?" In one move, Duane countered charges from southern Federalists that Gabriel, like Toussaint Louverture be-fore him, was inspired by "French" republican ideals, while denying Gabriel any real political standing—this "unfortunate black" merely misunderstood a mistaken Federalist diplomatic decision.[72]

Toussaint Louverture and the slave rebellion in Saint-Domingue met a similar fate. On occasion, the *Aurora* painted Louverture in a decent light, but for the most part, the paper viewed his particular uprising against tyr-anny only as a danger to white Americans. On August 14, 1801, the *Aurora* printed a reaction to the new constitution adopted in Saint-Domingue in July 1801. The article praised Louverture as a "truly great man" and contended that recent events in Saint-Domingue "demonstrate the progress of moral principles among all descriptions of men. They exhibit men hitherto dis-graced by their colour, throwing off their chains, and advancing to the enjoy-ment of freedom." But this romantic description of the new constitution was explicitly contradicted three days later: "through the whole of this new made monster," said the *Aurora*, "no man who regards human rights or free gov-ernment can discover any thing to admire." The 1801 constitution did have patently antidemocratic elements, as it bound former slaves to the land in order to restore the plantation economy, made Louverture governor for life, and allowed him to choose his successor. Yet it also abolished slavery and established formal racial equality. Duane was less interested in these contra-dictions than in the danger Saint-Domingue presented to white people. He thought that the constitution "may spread one day the storm of retaliating destruction upon the heads of the whites" in Saint-Domingue. Duane then turned to the "southern states" and their "security" from slave rebellion. As in his response to Gabriel's conspiracy, that security would be found through European immigration. He recommended that Congress quickly "open by every means the channels of population, to hold out invitation to emigrants from the nations of Europe"; the farther south the state, the shorter the period of "local naturalization" should be. "The whole of the union," warned Duane, "even those who may not be so immediately concerned are as seriously though collaterally involved in the effects apprehended."[73] Slavery was America's problem, and liberal naturalization was the solution. It was never clear what this would mean for the hundreds of thousands of slaves already in the South, though Duane's investment in diffusion suggested that they would be relocated westward. But none of these schemes imagined slaves as real political actors capable, through emancipation, of claiming standing in the republic. They were instead a danger that needed securing by an influx of white people.

Duane frequently made connections between Saint-Domingue, American slavery, and naturalization policy. As he claimed in a January 1801 letter to Fulwar Skipwith, American consul in France, and Joel Barlow, who was living in Paris at the time, Federalist diplomacy and commercial relations with Louverture had endangered American interests. "You who have considered the situation of the Southern States," he wrote, "will appreciate the fatal policy, if there were nothing worse, which could at this time set up a black power in our neighbourhood so formidable, while white population was retarded by every means that the ingenuity of Britain could divine or her emissaries could covet." Duane supported the American embargo of trade with Haiti in 1806, and was shocked that some American merchants wished to continue to trade with "*black emperors.*" The merchants had no shame, he claimed, since the United States might very well find itself faced with a slave rebellion some day, in which the slaves of the South rounded up all the white men in the nation ("and all the females above a certain age") and massacred them. Such fears echoed the anxieties of southern slaveholders in Congress, who likewise imagined scenes of American slave rebellion to garner support for the Haitian embargo.[74]

These racial fantasies were the reverse of Thomas Branagan's call for empathetic identification with the African slave, and Branagan indulged in them as well as Duane. In *Serious Remonstrances*, he sketched an elaborate fantasy in which the slaves of Delaware revolted, defeated their masters ("which is both probable and possible") and marched on Pennsylvania, where they would join a "brood" of local blacks and mulattoes and subdue the white population. These fears of a black uprising may have been motivated by everyday experiences in Philadelphia, or they may have been provoked by accounts of the massacres of white inhabitants authorized by Jean-Jacques Dessalines after Haitian independence. Branagan was also likely familiar with Bryan Edwards's history of Saint-Domingue, which instilled fear of slave rebellion throughout the Americas.[75] Whatever their source, in the context of Jeffersonian democracy, these fears of black rebellion had national political significance. White paranoia encouraged an ideological identification with slaveholders: if slaves in revolt would massacre all whites, then whites in a slave society presumably had a shared interest in restraining black freedom. Branagan presented his fears of slave rebellion in order to promote the eradication of slavery, but in practice such visions undermined the autonomy of free black communities in the North, by bolstering fears that supported racial exclusion.

The Pennsylvania legislature repeatedly debated bills to ban black migration into the state, culminating in the racist legislation proposed by Republican Jacob Mitchell in 1813, which sought to suppress runaways by forcing free blacks to carry certificates proving their status. Such projects not only mobilized northern fears, they embraced southern power, since slaveholders had long demanded similar restrictions on free black activity. Like Thomas Branagan, slaveholders also wanted to keep runaways out of the bowels of Pennsylvania, but not because they wanted to end slavery. Instead, they appealed to Pennsylvanians to expel runaways in order to help them maintain it.[76]

While the 1813 proposals were narrowly defeated, they testified to the influence of slaveholder power in northern polities, particularly in the mid-Atlantic. That power was felt in multiple ways, which were all too direct for black people: through the kidnapping of free blacks, the persistence of northern slaveholding, and the comity offered to sojourning southerners to temporarily bring their slaves with them to the northern states. But mastery was also felt, and in some sense sustained, in the minds of white northerners, who repeatedly came to terms with slavery and made allowance for its existence in their daily lives. In 1800, readers of the *Aurora* encountered the reach of slaveholder power in the paper's advertising section, which included notice after notice from masters in the surrounding states, soliciting assistance in recapturing runaway slaves. Fugitive ads came from northern masters as well as southern ones; an anonymous New Jersey slaveholder was particularly adamant that *Aurora* readers help "Stop the Runaways!" as the title of his recurring notice put it. Such notices indicated the extent to which slavery was still very much a national institution into the nineteenth century; New Jersey abolished the institution in 1804 but a form of slavery remained in the state down to the Civil War.[77]

Southern advertisements, by contrast, pointed to the relationship between the growing sectionalization of slavery and the national compact of Jeffersonian democracy. While immigrants like Duane claimed civic standing in the emergent free North, runaways encountered the long reach of slaveholder power. In the *Aurora*'s fugitive advertisements, slavery wore its true face as an institution founded on power and profit—on the ability to control chattels, people with prices.[78] Pennsylvania whites may have sought to exclude blacks as a group from civic standing, but runaway ads asked them to identify black people as individuals, to study their faces and clothing and behavior for telltale signs that their very specific bodies were not their own. To scan these advertisements was to know slavery as a system of individualized dominion. To scan them and to continue reading to Duane's indictments of Federalist power and celebrations of Thomas Jefferson was to experience the accommodation of slavery at the heart of early American democracy.

Thomas Jefferson, Illuminator of Benumbed Minds

Branagan knew the coercive authority of slavery well; Duane admitted it on occasion. Yet both men found themselves accommodating slaveholding power through the language of race. They likewise shared an appreciation of Thomas Jefferson, a political hero for both men. Jefferson more or less agreed with Duane and Branagan about black depravity, but that was not why they adored him. Instead, they saw in Jefferson a symbol of their own democratic aspirations for themselves, America, and the world. As Branagan put it with characteristic amplification, the Virginian was "a flame which will illuminate the benumbed minds of the enslaved, the wretched, the degraded sons of Europe, Asia, and Africa."[79] In the end, this enthusiasm for Jefferson played as important a role in checking the egalitarian potential of their political vision as their embrace of racism. It tempered their criticism of slaveholding power, while leaving their democratic idealism seemingly intact.

Branagan demonstrates this paradox nicely. Whether or not he read the *Aurora*, he appears to have agreed with Duane's portrait of Jefferson as antislavery stalwart, since he wrote to the president to ask him to subscribe to his publication of *Avenia*. "Of all the publications which may be productive of public

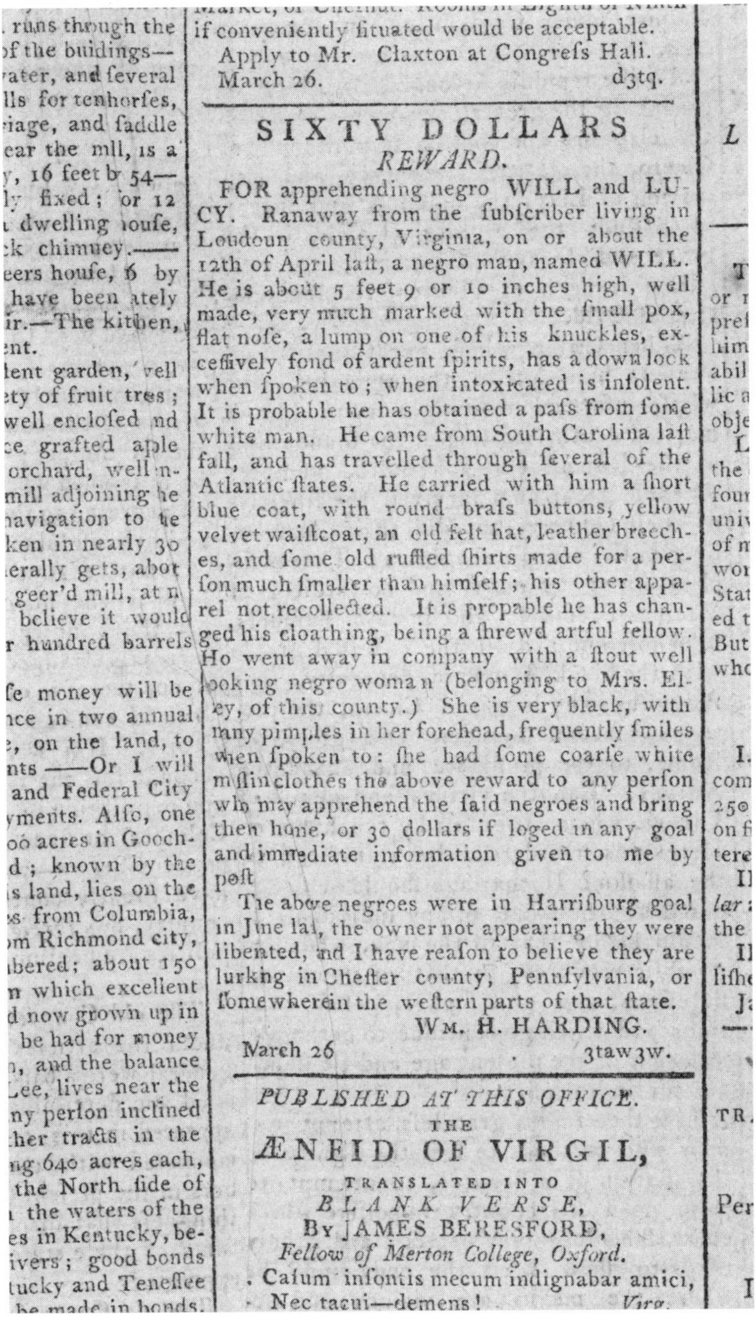

. runs through the
of the buildings—
rater, and several
lls for tenhorfes,
iage, and faddle
ear the mill, is a
y, 16 feet by 54—
ly fixed; or 12
t dwelling ioufe,
:k chimney.——
eers houfe, b by
have been ately
ir.—The kitchen,
:nt.

lent garden, vell
ety of fruit trees;
well enclofed nd
ce grafted aple
orchard, well in-
mill adjoining he
navigation to te
ken in nearly 30
erally gets, abot
geer'd mill, at n
believe it would
r hundred barrels

fe money will be
nce in two annual
e, on the land, to
nts ——Or I will
and Federal City
yments. Alfo, one
oó acres in Gooch-
d; known by the
s land, lies on the
ss from Columbia,
m Richmond city,
ibered; about 150
n which excellent
d now grown up in
be had for money
n, and the balance
Lee, lives near the
ny perfon inclined
her tracts in the
ng 640 acres each,
the North fide of
t the waters of the
es in Kentucky, be-
ivers; good bonds
tucky and Teneffee
he made in bonds.

if conveniently fituated would be acceptable.
Apply to Mr. Claxton at Congrefs Hall.
March 26.   d3tq.

SIXTY DOLLARS
REWARD.

FOR apprehending negro WILL and LU-
CY. Ranaway from the fubfcriber living in
Loudoun county, Virginia, on or about the
12th of April laft, a negro man, named WILL.
He is about 5 feet 9 or 10 inches high, well
made, very much marked with the fmall pox,
flat nofe, a lump on one of his knuckles, ex-
ceffively fond of ardent fpirits, has a down look
when fpoken to; when intoxicated is infolent.
It is probable he has obtained a pafs from fome
white man. He came from South Carolina laft
fall, and has travelled through feveral of the
Atlantic ftates. He carried with him a fhort
blue coat, with round brafs buttons, yellow
velvet waiftcoat, an old felt hat, leather breech-
es, and fome old ruffled fhirts made for a perfon much fmaller than himfelf; his other appa-
rel not recollected. It is propable he has changed his cloathing, being a fhrewd artful fellow.
Ho went away in company with a ftout well
looking negro woman (belonging to Mrs. El-
2ey, of this county.) She is very black, with
many pimples in her forehead, frequently fmiles
when fpoken to: fhe had fome coarfe white
muflin clothes the above reward to any perfon
who may apprehend the faid negroes and bring
then home, or 30 dollars if loged in any goal
and immediate information given to me by
poft
   The above negroes were in Harrifburg goal
in June laft, the owner not appearing they were
libeated, and I have reafon to believe they are
lurking in Chefter county, Pennfylvania, or
fomewhere in the weftern parts of that ftate.
                          WM. H. HARDING.
March 26   3taw 3w.

PUBLISHED AT THIS OFFICE.
THE
ÆNEID OF VIRGIL,
TRANSLATED INTO
BLANK VERSE,
By JAMES BERESFORD,
Fellow of Merton College, Oxford.
. Cafum infontis mecum indignabar amici,
· Nec tacui—demens!   *Virg.*

L

T
or 1
pref
him
abil
lic a
obje
L
the
four
univ
of n
wor
Stat
ed t
But
who

I.
com
250
on fi
tere
Il
lar:
the
Il
lifhe
Ja
—

TR.

Per

I

Figure 4. Runaway Advertisement for Will and Lucy, *Aurora General
Advertiser*, April 2, 1800. Courtesy of the Library Company of Philadelphia.

utility," Branagan immodestly told the president, "there is none more deserving of general attention; none more intrinsically [important] to the citizens of America!" Jefferson did not answer Branagan directly, nor did he officially subscribe to *Avenia*, but he was provoked by Branagan's request to send a response via Pennsylvania Senator George Logan, whom he asked to speak with Branagan in person to explain his refusal. As Jefferson told Logan, he "most carefully avoided every public act or manifestation on that subject" of slavery, but he was prepared, should the right opportunity arise, to "interpose with decisive effect." "In the meantime," he explained, "it would only be disarming myself of influence to be taking small means," like subscribing to Branagan's antislavery epic. Whatever Logan told him, Branagan was apparently convinced that Jefferson silently supported his cause. (Jefferson or Logan seems to have given him some financial support as well.) In an essay attached to *Avenia*, he wrote that he could "scarcely avoid almost idolizing the patriot" Thomas Jefferson and his ongoing battle against "the votaries of aristocracy and despotism."[80]

In many ways, this brush with idolatry made no sense, as Branagan's praise of Jefferson followed a chorus of denunciation of Virginia slaveholders and the three-fifths clause. Slaveholders, he claimed, had learned from an early age to "trample on the rights of their fellow men" and were unfit to govern a republic. "The idea of a slaveholder being a good legislator or governor," remarked Branagan, "is as inconsistent as to suppose a wolf would be a good shepherd." Yet by virtue of the three-fifths clause, slaveholders did govern the United States, and Branagan believed that Virginia, through the Louisiana Purchase and the expansion of slavery to the southwest, was "securing supreme influence" in the union at the expense of the northern states. Branagan called for the eradication of "the diabolical principle, which confers such a super-abundance of the paramount rights of suffrage and sovereignty, upon a part of the citizens, accordingly as they enslave and murder their fellow men."[81]

If Jefferson led the Democratic-Republican party, the political vehicle for most southern slaveholders, then how was he not, in some obvious way, the representative of "aristocracy and despotism"? The discrepancy seems astonishing, but it reflects the power, as much as the paradox, of Jeffersonian democracy. Northern whites with antislavery leanings could be contained in a movement in which slaveholders ruled because they loved Jefferson and often, like Branagan and Duane, feared black men. Likewise, slaveholders could embrace a president who was portrayed as an antislavery hero in Philadelphia, in good part because Jefferson knew where to draw the line—signing his name to Branagan's antislavery poem might endanger his standing in the South, just as rejecting Branagan outright would lose him an ally in the North. This delicate balance perhaps explains Jefferson's strange appearance in *Avenia*: in the midst of a rant about Virginia slaveholders, he is not included as a member of their company, but as a transcendent symbol of international liberty. Such contradictions were at the heart of democratic culture in the early nation, where white men learned to accommodate slavery even as they maintained egalitarian and antihierarchical political convictions. Thus *Aurora* readers would hear one day of John Randolph's attempts to suppress antislavery petitioning, and on the next that he was a great defender of liberty against autocratic power. In one issue, Duane prognosticated about the end of slavery in America, led by Thomas Jefferson; in another, readers scanned advertisements offering $60 for the capture of Will and Lucy, runaways from Loudon County, Virginia. To read such notices was to know that you lived in a slaveholding republic, in a polity that demanded of all its citizens some acceptance of bondage.

Branagan, Duane, and their fellow northern democrats helped create an image of Jefferson that persists to this day. As a 1799 Republican toast printed in the Aurora put it, Jefferson was "the virtuous and enlightened citizen who formed the declaration of independence which proclaimed to the universe, that America was free.[82] It is their vision of this freedom-loving president that serves as the counterpart to the slaveholding Jefferson in our ongoing discussion of the American paradox between freedom and slavery. To some extent this indicates Jefferson's charismatic power; to some extent it demonstrates that Duane and Branagan were remarkably inconsistent: after assaulting Washington for holding men in bondage, Duane glorified Jefferson for his vision of emancipation. Yet in the end, Jefferson was a symbol of unity, not contradiction. As a figurehead for the Republican coalition and emerging symbol of the American nation, Jefferson signified the complicated reconciliation between democratic conviction and the power of slavery in the political lives of men like Branagan and Duane. Never complete and subject to ongoing challenge, this reconciliation was nonetheless quite effective. In an era of political instability and in the shadow of the Haitian Revolution, the largest slave revolt in world history, the Jeffersonian coalition provided crucial institutional and ideological security for American masters.[83] Embracing Jefferson and the United States persuaded men like Duane and Branagan to accommodate slaveholder power by narrowing their cosmopolitan claims. They found a new civic life in the United States only through toleration, if not accommodation, of the perpetual social death of the enslaved. Their ability to portray this muddled situation as an egalitarian dream demonstrated the supple power of American democracy, which kept enticing Duane, Branagan, and so many other northern white men to be free.

CHAPTER 3

Jeffersonians Go to Washington

The election of 1800 marked a distinct shift in national political power, as the Democratic-Republicans took over the presidency and both houses of Congress. The Jeffersonian ascendancy was most obvious in the House of Representatives, arguably the most democratic branch of the federal government. Republicans moved from 43.4 percent of the House in the 6th Congress (1799–1801) to just over 64 percent in the 7th (1801–1803). Their share rose to over 80 percent of the House in the 9th Congress (1805–1807) before declining during the buildup to the War of 1812 and the war itself. But those declines proved momentary, and looking back from 1820, it was clear that the Jeffersonian "revolution" of 1800 caused a major realignment of power in the federal government.

Jeffersonian victories also revealed sectional discord in a new way, as the democratizing power of the Democratic-Republican coalition encountered the institutional power of slavery. This confrontation too was most obvious in the House of Representatives, whose democratic elements were intertwined with the least democratic feature of the United States Constitution, the three-fifths clause. As the national power of Federalism declined, the differences between the two wings of the Jeffersonian coalition, one tied to democracy and one tied to slavery, became more apparent, especially in confrontations over slaveholder power on the floor of Congress.

Republicans gained power across all sections of the country in the election of 1800. Northern Republicans increased their share of the House from just under 18 percent in the 6th Congress (1799–1801) to over 28 percent in the 7th Congress (1801–1803). But Jefferson's election also represented the consolidating power of the South in national politics, and this too was reflected in the changing nature of the House. In the 6th Congress, northern Federalists were the largest group in the House, with just under 35 percent of the whole, while southern Republicans held roughly 25 percent. Those numbers were reversed in the 7th Congress, as southern Republicans now controlled a plurality of the House that remained steady through the early Jeffersonian years: just under 36 percent in the 7th Congress, just under 40 percent in the 8th, just over 42 percent in the 9th. These southern Republican gains came at the expense of southern Federalism, which declined rapidly after Jefferson's election, from 23 seats (21.7 percent) in the 6th Congress to 12 in the 7th to 9 in the 8th and a meager 4 in the 9th. Thus Jefferson's first term saw the southern states grow relatively more unanimous in partisan orientation, while in the North, especially in New England, partisan competition remained divisive. The practical result of these patterns was that the South, aided by the additional power allotted by the three-fifths clause, often had a decisive role in the Republican coalition, in the House, and in the federal government.[1]

This shift in sectional power coincided with the removal of the national capital from Philadelphia to Washington in the fall of 1800. John Adams spent a brief season in Washington as president, but under Jefferson, the capital came into its own. Many early visitors to Washington were unimpressed by the capital city, then a small town of just over 3,000 people. It was a "wilderness city," said Eliza Quincy of Massachusetts; a "cemetery of all comfort," claimed her husband Josiah. In some respects, the privations of Washington were no accident. The capital embodied a republican critique of urban centers of financial and political power. Thus rustic Washington went hand in hand with Jefferson's greeting of Anthony Merry, the British ambassador, in his dressing clothes and the somewhat more extreme measures taken by a Republican convert who intentionally muddied his boots "when he attended Mrs. Merry's parties, in order to let it be inferred what a liberal he was." Skepticism of artifice, sophistication, and luxury was a hallmark of republican ideology and, when turned against British frippery, a defining trait of an emergent American nationalism.[2]

In reality, Washington was never as rustic as its detractors imagined it to be. During congressional sessions it hosted a national political society composed of elite men and women from throughout the nation. Jefferson may have offended the British ambassador by his manners, but he also gave dinner parties that brought congressmen together for reputedly sumptuous feasts. When one Massachusetts Federalist dined at the president's table in 1804, he found himself eating multiple dishes that he did not recognize and could not name. Jefferson's presidency, like his life at home in Monticello, never lacked sophistication.[3]

These displays reflected Jefferson's elite standing and the wealth made possible by slavery. Jefferson preferred to disguise his relationship to slaveholding while in Washington, relying primarily on white servants, but he could hardly disguise the capital's presence in slave territory. The main Jeffersonian newspaper, the *National Intelligencer*, regularly listed slave sales, as did the Federalist *Alexandria Advertiser*. The capital was governed by the slave code of Maryland, which made slaveholding congressmen feel far more secure about their human property than when they served in Philadelphia. In 1813, South Carolinian slaveholder and representative David Rogerson Williams attended a dinner party, only to be greeted at the door by his slave Alex, who had run away a few months previous and had found temporary refuge in Washington. As a racist southern historian later put it, "the lawful master reclaimed his chattel" and forcibly returned Alex to South Carolina.[4]

Williams would have had the same right to reclaim his slave in Philadelphia under the 1793 Fugitive Slave Act; he also would have received special exemptions to keep his slaves in Pennsylvania. But holding and recapturing slaves in northern vicinities could be difficult, as some southern masters learned in the 1790s. In Washington, by contrast, northerners complained about the presence and power of slavery. In the early days of Jeffersonian rule, northerners decried the coffles of slaves that passed through town, en route to sale; such complaints only escalated over the years, as Alexandria, Virginia, across the Potomac River from Washington, became a major depot in the domestic slave trade. The power of slavery appeared in a very different way in Congress. Southern Republicans did not bring gangs of slaves with them to Washington, but they represented slavery forcefully in debate, demonstrating the militancy of men who were accustomed to command.

As Federalist power declined after 1800, the problem of slavery within the Republican coalition became more apparent. Slavery was a constant political issue during the Jeffersonian years, as congressmen fought over the regulation of the international slave trade, the acquisition and governance of the Louisiana Purchase, the southwestern expansion of slavery, fugitive slaves, the three-fifths clause, and American policy toward the new nation of Haiti. Northern congressmen voted with the South on some of these issues, but on others they opposed southern interests, provoking confrontations with slavery's most powerful political ambassadors.

These confrontations destabilized the ideological accords formed by men like William Duane and Abraham Bishop in the election of 1800, and threatened to produce a new political attack on the coercive authority of slavery and the antidemocratic power of slaveholders. In the House, where northern democrats met slaveholders elected by virtue of the three-fifths clause, the contradictions of Jeffersonian democracy were revealed in their greatest clarity. The Republican coalition had been able to contain the antislavery sentiments of northern democrats as they imagined slaveholders from a distance; it now had to contain repeated conflicts over the governance of slavery in the halls of Congress. In many ways, that would prove a far harder task.

Southern Power, Northern Resistance

National conflict over slavery in the early republic was episodic but recurrent, exposing pronounced sectional differences over how the institution should be governed at the national level. The stereotypical narrative of southern thought about slavery—from "necessary evil" in the early republic to "positive good" in the antebellum era—tends to misrepresent the nature and the crucial stakes of these early debates, as well as long-term continuities in national political conflict over slaveholder power. Early sectional conflict focused not on what slaveholders felt about slavery but instead on their ability to control it as an institution. Many debates thus turned on the question whether or not slavery could be governed democratically by white men in the national legislature. Slaveholders were wary of granting non-slaveholders from northern states any role governing slavery at the federal level because, they claimed, northerners had no immediate interest in slavery.[5]

Southerners sought to do more than remove slavery from the federal agenda, however. They also demanded federal power to protect to their property rights in slaves.[6] This demand was most obvious in the case of fugitive slaves, but it became apparent in multiple ways in the Jeffersonian period. Slaveholders also sought to limit the political standing of free African Americans. Foreshadowing the dominant southern position during the Missouri Crisis, slaveholders argued that free African Americans were a critical threat to the slave regime. These arguments appeared self-evident to many southern Republicans but struck many of their northern counterparts as autocratic, unfit for a republic of free men.

In February 1790, during the second session of the First Congress, the House received two petitions from Quakers protesting against the African slave trade, and a third from the Pennsylvania Abolition Society, signed by Benjamin Franklin, which effectively proposed the gradual eradication of

Figure 5. William Russell Birch, *A View of the Capitol of Washington, ca. 1800.* Courtesy of Library of Congress, Prints and Photographs Division.

slavery in the United States. The petitions provoked a sectional showdown in the House, where James Jackson of Georgia, soon to be an ardent Republican, mounted a fierce defense of slavery. He claimed that slavery was sanctioned by the Bible, that the southern states would go to war to defend it, and that if Pennsylvania representative Thomas Scott brought his theories of judicial abolition to Georgia, he would probably be killed. Jackson was matched in the 1790 debate by South Carolina Federalist William Loughton Smith, and South Carolina Federalists remained the chief defenders of slavery at the national level throughout the 1790s. Meanwhile, Virginians tended to stay out of the fray, even while they acted decisively to limit Congress's powers when it came to slavery. In the 1790 debates, James Madison worked behind the scenes to lay down a firm position on the governance of slavery: the federal government had neither the right nor the power to interfere with the institution in the southern states. While Georgians and South Carolinians would always be far more aggressive than their Upper South counterparts, this core principle of federal noninterference—effectively, a claim that slaveholders should retain political control over slavery—emerged as a key element of southern unity during the Jeffersonian era. Virginia Republican John Randolph only repeated, if a bit more firmly, the Madisonian position in 1800, when he informed his fellow representatives that "the Constitution had put it out of the power of the House to do anything" when it came to slavery.[7]

Unfortunately for Randolph, northern antislavery groups and many northern members of the House did not agree. Most northerners agreed, in theory, that southern slavery was primarily the concern of the southern states, but they did not believe they were powerless over the institution. In contrast, they constantly harried the institution at its margins, in debates over fugitive slaves, the international slave trade, and the expansion of slavery. Southern masters, in contrast, could not tolerate even limited interference in slavery by northerners. At the same time, southerners also demanded greater federal power over the same three issues, but exercised on their own behalf. These fundamental disagreements ensured that there would be ongoing conflict between democratic governance and slaveholder power throughout the Jeffersonian period.[8]

The nature of that conflict changed significantly after 1800. In the 1790s, South Carolina Federalists were the most vocal proslavery force in the House, and northern Republicans could therefore associate the militant defense of slavery with Federalist resistance to democracy. In the Jeffersonian years, the pattern of national slavery politics shifted, and northern Republicans were repeatedly thrown into conflict with their southern allies. By the 9th Congress of 1805–1807, there were only four southern Federalists in the House, and thus the defense of slavery inevitably fell to southern Republicans. Partisan coherence in the South was complemented by relative regional unanimity as well. By the end of Jefferson's presidency, it became difficult to draw firm distinctions between the upper and lower South on slavery questions. Virginians continued to appear more moderate than their lower South counterparts, but when northerners tried to assert their right to make democratic decisions about slavery, southerners responded by coalescing around the principles of federal noninterference and slaveholder autonomy—the belief that slaveholders alone should control the regulation of slavery. Jeffersonian slaveholders disagreed about the ethics of slavery, but they by and large agreed that it should not be subject to national democratic rule. Practically, that entailed a proslavery, antidemocratic politics in defense of the master's ability to control his slaves as chattel.

Jefferson was inaugurated in March 1801, but the first session of the first Jeffersonian Congress did not begin until December, since Congress typically met from the late fall through the winter.[9] Five weeks after the commencement of the Republican-dominated 7th Congress, northerners faced a southern demand for a stronger fugitive slave law, and with it, a clear manifestation of slaveholder power. The proposed law originated in Maryland, where slaveholders petitioned their governor and council in early 1801 to complain of difficulties they faced recovering runaway slaves. They emphasized "the unwarrantable conduct of many of the inhabitants" of Pennsylvania, Delaware, and New Jersey. "Once they have got into the neighboring states," a petitioner complained, "every possible obstruction is thrown in the way of retaking them." Some masters who attempted to recapture their property were charged with "a supposed breach of the peace . . . and they have been obliged to give up their property to redeem themselves from jails." If something were not done to remedy this situation, "the slaveholders on this shore must be ruined."[10]

These difficulties were inevitable given the nature of the Fugitive Slave Act of 1793. On the one hand, the act clearly favored southern masters. It provided federal penalties for harboring fugitives, and enlisted federal, state, and local officials in the northern states to serve in the process of rendition. It did not acknowledge the right of fugitives to testify on their own behalf, favoring instead the testimony of slaveholders, which could be presented by an affidavit made in a slave state. This in turn made free blacks in the northern states vulnerable to kidnapping, without the capacity (in federal law) to challenge their status as presumed fugitives. Yet despite this southern bias, the 1793 act had to operate among states where slavery had either been abolished or was a more marginal institution than in the South, where growing free black communities could provide refuge to runaways, and where abolitionist societies interfered in the process of reception. Those states, as the Maryland petitioners knew from experience, could prove hostile to slaveholders. As the kidnapping of free blacks escalated after northern abolition, furthermore, the northern states moved, albeit slowly, to grant greater protections for free blacks. Pennsylvania passed an anti-kidnapping law in 1788 and the Pennsylvania Abolition Society attempted to aid free blacks who had been illegally detained as fugitives. More informal resistance to recaption, to judge by the complaints of Maryland slaveholders, likewise caused masters considerable frustration.[11]

The Maryland petitioners' complaints were brought to Congress by Republican Joseph Nicholson, one of the more important Jeffersonians in the House, who first proposed a bill to modify the fugitive slave law in February 1801. Nicholson's bill was finally debated in the House in January 1802, in a newly elected Congress where Republicans had a firm majority and southern Republicans held a plurality of House seats. But the subsequent debate exposed, in the words of Henry Adams, the "limit of Virginian influence," revealing sectional differences over the legitimate bounds of slaveholding authority.[12] Nicholson's bill compelled northern employers, under threat of a $500 fine, to advertise in two newspapers the name of any black person they hired, to ensure that they were not employing a runaway slave. All northern blacks, meanwhile, would have to carry a certificate verifying their status as freed persons, and could not work without one. These regulations asked northerners to presume that African Americans, unless demonstrated otherwise, were fugitives from southern masters. Southern congressmen found nothing amiss with this proposal, since the employment of fugitives was "a great injury" to slaveholders. Even recaptured fugitives caused considerable problems. They told fellow slaves of northern hospitality and assistance, "which excited a disposition in others to attempt escaping, and obliged their masters to use greater severity than they otherwise would." Thus "even on the score of humanity," said southern congressmen, it was "good policy in those opposed to slavery to agree to this law." In other words, northerners should submit to invasive federal restrictions and curtail the rights of free blacks in their states so that masters would whip their slaves less often. That argument proved unconvincing. The bill lost 43-46, in a sectional vote: five northern Republicans and a Vermont Federalist joined the South in supporting the bill, while two North Carolina Federalists voted with the rest of the North, Federalist and Republican alike, to oppose it.[13] The debate on the fugitive bill did not lead to any ongoing legislative crisis, and the rest of the session featured partisan conflict over taxation and the judiciary, in which southern and northern Republicans jointly opposed southern and northern Federalists. But sectional dissent over the fugitive bill suggested that northern Jeffersonians were prepared to oppose their southern colleagues, particularly when they felt threatened by excessive slaveholder power.

Of course, in a larger sense, northerners had accepted the institutional power of slavery by joining the Jeffersonian coalition and committing themselves to the political future of the United States. Such ambitions were increasingly difficult to separate from American slavery, which had begun to rebound from the setbacks caused by slave flight, disease and dislocation, and Loyalist outmigration during the Revolutionary War. Securing territory west of the Appalachians proved beneficial to upper South slaveholders, who throughout the 1790s relocated with their slaves to what would become the states of Kentucky (admitted 1792) and Tennessee (admitted 1796). The rise of short-staple cotton production in the lower South and the British demand for cotton imports propelled the expansion of slavery in Georgia and South Carolina, and set the stage for further expansion to the southwest. In the first decade of the nineteenth century, the American South had already become the dominant cotton supplier to Great Britain. Jeffersonian diplomacy and, eventually, military action helped the United States obtain the Louisiana Purchase, including the crucial port of New Orleans, and confirm territorial sovereignty over the future lands of the deep South. The intertwined relationship between American sovereignty, cotton production, and an expanding market in enslaved human beings made Jeffersonian slavery a fundamentally dynamic institution. Like Jeffersonian democracy, Jeffersonian slavery entered the nineteenth century bent on expansion.

Louisiana, the Expansion of Slavery, and the International Slave Trade

The Democratic-Republican coalition contained northern members galvanized by anti-elitist and egalitarian sentiment and southern members who were committed to maintaining and expanding American slavery and slaveholder power. That composition proved successful in the election of 1800, but it would be tested during the presidency of Thomas Jefferson, as two interrelated developments led to an escalation of congressional conflict over slavery. In the spring of 1803, Jefferson acquired the Louisiana Territory from France, through a treaty of cession that the Senate ratified in October. That December, South Carolina reopened the international slave trade from Africa, in part because of pressing demand for slaves from the South Carolina backcountry, where the development of short-staple cotton agriculture led to an expanding plantation frontier; in part because South Carolinians could now fill a demand for slaves in New Orleans. These two events reinforced a slave regime bent on expansion, and they were both subject to sustained congressional debate.

In January 1804, the Senate engaged in an extended debate over the government of the Orleans Territory, the southern segment of the Louisiana Purchase. Slavery took center stage when Connecticut Federalist James Hillhouse proposed to gradually abolish the institution in the new territory. Then, in February 1804, the House debated taking federal action against South Carolina's reopening of the African slave trade, by taxing imported slaves. Partisan and sectional alignment were not always straightforward in these debates. In the Senate, some northerners, Federalist and Republican alike, supported the expansion of slavery to Louisiana; in the House, South Carolina Federalists adamantly opposed northern Jeffersonian efforts to tax the African slave trade, while some Virginia Republicans lent limited support. But at crucial moments these legislative conflicts revealed a political rift that threatened to disturb the Jeffersonian coalition. Southerners began to coalesce around a defense of slaveholder autonomy, even as they disagreed internally about various points of policy regarding slavery. This foreshadowed later conflicts over the international slave trade, in 1806 and 1807, in which Republican unity fractured around the question of slaveholder power. In the northern states, Jeffersonians found various ways to accommodate slavery to defend the Republican coalition. In Congress, however, slaveholders were unwilling to accommodate democracy when it came to making decisions about slavery.

The public response to the Louisiana Purchase reflected both the power of Jeffersonian nationalism and its latent sectional strains. Northern Republicans celebrated the Purchase as the foundation for an empire of liberty, while lower South slaveholders projected an expanding republic of slavery. In the *Aurora*, William Duane contended that the Purchase would confirm American sovereignty and cause both Europeans and Native Americans to respect the power of the United States. In response to suggestions that Louisiana would prove ideal for the expansion of slavery, Duane argued that it would instead allow for "dispersing our present coloured population" and that it would eventually follow the path of the Northwest Territory, and become free altogether. In Connecticut, Abraham Bishop praised the Purchase to Republicans as "an assurance of long life to our cause." Louisiana would become "an asylum for the oppressed of all nations, without fear of an alien act," as the "whole western continent" would be "detached from the wars of the eastern, from its kings, its first consuls, and nobles, from vast plans of dominion by conquest." Meanwhile, in the South Carolina press, writers candidly discussed opportunities for slaveholders in the new territory.[14]

By 1803, the intertwined growth of cotton agriculture and British textile manufacturing prefigured slavery's ambitious future. Between the 1780s and the early 1800s, cotton goods became the dominant British export and the lower South emerged as Britain's chief supplier of raw cotton. This conjunction rehabilitated slavery in a region that had seen disastrous losses during the Revolution, and inspired backcountry planters in South Carolina, who gravitated to the Republican coalition, to push for reopening the international slave trade. In addition to the backcountry demand for labor, slave traders soon had a ready market in the plantation districts around New Orleans. Thus in contrast to Duane's antislavery projections, lower South slaveholders took decisive steps to expand slavery and cement its place in the American political economy.[15]

These contrasting visions of the American future became a political problem in early 1804 when Congress debated legislation for governing the new territory of the Louisiana Purchase. While much of the debate over Louisiana focused on how the territory would be governed and how its existing residents would be incorporated into the United States, the expansion of slavery to Louisiana became a significant problem in the Senate. The Purchase was divided at the 33rd parallel into a southern district, the "Orleans Territory," and a vast upper portion, the "District of Louisiana." The upper part of the purchase was placed under the authority of the territorial governor of Indiana, while Congress created a detailed structure of government for the Orleans Territory, much of it based on an original draft by Jefferson.[16] The problem of slavery expansion arose in the Senate debates over the government of Orleans Territory at the provocation of Connecticut Federalist James Hillhouse. At one point, Hillhouse attempted to gradually emancipate every slave brought into the Orleans territory, claiming he was "in favor of excluding Slavery from that Country altogether."[17] This would have been nearly impossible, given the sentiments of the planters who were already in Louisiana before the United States acquired the territory, whose slave property was guaranteed by the terms of the treaty of cession.[18] It was impossible in the Senate as well, as Hillhouse's proposal was quickly defeated, 17-11.

The Senate did agree, however, to ban the international slave trade to Louisiana. Despite strident resistance from Georgia Republican James Jackson and New Jersey Federalist Jonathan Dayton, the restriction passed by a wide margin, 21-6. An additional restriction proposed by Hillhouse sought to prevent the introduction of slaves who had previously been imported elsewhere in the United States. Senators openly acknowledged this provision as an attack on South Carolina's reopened African slave trade, and it too passed by a considerable majority, 21-7. But Southerners who objected to the international slave trade quickly reconsidered their support for a key provision in Hillhouse's amendment, an attempt to limit slave importation to a "bona fide owner" of slaves intending to settle in the territory. Any slave imported otherwise would be emancipated. On paper, this restriction would curtail the domestic slave trade to the territory, and it provoked a significant division in the Senate that transcended questions about managing the slaveholders already resident in Louisiana. Instead, the bona fide owner provision led to a debate about slaveholder property rights and the ability of masters to control the institution of slavery.

In objection to Hillhouse's amendment, James Jackson of Georgia reiterated his central contention from the debate over the international trade: "I again say that country cannot be cultivated without slaves—it never will." Kentucky Republican John Breckinridge, who opposed allowing the international trade to Louisiana, now argued that it would be "good policy to permit slaves to be sent there from the United States. This will disperse and weaken that race—and free the southern states from a part of its black population, and of its danger."[19] Furthermore, Breckinridge did not wish to "prohibit men of wealth from the southern States from going to settle in that country," an obvious misfortune. Breckinridge also took the opportunity to clarify the place of slavery in the United States. Responding to Vermont's Stephen Row Bradley, who had supposedly claimed "*that liberty cannot exist with slavery,*" Breckinridge was direct: "This is not correct—*it* exists in these states who have slaves. Our constitution recognizes *slavery*—it does more—it expressly *protects* it." North Carolina Republican David Stone later pointed out that there were "near 900,000 slaves in the U.S. and they are worth $200,000,000. Slaves are property." Given the protection of slavery in the Constitution, Stone could not understand why slaveholders should be "prohibited from sending and selling their slaves in Louisiana." As had been clear in the fugitive debates, and would become clear yet again in debates over taxing the international slave trade, most slaveholders were adamant that property rights in slaves, the essential foundation for the entire southern economy, had to be defended at the national level.[20]

Hillhouse's "bona fide owner" restriction survived by a narrow and mostly sectional vote of 15-13, but he then modified it to specify that only slaveholders who were also citizens of the United States would be allowed to bring their slaves into the Orleans Territory. A majority of the Senate (18-11) backed this new proposal, but not before a remarkable argument between Hillhouse and James Jackson. Jackson in other moments declared his wish to restrict rapid settlement of the new territory, but he could not agree to these dual restrictions on both immigrants and slaves. Jackson wanted to ensure that foreigners, and especially Englishmen, could settle the Orleans territory, slaves in tow. In response, Hillhouse described emigrants who left their countries as "the worst of men," an epithet possibly intended for Jackson, who had immigrated to the United States from England. The Georgian became predictably bombastic, and claimed that "the *friends of liberty only will come.* . . . The very best men will flee from Europe—for liberty exists only in this country." He then chided Hillhouse for being "*apprehensive of having too many Jacobins in this country.* The government and Congress were five years ago afraid of Jacobins—I hope we are not like them." Evoking Federalist repression in the 1790s, Jackson declared his sympathy for the vision of Pennsylvania Republicans like John Binns and William Duane, who wanted to open the United States to political radicals and European migrants. But he also demonstrated just how far apart northern and southern Republicans truly were when it came to the place of slavery in America. Jackson's imagined Louisiana would be filled with Jacobins and slaves, living side by side, in the only country where freedom truly existed. There was no contradiction in this vision, since Jackson believed slaves were ultimately "incapable of liberty." In addition to an "asylum for the oppressed," Louisiana would be an asylum for oppression.[21]

Hillhouse's limited restriction on slavery in lower Louisiana was not to last. Relating news from the territory in February 1804, Hillhouse's fellow Federalist Simeon Baldwin reported, "it would require an army to enforce a law excluding slaves a principle which the Senate have adopted."[22] Planters in the Orleans Territory opposed any restriction on slave imports and sent a remonstrance to Congress in late 1804 asking for full access to the African slave trade. In March 1805, Congress compromised by upgrading the Orleans Territory to the status of the Mississippi Territory, voiding the Hillhouse "bona fide owner" restriction. The new territorial act also did nothing to restrict the transshipment of African slaves from American ports, like Charleston, that permitted the international slave trade.[23] Although still prohibited from importing African slaves directly, Louisianans now had effective access to the trade by way of South Carolina. Approximately 50,000 African slaves arrived in South Carolina from 1804 to 1807, and slave traders were full of optimism. "Our market is at this moment extremely favorable for the sale of

Africans," wrote two Carolinian factors to their Rhode Island partners in November 1806, "as the demand from the backcountry and New Orleans is very
considerable."[24] Congress could do nothing to stop South Carolina from importing slaves, and it proved unable to constrain the domestic slave trade to
Louisiana. This was slaveholding autonomy in practice, as the lack of restrictions on slaveholder property rights allowed the relatively unfettered movement of human chattel from east to west.

The transshipment of Africans imported into South Carolina foreshadowed the rise of a national interconnected market in enslaved persons, which
grew considerably after the War of 1812. In the 1790s and 1800s, close to
100,000 Chesapeake slaves were subject to forced migration, to the new
states of Kentucky and Tennessee as well as to South Carolina and Georgia,
usually alongside their masters but also through sale. After the closing of the
international slave trade in 1808 and the confirmation of American sovereignty over the southwest during the War of 1812, the Chesapeake became the
principal source for a growing domestic slave trade to the emerging Deep
South, the cotton lands stretching from upcountry South Carolina and Georgia through Alabama, Mississippi, and Louisiana.[25] That trade was made possible by the relative autonomy of slaveholders in southern jurisdictions to
move, sell, and purchase slaves as they saw fit. It depended first and foremost
on the dominion of masters over their slaves, and secondly on their ability to
defend that authority at the state and federal levels.

As subsequent debates in the House over the international slave trade
would demonstrate, southerners by and large agreed that they needed to protect slaveholder power from outside interference. Thus while debates over
Louisiana may have turned primarily on an East-West axis, insofar as they
focused on the problems of incorporating new territory and foreign people
into the American republic, they also exposed North-South divisions in
Congress over the question of slaveholder power. That question repeatedly
came to the fore when masters sought to defend their interests in slavery,
which required maintaining their property rights in human chattel. Congressional conflict repeatedly tested the political power and political legitimacy
masters needed to maintain those property rights—to maintain the coercion
necessary to enslave. Put another way, it tested the illusions of northern Jeffersonians, who believed that their political commitments promoted the expansion of democratic freedom.

Republicans Attempt to Tax the
International Slave Trade

Under the Constitution, Congress was prohibited from outlawing the international trade until 1808. In the meantime, it could only express its disapproba-
tion by taxing the trade at a maximum of ten dollars per imported slave. In
contrast to the Senate, where a Connecticut Federalist attempted to limit slavery in the Orleans Territory, northern Republicans led the fight to tax the slave
trade in the House. On February 14, 1804, Pennsylvania Republican David
Bard, morally outraged by the African slave trade, proposed that Congress levy
the ten-dollar tax in order to "show to the world that the General Government
are opposed to slavery, and willing to improve their power, as far as it will go,
for preventing it." Bard was a Presbyterian, and like New England Baptist John
Leland, he had spent time as a missionary in Virginia in the late eighteenth
century and opposed slavery on religious grounds. Like fellow Pennsylvanians
John Binns and William Duane, he also believed the American nation-state
was a haven for political freedom. As Bard saw it, "the Americans . . . certainly
enjoy the greatest share of liberty, and understand the principles of rational
government more generally than any other nation on earth." For Bard, these
principles made the slave trade, as well as slavery itself, anathema. The Americans, said Bard, perhaps hearing the sarcastic voice of Samuel Johnson in his
head, "have denounced tyranny and oppression; they have declared their country to be an asylum for the oppressed of all nations. But will foreigners concede
this high character to us, when they examine our census and find that we hold
a million of men in the most degraded slavery?" Furthermore, Bard argued, the
slave trade violated "a law paramount to all human institutions," Christ's injunction to "do unto others as you would that others should do unto you." Taxing such an iniquitous trade was not only "justified on the ground of sound
policy," it was "supported by every principle of virtue."[26] Slavery was a national
moral problem, and the African slave trade its most egregious feature. Thus
South Carolina's actions required a response from Congress.

Other northern Republicans developed a more practical attack on the
slave trade, employing another cardinal principle of Jeffersonian democracy,
anti-elitism. In response to southern suggestions that Bard's proposed tax
would burden "agriculture" and that slaveholders suffered considerable "misfortune" and "poverty" because they held slaves, northerners argued that they
simply wanted to tax the rich. Samuel L. Mitchill, a Republican from New

York, compared the modest surpluses of a northern farm to the "enormous income derived to the proprietor of an estate employed in the culture of tobacco, rice, cotton, and sugar." John B. C. Lucas argued that since "no article imported into the United States gives a greater profit, so no article can better bear a tax." Joseph Stanton of Rhode Island "consider[ed] slaves a luxury." And he reminded the House that they were a political as well as an economic luxury, since "they are considered by the Constitution, three-fifths of them, to give a Representative." Northerners admitted the South Carolinians might import slaves as they saw fit, according to the Constitution, but many among them agreed with Henry Southard of New Jersey, who "thought they ought to be made to pay for it."[27] In the 1790s, Republicans had relied on antielitism, evangelical Christianity, and idealization of the American nation-state as an asylum for freedom in order to build the Jeffersonian coalition in the North. But now, confronted with the institutional power of slavery in Congress, those same convictions seemed liable to undermine partisan bonds.

There were, however, some signs that upper South slaveholders might support the northern demand to tax the slave trade. Virginian Josiah Parker had first introduced a proposal to tax the international trade, back in 1789, with sentiments very similar to those of David Bard in 1804.[28] In addition, Congress had been close to unanimous in outlawing American participation in the international slave trade to foreign nations in May 1800.[29] Multiple southern state legislatures condemned South Carolina's reopening of the international trade, and many upper South masters made a critical distinction between domestic American slavery and the African slave trade: the first was an institution that slaveholders inherited and managed as best they could, while the second was a moral crime. Such distinctions likely persuaded some Virginia Republicans to support the call for the slave trade tax, and Virginia Jeffersonians John Wayles Eppes and John Jackson defended the proposed tax in the course of debate.[30]

But by 1804, southern opposition to the international trade rarely implied a practical antislavery politics. Virginia had a clear economic interest in outlawing the international trade, as the state had a relative surplus of slaves. As William Plumer observed, while recording the Senate debates over the Orleans Territory, "it is obvious that the zeal displayed by the Senators form the Slave States, to prohibit the foreign importation of Slaves into Louisiana, proceeds from the motive to raise the price of their own slaves in the markett." Banning the international trade would help provide an outlet for that surplus through an emerging domestic trade, which in turn would help maintain the value of slave property. Furthermore, moral opposition to the international trade often helped justify slaveholding paternalism. In the nineteenth century slavery became "domesticated," as Willie Lee Rose has argued, as masters attempted to render the institution more stable and, in their own eyes at least, more humane. Yet paternalists shared a common value with other masters: they would not allow non-slaveholders to control slavery in the United States.[31]

This principle of slaveholding autonomy ultimately persuaded the House to reject David Bard's slave trade tax. A narrow majority of southerners defended the right of South Carolina and, implicitly, of all slaveholders to be free from outside interference, and only two southern Republicans supported the northern position in open debate. As Republican Speaker of the House Nathaniel Macon put it, the tax would "look like an attempt in the General Government to correct a state for the undisputed exercise of its Constitutional powers." To chastise South Carolina "appeared to him like putting a State to the ban of the empire." And "to this . . . I can never consent." For Macon, maintaining the autonomy of the states was more important than national condemnation of the international slave trade. Benjamin Huger, a South Carolina Federalist, agreed with Macon. "Let us alone," he told northern supporters of the tax, "and we will pursue the best means the nature of the case admits of. Interfere and you will only increase the evil; for, whenever the Government of the Union interfere in the peculiar concerns of a State, it must excite jealousy and a spirit of resistance." Huger then extended this argument for noninterference to slaveholders themselves, by way of analogy: "Do we not all know, that by interfering between a man and his wife, we only aggravate the difference; and do we not likewise know that any interference between a master and his slave induces the former to be more severe." The southerners who objected to Bard's proposed tax did not have elaborate defenses of slavery to match his idealistic condemnations. They did not need them, because they were not interested in debating the morality of slavery with a man like Bard—they merely wanted to make sure he left them alone to treat their slaves (and their wives, no doubt) as they thought appropriate.[32]

Such sentiments reflected the nature of slavery as an institution, "a system of extreme personal domination" in the words of historian Steven Hahn, which depended first and foremost on the individual master's authority over his slaves. Protecting that power meant protecting slavery. For many slaveholders, this entailed restricting the ability of non-slaveholders to control an institution in which they had no legitimate interest. Sometimes masters made this point by arguing that slavery was properly a "municipal" concern, subject to regulation by state governments alone. But this was often a second-ary argument compared to the more immediate and fundamental political relationship that sustained slavery: mastery over another human being. Thus when presented with a Quaker antislavery petition in the Senate in early 1805, Southerners argued "that the Quakers were not interested in the question of slavery, for they had no slaves—*& ergo* they had no right to petition." After listening to these contentions, William Plumer recorded a premonition that would soon be all too commonplace: "this very subject of Negro slavery will I am convinced produce a division of the United States."[33]

In debates over the fugitive law in 1801, northerners resisted the extension of slaveholder power into their own locales. Yet when it came to resisting the expansion of slavery or indicting the international trade, they had far less success. Hillhouse won his limited amendments blocking the full-fledged introduction of slavery to Louisiana, but they were paper rules that were overturned within a year. On February 17, 1804, supporters of Bard's slave trade tax managed to defeat an attempt to postpone his motion until the next Congress, but they could not keep his proposal on the House floor.[34] The slave trade faded into the legislative background, as the House turned instead to what many members no doubt saw as more pressing matters: debates over the Yazoo Purchase, a land speculation scheme in western Georgia; the government of Louisiana; and impeachment proceedings against Supreme Court Justice Samuel Chase. Congress never acted on Bard's motion before adjournment. Unlike the antebellum period, there was no organized outside group fighting to keep the problem of slavery on the floor of Congress. Meanwhile, the connection between slave trading, southwestern expansion, and cotton agriculture only continued to grow stronger. It remained to be seen whether northern Republicans could mount any serious challenge to Jeffersonian slavery.

Partisan Unity and Emerging Discord

Congress did not act on Bard's motion to tax the international slave trade in 1804, partly under the illusion that South Carolina would end the trade. That did not happen, and Congress did not return to the problem of the slave trade for two more years. In February 1805, in the second session of the 8th Congress, Henry Southard of New Jersey tried to reintroduce a resolution to tax slave imports. The House referred the resolution to a Committee of the Whole, but never took up the subject. In March of that year, Joseph Bradley

Varnum introduced a proposal from the Massachusetts legislature for a constitutional amendment giving Congress immediate powers to end the international trade, but it was laid on the table.[35] In the meantime, denunciations of South Carolina filled the national press, both North and South. By the fall of 1804, Duane's *Aurora* openly called for Congress to find some means of "counteracting the barbarous traffic of human beings, which had been recently permitted by South Carolina." Yet as they focused their antislavery arguments on South Carolina, northerners continued to persuade themselves that the nation as a whole was opposed to slavery. As the *Aurora* put it in November 1804, "in the majority of the southern states, a universal disposition prevails to follow by degrees the example of Pennsylvania" and establish gradual emancipation. Two months later, the *Aurora* condemned South Carolina for allowing "the foul blot" of the slave trade to remain on its "character," and then exculpated the rest of the United States from any responsibility for South Carolina's actions.[36] This allowed Republicans to contain the rapaciousness of slavery into one errant state, and ignore the emerging southern consensus around the principle of slaveholder autonomy. It likewise let men like Duane believe that a western empire of liberty was still plausible, once the nefarious actions of South Carolina were constrained.

Partisan politics reinforced this optimistic Jeffersonian nationalism, in part by marginalizing Federalist criticism of the institutional power of slavery. In the summer of 1804, Massachusetts Federalists began their ill-fated campaign to abolish the three-fifths clause, which led to a chorus of condemnation throughout the northern Republican press. Between South Carolina slaveholders and New England Federalists, northern Jeffersonians occupied an ideological spectrum in which their vision of the American future appeared humane and rational, even as they made allowances for the institutional power of slavery. A Republican-led committee in the Pennsylvania state legislature first denounced the Federalist plot to repeal the three-fifths clause, and then explained that the southern states—other than South Carolina—were "deeply sensible of the immense evil and danger relating to them, from the number of their slaves; and we are persuaded, are more anxious for their emancipation, than even the eastern and northern states." The committee was therefore convinced that Congress would impede the importation of slaves into Louisiana.[37] But this proved to be wishful thinking. Instead, Congress changed the status of the Orleans Territory, and opened the door to the international slave trade via Charleston. As the record in Duane's *Aurora* suggests, northern Republicans were aware that African slaves were being landed in Charleston harbor.[38] But they did not draw clear lines between the international trade and southwestern expansion, in part because they continued to tell themselves, and the northern public, that territorial expansion furthered the cause of republicanism and human freedom. In conjunction with Republican hostility to Federalist antislavery measures, such sentiments sustained a Jeffersonian nationalism that allowed slavery considerable freedom to expand.

But other episodes demonstrated that northern Jeffersonians would continue to contest slavery, and continue to interfere with the prerogatives of southern masters. In January 1805, James Sloan of New Jersey offered a volatile motion when he proposed that Congress gradually emancipate all the slaves in Washington, beginning on the Fourth of July that year. The appeal to the anniversary of independence, like Bard's speech against the international trade, demonstrated an attempt to identify antislavery principles with American nationalism. It is not clear why Sloan raised this issue, later to be a central goal of antebellum abolitionists. Given the nature of congressional debate on slavery before 1805, it seems unlikely that Sloan believed his gradual emancipation proposal would succeed, and he probably intended to provoke. The motion to consider Sloan's proposal was rejected 65-47, and the motion itself was rejected 77-31, with 24 northern Republicans, including Bard, in favor.[39] There was little debate recorded in the *Annals of Congress*, but it was obvious that northern Jeffersonians like Sloan were growing restive with southern power, and that they were not heeding Huger's request to let the masters alone. Although Sloan's proposal received only minority support, it was dangerous enough in the mind of Peter Early, a Georgia Republican. A year later, he would class Sloan's proposal alongside the 1790 slave trade debates as an example of the terrible disruption produced by antislavery politics.[40]

Republicans like Sloan defined the conflicted contours of northern Jeffersonian thought on slavery. When the Republicans came to power in New Jersey in 1803, Sloan was elected to the House and arrived in Washington that winter to take his seat.[41] He continued to oppose Federalism at the national level, but he also did not hesitate to attack slavery, and he soon found himself in heated debate with southern Jeffersonians. While many Federalists in Washington belittled Sloan, as Samuel Taggart of Massachusetts put it, as "the small end of small things," conflict over slavery often suggested possible points of agreement between antislavery Federalists and Republicans. In January 1806, Sloan rose to reintroduce a bill to tax slave imports. He had brought the subject before the House at the beginning of the session in December 1805, but agreed to a postponement when David Rogerson Williams of South Carolina explained that his state legislature was considering the subject that very moment, and would probably move to reimpose a ban on the international trade (which Huger had likewise claimed in 1804). But South Carolina did not do so, and the House began a new round of debates on the slave trade tax on January 20, 1806.

In contrast to the previous debates on the slave trade tax, where Virginians supported Bard's motion and South Carolina Federalists manned the southern barricades, Republicans now fought mainly amongst themselves. Roll-call votes indicated that some upper South Republicans continued to support federal attempts to tax the trade, but in debates on the House floor, lower South Republicans, as opposed to Federalists, now took the lead. Major opponents of the tax included South Carolina Republican David Rogerson Williams and Georgia Republican Peter Early (by birth a Virginian), both of whom would play a significant role in debates over ending the international trade the following year. As in the debates over Bard's tax, opponents hoped the federal government would not, as Early put it, point "the finger of scorn" at South Carolina.[42] But Early also emphasized a broader point: that the question of slavery "ought never to be stirred in our national councils," because it inflamed sectional bitterness among members of Congress. This amounted to a somewhat milder rendering of the doctrine of noninterference: non-slaveholders should not concern themselves with slavery, lest they "disturb the public harmony." He promised to give Sloan's resolution "a more hearty negative than I have ever before given in my life."[43]

Suppression of debate on slavery soon became personal, offering members an object lesson in southern intimidation. A young Delaware Federalist, James Madison Broom, rose to speak on behalf of Sloan's tax and proceeded to point and wag the finger of scorn in the direction of South Carolina. Returning to the economic arguments raised by northern Republicans in the 1804 slave trade debates, Broom expressed disbelief that anyone would hesitate to tax slaves, "who so far from being owned by the poor, are the exclusive property of the rich." "I do not know why," said Broom, "we should trample on the poor in order to privilege the rich." Such frank anti-elitist sentiments provoked southern ire. Peter Early accused Broom of "wounding the feelings of South Carolina," libeling the state with "every term of reproach which his imagination could bring to his aid." O'Brien Smith, a South Carolina representative, sent Broom a note "requesting an explanation" for his remarks, a typical formality en route to a duel; the following day, Broom apologized to the House, which, according to William Plumer, "fully satisfied Mr. Smith."[44]

David Rogerson Williams was not satisfied, however, and later rose to defend his native state from those who "had painted her conduct in the most odious and detestable colors their ingenuity could invent" and who had "cast on that community, in a most unmanly manner, all the opprobrium applicable to an inhabitant of Newgate." "South Carolina," he instructed the House, "deserved a far different character from that given her by those gentlemen who had taken upon themselves the task of abuse."[45] In many ways, these theatrics restated Huger's doctrine of noninterference, as lower South Republicans sought to browbeat and threaten Broom into silence.

Much as Early had promised, debate over slavery had excited sectional passions, causing discord among the Republican coalition. But on February 25, members North and South reunited toward the end of the debate on the slave trade to pass a key objective of southern slaveholders, an embargo on trade with the new nation of Haiti. The policy marked the culmination of a shifting course by Republicans in response to the Haitian Revolution. During the Adams administration, Republicans like Albert Gallatin had criticized Federalist efforts to open trade to Saint-Domingue. On first assuming office, Jefferson indicated that he might reverse Federalist support for Toussaint Louverture, and offered to aid the French in subduing him. Instead, he allowed American merchants to continue to trade with Louverture, a decision that proved of great benefit when Napoleon attempted to reconquer Saint-Domingue, a plan Americans feared might be a prelude to French recolonization of Louisiana. While the French General Charles LeClerc managed to capture Louverture in 1802, a combination of tropical disease and black military resistance defeated his expedition to seize control of Saint-Domingue. That led Napoleon to abandon plans for Louisiana, which he then sold to the United States. The preservation of Saint-Domingue's independence from France thus helped preserve American interests in the southwest. But instead of maintaining commercial ties with an independent Haiti, Republicans in Congress first fought to limit American trade to the island and then to outlaw it altogether, with the aim, said some members, of undermining the new nation.[46]

In December 1805, Georgia senator James Jackson demanded an embargo to prevent "brigands" from Haiti from traveling to the United States. He warned that trade with Haiti would create a precedent that European nations might follow should a band of slave rebels ever gain limited autonomy in the United States. A year prior, Virginia Republican John Wayles Eppes, Jefferson's nephew and son in law, reputedly said he "would venture to pledge the Treasury of the United States, that the Negro government should be destroyed."

Supporting the embargo in the House in February 1806, he now dared any
member of Congress to come forward and "declare St. Domingo free." Whoever should do so "would cover himself with detestation" for accommodating
"a system that would bring immediate and horrible destruction on the fairest
portion of America." Such comments no doubt evoked memories of the massacres of white residents carried out in newly independent Haiti, which were
widely reported in the American press in the summer of 1804. The fair white
people of America could not suffer an independent black state.[47]

Most northern Republicans eagerly joined ranks with their southern
counterparts to support the embargo on trade with Haiti. Pennsylvania Republican George Logan first proposed the embargo in the Senate, while in the
House, fellow Pennsylvanian John Smilie denied "that the inhabitants of St.
Domingo are a nation." Smilie argued that the United States must follow the
dictates of France when it came to trade with the island; his less politic colleague Joseph Clay claimed that trade with Haiti was "a sacrifice on the altar
of black despotism and usurpation." Massachusetts Federalist William Ely,
perhaps inured to supporting lost causes by the fate of his attempt to repeal
the three-fifths clause, spoke with conviction on behalf of the Haitians and
against subservience to Napoleonic France, but to no avail. He was joined by
only two northern Republicans (and two maverick southern members, including Matthew Lyon, now of Kentucky), along with the bulk of the Federalist contingent of the House. That made for a very poor showing, and the
Haitian embargo passed by a large margin, 93-26.[48]

In practice, the embargo proved relatively weak, and trade with Haiti did
not decline significantly until after Jefferson's general embargo on American
commerce went into effect in 1808.[49] Ideologically, however, opposition to
Haiti played an important role in the Republican coalition. Northern and
southern Jeffersonians found common ground in their shared hostility toward an independent black nation, even as they divided over the regulation
of the international slave trade. When debate on the embargo began, Sloan
had been brusquely pushed aside by Peter Early of Georgia. Sloan had risen
to request the third reading of his bill on the slave trade tax, but Early interrupted him to direct the House to the more pressing business of the embargo.
Despite this object lesson in how southern demands took precedence over
northern concerns about the politics of slavery, Sloan too voted for the ban.
In the House, northern Republicans agreed with their southern counterparts
that Haiti was a danger that had to be contained.

While the House acted decisively on the Haitian embargo, southerners repeatedly tried to deter consideration of the slave trade tax. On February 4, John Randolph of Virginia had moved that the Committee of the Whole considering the tax should rise, "with a view," he explained, "of getting rid of the business." But that motion and two subsequent attempts to postpone debate failed, in part because enough southerners voted with a majority of northerners to keep the issue before Congress.[50] On March 4, Sloan returned an amended bill to tax the international trade. Calls for rejection and postponement immediately ensued, with David Rogerson Williams moving "to make it the order for the 4th of July." That would have made for a stirring example of antislavery patriotism, except for the fact that congressional sessions usually ended by April. Only thirty-four members rose to support Williams's mock proposal. Instead, the bill was made the order of the day for the following Monday. However, as had happened to Bard's proposal in 1804, Monday came and went, and the bill was never read a third time. Instead, the House turned to a long debate on the non-importation of select British goods, a legislative response to recent British incursions on American shipping. While calls for postponement had failed to suppress debate on the international trade, many Republicans were apparently willing to overlook South Carolina's intransigence in the face of threats to national sovereignty. As David Rogerson Williams put it, "Shall a man spend time in adjusting the tie of his cravat when the hangman's noose is at his neck? Shall we be engaged in our little divisions when the enemy is at our door?" Whether or not Williams's analogy convinced, much of the rest of the session was spent trying to respond to British threats to American commerce—rather than in confronting the commerce in slaves at the Port of Charleston. Williams did attempt to close the so-called South Carolina loophole, which allowed African slaves to be sent to New Orleans after a brief stop in Charleston harbor, but he opposed northern attempts to interfere in the internal affairs of South Carolina. Like the South Carolina Federalists before him, he did so successfully.[51]

In 1804, northern Democratic-Republicans might have told themselves that South Carolinians were separate from the southern mainstream; now in 1806 they encountered a broader coalition of southern voices opposed to northern sentiment on the slave trade tax. Among the South Carolina contingent, moreover, the torch had passed from Federalists like Benjamin Huger to Republicans like Thomas Moore and David Rogerson Williams. As it turned out, Huger was the last South Carolina Federalist to ever serve in the House. (He would return for one final session in 1815.) From the 9th Congress of 1805–1807 onward, the South Carolina contingent was dominated by Republicans, reflecting internal changes within the state. As cotton production expanded in the South Carolina upcountry, new men came into power through slave-produced wealth. They gravitated toward Republicanism, and opposed the low-country Federalists who dominated state politics. In 1808, Republicans in South Carolina won a more even apportionment of the state legislature (although one still based on wealth) and by 1810 they had achieved white manhood suffrage. New political figures, like John C. Calhoun, rose to prominence as upcountry Republican leaders. In contrast to both South Carolina Federalists, who hated democracy as much as they reviled northern antislavery sentiment, and Virginia gentry like Jefferson, who acted the part of benevolent patrons of northern freedom, lower South Republicans anticipated the complex mix of egalitarian sentiment, masculine aggressiveness, and slaveholding dominance that coursed through antebellum southern Jacksonian democracy. Williams (or "Thunder and Lightning," as he was later known, for his oratorical bombast against Great Britain during the War of 1812) was both a committed Republican and a committed defender of slavery. In 1814, he became governor of South Carolina, confirming the triumph of the Democratic-Republicans in his state.[52]

The decline of southern Federalism was a direct result of the national ascendancy of Jeffersonian democracy. Republicans followed their success in 1800 with even more far-reaching electoral victories in 1804. Yet such success also revealed internal tensions, and by the winter of 1805–1806, the Democratic-Republican party was splintering in multiple directions. Virginia Republican John Randolph was soon in open conflict with the administration, driving Congress to distraction, and he attracted a small but dedicated following, including, for a time, Williams, who spurned a dinner invitation from President Jefferson to demonstrate his resistance to executive power. Randolph's constant attacks catalyzed northern sectional resentment that often had little do with slavery, as he alienated multiple members of the Jeffersonian alliance in debates over the Yazoo Purchase and the impeachment of federal judges. As early as February 1804, Federalist Samuel Taggart heard a Massachusetts Democrat remark, after a typical Randolph tirade, "d-m the Democrats, if this is democracy I have done with it." In the same year, New Hampshire Senator William Plumer reported that "some of the democrats in the hearing of federalists said that *Randolph was assuming & very arrogant & that they hated him.*"[53] Randolph was soon out of favor with Jefferson, but his hectoring pointed to the potential for sectional rupture in the Republican coalition. To the extent that Randolph was viewed as an eccentric, he functioned much like South Carolina in the Republican imagination, as an extreme case who proved the moderate center of the party to be rational and humane. But in pivotal debates over slavery, first in 1807 and then again during the Missouri Crisis, Randolph moved from the margins to the center, giving voice and form to the fundamental political objective of slaveholders: to retain control of their slaves.

The End of the International Slave Trade

In the winter of 1806–1807, encouraged by a message from President Jefferson, the House debated and then passed a bill to prohibit the international slave trade beginning January 1, 1808. Recent historians have argued that the abolition of the international trade demonstrated a limited national victory against slavery, one that was ratified over time by increasing penalties against participation in the trade. That position has merit, since although illegal traders continued to violate the slave trade ban down to the Civil War, the absolute number of foreign slaves imported into the United States declined significantly after 1820. But the counterpoint to American prohibition of the international trade to domestic ports was the federal government's glaring weakness when it came to preventing the foreign slave trade to other nations, which American seamen and merchants continued to participate in despite its illegality. Furthermore, because of American resistance to bilateral agreements with Great Britain to police the trade, the American flag served as cover for slave traffickers to the Caribbean and Brazil for decades.[54]

Within the United States, moreover, banning the international trade coincided with the rise of an internal, domestic slave trade. That internal trade was driven by the expansion of slavery, which northerners in Congress did little to check during the Jeffersonian years. When they endorsed the Louisiana Purchase, they sanctioned the acquisition of New Orleans, which would be a principal port for both slave-grown exports and the domestic slave trade throughout the antebellum period. While the common image of the domestic trade is the slave coffle, slaves also traveled by ship throughout the antebellum period, bound in an American seaborne slave trade from eastern ports through the Gulf of Mexico to New Orleans. Thus as one slave trade came to a fitful end, another expanded, secured by the expansion of American power to the southwest and the ability of slaveholders to control their property rights in slaves in the American political system. The domestic slave trade, as Steven Deyle has argued, knit together masters from different regions of the South, as demand for slaves in the Southwest buttressed slave prices in the Chesapeake. Thus rather than a culmination of a glorious struggle against slave trading, the prohibition of the international trade instead marked a key transition in American slavery. Coerced migration through the domestic trade grew in intensity in the years after the ban went into effect, a crucial foundation for the antebellum slave empire.[55]

Thus while a majority of members of Congress opposed the international slave trade, there was no real antislavery consensus against slave trafficking per se within the Jeffersonian United States. Nor was there much consensus on the governance of slavery within Congress. Instead, the final round of debates over the international trade evoked the same divisive question as previous conflict over the slave trade tax, the prerogative of slaveholders to control the politics of slavery. On paper, the outcome of the 1807 debates was a law banning the international slave trade to the United States. But in the House, the outcome was southern predominance on almost every legislative provision, an institutional victory that matched the defense of slaveholder power that southerners articulated throughout the course of debate.

Conflict over slave trade prohibition focused on two main questions: One, what should the federal government do with the slaves taken from a vessel captured as a result of interdicting the international trade? Two, how should slave traders be penalized? James Sloan instigated conflict on the first question on December 17, 1806, when he moved that any person "forfeited" by capture (the term came from the fourth section of the House bill) "should be entitled to his freedom." Georgia's Peter Early, who had drafted the House bill, quickly explained to Sloan that any slaves captured by the government could not be emancipated. They had to "be sold as slaves, and be afterward kept as such." Early lamented this "melancholy" necessity, but could see no other way to enforce the prohibition. No southerner would support a law that might lead to the introduction of emancipated Africans into their states. Slavery was a great evil, granted Early, but the presence of free blacks in a slaveholding society was "an evil far greater than slavery itself. Does any gentleman want proof of this. I answer that all proof is useless; no fact can be more notorious." He then threatened that southerners would have to kill any free blacks released into their states, out of "self-preservation." "Not one of them would be left alive within a year," he promised.[56] There was no better demonstration of the fundamental divide between antislavery and proslavery visions of the end of the slave trade: Sloan wanted to liberate African captives; Early wanted to ensure that no liberated slaves would be allowed into the slaveholding republic, lest they threaten the security of the masters.

Many northerners rose in support of Sloan's motion, but in contrast to Early's proposal, which specified an exact procedure for handling captured slaves (customs officers would sell them at auction), they could not agree on an alternative plan. Massachusetts Republican Barnabas Bidwell suggested that the contraband slaves could be left to the disposition of whatever state they happened to be captured in, in order to prevent the federal government from taking on the role of a slave trader. Bidwell and other northerners did not even want the word "forfeiture" in the bill, since the term itself implied a federal recognition of property rights in slaves, "which neither the Constitution nor the laws of the United States, have ever authorized." This argument for an antislavery constitutionalism, whatever its legal and historical merits, was fairly weak in a tactical sense. In his effort to rid the bill of the taint of slavery, Bidwell threatened to sacrifice any capacity to control the slave trade. His Federalist counterpart Josiah Quincy pointed out that Bidwell's plan would probably not prevent subsequent sale into slavery, since most illegally traded slaves would be captured in or near southern ports. If the national government did not take possession of them, they would be retained as slaves. Sloan then modified his original proposal so that any slaves imported into free states would become free, while those imported into slave states would be sent back to Africa or "bound out as apprentices." The motion gained little traction, but it foreshadowed a future ground of agreement between white men in the North and upper South. After the American Colonization Society received federal funding in 1819, enslaved people captured through slave trade interdiction efforts were returned to Africa. In 1807, Sloan's proposal to send slaves to Africa mainly indicated northern inability to agree on a definitive plan to police the international trade. Sloan's first amendment, to make all persons captured "free," but with no practical plan on how to do so, gained only nineteen votes, and Bidwell's proposal only thirty-six. In the face of northern confusion, the southern position represented by Early seemed impregnable.[57]

On January 7, 1807, however, northerners joined forces when Bidwell moved that the bill be amended by adding the following proviso: "that no person shall be sold as a slave by virtue of this act." Southerners, who saw the international trade as a separate issue from domestic slavery, stood their ground. Many masters supported abolition of the international trade primarily to render domestic slavery a more stable institution. And a federal government that had the power to set slaves free did not ensure the stability of slavery. The northern proposal to prevent anyone from being sold as a slave, said southern representatives, would "affect nine-tenths of the property of the southern States, and might in its effects strike at all the property held in slaves; that consequently it became their duty to resist it." In contrast, many northerners believed that ending the international trade was the first step in abolishing slavery altogether. Legislation that would sell contraband slaves into bondage hardly fulfilled that objective. The House eventually split over the Bidwell amendment, 60-60. The roll call on this vote indicated that northern Federalists and Republicans were now in better agreement on the politics of slavery than they had been in previous years. But southerners were also much more cohesive. Only six southerners (including Broom of Delaware) voted with the North. Upper South slaveholders had considered backing northern attempts to tax the international slave trade in 1804, but they were far less interested in adding to the free black population of the southern states in 1807. The even division of the House left only one vote outstanding, and it belonged to the speaker, Nathaniel Macon of North Carolina. Although Macon had told the House a year previous that "no one regretted the evil [of slavery] more than he did," he too voted with the South not to set captured slaves free.[58]

Northerners did not rest after losing this vote. When the bill was read for a third time on January 8, they pressed to send it back to committee. "So as to save the United States from the humiliation and disgrace of sanctioning a principle at which the strongest feelings of humanity, as well as the plainest dictates of reason, revolted," they asked southerners to ensure that that any person taken while enforcing the prohibition should not be made a slave. They also complained that Peter Early, the proslavery Georgian, had controlled the drafting of the bill, and requested a new committee composed of a member from each state. Southerners, for once, endorsed majority rule when it came to slavery politics. After the northerners had lost a direct vote, they wondered, "What more can they ask?" To Early and other southern members, northern arguments that the bill would violate certain cherished values simply made no sense. The bill would not operate among the northern states, but in the South, since the great majority of illegally imported slaves would arrive there. Once again, southerners demanded national deference to their prerogatives as masters.[59]

That demand was likewise evident in debates over the penalty provision of the bill, although sectional divisions were less distinct on this question. A solid contingent of northern Republicans and Federalists supported a death penalty for slave trading, while Early and other southerners favored a prison term between five and ten years. As Early explained, the death penalty suggested that the enslavement of Africans was a great moral evil. And most southerners, Peter Early explained, "do not consider slavery as a crime. They

Table 1: Roll Call on Bidwell Amendment "that no person shall be sold as a slave by virtue of this act"

	For amendment (60)	Against amendment (60)
Northern Republican	39	9
Northern Federalist	15	4
Southern Republican	5	44
Southern Federalist	1	3
Total northern votes	54	13
Total southern votes	6	47

Tie broken by Nathaniel Macon (R-N.C.) against amendment. Numbers from *AC*, 9th Cong., 2nd Sess., 267. Party affiliations from *Biographical Directory of the United States Congress* (bioguide.congress.gov).

do not believe it immoral to hold human flesh in bondage. Many deprecate slavery as an evil; as a political evil; but not as a crime." James Holland of North Carolina and Edward Lloyd of Maryland were so far from considering slavery a crime that they argued only a small minority of slaves taken from Africa were truly "kidnapped and carried away from a state of freedom." Most were slaves already, they explained, and under far worse masters than those of the southern states.[60]

In contrast, while northerners too felt that slavery was a "political evil," many among them were also prepared to define the slave trade as a moral crime. Connecticut Federalist Theodore Dwight tried to cite Jefferson's message to Congress on the trade in order to prove that the slave trade "was a violation of human rights"; he then asked any gentlemen holding Early's view of the matter to "lay his hand on his heart; let him ask his own conscience, if it is not a violation of human rights, if it is not immoral, thus forcibly to carry these wretches from their home." Sloan pleaded the cause of sympathy, and asked the House to see slaves not as enemies, but as victims: "the poor and needy, the dumb and the lame, and those who cannot plead their own cause." He received little hearing, and was later shouted down when he tried to relate stories he had heard from slaves imported into New Jersey, who described the terrors of kidnapping, and the relative paradise of Africa compared to being a slave in America.[61]

Sloan's suppression fit a wider pattern. In the end, the proslavery position represented by Early prevailed on almost every count. Sloan and his

supporters lost the death penalty provision, 53-63, in part because 29 northerners (23 of whom were Republicans) voted with Early. Antislavery northerners did win their fight to recommit the House bill, however, and debate
resumed on February 9th over a new provision that would place slaves captured through interdiction in a free state, where they would serve as indentured servants or apprentices for a term of years. Early could not tolerate
liberated slaves, even at distance, and again threatened violence. "The inhabitants of the southern states," he promised, "would resist this provision with
their lives." In response, he adopted the proposal first put forth by Massachusetts Republican Bidwell: that captured slaves should be left to the disposition
of the state into which they had been illegally imported. As Sloan noted ironically, southerners had decided "to give up the question, whether the United
States shall sell the negroes as slaves; and for what? To sell them themselves.
This is mighty condescension indeed."[62] Early's position did not win out in a
direct vote, but it did prevail. The House decided to adopt a bill from the
Senate in place of their own, and it contained a similar provision to Early's.[63]
After some final jockeying, the House passed the bill prohibiting the slave
trade by an extremely large majority, 113-5, on February 13, 1807. Historian
Don Fehrenbacher described the vote as "the closest approach to unanimity
ever recorded in a congressional roll-call vote on a significant slavery issue."
But the record of the debates tells a different story: Antislavery northerners,
having lost most of the provisions they argued for, acquiesced in the limited
attack on the slave trade proposed by Early and other southerners. They
could not have left the congressional session with any sense that they had
passed powerful antislavery legislation, nor with any feeling of sectional accord.[64] Instead, the slave trade debates revealed powerful differences between
northerners and southerners when it came to regulation of slavery.

However, little of the sectional conflict in Congress, with some important
exceptions, made it into the Republican press.[65] Instead, northern Republicans celebrated the abolition of the slave trade as the first step in the gradual
end of slavery in the United States. In the *Democratic Press*, John Binns
praised Jefferson for advocating legislation to end the slave trade, and declared, "*the axe is therefore at length, effectually laid to the root of slavery*."[66] In
December, Binns reported on plans for celebrations by African Americans in
Philadelphia and New York on January 1, 1808, the day when the international trade would become illegal. This was one of the more ironic outcomes
of the slave trade debates: southerners fought to ensure that interdiction of
the slave trade would never grant freedom to Africans within the United

States, while free blacks in the mid-Atlantic and New England celebrated the end of the international trade and commemorated January 1 in order to perpetuate the message of antislavery reform. This seeming disconnect between what was said in Congress in 1807 and what was said in the churches and on the streets of New York and Philadelphia in 1808 demonstrated less that the slave trade legislation had, as Binns reported, "wipe[d] off a foul blot which has too long stained our national character," than that the international trade remained a fundamental issue, both symbolic and real, in the ongoing struggle against slavery. Southerners in Congress were right to fear that a sustained federal commitment to interdicting the slave trade and liberating African captives in America threatened slavery itself. Even the very weak legislation that passed in the spring of 1807 helped free black communities mobilize, develop a collective consciousness and pride in their African past, and solidify political claims on the United States. Such living, breathing antitheses to the slaveholding order of things represented a real threat to the ability of masters to control the politics of slavery.[67]

So too did indications that northerners in the 1807 debates might overturn the cardinal principle of noninterference with domestic slavery. The bitter sectional disputes in Congress did point to the distant possibility of undermining American slavery, not through a national antislavery consensus, but through exposing the nature and limits of slaveholder power. In some respects, the debates helped clarify that the problem of American slavery would not be solved by interdicting the international slave trade. The real obstacle to antislavery reform was the political authority of masters within the United States.

"Let Union Kick the Beam"

Despite Peter Early's success in preventing Congress from freeing slaves, one southerner saw a precedent so dangerous in the slave trade legislation that he promised to openly defy the new law. The Senate bill adopted by the House included two provisions that could be seen as favoring moderate antislavery voices from the North. First, the bill required ships transporting slaves from one part of the United States to another to provide a manifest detailing the human property on board. Second, ship captains had to swear to the fact that the transported persons had not been imported after January 1, 1808, and that they were legally slaves within the United States. Both provisions were meant to constrain smuggling; the second, as historian Nicholas Wood suggests, was probably intended to prevent kidnapping of free blacks as well. The manifest provision also had an important if somewhat unintended consequence, insofar as it created a body of sources detailing an American middle passage from eastern ports to New Orleans. An 1839 manifest for the "Brig Uncas," for example, had signatures from the ship's master and the shipper, notorious Washington, D.C. slave trader William H. Williams, swearing to the fact that "the Negroes herein set forth" had not been illegally imported and were legally slaves. It then listed 49 slaves bound from Alexandria to New Orleans by name, age, height, and color, including Dorcas Hawkins (twenty-five, just over 4 feet tall, "dark"), her children Sarah (age two) and Lewis (three), Izabella Peterson (sixteen, 5 feet and ½ inch tall, "black"), and an unnamed six-month-old female "infant."[68] This record, generated by the interdiction of the international trade, is but one piece of evidence from the massive internal slave trade that sustained the cotton empire of the antebellum United States. Although congressmen were aware of that burgeoning domestic trade in 1807, they did not confront it directly in the course of debate. But they did confront the principle that made it possible, the principle that allowed Williams to ship a six-month-old child from Virginia to Louisiana: the master's authority over enslaved people.

The extent to which some southerners would go in defense of that power became clear when the House confronted the second moderate antislavery provision from the Senate bill. In order to prevent smuggling of imported slaves, the Senate proposed placing a lower limit on ships engaged in domestic transport of slaves (technically, on transport of slaves "to any port or place whatsoever"). The bill proposed a limit of fifty tons, to which Early responded with a detailed amendment specifying that the "nothing in this section shall extend to prohibit the taking on board or transporting any negro, mulatto, or person of color, (not imported contrary to the provision of this act,) in any vessel or species or craft whatever, from one place to another, within the jurisdiction of the United States." The amendment seemed intended to clarify that an American master could transport his legally held slaves wherever and however he pleased. That is how David Rogerson Williams and John Randolph interpreted it, and they were outraged when they learned on February 18 that the Senate had disagreed to Early's amendment. The show of unanimity the House had demonstrated five days earlier in passing the slave trade bill threatened to break down into sectional rancor. Williams claimed that "the bill without the amendment would provide that no negroes shall be transported from one State to another to be sold or held in service." That was a considerable overstatement, but Williams was clearly worried about his property rights in slaves. So was Randolph, who had been silent for most of the debate over ending the international trade. He threatened to personally violate the fifty-ton limit to defend "the rights of slaveholders" if the bill passed without Early's amendment. Early rose in support of his amendment as well, and the House was persuaded to request a conference with the Senate to revise the bill.[69]

The conference produced a forty-ton limit as a compromise measure and specified that masters were free to transport slaves in vessels of any size on "any river, or inland bay of the sea, within the jurisdiction of the United States."[70] This new restriction did not pass without incident. On February 26, Early claimed he was "decidedly hostile to the provision" and John Randolph rose again to defend the power of masters over their slaves. The restriction might someday lead to "universal emancipation," he warned, and declared he "would rather lose every bill passed since the establishment of the Government, than agree to the provision contained in this slave bill. It went to blow up the Constitution in ruins." The following day, Randolph delivered "an animated speech" in which he told his fellow southerners that the forty-ton limit would curtail their ability to sell their property, and that "by depriving a man of the right to sell his property it ceased to become property." Referring to the sectional and antislavery passions on display in the previous few weeks, Randolph wondered if southerners were willing "to rest the security of their property upon the two Houses of Congress." "There appeared to be a portion of that House," he said, "small in point of abilities, who were opposed to the present state of things in the southern states." Randolph never had much respect for northern Republicans, whom he insulted throughout his long congressional career. But he was now convinced, not without evidence, that they intended to use their small abilities to challenge the sovereignty of slaveholders.[71]

The end of the slave trade debates brought things full circle, demonstrating again the conflict between slaveholder autonomy and national democratic decision making. If the forty-ton limit passed, Randolph predicted that no southerner would return to take his seat in Congress. "If the entering wedge is to be driven," he said, "let us secede, let us go home." Pennsylvania's John Smilie responded in frustration that if the southern states "do not like the union, let them say so—in the name of God let them go—we can do without them." Randolph rose to clarify his position, lest it be misinterpreted by congressional reporters: he was an advocate of union "as the means of our liberty, happiness and safety . . . but if union and the manumission of slaves are to be put into the scale, let union kick the beam!" No one had yet been quite as explicit about the political contest at the heart of the slave trade debates. Randolph demanded and quickly drafted an amendment stating that no section of the bill abolishing the international trade "shall be construed to abridge, modify, or affect, in any manner whatever, the full, complete, and absolute right of property of the owner or master of any slave." But here southern unity failed Randolph, Early, and Williams. Enough members from the upper South broke ranks to join a northern majority, first to adhere to the forty-ton limit and then to deter consideration of Randolph's amendment.[72]

This small victory could not have provided much recompense to northerners in 1807, who had lost their more important amendments to the slave trade bill. Members had been listening to Randolph rave on many other subjects all throughout the session, but now they heard him as the voice of the unrepentant master, in defense of his exclusive power. Such performances might be attributed to Randolph's eccentricities, but when it came to slavery, Randolph was exemplary rather than idiosyncratic. His defense of slaveholder property rights was not rooted in proslavery zealotry: Randolph opposed attempts to overturn the ban on slavery in the Northwest Ordinance, he condemned the domestic slave trade, and he wrote a will freeing his slaves at his death. Randolph agreed with Early that slavery was a political evil, not a moral crime, an institution that southerners had been born into, rather than one that they had actively built.[73] Such beliefs evaded the ethical problem of slavery, but they did not constitute an ethical defense of the institution. What Randolph defended absolutely was his power, not his virtue. Like most southern masters, he was unwilling to allow northern non-slaveholders to control the regulations that governed slavery. This inevitably created problems for the Jeffersonian alliance, because while northerners were willing to cede extensive authority to slaveholders, they were not willing to cede everything. When they made limited attempts to restrain an institution that in most respects they had allowed to expand unchecked, they were vehemently rebuffed. Such discord weakened Jeffersonian bonds and undermined the nationalist myth of a gradual end to American slavery.

Removal of the Capital

The fallout from the slave trade debates did not travel far beyond Congress, and the summer of 1807 witnessed a return to Jeffersonian nationalism in response to the *Chesapeake* affair, a diplomatic crisis caused when a British ship fired on the American vessel the *Chesapeake*, and then removed from its crew four seamen claimed as deserters from the British navy. Instead of arguing with each other over the slave trade, Americans North and South spoke openly of defending their national honor by going to war against Great Britain. Instead of condemning slavery, they condemned what many deemed the far worse practice of naval impressment. But the sectional animosity evident in the slave trade debates did not disappear. Jefferson's response to British aggression provoked disaffection toward southern predominance in Washington and in the Republican coalition. When Congress passed a commercial embargo on American exports in December 1807, more northern Republicans began to reconsider their political ties to the South. By early 1808, there was an active movement to support a northern candidate, Vice President George Clinton of New York, at the next presidential election. In this heightened partisan context, James Sloan proposed that Congress should remove the capital of the United States to Philadelphia. Sloan would soon declare his support for Clinton, and his removal proposal was therefore likely intended as a ploy to catalyze northern dissent in Congress. But it was also a testament to Sloan's years in Washington, which had featured constant debate with southern members over the institution of slavery. In proposing the removal of the capital northward, Sloan was striking a symbolic blow at the power of slaveholders in the federal government.

On February 2, 1808, "impelled by the love of that country which gave me birth" and "considering the situation of the seat of Government at this place as one of the greatest evils under which the people of the United States do now suffer," Sloan offered a resolution to remove the capital to Philadelphia. A pamphlet published shortly after the debate summarized Sloan's major reasons for removal: that the capital was in an inconvenient and unhealthy location, that it was expensive to administer, that it gave the President too much power, that it deprived the citizens of Washington of a "republican form of government," and that it was "surrounded by an old, worn out, impoverished country, thinly inhabited by freemen, but abounding with slaves." Sloan imagined "a real whig of '76" traveling to Washington only to be overcome by "disgust and indignation." "Would he believe that the wise, the virtuous, and economical *Jefferson*, and his supporters, had lavished away millions upon so absurd, extravagant, and hopeless a plan?—A plan to raise in the centre of the republic, costly monuments similar to those formerly erected in what is now termed the dark ages of the world, by tyrannical despots to perpetuate their crimes?"[74]

In the House, Sloan's proposal led to a fairly dissolute debate, mostly framed around the virtues and vices of cities. Matthew Lyon, who recalled all "the insults I received in Philadelphia whilst in the minority," said he would rather remove into a wilderness. Nathaniel Macon likewise recalled the bitterness of the 1790s, "when the name of Republican and Democrat was accounted a disgrace," and recommended moving "over the Alleghany" to escape the influence of cities and the Bank of the United States, based in Philadelphia. Later in the debates, John Taylor of South Carolina spoke of another evil of Philadelphia: its lack of sympathy for "a certain subject, in which the Southern States are deeply interested. When formerly there, one Warner Mifflin, and his associates, continually kept Congress in hot water, by teasing and pestering them with something about slavery. They had no regard for our feelings."[75] For Taylor, a capital surrounded by slaves was much preferable to one filled with Quakers and abolitionists.

Everyone's feelings seemed to suffer in the course of the debate. Lyon and Taylor recalled the insults they had received in Philadelphia, because they were Republicans and because one of them held slaves, while Sloan recounted being accosted on his way to the current debate "by a parcel of boys, who cried out 'There goes the old Quaker rascal, he ought to be hung.'" Barent Gardenier of New York rose to defend northern cities from vilification by Macon and Philip Barton Key, a Maryland Federalist, which provoked John Wayles Eppes to declare that cities had consistently opposed "the rights of the nation."[76] The debate ended bitterly, and without resolution, yet it indicated the potential for sectional passions to overcome partisan ties. As Benjamin Tallmadge of Connecticut remarked, "I have rarely noticed a question agitated in this House, when party distinctions have been more thoroughly lost in the subject."[77] The motion to commit Sloan's resolution to a Committee of the Whole lost 61-63, mainly along geographical lines: 21 northern Federalists, 31 northern Republicans, and 9 southern Republicans supported the motion, while 44 southern Republicans, 15 northern Republicans, and 4 southern Federalists opposed it. As had happened in the slave trade debates the previous year, northerners threatened to unite along sectional lines and to overlook, however temporarily, the partisan disputes that sustained Jeffersonian democracy. Slavery was not at the forefront of debate, but it hovered on the margins, an inevitable issue for northerners like Sloan, who worried about being surrounded by slaves, and southerners like John Taylor, who worried about losing them.

More apparent was an emerging conflict about the nature of sectional power in the United States. Some voting with Sloan no doubt mostly wished to escape the boarding houses and miserable roads of Jeffersonian Washington, but a vote to remove was also a vote to return the seat of national power to the North. This reflected a wider and growing sense of northern resentment at a perceived imbalance of sectional power in national politics. Thus in some respects, James Sloan's Jeffersonian odyssey culminated in a simple desire to return home. Washington had not been the scene of endless celebrations of liberty led by Thomas Jefferson, but instead played host to repeated confrontations between men like Sloan and the slaveholding South. Sloan and other northerners therefore sought to remove the capital to a free state, to leave Washington behind. This was a very different type of antislavery claim from David Bard's argument, in the first round of debates over taxing the slave trade, that the founding ideals of America opposed slavery, and that Americans should try to live up to them. Sloan was no longer making an argument about ideas. He was trying to alter the federal government as an institution, to literally reverse its course from Jeffersonian Washington to Federalist Philadelphia. The magnitude of that task indicates just how difficult it was to challenge the expanding power of American slavery.

CHAPTER 4

The Idea of a Northern Party

The Democratic-Republican party grew impressively after the election of 1800, and by Jefferson's second term it was the dominant force in national politics. But success came with a price, as the relative decline of Federalism exposed internal tensions at the state and national levels. In Pennsylvania, Republicans began to divide almost immediately after 1800; in New York, factional rivalries dominated state politics, and in Congress, sectional divisions caused some northern Jeffersonians to rethink their alliance with the slaveholding South. The final years of Jefferson's presidency only escalated these internal divisions, as Republican economic and diplomatic policies led to widespread disaffection in the North. In 1808, the presidency passed from Jefferson to James Madison, but not without incident, as New York Republicans attempted to nominate George Clinton, while Republicans in Virginia, including John Randolph, sought to nominate James Monroe. Thus Madison took office as head of a coalition riven by internal strains, and schisms only deepened over the next four years. Federalists took advantage of Republican disunity and regained power in Maryland and states northward. By 1812, dissidence had broken out on multiple fronts, as northerners turned against the presumed dominance of Virginia in national politics.

As in the 1790s, international issues catalyzed partisan bitterness in the era of the War of 1812, especially in the North. Federalists condemned Republicans as tools of Napoleonic France, while Republicans accused Federalists of tacitly supporting British power against American interests. These mutual attacks escalated after the passage of Jefferson's embargo in 1807 and ran through the War of 1812, as Federalist New England openly flaunted the federal government. But unlike during the 1790s, the Republican coalition also faced significant internal dissension, as a number of northern Republicans considered alternatives to Jeffersonian rule. The complicated diplomatic situation faced by the United States during the Napoleonic Wars, caught between the powerful French and British states, thus had an important domestic political counterpart. As diplomatic crises intersected with partisan discord after 1807, the political order forged by the Republican revolution of 1800 threatened to unravel.

Slavery was not the most important problem for these Republican dissidents, who often focused instead on a perceived imbalance of sectional political power, but once they began to think in sectional terms, they opened the door to indictments of southern mastery. Those who also questioned the legitimacy of democratic rule by slaveholders challenged the ideological bonds forged in the 1790s and ratified by the election of 1800.

Northern Republican dissent was a complex movement, marked by internal variation and tension. Some Jeffersonian dissidents were as skeptical of the advance of democracy as they were of the power of slavery, and easily reconciled with a conservative Federalist worldview. Others, however, broke with southern Republicans because democracy and slaveholder power proved irreconcilable, as session after congressional session demonstrated. Such Republicans sometimes shared ground with Federalists when attacking southerners in Congress, but they did share Federalist conceptions of the ideal American polity. Likewise, many Federalists hesitated to embrace dissenting Republicans like James Sloan, because they abhorred the middling men who rose to prominence in the Jeffersonian coalition. The persistence of Federalist-Republican antagonism in the North made sectional unity against the southern-led Republican coalition a difficult prospect.

At the same time, northerners who remained loyal to the Republican coalition escalated their attacks on a reviving Federalist party. The deteriorating diplomatic situation raised the stakes of those ideological battles, as Republicans sought to defend the American nation-state against British power. In contrast to Republican dissidents, a number of elite Federalists embraced the Republican party after 1807 because they viewed Federalism as insufficiently committed to the cause of American nationalism. This foreshadowed an important source of Republican resilience. After the onset of the War of 1812, Republican stalwarts condemned criticism of the Madison administration as submissiveness to Britain bordering on treason. The war, the political moderation of Virginians like Madison and Monroe, and the internal weaknesses and tensions of northern dissent set the stage for the resurgence of Jeffersonian nationalism, as Republicans unified around a nation threatened by internal and external enemies.

These complex relationships between section, nation, democracy, and slavery shaped the alignment of political forces on the eve of the War of 1812 and for decades afterwards. The quick passage from nationalist unity at the end of the war to the divisive Missouri Crisis of 1819–1821 demonstrated the ongoing instability of the Jeffersonian political order, while the resolution of the Missouri Crisis after two years of sectional bitterness likewise demonstrated the resiliency of Jeffersonian nationalism. That alternation between crisis and resolution would have been familiar to northern dissidents between 1807 and 1812.

As they attempted to challenge the political power of slavery in the United States, dissidents struggled to develop a counter-narrative and a sustained movement that could unify northern dissent. Federalist-Republican antagonism proved difficult to overcome, while Jeffersonian nationalists revived and reinvented the democratizing spirit of the 1790s in new forms. In a sense, then, the largest obstacle faced by dissidents was composed of their own past sentiments and choices, the combination of desiring freedom and tolerating slavery that made Jeffersonian democracy possible.

A Tale of Two Apostates

America's vexed international situation before the War of 1812 led to alternating bouts of nationalist fervor and bitter criticism of the federal government among northern Republicans. The long conflict between Britain and France, exacerbated by the French Revolution and the rise of Napoleon, entered a new phase in late 1805 after the battles of Trafalgar and Austerlitz. Britain had naval supremacy, while France controlled much of the European continent. Both nations attempted to restrict commerce to their respective enemy, which undermined the ability of American merchants to act as neutral carriers, an important source of national wealth in the early republic. The British *Essex* decision of 1805 constrained the American carrying trade from the Caribbean to continental Europe, by outlawing the practice of the "broken voyage," whereby American ships would theoretically "neutralize" their cargo by first bringing it to an American port. This foreshadowed the Orders in Council of 1806 and 1807, the first of which declared a blockade on ports in northern Europe, while the second effectively prohibited any American ship from trading with Europe without first stopping in a British port. France, meanwhile,

passed the Berlin Decree in 1806, placing a paper blockade (relatively unen-
forceable, given the weakness of the French navy) on England, and outlawing
trade in British goods or from British ports to Europe. In 1807, Napoleon issued the Milan Decree in response to the recent Order in Council by declaring
that any ship that followed the new British rule (or had been searched by a
British ship) would be subject to seizure by France. Thus both French and
British policy undermined American independence and neutrality and sought
to constrict an important source of American mercantile wealth.[1]

To many Republicans, Britain was the more dangerous and immediate
enemy. British naval power extended across the Atlantic, and Britain impressed seamen serving on American ships, including naturalized American
citizens, to meet increased manpower needs during the Napoleonic Wars.
Control of the Canadian provinces, furthermore, gave Britain a firm presence
on the northern frontier of the United States. Finally, Jeffersonians had been
steeped in Anglophobia since the 1790s, and took occasion every Fourth of
July to commemorate the American Revolution as a virtuous struggle against
British tyranny.[2]

The reach of British power was obvious in the *Chesapeake* affair of June
22, 1807, when the captain of HMS *Leopard* engaged the USS *Chesapeake* ten
miles off the Virginia coast, and demanded to board in order to search for
deserters from the British navy. When the request was refused, the *Leopard*
opened fire on the unprepared *Chesapeake*, killing three men and wounding
eighteen. The British then boarded the ship and removed four men: David
Martin, William Ware, and John Strachan, all of whom were American born
but claimed as deserters from the HMS *Melampus*, and Jenkin Ratford, a de-
serter from the HMS *Halifax* who was born in Britain and thus claimed as a
subject by the British crown. The resulting fury in the Republican press knew
no bounds. On July 1, 1807, one "Timothy Spintext" cataloged the terrors of
British power for readers of John Binns's *Democratic Press.* "The British nation," he declared, "sought to make us slaves of their despotic power." They
intended to treat the United States as they had Ireland, Scotland, Asia, and
Africa, as an imperial satellite controlled by force and violence. The attack on
the *Chesapeake* was "the most wanton, the most daring outrage . . . which
stands recorded on the page of history." For the *Democratic Press,* "Bloody,
bloody Britain!" was an enemy not only to American independence, but to
human freedom around the globe.[3]

Binns's Anglophobic alliteration reflected a central tenet of Republican nationalism: that the United States must be an asylum and arsenal of democracy. The American struggle against Britain was often tantamount, Binns and others suggested, to a worldwide contest between freedom and slavery.[4] Although these arguments can seem grandiose in retrospect, Jenkin Ratford (the alias of one John Wilson) no doubt would have found them convincing. Ratford relished his temporary freedom in what he called "the land of liberty," where he took occasion to publicly spurn British authority. For his transgressions, Ratford was hanged on board the HMS *Halifax* on August 31 in the harbor of Halifax, Nova Scotia. His execution, claimed the judge who sentenced him, would serve to convince other seamen of the "heinous crime of desertion," made all the worse by "mutinous and contemptuous behaviour to your Officers." Republicans quickly condemned this object lesson in British authority.[5]

Some Republicans argued for war in response to this violation of American sovereignty, and growing outrage against Britain inspired a few renegade Federalists, like John Quincy Adams, Charles Jared Ingersoll, and William Plumer, to embrace the Jeffersonian coalition as defenders of the American nation-state. Instead of war, Jefferson and Republicans in Congress responded to British aggression with the embargo, signed into law in December of 1807. The embargo attempted to halt all American exports in order to force England and France to recognize the rights of the United States as a neutral shipper, and to end the British practice of impressing American sailors. In conjunction with the nonimportation of select English goods, Jefferson and Madison thought that the embargo would cause enough economic damage to Britain to gain concessions for the United States. Federalists quickly criticized the measure, entertained plans for state-level resistance, and argued that the northern states had to unite with each other to protect their commercial interests. Although he was skeptical of the embargo's efficacy, Adams supported the administration, and finalized his break from the Federalist party by joining the Republican caucus in Congress to nominate Madison for the presidency in January 1808. In a public letter to Massachusetts Federalist Harrison Gray Otis, Adams criticized fellow senator Timothy Pickering, detailed the horrors of impressment, and argued for political unity to resist Federalist attempts to return the United States to "a state of national vassalage."[6]

While diplomatic crisis persuaded Adams to join the Republican party, it provided James Sloan of New Jersey with the final motivation to leave it. The embargo, which threatened northern merchants, export-oriented farmers, and the economies of port cities, provoked Republicans throughout the North to question the utility of their alliance with the South. It also led to widespread smuggling, in response to which Jefferson proposed enforcement measures that, on paper, gave the federal government excessive powers to control the behavior of individual citizens. In December 1808, James Sloan told Congress that, compared to Jefferson's enforcement measures, "the Alien and Sedition laws were humane and just."[7] Like Adams, Sloan joined the Republican caucus in Congress that nominated James Madison for the presidency in January 1808, but he soon revoked his allegiance and declared his support for George Clinton of New York, Jefferson's current vice president. In a widely copied letter first published in April 1808, he criticized the caucus as an attempt to prevent a thorough democratic review of presidential candidates, and repeated his argument for removal of the national capital from Washington.[8] In doing so, he challenged the ability of the Republican coalition to continue to control national politics.

The caucus was an important institution of Democratic-Republican organization at the national level: composed of Republican senators and representatives, it successfully proposed the Republican candidate for president until 1824, when Republicans throughout the country abandoned the caucus nominee, William Crawford, arguing that the institution was inherently antidemocratic. Tensions over the caucus began much earlier, driven by personal and regional jealousy. In January 1808, most New York members refused to attend the caucus, while George Clinton, according to fellow New Yorker Samuel L. Mitchill, "considered himself treated with great cruelty and disrespect" by the Republicans who did attend and nominated Madison.[9] Clinton's hurt feelings notwithstanding, the true injustice of the caucus was sectional rather than personal, as historian Leonard Richards has shown. The three-fifths clause, in conjunction with the national politics of democracy, institutionalized southern preponderance in the Jeffersonian coalition. Additional power in Congress, paired with relative partisan unity in the South and relative disunity in the North, gave southern Republicans an edge in every caucus through the War of 1812.[10] Dissidents like Sloan thus faced a daunting task.

Northern Republicans were not the only critics of the caucus and Madison's nomination. Southern Republicans led by John Randolph tried to nominate James Monroe, and for a moment the election of Madison seemed doubtful, as the Republican coalition frayed at both ends. George Clinton did not mount much of a campaign, but for a few months, he served as a focal point for the expression of multiple resentments against the Republican party and the relative power of Virginia in national affairs. Madison ultimately prevailed, in part by containing his rivals within the administration: Monroe became secretary of state, and George Clinton remained as vice president. But disaffection continued to fester, especially in the North, and DeWitt Clinton would draw on mounting sectional resentment in his far more successful presidential bid in 1812.

Neither Clinton campaign stressed opposition to slavery as a major cause. Instead, Clintonians argued that Virginia had controlled the federal government for far too long, to the detriment of northern (and especially New York) political and economic interests. But by disrupting the unity of the Republican party, the Clinton campaigns provided political space for Democratic-Republicans to express sectional and antislavery sentiments, and thus to challenge the partisan and ideological accords of Jeffersonian democracy.

The extended diplomatic crisis from 1807 to 1812 created obvious opportunity for northern dissidents. In opposition to Virginia slaveholders, Republican rebels like Sloan mounted a compelling argument in favor of northern power. But crisis also bolstered the cause for Republican and national unity. In contrast to men like Sloan, dissident Federalists like John Quincy Adams and William Plumer, previously frank opponents of the three-fifths clause and the Republican coalition, pointed to the powerful countervailing force of American nationalism. As Adams told New Hampshire Republican Nahum Parker in December 1808, "every man must set himself and his pretensions aside, before the great interests of the Nation."[11] The ideological tensions of Jeffersonian democracy before the War of 1812 thus became a contest over the terms of American nationalism, as dissidents challenged the Jeffersonian consensus and Republicans new and old fought to defend the Republican coalition from internal and external threat.

Federalist Rebirth?

While Jeffersonian foreign policy led to an increase of Republican dissidence after 1807, hostility to Virginian rule and southern slavery had influenced Republican dissenters since Jefferson's first election. New England Federalists attacked the political power of Jeffersonian slaveholders after the election of 1800, prompting nationalist defenses of Jeffersonian rule by men like Abraham Bishop and John Leland. But not all their Republican counterparts were so charmed by the Jeffersonian ascendancy. A case in point was Francis

Blake, a Massachusetts Republican and the first editor of the Worcester *National Aegis*. Blake began political life as a fairly typical Jeffersonian, filled with ardor for the French Revolution and the international progress of liberty. In a July Fourth address in 1796, he defended the Terror as a "transitory frenzy" and promised the tyrants of the world that they would soon "be cast down to hell." "The grand political millennium is at hand," he exclaimed, "when tyranny shall be buried in ruins; when all nations shall be united in ONE MIGHTY REPUBLIC!" He was more restrained as editor of the *Aegis*, yet he remained an enthusiastic partisan. In a prospectus for the new paper issued in the fall of 1801, Blake (writing under the pseudonym "Hector Ironside") warned that "the spirit of oppression . . . is yet stalking abroad in our land. Sullen and revengeful it will never be appeased but by the immolation of liberty itself." The *Aegis* would be a shield against such an implacable enemy; it would seek "to exhibit truth as it is; to expose the fallacy of pretended federalism; to increase the energy of republican principle."[12]

A few years later, Blake's Republican enthusiasm had run dry. A series of local political conflicts compelled him to leave the *Aegis* in April 1804, and he spent much of the next two years traducing his former partisan allies in print. By 1806 his apostasy was confirmed in the *Aurora*, where William Duane declared him a Federalist. This followed an extended public dispute with Edward Bangs, a Worcester Republican who wrote for the *Aegis*, which began when Blake filed suit to recover the *Aegis*'s type and printing press.[13] In public, Blake's falling out with the Jeffersonian coalition seemed the result of petty local rivalries, but in private, Blake confessed deep-seated anxieties about the "wild & ruthless & overwhelming ambition of Virginia." "I have long discerned in this haughty & <u>aristocratic</u> section of the Continent," he told his friend Jabez Upham in 1804,

> a disposition to prostrate the power & wealth & influence of the smaller states at the footstool of her own potent authority. I believe her boasted democracy consists in a propensity to aggrandize herself by destroying the commerce of New England. I am convinced it is time to make a stand & to defend ourselves agt. this alarming spirit of encroachment.

Blake hoped that a third party would arise in the "Eastern states" to defend their prerogatives against "the Southern tide of usurpation." To Blake, such a party would still be "Republican," but it would represent "New England

Republicanism," and "be equably opposed to the dangerous doctrines of excessive Federalism, & the fallacious theories of Southern democracy."[14]

It was telling that Blake chose to confide in Upham, a Federalist and
friend of Josiah Quincy's. Blake's skepticism about Virginia was married to a
distaste for the egalitarian tendencies of northern Jeffersonian democracy.
"By democracy," Blake explained to Upham, "I have never meant the government of the rabble." Then followed a rant against populist democrats "who
will make every 'bricklayer a legislator because there is no better sign of a
brave mind than a hard hand,'" and otherwise upset the social order. "I should
even choose to bow down the kneck under the heavy & galling yoke of Anglo
Federalism," declared Blake, "rather than trust to such a revolution & commit
myself to the mercy of such reformers."[15]

Blake eventually did bow down his kneck and join the Federalists, and he
was elected as a Federalist member of the Massachusetts Senate in 1810.[16] His
newfound conservatism coincided with a revival of Federalism throughout
the North, in response to the embargo and the deepening diplomatic crisis
with Britain. Spurred on by a new generation of leaders who embraced democratic politics, if not democratic ideals, younger Federalists fomented partisan conflict, instead of retreating into elitist disdain, and regained significant
political power north of the Potomac after 1807. Blake's local antagonist Edward Bangs anxiously watched the resurgence of Federalism in Massachusetts. During a visit to Boston in June 1808, he was alarmed at "the untoward
ascendancy of federal or British politics." He begged his Republican comrade
Nathaniel Howe to write newspaper editorials to "counteract the effects of
the Embargo upon the ignorant, and stir up every wavering Democrat."[17]

While many Federalists, like Blake, condemned excessive popular sovereignty, in practice, disputes over Jeffersonian foreign policy invigorated partisan competition and increased electoral turnout. The Federalist revival,
ironically, helped expand democracy. In Massachusetts, this new, aggressive
confidence helped Federalists turn back the gains of Republicans after 1800,
and during the War of 1812, they consolidated power under a regional attack
against Republican foreign policy, the threat of Napoleonic rule, and the
dominance of Virginia in the federal government.[18]

The Federalist renascence allowed Blake to complete his passage from
youthful Republican ardor to older and more bitter conservatism. In 1808,
Blake's rivalry with Bangs continued, but now over national and international
issues, as Blake organized a July Fourth celebration to attack the Jeffersonian
embargo, while Bangs helped organize a counter-celebration led by Republi-

cans.[19] Four years later, Blake was once again involved in dueling Independence Day celebrations. On July 4, 1812, Blake publicly repudiated his earlier endorsement of the French Revolution and claimed that an "overweening partiality for FRANCE" had a negative effect on American politics and foreign policy. In 1814, he joined the Federalist attack on the political power of the South, and in an October speech in support of the Hartford Convention, he called the three-fifths clause "an original and radical defect in the form of government, and, perhaps, one of the primary causes of our misfortunes." Reversing course entirely, he now praised England for contributing what good there was in American life and, according to the Republican press, reportedly claimed *"he was ready to change this Constitution for that of Great Britain, MONARCHY AND ALL."*[20] That may have been a prejudicial paraphrase, but there was no doubt Blake had renounced his prior commitments to the Republican coalition and his youthful passions for revolutionary France.

Republicans, of course, thoroughly denounced Blake for such Anglophilic sentiments, and his dissidence served to catalyze Jeffersonian solidarity. In his widely read unionist pamphlet *The Olive Branch*, first published in 1814, Pennsylvania Republican Matthew Carey condemned the "outrageous violence" of the *"quondam democrat"* Francis Blake.[21] That Jeffersonians regarded Blake's partisan conversion with disdain rather than anxiety suggests the limits of the Federalist revival. On their own, Federalists never became a substantial threat to the Republican majority at the national level. Their numbers in the House of Representatives recovered from a low point in the Ninth Congress (1805–1807), but they never managed to gain more than a 38 percent share of the House. Outside Maryland, furthermore, they made very limited inroads in the South. In the North, Federalists were more successful, but their gains often helped repair internal Republican divisions that had grown more prominent in the absence of an external rival. In returning to Federalism, Blake helped confirm the longstanding Jeffersonian message that sectional disputes, especially about slavery, were fueled by the antidemocratic passions of a regional elite. That argument was essential to Jeffersonian nationalism, and as long as there were Federalists willing to berate Republicans, it retained legitimacy.

Thus Blake's Worcester counterpart Edward Bangs, who wrote for and occasionally edited the *Aegis* after Blake's departure, spent the years between 1807 and 1812 in a state of rising partisan fervor, driven to defend Republican nationalism from Federalists, Great Britain, and Blake. In a series of letters to his friend Nathaniel Howe, Bangs expressed a fierce commitment to

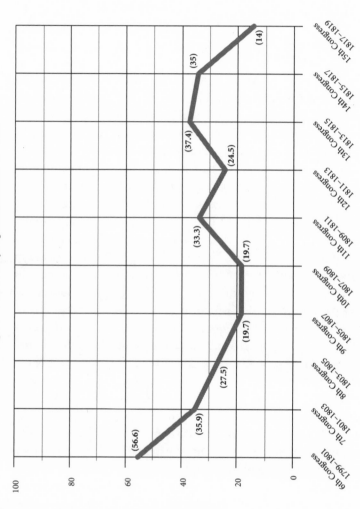

Figure 6. Federalist strength in the House of Representatives, 1799–1819. Congressional data from Kenneth C. Martis, *The Historical Atlas of Political Parties in the United States Congress, 1789–1989* (New York: Macmillan, 1989), and *Biographical Directory of the United States Congress* (bioguide.congress.gov).

maintaining the Jeffersonian standard as regional opposition grew more powerful. "The Aegis," he promised in the fall of 1807, "increases within a few weeks very fast in the number of its subscribers and bids defiance to the malice of federalism." By the following summer, Bangs was engaged in an ideological war with Francis Blake, and preparing himself for a military one with Britain. "Party rage is higher here than ever before," he wrote Howe from Worcester in July 1808. But he had grown sanguine since his encounter with Boston Federalism a month previous. "The tories are busy and audacious and I am pleased to find that they have been met with a spirit, which may be an useful lesson to teach them that Republicans will never be trampled on." In particular, he noted that the *Aegis* had attacked Blake's anti-embargo Independence Day event and promised that the Republican apostate would continue to receive "a pretty severe flogging in our paper." Meanwhile, the "Democratic Celebration" of Independence "was conducted with unprecedented eclat." Bangs anticipated "becoming a military man," prepared to "serve my country if occasion calls." Bangs's combination of partisan fervor and militant nationalism anticipated the main Republican response to Federalist criticism in the years before the War of 1812. Uniting party and nation, Republicans called on all true democrats to defend both.[22]

Federalist gains over the next few years only hardened Bangs's devotion to the Republican cause. "The malice and violence of federalism are now at their utmost height," he wrote to Howe in December 1811; he deemed it "indispensable" for Republicans to "leave no single step untrodden, no single measure neglected that can possibly conduce to our victory over our furious antagonist." While Republicans were mostly unsuccessful in Massachusetts, where Federalists won the race for governor and took over the lower house of the state legislature in the Spring of 1812, Bangs's fervor was replicated throughout the North on the eve of conflict, in heartfelt calls for Republican unity and commitment that evoked the partisan strife of the 1790s.[23] Republicans returned to their roots, as the menace of Federalist resurgence revived the central passions of Jeffersonian democracy.

The Clintonian Moment

Between 1807 and 1812, however, mainstream Republicans had to contend not only with conservatives like Blake but also with committed democrats who had grown disenchanted with slaveholder power. Throughout the North,

a number of disaffected Republicans began to seek an alternative to Jeffersonian rule, not in Federalism but in a northern-oriented coalition opposed to
southern power at the national level. Such internal Republican dissension
was more dangerous than Federalist resurgence when it came to the national
hegemony of the Democratic-Republican party.[24]

Francis Blake's imagined party of the "eastern states," opposed to Virginia
rule, was thus a distinct possibility in the years after 1807, and its advocates
included not only bitter ex-Republicans animated by sectional pride and disgust with democracy, but men who no longer believed that the Jeffersonian
coalition fulfilled their democratic and partisan aspirations. Among the disaffected were radical democrats like James Sloan and, briefly, William Duane,
as well as moderate northern Republicans who believed that southern Republicans were inherently hostile to northern commerce and political power.
Both groups pointed to slavery as a root cause of southern behavior. Dissidents like Sloan focused their criticism on slavery itself, and revised longstanding Federalist objections to slaveholder power in democratic terms.
Moderate Republicans pointed less to slavery's inherent antidemocratic tendencies and more to southern (and especially Virginian) power in the federal
government and southern antagonism to northern political and economic
interests. Together, these two strains of Republican dissent suggested the potential influence of northern sectionalism in national politics well before the
more divisive Missouri Crisis of 1819–1821.

Unlike Massachusetts Republican turned Federalist Francis Blake, James
Sloan never abandoned his attachment to democracy, while most Federalists
never abandoned their disgust for Sloan. In many ways, this made Sloan a
greater danger to Republican unity than a man like Blake. Because he remained a democratic enthusiast, Sloan could not be written off as a hack-
neyed Federalist conspirator. Instead, he spoke with the bona fides of a true
Republican convert, but one who no longer believed that democracy could
survive in alliance with slavery.

After proposing the removal of the national capital to Philadelphia in February 1808, and then abandoning Madison for George Clinton, Sloan returned
to Congress the next fall prepared to indict the Republican administration. Addressing the House on December 27, 1808, Sloan claimed the embargo was now
"the greatest evil these United States suffered." When Thomas Gholson of Virginia chided that northern fishermen should spin cotton and northern merchants turn to the plow in order to survive the economic crisis caused by the
embargo, Sloan responded with a tempestuous attack on southern slavery.

Such a plan was "well adapted to the meridian of a government where *slavery* and *unconditional submission* is the order of the day," he retorted, before turning to Georgia's George Troup, who had told the House to place their trust in the "honorable" and "enlightened" people of Virginia, rather than the "depraved of the cities" in New England. Sloan might have agreed with Troup's assessment back in 1800, but he no longer believed in an enlightened Virginia. "I will never *appeal* or *look up for example*," he confessed,

> to any state government, under which *three hundred forty-six thousand nine hundred and sixty eight HUMAN SOULS* are kept in a state of *perpetual bondage,* and used as an article of *traffic*, in common with a bale of goods, or a beast of the field . . . I will never hold up as an *example* any government, where the choicest of all earthly blessings, "*liberty*," is extended only to a chosen few, and withheld from the many; where a great majority of those *called* freemen, who are compelled in case of war to risque their lives in support of the property of the rich, are denied a voice in making the law that so compels them, or any others.

Sloan, once a defiant Jeffersonian, could no longer restrain sectional and antislavery sentiments that placed him in direct opposition to his southern colleagues. That endangered the ideological system he had helped build in 1800, in which northern white men pursued their democratic freedom while suppressing open hostility to southern slavery. Now he viewed slaveholders, especially from Virginia, as a fundamental danger to democracy—not only because they held dominion over slaves, but also because they limited the political power of ordinary white men.[25]

Sloan contrasted Virginia with New York, where the Declaration of Independence was "reduced to a practice," and the "power of the poor man to guard his ewe lamb, is equal to that of the rich over his flock." Simple arithmetic defined New York's difference from Virginia, whose national power depended on the three-fifths clause. Thomas Jefferson's state had 22 congressional representatives, yet a recent election saw only "between twenty and twenty-five thousand votes"; New York and its eighteen representatives, by contrast, could "boast *one hundred and eleven thousand* free and independent voters."[26] Such comparisons established the obvious: slavery was antithetical to democracy. Sloan turned Republican antiaristocratic language against southern slaveholders, while rephrasing traditional Federalist complaints against the three-fifths clause in democratic terms. He sought an alternative to Virginia rule based on a practical application of the Declaration of Independence, by which he meant an egalitarian political system in which population, not wealth, determined representation. Endorsing New York state as an exemplar of democracy was somewhat naïve, given the restrictions on suffrage and popular election within the state and the persistence of slavery, which had been abolished only recently (in 1799), and only on the most gradual terms.[27] But in terms of national politics, New York presented a potential alternative to Virginia—not only to Sloan, but to a number of dissident Republicans between 1807 and 1812.

In New York, where dissenting Republicans hoped to use criticism of the embargo to aid the electoral prospects of George Clinton in 1808, Jeffersonian commercial policy was represented as a larger southern project to check the growing economic and political power of the northern states. One of Clinton's most important ideological supporters in 1808 was, like Sloan, a very disaffected Republican. He was also Clinton's son-in-law. After setting the United States afire with political controversy in 1793 by catalyzing the growth of Democratic-Republican societies and American ardor for the French Revolution, "Citizen" Edmond-Charles Genet settled down to a quieter life in Greenbush, New York, just south of Albany, as the husband of George Clinton's daughter Cornelia. He returned to political controversy in 1808 an older and more bitter man, disillusioned with both the French Revolution and the Virginia Republicans who had come to power in the United States. Genet argued that the election of Madison in 1808 "would not only be extremely detrimental to the welfare of the United States, but also to the cause of republicanism." He attacked the congressional caucus that nominated Madison as an undemocratic institution that aimed "to perpetuate the Presidency in the hands of Virginia." Virginia's ambition threatened both sectional unity and the health of the American economy, Genet explained, because the embargo, "the undisputed property of a few southern systematic politicians," had become a disastrous impediment to northern commerce. Southern agrarianism falsely envisioned "agriculture as the paramount source of the wealth of nations," and "commerce and navigation as mere subaltern agencies."[28] For George and DeWitt Clinton, such disregard for commerce was especially apparent in the unwillingness of the national government to support defensive preparations for the harbor of New York. Indeed, George Clinton told Samuel L. Mitchill in February 1808 that Thomas Jefferson was personally responsible for keeping the harbor unprotected.[29]

Similar claims echoed during DeWitt Clinton's presidential campaign, anticipating the developmental ethos of antebellum Whigs. The *Columbian*, the main Clintonian paper during the election of 1812, printed articles emphasizing that New York, unlike Virginia, was constituted of a mixed economy of commerce, agriculture, and manufacturing. Edited by Charles Holt, who began his career as a Jeffersonian printer in Connecticut, *The Columbian* also endorsed plans for a canal between the Hudson River and Lake Erie.[30] Clinton had been appointed to the board of canal commissioners in 1810 and toured the prospective route through the Mohawk Valley. Support for the canal brought together elite Federalists and Republicans in New York, as was obvious in late 1811, when DeWitt Clinton traveled to Washington with Gouverneur Morris to ask for federal funds to support the canal. Some observers in the capital tied Clinton's Washington visit to his presidential aspirations, linking his advocacy of economic development with New York's resentment at Virginia rule.[31] Rebuffed by Congress and Madison, the two men returned home, where Morris recommended that New York undertake canal construction on its own behalf. The War of 1812 interrupted Morris's ambitious plans, but Clinton revived them in 1815 and the New York Legislature eventually agreed to support the canal project. After completion in 1825, the Erie Canal proved to be far more productive than imagined, a dramatic example of how internal improvements could catalyze widespread economic development.[32]

The extent to which defending commercialized agriculture and the dignity of New York might lead to open attacks on slavery remained unclear. In 1808, Genet censured the "indolent slave-holders" of Virginia and warned that the election of Madison would mean "the maritime states humbled and empoverished, Virginia, resting on the arm of slavery, ruling the union in peace."[33] But he also hoped to reach out to dissident Virginia Republicans— despite his focus on the northern states, he proposed James Monroe as George Clinton's vice president—which constrained strong antislavery claims. Like many elite New Yorkers, furthermore, Genet and George Clinton were quite comfortable acting the part of the master. In 1795, Genet offered to sell a young slave to his father-in-law; ten years later, he threatened to sell a disobedient servant.[34] He was hardly an isolated case, since New York's gradual emancipation law allowed masters to retain their current slaves for life, and their progeny for over twenty years. As late as 1810, there were over 15,000 slaves in the state.[35] The slow decline of slavery in New York and New Jersey impaired the sincerity of northern indictments of "indolent slave-holders." Given this local context, it was not surprising that neither Clinton campaign made slavery the central issue in national or northern politics.

The Clintonian moment, like later, more forthright attempts to build antislavery political coalitions in the North, was not rooted in ideological purity. In 1812, when DeWitt Clinton ran for president, critics complained that he was simply an unprincipled office-seeker, constantly shifting positions for tactical advantage. While partly true, the 1812 campaign also managed to unite a diverse set of actors in an attempt to undermine the national power of the Virginia Republicans. The variety of interests in Clinton's camp made conflicting claims inevitable, but it also expressed the main electoral strength of the Clintonian coalition, the possibility that northern Republicans and Federalists might unite along sectional lines. And in that respect, regardless of the sincerity of their antislavery commitments, Clintonian dissidents threatened the Jeffersonian coalition and the security of slaveholders in the federal government.

For most northerners, disaffection from the Democratic-Republican party was driven by sectional grievance, not antislavery argument. Like Genet, they worried about a presumed southern threat to northern economic development and political preeminence. These sectional sentiments grew in intensity from 1809 to 1812, as diplomatic relations with Great Britain worsened. In New York, DeWitt Clinton first backed away from the sectional attacks of 1808, and sought to reunite with the Madison administration in order to secure federal patronage and maintain power at the state level. But as criticism of Madison mounted after 1810, Clinton moved toward an open break with the Republican coalition.[36] By May 1812, when the New York legislature nominated Clinton for the presidency, sectional resentment threatened to undermine Democratic-Republican support throughout the North.

Nicholas Gilman, senator from New Hampshire and Clinton supporter, was one of the more well-known northern dissenters, or "malcontents," of 1812. Though he had always been something of a maverick, shifting from a moderate Federalist position in the 1790s to moderate Republicanism in the 1800s, Gilman remained an advocate of Jefferson's diplomacy through at least 1806. In the spring of that year, he wrote to a friend in support of the nonimportation of British goods (a prelude to the embargo of 1807), which was under debate in Congress. But by the end of 1808 he had begun to doubt the wisdom of the administration, and wondered whether Jefferson and Madison would ever develop a coherent foreign policy. By 1812, his doubts had blossomed into a strong case of sectional resentment. As Congress debated declaring war against Great Britain that spring, Gilman decisively opposed the southern leadership of the Republican party. On May 1, he complained of "The mean degrading prejudices entertained and inculcated by Thomas Jefferson & others against merchants and merchantile cities," which had "been so long in fashion at the seat of Government as to be infinitely injurious to that [mercantile] interest and, as I believe, to the general interest of the nation." Gilman doubted whether "commerce shall ever receive a fair and reasonable protection from the general government . . . unless we can have a President from one of the States north of the Potomac." By the end of the month he wrote in favor of DeWitt Clinton.[37]

Sectional strains were apparent even in Madison's cabinet. In March 1810, Gideon Granger, Connecticut Republican and postmaster general, had written directly to Clinton in support of his candidacy. Granger was convinced that "if the dominion of Virginia be continued or any Executive power given South of the Potomac" war would result before the end of the next administration. Granger had long been inclined to a northern view of American politics. In 1804 he wrote to DeWitt Clinton that "the strength of the nation this day is East of the Delaware [river]," and that the Northeast, because of its stronger commercial and financial institutions, would form a powerful alliance with the new territories west of the Appalachians. At the time, Granger was worried that the Republican party might fragment because of the ideological extremism of southerners like John Randolph. By 1810, however, Granger hoped for just such a realignment. When the New York legislature met to consider nominating DeWitt Clinton for president in 1812, Granger sent letters from Washington declaring his preference for a northern candidate, and apparently helped tip the balance in favor of Clinton.[38]

Such northern men were not the only threat to Madison's reelection. His administration was beset by internal dissension from the outset, pulled apart by warring factions and interests. In the southern states, John Randolph opposed him as a betrayer of true Republican principles, while the Smith family of Maryland (Samuel Smith, a powerful senator, and Robert Smith, secretary of the navy from 1801 to 1809 and Madison's secretary of state until 1811) plotted to undermine Madison and win the presidency in 1812.[39] Men like Granger, Gilman, and DeWitt Clinton were likewise involved in a struggle for personal power and influence as much as an ideological conflict over Virginia's predominance in the federal government. Nor did they openly attack slavery to the same degree as men like Sloan. Instead, they emphasized

southern threats to northern commerce and expansion. The Clintonians
were hardly an antislavery force. Yet by disrupting the Jeffersonian coalition
they created political space for northerners to challenge the supremacy of
Virginia and the power of slavery in national politics.

Some Federalists perceived the Clintonian movement as an opportunity
to regain power and rehabilitate the northern states from the delusions of
Jeffersonian democracy. At a national meeting of Federalists in New York,
September 15–17, 1812, Massachusetts's Harrison Gray Otis spoke in favor of
Clinton and against those men, especially Rufus King, who wanted a Federalist to contend against Madison. No firm decision was made to back Clinton,
but the Federalist convention agreed to a vague resolution not to back one of
their own and to support whomever would "pursue a different course" from
James Madison.[40] Well into the fall, some Federalists believed Clinton's campaign would redeem the northern states from Virginia rule. Edward St. Loe
Livermore (whose brother Arthur would be an important antislavery Republican during the Missouri Crisis) served two terms in Congress as a Massachusetts Federalist from 1807 to 1810 and supported Clinton in 1812. He wrote
to Connecticut Federalist Timothy Pitkin in November 1812 to report that
Massachusetts and New Hampshire would give their votes to Clinton. "It will
be a great satisfaction," he noted, "to find that the people have discarded
those foolish miserable dupes to the Virginia slave drivers through whose aid
in a great measure they have lorded it over the U.S." In 1800, New England
Republicans believed that Jefferson would liberate them from Federalist tyranny. In 1812, Livermore hoped DeWitt Clinton would emancipate New England from the despotism of slaveholders.[41]

As a New Yorker representing an important contingent of the state's Republicans, Clinton offered Federalists a viable opportunity to regain influence at the national level.[42] The Clinton campaign also enabled Federalist
criticism of the three-fifths clause to resurface, now not simply as resentment
at Jefferson's election, but as part of a broader regional argument in favor of
northern power. Sereno Edwards Dwight, the son of Timothy Dwight,
penned one of the more powerful antislavery attacks in support of Clinton.
In October 1812, the *Connecticut Journal* ran two articles by Dwight that explained in great detail how the three-fifths clause gave the "Slave Country"
unwarranted political power, and called for the "Men of the North" to reject
the authority of the *"Representatives of Negro Slaves."* As historian Matthew
Mason has shown, some Federalists, like New York's Gouverner Morris, believed that new "geographical divisions" based on opposition to the

three-fifths clause might trump the partisan divisions of Jeffersonian democracy.[43] Such visions were not entirely fanciful. Federalists received Republican support in the Massachusetts Assembly for a resolution opposing
"offensive war," and opposition to Madison helped them regain the Massachusetts governorship and a majority in the New York Assembly in 1812.[44]

Some historians have thus seen in the Clinton campaign little more than
Federalism in a new guise. But northern dissent in 1812 extended far beyond
the reviving Federalist party. Republican dissidents like James Sloan pointed
to a new, sectional attack on slavery, one that recast Federalist criticism of the
three-fifths clause and slaveholder power in a more democratic vein.[45] In
doing so, Republicans like Sloan undermined the ideological commitments
that had sustained Jeffersonian democracy, much as the idea of a northern
party threatened the partisan alliance between northern democrats and
southern slaveholders. Such sectional antislavery thinking remained on the
margins of Clinton's 1812 campaign, but at moments, it indicated the real possibility (and the real danger to the Republican coalition) of a significant realignment in northern democratic thought.

William Duane, once the scourge of Federalism and leading printer of the
Republican coalition, provides perhaps the best evidence of how dissidence
could transform Jeffersonian adherents into bitter opponents of the South.
Duane's hostility to Madison grew out of state-level disputes in Pennsylvania,
where Republicans had begun to fragment soon after Jefferson's election, di-
viding first into "Quids" and "Democrats," the supporters and opponents of
Governor Thomas McKean, who proved too conservative for Duane's taste.
Duane and his Philadelphia partner Michael Leib soon joined forces with a
pair of rural counterparts, Simon Snyder and John Binns, who edited the
Republican Argus in Northumberland, Pennsylvania, from 1802 to 1807. Together, they worked to replace McKean with Snyder, which they did successfully in 1807. But the alliance was uneasy from the outset, and began to
fragment when Binns moved to Philadelphia and commenced publishing the
Democratic Press in 1807. The Republicans divided again, now between a
"New School" tied to Snyder and the "Old School" led by Duane and Leib. In
contrast to William Duane and the "Old School," New Schoolers had stronger ties to rural Pennsylvania, they looked more favorably on capitalist development, they opposed radical changes to the state's legal system, and they
were more willing to embrace the Quids, the Republican gentlemen of the
1790s. Pro-manufacturing Republicans like Tench Coxe and Matthew Carey
joined the New School movement, as did more elite Republicans like Richard

Rush and Charles Jared Ingersoll. Duane, in contrast, was hardly an economic radical, but he did oppose concentrated economic power, and he
fought successfully to prevent the recharter of Alexander Hamilton's Bank of
the United States in 1811.[46] That fight, which pitted Duane against treasury
secretary Albert Gallatin, left him embittered with the Madison administration. Like a number of northern dissidents before the War of 1812, he turned
to sectionalism to clarify his opposition to the Republican coalition.

Internal Republican disputes led to more strident sectional attacks because the Republican party was so closely identified with Virginia at the presidential level. Duane resented Gallatin because of his ties to the Quids and
the New School, and because (thought Duane) Gallatin had denied him merited federal patronage after the election of 1800. But after the bank fight,
Duane's hatred of Gallatin reached new heights, and soon led to a general
indictment of Madison's administration. By early 1812, the *Aurora* was publicly calling Gallatin "The Rat in the Treasury," and running pro-Clinton editorials from New York papers. For much of the winter and spring of 1812,
Duane appeared to be seeking Madison's removal from office, and he openly
claimed that any administration that countenanced Gallatin could not maintain the confidence of the people.[47]

Duane's hostility toward Madison threatened to become a full-fledged
criticism not simply of men and measures in Washington, but of the power of
the South and slaveholders in national politics. In the Clintonian moment
before the War of 1812, he seemed liable at times to join a wider movement
for northern power. In February 1812, for example, Duane ran a bitter attack
on the political culture of Virginia. Provoked by the lack of direct representation in the state legislature, Duane indicted Virginia as a polity that did not
acknowledge "the rights of man," as it was organized on the "principles of the
British borough system," in open defiance of majority rule politics. For
Duane, these antidemocratic measures ensured that Virginia, "instead of
being populous, in a free, hardy, and industrious race of freemen, is accursed
with a mass of slavery and shame—its sterility, poverty, and danger." Instead
of drafting apologetics for the Virginia gentry, as he had after the election of
1800, Duane now condemned the state's elite as the chief obstacle to promoting democracy, and thus ending slavery. He admitted that they might have
"kind manners and generous hearts," but described the government of Virginia as an "aristocracy" that was "at open variance" with the foundational
principles of the Declaration of Independence. "The white artisan," he explained, would never wish "to settle in a state in which he either has no rights,

or is treated like a slave." Duane closed with an excoriation of John Randolph, "that *miserable misanthrope*." There were too many men like Randolph in Virginia, who "would prefer to be the *lord over a plantation* of negroes, than a free citizen among men who perform the functions assigned them by the creator, and eat their bread which they have themselves earned." Duane predicted that Virginia "will fall behind her sister states . . . should she adhere to the errors of her present constitution."[48] In 1800, Duane had looked to Virginia to redeem the United States from Federalism. He claimed that Virginia had inspired abolition in Pennsylvania and he glorified the young John Randolph in the *Aurora*. Now in 1812, at odds with the Madison administration and as intemperate as ever, Duane reversed course. Randolph was a misanthrope and Virginia was a hindrance, not an inspiration, to political freedom.

James Sloan, by now out of Congress and a confirmed opponent of the Madison administration, found in DeWitt Clinton's campaign another opportunity to vent his resentments against Virginia and the Democratic-Republican party. In the fall of 1812, contradicting reports of his death a year earlier, Sloan published a pamphlet supporting Clinton for president. As in his 1808 speech against the embargo, the pamphlet constituted an inversion of northern Jeffersonian ideology. Instead of decrying Federalism, as he had done vigorously during Jefferson's first term, Sloan bluntly attacked the Democratic-Republican party. In part, his objections were based on traditional republican anxieties about the impending expansion of the American fiscal-military state on the eve of the War of 1812. Ultimately, however, Sloan believed that the abusive power of Madison's administration reflected the sectional imbalance of the American political system, in which a southern minority, already larger than warranted due to the three-fifths clause, dominated the federal government and undermined the interests of the "Middle and Eastern states." Southerners, claimed Sloan, were unfit to govern "a great, free, and enlightened, agricultural and commercial people." They might claim to be devotees of liberty, but their "conduct proves them unjust, tyrannical oppressors of the human species!" Yet these representatives of a slave society remained in control of national politics, through "the weight of Executive influence" and "the virulence of party politics." Many northern Democratic-Republicans, Sloan argued, had been induced to support Madison for president in 1808, "contrary both to the interest of their constituents, and their own judgment and inclination," all the while "attempting to cover their breach of trust and injustice, under the specious pretex[t] of unity to prevent the Federalists from obtaining their former power."⁴⁹ In 1801 and 1802, an enthusiastic Sloan argued that Jeffersonian democracy would free northern men from Federalist power. In 1812, he contended that partisan politics suppressed legitimate sectional grievances and allowed slaveholding tyrants to remain in power.

Sloan proposed a counterfactual that expressed his vision of a republic redeemed by the North. "Had an eastern President been chosen last election," Sloan declared,

> and the seat of government removed to Philadelphia, where the Representatives of the people could have had correct information of the opinion of their constituents, and legislated publicly before a free people, procuring their bread by some useful occupation; instead of secretly with closed doors, surrounded by slaves and slave-holders, and a set of war hawks, and other idle drones; . . . I am fully convinced, had that been the case, that instead of the deplorable situation to which we are reduced, our public debt would have been principally discharged, and a surplus in our treasury to have applied to the improvement of canals, and roads, whereby our citizens would have been united together, and the inestimable blessing of peace, love, and harmony, would have smiled on our land!⁵⁰

Sloan's alternative vision of the United States emphasized government transparency, the nobility of labor, and federal support for internal improvements. In contrast to men like Clinton, for whom sectionalism often meant advancing personal and regional power, Sloan's sectional vision also had a distinct antislavery message. Like other moments in the campaign of 1812, it suggested the outlines of a northern antislavery argument that would return with force during the Missouri Crisis, when some northerners looked again to DeWitt Clinton to unseat a Virginian president.

The Limits of Northern Dissent

Sloan's dream of a capital in Philadelphia and ample funds for internal improvement was not to be. Instead of peace, love, and harmony, on June 18, 1812, the United States chose war against Great Britain. It was one of the more divisive military decisions in American history, opposed by Federalists and dissenting Republicans alike. But war ultimately proved a unifying cause for the Republican coalition, as the threat of British invasion revived foundational ideals of partisan and national union.

Those ideals persisted in part because Federalist-Republican antagonism could not be muted by the likes of DeWitt Clinton. On the one hand, Republican nationalism, fired by war, restrained internal dissent and defined Federalist criticism as anti-patriotic subversion. On the other hand, as the case of James Sloan suggests, reconciliation between northern Federalists and Republicans had distinct limits, given persistent Federalist disdain for northern democrats.

Just before James Sloan began to break openly from Republicans in Washington, he was subject to public humiliation throughout the northern press, for an incident involving his servant and a horse. The story was first told in the Federalist *United States' Gazette* on Christmas Eve, 1807. Apparently Sloan's son instructed the servant to ride an old mare to a ferry crossing at the Delaware River, and ask the ferryman to send a letter for Sloan on to the Philadelphia post office. Instead, the servant (one "Dutch boy") tried to have the letter and horse sent together. He assured the ferryman that the horse should be sent for free, because Sloan was a member of Congress, and therefore had a franking privilege that allowed him free use of the post. The mare made it as far as the Philadelphia post office, and was slated to be hitched to the next post wagon heading for Washington, before Sloan's son found out the mistake and retrieved her. To avid readers, the scene must have seemed like a page from Hugh Henry Brackenridge's novel *Modern Chivalry*, a satire of early national politics composed of the misadventures and malapropisms of the "bog-trotter" (that is, Irishman) Teague O'Regan. The story of "James Sloan's Mare" classed Sloan alongside his servant, as but a somewhat lighter shade of idiot.[51]

Teague O'Regan was the butt of jokes not only about incompetent foreigners, but also about democracy. He was an object lesson in how an expanded electorate and the lack of prescriptive qualifications for office could undermine rational government. To many northern Federalists, James Sloan had long played a similar role. His revolt against Madison thus hardly ensured that he would be welcomed with open arms by Federalists. In response to his pro-Clinton pamphlet in 1812, Sloan was met with derision by George Helmbold, alias "Toby Scratch'em," in *The Tickler*, the Federalist Philadelphia magazine. Toby would have no business with "James Sloan, a man who has ever been the standing joke of the Jerseys." Sloan's dissidence, claimed *The*

Tickler, was fueled by his resentment at not receiving patronage from Madison, and his desire to obtain a local appointment in New Jersey. That was partly true, but hardly differentiated Sloan from most other congressmen in the early 1800s. What made him different, in Helmbold's estimation, was his degraded status: "Any person not totally blinded by party zeal may see the object of the little chattering Jersey hog merchant, whose shamble in the Jersey market will no doubt be well stocked tomorrow with his *book*, and his puddings, and his pork." Ultimately, Sloan was and always would be a contemptible, dishonorable person.

> However *politic* many gentlemen may suppose it to receive the honorable James Sloan into the federal ranks, we cannot but consider it as disgraceful; and it is a well known fact, that this practice of receiving democratic apostates into the ranks of federalism, has done more injury to the cause than all the power and all the arts of united democracy; and what is to be expected from the exertions of *Sloan*, but that all his nonsense and folly will be ascribed to the federalists, and instead of weakening, add strength to the democratic warhawks in New Jersey?[52]

The Tickler's strategy of pure Federalism may have preserved its distinctive oppositional voice, but it had long been proved a political failure. Even as Federalists made gains from the embargo onward, they lost moderate adherents like John Quincy Adams and William Plumer to the appeal of Republican nationalism. Some Federalists may have embraced the techniques of democratic politics, but persistent disregard for the political abilities of ordinary men made cooperation with Republican dissidents like Sloan and Duane difficult. And Federalist attacks on democracy only provided fuel for Republican stalwarts, who pleaded for Republican unity in opposition to Federalist schemes for regaining power.

Those demands for unity were heightened after 1807, as Jeffersonian nationalists accused Federalists of abetting British schemes to dismantle American independence. For a number of Republicans, politics took on a new, vital character in the lead-up to the War of 1812, as they fought not simply to retain Republicans in office but to maintain the independence of the United States. In Worcester, Massachusetts, Francis Blake's nemesis Edward Bangs grew more zealous in the face of potential conflict with Great Britain. Defense of Republican political principles became absorbed into defense of the

American nation-state. "British aggressions upon the United States are every day assuming a deadlier cast," he warned Howe in September 1811. By the next June, days before the official declaration of war with Britain, Bangs was prepared for sustained military conflict. Given the "present situation of our beloved country," he explained, "I shall look upon war as a blessing." Along with other young patriots, he had volunteered for military service, and was prepared to "march wherever I am ordered."[53] Identifying self and nation, Bangs found motivation to resist challenges to Republican power.

In the summer of 1812, soon after the congressional declaration of war, Bangs and his fellow Republicans prepared a July 4 celebration in Worcester in order to "confront" a grand Federalist assembly, at which Francis Blake was to deliver the oration. While Blake spoke of his disillusionment with the French Revolution, the Worcester Republicans expressed their desire to go to war against Britain, in defense of the American republic. The *National Aegis* prefaced its account of the Republican celebration with an excerpt from an English version of "The Marseillaise": "To Arms, To Arms, ye brave / The avenging sword unsheath / March on! March on! All hearts resolv'd / On VICTORY or DEATH." The Republican orator at Worcester, Enoch Lincoln (son of Levi Lincoln), likewise took a martial tone in an otherwise florid speech. Ignoring Federalist criticism of the three-fifths clause, he defined the American Republic as the antithesis of tyranny, based on "equal representation" and the "Rights of Man." This egalitarian foundation made the United States exceptionally strong. The "citizen soldier" he believed, would defend the nation at all costs, thus providing a sure safeguard against invasion. "To Arms," cried Lincoln; "Union be the watchword, Victory or Death the end!"[54] Such injunctions indicated the heightened stakes of partisan conflict in 1812. Taken at their word, Republicans were willing to die for the United States. These emotions displaced the challenge of Federalism and Clintonianism, as Jeffersonians like Lincoln sought a world-historical stage, arms in hand. They fought to defend themselves and the very existence of the republic.

The War of 1812 produced similar nationalist sentiments in abundance, exposing the liabilities of Federalism when it came to challenging southern power. The conflict provided many justified occasions for dissent, and Federalists in New England helped undermine the wartime objectives of the Madison administration. But Republicans used the war to claim a nationalist sanction for their control of the federal government. Many northerners who supported Clinton in 1812 returned to the Republican coalition, and the sectional attacks of the prewar years were drowned out in a patriotism based on

American grievance and desire for vengeance. Criticism of slavery was once again closely tied to Federalism, and particularly to New England elites, who were cast as traitors to the nation. The brief moment of potential agreement between Federalist and dissident Jeffersonian critics of Republican rule was lost in the nationalist politics of the conflict. Federalists continued their war against the three-fifths clause, which they elevated to a major cause of regional dissent at the Hartford Convention of fall 1814. The subsequent demonization and belittling of the convention in the Republican press made protest against slave representation appear to be little more than regional bitterness. Yet just a few years previously, agitation against the three-fifths clause and sectional inequality had appeared to be a shared grievance between Federalists and dissident Republicans. This ideological transition demonstrated the ability of wartime nationalism to shift priorities and renew the Jeffersonian reconciliation with the institutional power of slavery.

The war also helped reconcile white Americans to slavery through the politics of race. At the time of the *Chesapeake* attack in June 1807, the whiteness of the American nation-state was hardly taken for granted, as the public response indicates. Two of the three American seamen taken by the British, David Martin and William Ware, were men of color, yet Republicans defended them as citizens of the United States whose rights had been violated by British power. William Duane's *Aurora* (at the time, a defiant nationalist paper) printed detailed depositions to establish the nationality of the *Chesapeake* captives, in turn establishing that Ware was the child of a white man and an enslaved black woman.[55] In their efforts to defend victims of British oppression, Republicans seemed liable to undermine racial boundaries of belonging.

As war became more imminent, however, whiteness became more, rather than less powerful. The call to arms was in many ways already racially exclusive, since African Americans were commonly barred from state militias, a practice complemented by federal law, which required that "every free able-bodied white male citizen . . . be enrolled in the Militia."[56] Fighting on behalf of an expansionist, slaveholding nation also promoted racial exclusion and white supremacy. During the war, slaves in the Chesapeake and the Southeast fled from their masters and joined British forces; some returned in arms to attack the United States. The paranoid fantasies about slave rebellion that Republicans like Duane had generated in response to the Haitian Revolution appeared to be coming true, and northern and southern Jeffersonians expressed their shared dread of black resistance. Violent conflict with Native

Americans on frontiers North and South was an even more powerful motivation for white men to stand together in solidarity. Northerners in Ohio and the Indiana Territory had fought to keep the Northwest Territory free from slavery for years preceding the War of 1812, at times openly indicting the evils of slaveholder power. Their achievement proved essential in perpetuating a sectional division between slave and free territory beyond the Appalachians.[57] But during the war, these sectional divisions mattered much less to white Americans who perceived a common enemy in the Shawnees, Creeks, and other Native American tribes loosely allied with the British. Horror stories of Native American attacks, as they had during the American Revolution, provided cause for unity, and mobilized a powerful sense of vengeance. Racialized visions of the nation in turn helped buttress arguments that African American slaves were enemies who had to be contained and free African Americans were an alien presence within the United States.

Throughout the conflict, these sentiments of vengeance and exclusion were married to democratic idealism. The War of 1812 provided Republicans who had not experienced the American Revolution firsthand the opportunity to reenact it, and claim national independence for themselves. Individual liberation, Republican power, and national defense merged in the hazards of war, as Republicans took the ideological offensive against their many enemies. Opposition to Britain and defense of the American nation-state proved a remarkably unifying cause, bringing together elite Republicans like Elbridge Gerry, ex-Federalists like John Quincy Adams, and rabid democrats like Duane in defense of the autonomy of the United States.[58] In the end, war revived the ideological unity of the Republican party, and suppressed the idea of a northern one.

CHAPTER 5

Republican Nation: The War of 1812

The American entry into the War of 1812 was driven by the long-term diplomatic crisis caused by the French Revolution, the rise of Napoleon, and British attempts to constrain the expanding power of the French state. But the war also demonstrated the growing power of American nationalism and its pivotal role in partisan conflict, both between Federalists and Republicans and within the Jeffersonian coalition. As the postcolonial United States struggled to establish its sovereignty in European and especially British eyes, Jeffersonians were likewise engaged in an ideological project of national self-definition, one that projected the American state as the guardian of universal democracy. During the War of 1812, that nationalist project became inextricably bound up with slavery because of the nature of the Jeffersonian coalition and expansionist objectives of the United States in the southwest. Enslaved people were certainly aware of the ties between American masters and the American state, and throughout the war thousands seized opportunities to flee the republic.

The diplomatic crises that followed the French Revolution had an important influence on the formation of the Democratic-Republican party. France objected to the 1794 Jay Treaty with Great Britain on the grounds that it violated earlier accords between the French government and the United States; at home, opposition to the treaty mobilized an emerging Republican coalition in Congress. In 1798, after reports of the XYZ affair reached the United States, John Adams authorized a "Quasi-War" against French ships in the Caribbean; domestically, Federalists set out in 1798 to repress the burgeoning Republican party, particularly its immigrant and radical democratic wing. When Jefferson came into office, there was a brief lull in foreign affairs, as France and Britain were at peace from 1802 to 1803, under the Treaty of Amiens. But then war resumed, and by 1806, events were turning again toward crisis, especially on the Atlantic Ocean, where American shipping was caught in a vise between French and British maritime policy and American seamen were impressed to serve the increased needs of the British navy. Jefferson and Republicans in Congress sought to defend American interests by passing the Embargo Act of 1807, but the legislation failed to improve relations with Britain and France and internal Republican dissent. When James Madison became president in 1808, he faced a deteriorating diplomatic situation alongside multiple political challenges from within the Republican party.

Jefferson's embargo was repealed in March 1809 after considerable protest in the northeastern states. Republicans adopted a policy of non-intercourse in its place, curtailing commerce only with Britain and France, but it was easily evaded. The following May, 1810, they passed legislation that reauthorized commerce with Britain and France but allowed the president to impose nonimportation under certain circumstances. If either Britain or France agreed to respect the neutral rights of American merchants, the United States would impose nonimportation on the other nation. Madison seized on a vague promise by Napoleon to respect American merchants and imposed nonimportation on Britain beginning in February 1811, but to little avail. Neither France nor Britain changed stance on American commercial rights and Britain continued to impress American seamen.

Britain remained the more dangerous enemy to many Republicans, for both ideological and practical reasons. British control of Canada ensured that commercial restrictions were easy to evade and threatened American economic and political power in the Northwest. Many Republicans also blamed Britain for encouraging Native American resistance to western expansion. These complaints only escalated when the United States entered into open conflict with followers of the Shawnee leaders Tenskwatawa and Tecumseh in the fall of 1811 in what was then the territory of Indiana. Although indictments of "British savages" ignored the roots frontier conflict in settler expansion, they encouraged white Americans to view British power as encircling the republic and threatening to undermine its independence.[1]

Having achieved little success with their commercial diplomacy, Republicans increasingly pressed for war. Much like the ensuing conflict, the push for war was halting, marked by embarrassments and administrative difficulties. Clintonians, "malcontent" Republicans, and Federalists in Congress stalled legislative preparations for war, while pro-war Republicans balked at imposing taxes to finance military preparation. Thus, in some respects, the declaration of war on June 18, 1812, was a desperate act. Britain finally repealed the 1807 Orders in Council on June 23, somewhat moderating its commercial policy toward the United States and thus removing a major cause for war. But by the time news of the repeal reached Washington, conflict had begun along the northern frontier.

In practical terms, the decision for war can seem foolhardy. Yet from an ideological perspective, the conflict made eminent sense to those northern Republicans, especially in Pennsylvania, who helped push the declaration of war through Congress. While northern Jeffersonians were concerned about American expansion and mercantile rights, they were most concerned with preserving their own political power and defending American democracy against the British state, a principal objective for immigrant radicals in the Jeffersonian coalition.

The war helped resolve the ideological and political difficulties faced by Republicans in 1812, when the party divided over the reelection of Madison, by giving nationalism a new motive force. Although the conflict itself often demonstrated American military ineptitude, even defeat sustained Republican nationalism, by tying patriotism to sentiments of vengeance and hatred, and fears of oppression and control. Militant patriotism restored an ideological basis for Republican unity, one that had been absent for most of Madison's first term. Institutionally, Madison struggled throughout the war to manage Congress, his own cabinet, and relations with the state governments; all these difficulties ensured that the administration never acted with the confidence projected by Republican ideologues.[2] In the near term, the war did not help the Republicans gain additional power, as Madison only narrowly defeated DeWitt Clinton in the fall of 1812, and Republicans lost power in the House, the Senate, and a number of state legislatures.[3] Yet despite these institutional failures, the war was an ideological success. The Republicans of 1812 crafted a sense of nationalism that kept Madison in office and affixed the tenets of Jeffersonian democracy firmly to the American nation-state.

Wartime nationalism worked to suppress Jeffersonian dissent, particularly on the subject of slavery. During the war, runaway slaves joined British forces in the Chesapeake and along the Gulf Coast, in what became an open fight for emancipation. Americans responded by fighting to maintain slavery, much as they had during the Revolution. Republicans deplored British raids in the Chesapeake, eliding the causes of slave resistance and emphasizing British brutality and the danger of black men in arms. Opposition to African American enemies and maintenance of slavery became embedded into the national cause. Meanwhile, dissenting Federalists rebuked the wartime government and continued to assault the political power of slavery and the three-fifths clause, given a privileged place in the list of grievances at the Hartford Convention. In response, Republican nationalists attacked Federalist antislavery criticism as borderline treason. The war consistently required the practical and ideological defense of slavery.[4]

Although Americans frequently cast the war as a defensive effort against the power of Great Britain, on northern and southern frontiers, it was a war of aggression against Native American opponents. The conflict revived and gave renewed national sanction to racialized narratives of the United States as a land threatened by Indian "savages," as Republicans North and South justified destruction—extermination, many said openly—of Native groups like the Shawnees and the Red Stick Creeks who threatened an expanding American nation. That racist, violent sense of nationhood directly abetted slavery in the Southwest, as Andrew Jackson fought to control territory essential to an expanding cotton empire. Violent nationalism also helped reconcile northerners to slavery, as rebellious slaves and Native enemies were depicted as dangerous opponents of white freedom.[5]

During the war, white Republicans refused to admit that slaves might seek justified liberation from their masters by aiding the British cause, and they dismissed black political agency. In contrast, Republicans elevated white impressed seamen to a pedestal of democratic martyrdom. The figure of the white slave, so prominent in early Republican ideology, returned, but now his master was the British state rather than the Federalist party. As had been true in prior appropriations of slavery to describe white oppression, Republicans once again displaced the ideological problem of black slavery in the South. Impressment embodied the political tyranny Republicans fought to overcome, while rebellious slaves were defined as a savage threat manipulated by the British, with no inherent politics of their own.

The Republican vision of a resurgent United States, at war with imperial Britain for the sake of democracy, provided the ideological faith the Jeffersonian coalition needed to survive the diplomatic and sectional crises of Madison's first term. Jeffersonian nationalism galvanized critical supporters throughout the North, and helped Madison win Pennsylvania, and thus the presidency, in 1812. In the longer term, wartime Republicanism would lead to the dissolution of Federalism and the regeneration of Jeffersonian democracy in Jacksonian America. The war propelled Jeffersonian ideals and fantasies to new heights. Arguments that in the 1790s belonged to a minority coalition struggling against Federalist rule were transformed in the course of conflict into national myths. In addition to fighting the war on the ground,

Republicans were also engaged in a crucial ideological contest, a war of ideas over the nature of American nationalism and its relationship to slavery.

The Nation and the Enemy

The War of 1812 presented a problem for Republicans like William Duane, an open critic of the Madison administration. In the winter of 1812, Duane printed strident antislavery attacks on Virginia and countenanced a DeWitt Clinton presidential campaign. But Duane's transatlantic politics made sustained resistance to Madison difficult after the declaration of war in June, and he soon rejoined the Republican fold. Duane had attacked Madison for lackluster diplomacy, but he never condemned militant opposition to Great Britain, the enemy of American and Irish independence. To the contrary, he was an early advocate of invading Canada, reprinting bellicose editorials on the subject in the fall of 1811.[6] Explaining his return to the Republican mainstream in the fall of 1812, Duane argued that once war had been declared, the only choice that mattered was "between honor and dishonor; between the nation and the enemy." He then launched into a tirade against Great Britain, whose "humiliating arrogance and insolence . . . has been felt for two centuries by every civilized people, and which has become at this time an intolerable cancer in the social body of this nation." Given a conflict between America and Britain, Duane chose America. "The executive which declared the war," he exhorted, "should be supported in the measures, and furnished with every means that the whole energy of the nation can call forth to bring it to a complete termination."[7] A defiant critic became an administration champion, a clear sign of the persuasive power of wartime nationalism.

In ideological terms, the war helped revive the political passions and the sectional alliance of the early Jeffersonian years. For northerners who believed the nationalist message of the Republican party, Virginian dominance of the federal government was a less significant threat to American democracy than the discontented Federalists of New England and the imperious schemes of Great Britain.

In New England, where Federalists saw the war as a political opportunity to regain influence and power, many Republicans remained stalwart, unmoved by either Federalist dissent or Clinton's sectionalist appeal. Joseph Story, a longtime Jeffersonian with a nationalist bent, had been appointed to the Supreme Court by Madison in 1810, despite Jefferson's skepticism of his attachment to the Republican cause.[8] Jefferson's wariness was not without foundation, but the onset of the War of 1812 found Story an ardent partisan, extolling Republican unity in the face of Federalist dissent. He opposed Federalist attempts to "inflame the mind against the whole Southern states" and he was appalled that New Englanders might turn against the American nation-state. As he told his friend Nathaniel Williams in August 1812, he was

> thoroughly convinced that the leading Federalists meditate a severance of the Union, and that if the public opinion can be brought to support them, they will hazard a public avowal of it. . . . Gracious God! That the people who led the van in the Revolution, should be the first to sell their liberties to a few designing, ambitious men, who hate even the name of patriotism![9]

Story's law student John Gallison felt similarly. Even though he opposed the war "as a measure of policy," he "believe[d] however that the wrongs, which we have sustained from G. Britain abundantly, justify it as a measure of right." Once begun, military struggle demanded national unity: "When our Country is at war but one voice should be heard & that should be the voice of Union & Patriotism. I am in dread lest by opposition the Federalists should bring on us the horrors of civil [turmoil]."[10] Thus neither Story nor Gallison was inclined to support the Clinton campaign. As Story told Williams, he did "not want to reproach Clinton, but I will say, that the present was the last occasion which patriotism ought to have sought to create divisions." War demanded national unity.[11]

Massachusetts Republican Elbridge Gerry was naturally opposed to DeWitt Clinton, as he was running as Madison's vice president in 1812. Gerry was likewise a bitter opponent of Massachusetts Federalists, who had condemned his recent tenure as governor (1810–1812). During his time in office, Republicans had loosened laws requiring tax support of the Congregational Church, promoted prosecutions for libel against the Federalist press, and supported redistricting of the state senate in favor of Republican candidates, thus helping to create a longstanding neologism in American politics, the "gerrymander." In response, Federalists drove Gerry and the Republicans from office in the spring of 1812, electing Caleb Strong governor and taking control of the lower house of the legislature.[12]

In the context of looming conflict with Great Britain, Gerry's opposition to Federalism embraced a militant nationalism bordering on paranoia. In a

January 1812 address to the state legislature, he attacked Britain and Federalist dissent, which he claimed descended directly from "royalist" opposition to the American Revolution, and appealed for national unity in defense of the country and the Constitution. Gerry, in fact, had once opposed the Constitution as well, refusing to ratify it in part because of objections to the three-fifths clause. Those complaints were now forgotten in his nationalist diatribe. Instead of worrying about the power of slaveholders in the federal government, Gerry feared that Great Britain might reduce the United States to slavery. Turning to a comparison that had become commonplace in the Republican press, Gerry charged that Britain had "doomed" impressed American seamen to "exile, slavery, and death" and warned that if the United States did not now rise to defend itself, it would be forced to submit to "the *title* and *treatment of slaves.*" He also claimed that he had been threatened with assassination for his support of Madison and the federal government, thus justifying, in his own mind at least, a life and death struggle for the republic.[13]

As Congress moved towards a declaration of war in June 1812, Gerry seemed certain that the Federalists intended alliance with Britain and rebellion against the Madison administration. Two days before the declaration of war, he told Richard Cutts, a fellow New England Republican and Madison's brother-in-law, that the Federalists sought to install a national administration "devoted to the interest & Government of Great Britain." Such anxieties inclined Gerry to see Federalists as internal enemies who threatened the survival of the nation. "War is declared by our national government," Gerry wrote to a friend ten days later, "& rebellion by our tory papers. This must be immediately suppressed, crushed in embryo, for a delay may produce a civil war." He then related a detailed plan to make a list of supporters and opponents of the administration throughout Massachusetts, and to arm committed Republicans to be "ready for action at a moments warning." All this had to be done without the support of the state government, currently controlled by the Federalists. "It would be unpardonable neglect," Gerry told Madison in July, "for the republicans in this state, with folded arms, to leave it in the power of such a disaffected Executive, to deliver up our fortress to the Enemy."[14] For Gerry, the War of 1812 provided occasion to unleash a militant nationalism bent on suppressing Federalism for good.

Gerry was somewhat extreme among wartime Republicans, but he was hardly alone. On June 29, 1812, Thomas Jefferson, echoing a Senate speech by Maryland Republican Robert Wright, instructed James Madison on how to suppress Federalist resistance: while southern Federalists could be dealt with by "a barrel of tar to each state," northern Federalists might require "the rougher drastics of Gov. Wright, hemp and confiscation." In other words, Federalists should be hanged as traitors and their property seized. Pennsylvania Republican Richard Rush indulged in violent metaphors when describing his plans to destroy the Federalist opposition. His fellow Philadelphian Matthew Carey became so incensed at Federalist dissent that he drew up plans for an "Association of Unionists," sponsored by President Madison, which would constrain Federalist elites in New England. He also wanted Congress to criminalize advocacy of separation of the Union. In Baltimore in June 1812, anti-Federalist violence was not just metaphorical, as a Republican mob destroyed the offices of the *Federal Republican* after the paper criticized the decision for war. Undeterred, the editor, Alexander Hanson, began publication at a new office on Charles Street in late July, leading to a standoff with another mob. Hanson and Federalist supporters fired at rioters as they attacked the office, killing one Thadeus Gale, who had exhorted the crowd to hang the "Tories." Eventually Hanson and his associates were taken into custody, but a new mob stormed the jail the next day, no doubt inspired by Republican editors who had called for the death of the "murderous traitors." A few Federalists managed to escape in the confusion, but those who did not, including Hanson, were viciously beaten. James Lingan, a Revolutionary War general, was stabbed to death, as historian Donald Hickey recounts, "amid cries of 'Tory.'"[15]

The violence in Baltimore frightened moderate Republicans like Boston's John Gallison. He was overcome by anxiety at a Federalist meeting at Faneuil Hall in early August, imagining that a mob led by "some bloodthirsty democrat" would soon storm the hall and perpetrate "an indiscriminate slaughter." Yet such fears did not temper Gallison's attachment to the Republican leadership, nor did the mayhem in Baltimore lead to any marked decline in Republican calls for the proscription of Federalists. Joseph Story argued for a sedition law to suppress Federalist dissent, and while no such legislation was passed, Federalist editors outside New England were intimidated by Republican militancy.[16]

The violent paranoia of men like Rush and Gerry mobilized commitments to national union and Republican cohesion, while maligning Federalist dissent. This helped suppress antislavery and sectional arguments, since Federalist opponents of the war frequently criticized the political power of southern slavery. In the ideological conflict of 1812, those arguments were effectively identified with treason. But Republican nationalism also had a positive, affective side, one that mobilized commitments to a Jeffersonian vision of the United States. Demands for wartime unity helped contain internal Republican dissidence, while projecting the United States as the last best hope of democratic emancipation from imperial power. Idealist visions of American freedom were deeply entwined with Republican paranoia and militancy. This potent combination of hope and fear helped rebuild Jeffersonian unity during the war.

Republicanism Renascent

In many ways, the War of 1812 allowed the Republicans to relive the passions of their formative years in the 1790s. This was especially obvious in the sectional politics of the war, which helped cement ties between a committed group of northern Republicans and their southern colleagues. The vote for war in the House was 79 for and 49 against; among the northern states only Pennsylvania (16-2), Vermont (3-1), New Hampshire (3-2), and Ohio (1-0) recorded majorities for war; New York (2-12), New Jersey (2-4), Massachusetts (6-8), Connecticut (0-7), and Rhode Island (0-2) voted against the declaration. The overall northern vote was 34 in favor (31 Republicans and 3 Federalists) and 37 opposed (15 Republicans and 2 Federalists). Northern Republicans who supported the war could once more consider themselves a virtuous minority struggling against an Anglophilic elite. As had been true of the early days of Jeffersonian democracy, they triumphed through their alliance with southern Republicans, who voted 44-3 in favor of war (the overall southern vote was 45-12).[17] This was especially true of Pennsylvania Republicans, who, as in the presidential election of 1812, held the balance of power between North and South.

One of the few negative votes from the South belonged to John Randolph, bugbear of the northern Jeffersonians. Randolph had long parted from the Republican leadership, and his war vote confirmed him as a pariah, as he now broke from old friends like Nathaniel Macon and took up a friendly correspondence with Josiah Quincy, arch-Federalist of New England. Northern Republicans, immersed in the surge of wartime nationalism, came forth confidently to attack Randolph in debate. In his first session in Congress in the fall of 1811, Pennsylvania's Jonathan Roberts confessed to an "unresistable temptation" to confront Randolph; by early 1813, he found Randolph "a man of inferior grade," isolated and without his usual power to command the

House. John Binns, meanwhile, who had been publishing insults of Randolph in the *Democratic Press* with material supplied by Roberts, termed the Virginian "a Coward" and declared, "I despise him heartily." Richard Rush, who also arrived in Washington in 1811, likewise gloried in what he termed "the anti-Randolph heights."[18]

During the 1806–1807 slave trade debates Randolph had appeared as the unsettling voice of southern mastery. Scorned by a robust Republican nationalism in the lead-up to war, Randolph's pro-slavery hectoring was less confronted than forgotten. In defense of the nation, northerners could suppress misgivings about slavery. Rush, a dedicated wartime nationalist, criticized Federalist antislavery dissent much as he rebuked Randolph. Rush decided that he would henceforth call the New England states the "rogue states," because New Englanders had the temerity to refer to the South as the "slave states." The only man Rush despised more than Randolph was Josiah Quincy, who had opposed Randolph in the slave trade debates, and who savaged southerners during the War of 1812. Republicans north and south spurned Quincy as a traitor. "The democratick lion," said Rush in August of 1812, was "determined to grapple with the foreign bull and all the Quincys of New England and the peaceable DeWitts of New York and elsewhere will not, as I now believe, prevent it." Infused with wartime nationalism, Republicans condemned Federalist skeptics and suppressed sectional discord over slavery.[19]

Outside New England, Republican nationalism faced its toughest test in New York, where the Clintonian threat was at its strongest. New York was also a theater of war, and the early campaigns on the Niagara frontier in 1812 fared poorly, generating more resentment than patriotism. Republican disunity and military failure allowed Federalists to keep control of the state assembly in the spring elections of 1813.[20] At the end of 1813, after another fruitless summer on the Niagara frontier and December attacks in which the British burned Lewiston and Buffalo in New York, a constituent of Republican Representative John W. Taylor complained that "there are many of our good republican citizens that feel depressd and almost loose their confidence in Government." But in a pattern that was to be characteristic of the conflict, defeat was transformed into motivating force, as Republicans accused the British of barbarism, particularly for bringing their Indian allies into New York, and sought vengeance.[21] As the Clintonian threat of 1812 faded, the war helped to bring key Republicans back into the party fold by generating powerful commitments to the American nation.

John W. Taylor, who lived in Ballston Spa, New York, is a good example of this process. He had been a moderate yet committed Clintonian, but given the chance to run as a Republican for Congress in December 1812, he pledged his support to the Madison administration to counter local antagonists who questioned his loyalty. He promised never to abandon the "cause of republican principles or the right of the nation for which we are now contending against the Tyrant of the Seas."[22] Taylor narrowly won election on December 15, 1812, and came to take his seat in Washington for a special session in the spring of 1813.[23] He was soon receiving vigorous letters from home, advising a stronger prosecution of the war.

In the summer of 1813, Taylor's constituent Thomas Palmer called on Congress to raise an army in order to successfully invade Canada. He claimed that "the Republicans in this county were never more united in supporting the war," and that he would happily pay taxes to see it through to the end. Even the embarrassing losses of 1812 and 1813 could not quiet Republicans' martial ardor. Salman Child, who complained that New Yorkers were losing faith in the federal government, found hope in the very military defeats he bemoaned. "There is a general burst of Indignation against the enemy," noted Child, who was "not without hopes that the late masacres will in the end promote the best Interest of our Country . . . and our poor suffering frontiers be forever relieved from the hostile ravages of the Murderous savages and their more criminal allies." Child exemplified a general pattern among advocates of the war, who often alternated between despair and demands for more militant prosecution of the conflict. In early 1814, Barry Fenton, a veteran of the Revolution, wrote to Taylor to demand "energetic measures from Congress" and suggested that "the tories or federalists . . . should be punished treasonably." Anxiety for the republic's survival endorsed militarist ambitions: "unless there is energetic measures pursued and the war with England rigorously carried on and the Canadas taken," said Fenton, "farewell to our government." A year later, just before news of Jackson's victory at New Orleans reached the Northeast, Fenton was in despair over the behavior of "the minority in Congress that is to say the federals the tories the adherents to the prince regent or the prince of darkness." He now offered to help fund the war himself (at fifty dollars a year) and, though he was "above fifty years of age," to leave home "and take the field again for my country." In other words, he was willing to relive the American Revolution in fact, just as many Republicans sought to relive it symbolically. Such sentiments endorsed a martial Republican nationalism, reunited New Yorkers to the national administration, and made the cause of the war a personal struggle for security and power.[24]

Taylor was a moderate nationalist compared to the war hawks of 1811 and 1812 who had fomented conflict with Britain, yet it was clear that the war touched deep roots in his political sensibility. He had long understood the United States in terms of its opposition to Britain. In a July Fourth oration from 1803, a young Taylor claimed, "Britain never had a right to this country," since the American nation was "the gift of heaven . . . designed by its beneficent creator as an asylum for the oppressed." Such views of American independence, echoed in countless speeches and toasts every Fourth of July, made hostility toward England a central tenet of Republican nationalism. As conflict with Britain escalated leading up to the War of 1812, men like Taylor only became more militant. In the 1810 New York gubernatorial race, he suggested that voting for Federalist candidate Jonas Platt meant "acknowledging the magnanimity & honorable sense of Justice of the British Crown." Backing Clinton in 1812 turned him, briefly, against the Republican leadership in Washington, but not against his core nationalist beliefs. Like a number of northern Republicans, he claimed to have endorsed Clinton because he believed the New Yorker would ensure a more "vigorous preparation" for war.[25]

In Congress in early 1814, he echoed constituents like Fenton, Palmer, and Child, defending the war and the invasion of Canada. In response to Federalist suggestions that New Yorkers did not favor the war, Taylor offered a grand vision of national defense and expansion. Americans sought security in ridding their northern frontier "of the unfriendly influence of a foreign power," Taylor explained. "Fathers & Mothers began to see their children & their children's children to the fourth generation spreading along the public & healthful regions of the North & west secure forever from the tomahawk of the savage Indian stimulated by the jealousy & hatred of the more savage Briton." "In the district I represent," he told the House, "the heart of the people is in the war—When Gov. has called for a few men they have volunteered by <u>companies</u> not to march to the lines & there stand like men of straw to scare the enemy but to cross the line & conquer Canada."[26] By the fall of 1814, after another disastrous summer that saw no progress in the conquest of Canada and British troops rampaging throughout the Chesapeake, Taylor was more resigned. In a letter to his wife, Jane Taylor, he despaired of a Congress riven by sectional resentments, and cast himself as a virtuous nationalist, struggling "to heal the soreness of personal & political resentments & to produce a spirit of patriotism & self denial in place of the intolerance of party & pride." Yet despite the divisions in Congress and the dejection brought on by three summers of inconsequential war, Taylor and his fellow representatives could still find moments of unity in martial sentiment. "Men of all parties," he told Jane, agreed that the United States must "fight manfully for their preservation."[27]

Such militarist emotions formed a dominant component of Republican ideology during the war, prompting men like Taylor, who was fairly placid and generally opposed to violence, to endorse aggression in the name of national freedom.[28] Martial nationalism, driven by outrage and the desire for vengeance, ultimately had a twin effect on the Republican mind: it revived fears of oppression and control—of slavery, as many Republicans openly claimed—that had marked Jeffersonian ideology in the 1790s and early 1800s, and it legitimized national and partisan solidarity with the force of armed conflict.

In Defense of the Naturalized Citizen

It did not require direct contact with the British enemy to adopt the martial vision of wartime Republicans. The strongest base of Republican nationalism in the North lay in Pennsylvania, a state that did not see active conflict during the war. Pennsylvania Republicans had provided the largest number of northern votes in support of war in June 1812, and they articulated a militant ideological vision of national and partisan unity. In Washington, Madisonians worked to retain the loyalty of the Pennsylvania nationalists, cementing their ties to the "New School Democrats," the men who backed the state's Republican governor, Simon Snyder, and his more moderate democratic politics. Relations with the "Old School," led by William Duane and Senator Michael Leib, were far more tenuous, and internal Republican divisions threatened to erupt throughout the war. Madisonians and New Schoolers alike were outraged when Secretary of War John Armstrong appointed Duane adjutant general of the fourth military district in 1812, and both men were eventually driven from their positions; when Gideon Granger appointed Michael Leib postmaster at Philadelphia in February 1814, Granger, who had been a prominent Clintonian, was dismissed the next day.[29] Yet these bitter internal divisions did not undermine a shared sense of the politics of democracy and American nationalism. Both Duane and his opponents built a romantic vision of the United States as a haven for democratic governance from the imperial power of Britain. This concept of the nation became the foundation for a sectional reconciliation during the War of 1812 that checked the threat of Republican dissidence in the North, and therefore worked to suppress interrogation of slavery in national politics.

For immigrant radicals like Duane, Republican nationalism grew out of a long history of ideological conflict and political repression dating back to the 1790s. Duane and Binns had suffered at the hands of the British state and the Federalist party, and this history of abuse increased the motivating force of Republican nationalism during the war. As Irish Americans, they had distinct and powerful grievances against England, which gave substance to a more generic Republican Anglophobia. Binns and Duane understood Britain as a burgeoning imperial power, resistant to democracy at home and abroad. They sought to fashion the United States as the democratic opponent of imperial Britain, in order to protect their own standing in American politics and to advance their transatlantic republican agenda. For Duane and a number of immigrant editors, defeating Federalism in the 1790s had been essential, because they depended on a free press and more open citizenship laws to continue their lives and careers in America. Somewhat higher stakes confronted Irish and British immigrants during the War of 1812, as British aggression forced a renewed defense of American citizenship and a pro-immigrant political culture. While Federalists returned to the nativist attack, complaining that the war was the project of foreign radicals like Binns and Duane, Great Britain threatened immigrants and naturalized Americans with dispossession and death.

The War of 1812 drew attention to one of the major achievements of Jeffersonian democracy, the repeal of Federalist naturalization policy and the incorporation of thousands of foreigners, many of them former British subjects, into the United States. In October 1812, the prince regent of Great Britain declared that all British subjects found in arms during the conflict would be treated as traitors and summarily executed; since Britain did not recognize the validity of American naturalization for subjects of the Crown, whose allegiance was deemed perpetual, such a policy openly threatened the lives of naturalized Americans. Under those terms, Duane, who was a naturalized citizen (but born a British subject) and who took part in the war effort, presumably could have been executed for treason had he been captured during battle. That ominous possibility loomed over twenty-three naturalized Americans who were captured during the Battle of Queenston Heights in November 1812 and sent to Britain to be tried for treason. Binns organized a protest meeting in Philadelphia and drafted public letters to Richard Rush and

Madison protesting the "barbarous policy" of the British. In March 1813, Congress gave the president power to retaliate in kind should American prisoners be executed. Fortunately, reciprocal mass executions were forestalled, as the British declined to prosecute the original twenty-three men captured at Queenston.[30]

The entire episode made obvious "the key issue of the war," as historian Alan Taylor argues, the conflict between citizen and subject, volitional and perpetual allegiance. For Binns and other naturalized Irishmen, it also made obvious the commitment of Madison and the Republicans to protect naturalized Americans. Richard Rush, Binns's close colleague in Pennsylvania politics, said the United States intended to place a "shield of inviolability" over naturalized citizens. Binns, who had been imprisoned by the British state in 1799–1801, now had an ear in the highest circles of the Republican government. This helped cement Republican bonds, particularly as Federalists showed little concern for the fate of naturalized Americans. At the Hartford Convention, which assembled in late 1814 in protest of the war, they recommended no naturalized citizen be allowed to serve in Congress or hold "civil office under the authority of the United States." Such persistent nativism only encouraged northern immigrants to keep faith in the Jeffersonian coalition and the Republican vision of the nation.[31]

Binns's hero of the War of 1812 was a fifty-five-year-old Irishman named John O'Neill, who had become a naturalized citizen of the United States. On May 3, 1813, O'Neill fought to defend the town of Havre de Grace, Maryland from an invading British force, continuing to man a cannon singlehandedly until he was captured. At first the British threatened to treat him as a traitor to the Crown, but then decided to parole him. His story quickly made the national Republican press, where Binns called him "The Hero of Havre de Grace." A group of Philadelphians were so impressed with his bravery that they sent O'Neill an engraved sword with a note of commendation; in response, O'Neill claimed he hoped to put the sword to use "in defence of my adopted country." Binns joined with Philadelphia Republicans to send O'Neill $215, prompting O'Neill to write back in gratitude, only lamenting that as a paroled prisoner, he could not continue his fight against "the oppressors of the human race, and particularly of my native country, Ireland." As an Irish American hero, O'Neill was the ideal embodiment of the republic of freedom imagined by Binns and Duane. Choosing the United States, and choosing to defend his volitional allegiance by force of arms, O'Neill personified the Republican

Figure 7. John O'Neill's sword, from Benton J. Lossing, *The Pictorial Field Book of the War of 1812* (New York: Harper, 1868), 673.

nation as virtuous and aggrieved, struggling to defend itself from what Binns called "a species of predatory warfare disgraceful to a civilized people."[32]

O'Neill's transfiguration testified to the importance of immigrant nationalism for wartime Republicans. But it also masked the complicated reality of war in the Chesapeake. While O'Neill sought to defend his civic life in the United States and his rebirth as a naturalized American, over 3,000 African American slaves ran to join the "predatory" British invaders, seeking freedom from their masters in the slaveholding republic. If the American government placed a "shield of inviolability" over O'Neill and his immigrant brethren, incorporating them into the polity, it built a barrier for enslaved people. They were not incorporated but confined within the republic, in a permanent state of alienation. When slaves perceived openings, they ran.

No Longer Colonies: Militant Nationalism in Pennsylvania

The visceral relationship between life, nation, and democracy grew stronger for many white Americans during the War of 1812. The conflict provided occasion for those who had not had Binns's personal experience with British justice to act the part of the abused democrat resisting English lords. Pennsylvania Republican Jonathan Roberts rose to national prominence through his advocacy of an aggressive stance against Britain in 1811 and 1812. Roberts, like Binns, supported the tanner turned governor Simon Snyder, and he made his way from the Pennsylvania state legislature to the House of Representatives and eventually to the Senate. Since reading Paine's *Rights of Man* at eighteen, Roberts had given up "every tolerance for Kings & old political institutions"; in the face of British aggression, he could now put those

sentiments into practice and defend the republic. In an April 1812 public letter to Paschal Hollingsworth, a Federalist merchant and critic of Madisonian
policy, Roberts claimed that the United States had "no choice but open war or
submission to a doctrine of absolute recolonization." His friend Thomas J.
Rogers, a Republican printer and Irish immigrant in Easton, Pennsylvania,
agreed. In a note thanking Roberts for his reply to Hollingsworth, Rogers
brought together three dominant themes of Republican nationalism: repression of domestic political opponents, hatred of the British, and fear of Indian
warfare on the frontier. "It is the duty of every good citizen to support the
measures of the government," he wrote, "and those who do not, when war
takes place, ought to be considered enemies."

> The American government have done everything which human pru-
> dence could devise to avert war. They have even put up with more
> than any other nation would be willing to put up with, and since our
> common foe will not do us justice, let us endeavor to chastise him for
> it. It is time that we should drive them from Canada, for as long as
> they possess the Canadas so long will they intrigue with the Indians.
> Therefore let us declare war without any longer hesitation.

Republicans in 1812 did not only dream of a coming secular millennium of
political freedom, as they had in the 1790s. Instead they sought to confront
internal and external enemies with violence, to ensure that the republic
would survive.[33]

Such sentiments were widely shared by Pennsylvania Republicans, like
Richard Rush, who had received an appointment to the Treasury Department
in part to help solidify Madison's ties to the Keystone State, and his friend
Charles Jared Ingersoll, a Federalist who had become a Republican and a pronounced nationalist after the *Chesapeake* affair. Rush, the son of Benjamin
Rush, was a far more elite member of the Republican party than Binns, yet he
too identified with the Republican narrative of political virtue defying repression. He had his own bitter memories of the 1790s, when "it was attempted in
Philadelphia to ram federalism down the throat of every youth who wore a
decent coat, at the point of General Washington's sword . . . how I gagged at it,
and how strong were my suffering sympathies too with the persecuted republicans." In the spring of 1812, Rush would echo Roberts's postcolonial anxieties,
claiming to Ingersoll that the United States would "never cease to be colonial"

until it fought a war with Britain. Rush encouraged Ingersoll to write a nationalist pamphlet titled *No Longer Colonies*. He promised that it would serve as a second *Common Sense*, stirring Americans to great feats of military and political valor, which for Rush included "stamping upon the very neck of federal toryism." Together these men worked to articulate an understanding of the United States as a nation militantly committed to democratic governance, struggling to establish its independence in a world dominated by aristocratic regimes and the love of power.[34]

Pennsylvanians were among the strongest proponents of the Republican nation. In the fall of 1811, when the new "war hawk" Congress sat in Washington, many Pennsylvania Jeffersonians were more than ready to commit to war with Britain. Thomas J. Rogers wrote numerous irate letters to Jonathan Roberts on the subject. Late in the fall of 1811, the British finally offered an apology for their 1807 attack on the *Chesapeake*, but Rogers was not swayed. As long as impressment continued, said Rogers, he was for war. "We have lost one hundred vessels within the last six months, taken by the British," he complained, "and they are impressing our seamen every day, and yet we wait negociation. Why not retaliate? A hand full of Americans would secure Canada. Upper Canada, the moment the signal is given, would join the American banners." Such militarist dreams were widely shared among nationalist Republicans in the months before the declaration of war, most infamously by Jefferson himself, who told William Duane that the conquest of Canada would be a "mere matter of marching."[35]

The projected ease of conquering both Upper and Lower Canada (John C. Calhoun offered one of the more conservative estimates, suggesting it would take four weeks) illustrates Republican hubris entering the War of 1812. Federalists mocked these visionary military schemes. William Stedman of Massachusetts sarcastically asked Timothy Pitkin to reply to his April 1812 letter "before you take Canada or at least before Congress adjourns."[36] Yet the implausibility of conquering Canada, which reflected the implausibility of the war as a whole, pointed to Republican strengths as well as weaknesses. Although they lacked military capability, Republicans had deep reservoirs of ideological commitment. In their minds, Canada was simply the most convenient site where the emergent democracy could engage the British Empire. Anticipating a violent conflict between democratic freedom and monarchical power, Republicans like Rush were delighted. "We shall be the first genuine democracy engaged in a war since the antients," said Rush in April 1812; he confessed he almost wished that the British might attack Washington so that he could turn soldier himself. For such Republicans, the war began as theory, as they imagined the virtuous exploits of a democracy in arms. Rush staved off anxieties that the United States was not prepared for war by citing Edward Gibbon's history of the Roman Empire, rather than battle plans or financial reports. The First Punic War, he believed, provided good evidence of "the energies of a republick once in motion," particularly when opposed by a state with a strong navy. While the analogy was not without merit, there was perhaps no better evidence that Rush, the comptroller of the Treasury, was fighting the War of 1812 first and foremost in his own mind.[37]

Doing so was not entirely inappropriate, since for Rush, as for many Republicans, the War of 1812 was primarily a war of ideas. As he explained to both Ingersoll and Madison, "being the only republick, the destinies of that sort of government are in our keeping. Should we stand by and see it longer debased by submission, or sordid avarice, its cause is gone forever." The romance of the "republick" at war would fade quickly once actual conflict began, and American forces suffered numerous defeats on the northern frontier. Rush's martial optimism turned to despair when he heard that General William Hull had surrendered his army at Detroit to a much smaller force led by Isaac Brock on August 16, 1812. Hull was perhaps influenced by narcotics and perhaps by paranoia about Indian attack, and he was definitely compromised by a lack of clear institutional authority in the federal government, which plagued American war aims from the beginning. The democracy, it seemed, was unprepared for serious military conflict. In a letter to Ingersoll, Rush described his mortification at seeing "Republican America exposed to the sneers of federalists, the exultation of tories—the contempt, the deserved contempt, of the British here and in Europe, of the very Indians! It is sorrow indeed." But Rush had already anticipated how nationalism might be salvaged even from so inglorious a defeat. It was "the peoples war," he explained earlier in the summer, and defeat would therefore inspire popular hatred and bolster support for the Republicans. "If they meet disaster," he predicted, "I firmly believe they will react with more vengeance and give Mr. Madison more votes; let a fleet burn Falmouth again. . . how we shall all vow vengeance! damn them, curse them, blow'em all up will be heard from a million tongues." This was just the course Rush himself took in response to Hull's debacle, explaining to Ingersoll that the Federalists now had to be destroyed. "We must be resolute even to death. We must vanquish and tread upon this English faction or they will use us, and with us the country and all its valuable principles. We must beat them to pieces or they will tomahawk and hatchet us."[38] Dreams of martial grandeur for the democracy became, in the aftermath of actual and humiliating attack, plots for populist retribution.

On the one hand, such intemperance reflected Rush's naiveté, the sort of cavalier attitude that led men like Jefferson to declare not only that Canada might be conquered by mere marching, but that New York and perhaps Boston would be burned in the course of the war, after which America would find retribution when London was set afire by its own oppressed denizens.[39] Yet Rush was not living in a world of fantasy; to the contrary, he and other Republicans recognized the importance of emotion and feeling in mobilizing nationalist morale and ideological conviction. As Nicole Eustace has argued, William Hull's want of "ardor" and his inability to sustain the same in troops under his command became a principal charge (made especially by the young Republican Lewis Cass) in his trial for treason. Meanwhile, Republicans sought to counter military defeat at Detroit by turning Hull into a scapegoat and instilling patriotic sentiment throughout the nation. Madison endorsed Rush's narrative of nationalist commitment rising from the ashes of military loss, claiming that the fall of Detroit "inspired everywhere new ardor and determination." Republicans continued to find ideological resolution in the wake of military defeat throughout the war, which helped them frame the conflict as a whole, despite its many humiliations, as a triumphant defense of the American nation. It was, but in expressions of ardent feeling far more than in acts of military valor.[40]

As Eustace has shown, feeling and emotion had crucial political valence for Republicans, who fought the War of 1812 through poetry, pamphlet, and song as well as on the battlefield. This was true not only in terms of a national contest over public opinion but in terms of the political control of the United States. Republicans forced the declaration of war through a hostile Congress, on a nation whose desire for conflict, considering the country as a whole, was temperate at best. They used the war to demand ideological purity, suppress dissent, and undermine their opponents. "I tell you Sir, a war is necessary to purge the country of the foul and wicked stuff which presses upon it," wrote Binns to Jonathan Roberts in May 1812. The Federalists, he declared, in a transatlantic metaphor, were as much "a band of factious aristocrats of intolerant overbearing persecutors as the Orangemen of Ireland." Then followed a detailed projection of the electoral map in the upcoming presidential contest. Binns was certain that Pennsylvania would remain firm for Madison, but urged Roberts to persuade Congress to declare war, to ensure that "the democratic party" remained strong and defiant. "The honor of the Nation and that of the party are bound up together and both will be sacrificed if war be not declared," he warned two days later.[41] The sentiment here was as much pragmatic as romantic. As Thomas J. Rogers put it, "the people look for a declaration of war and unless things are brought to a crisis we shall be induced to believe that Congress are not in earnest. . . . Therefore let them [Congress] convince the people that our wrongs shall be revenged, that our rights shall be respected in future, and that we are determined to protect our seamen, and the people will go with them." War would enlist popular support for the administration, and it would repair divisions in the Republican coalition that tended to "weaken the energies of the party." Declare war, and only the "tories" would be left in dissent. As Rogers promised, "we shall know how to dispose of them."[42]

Rogers's rhetoric echoed Jefferson's 1802 letter to Levi Lincoln, promising to drive Federalism into an abyss. Such sentiments are often taken as evidence of lack of understanding of or commitment to a "party system" in the early republic. Republicans believed they represented the true interests of the nation so Federalists were an illegitimate force not to be destroyed, a legitimate opponent in a stable system of party competition.[43] Yet men like Binns and Rogers were deeply concerned with practical politics and used nationalism toward self-consciously partisan ends. They demanded Republicans in Congress use their political will to force the issue of war, so that editors like themselves could inflame popular sentiment, secure Madison's election, and remain in power.[44] Binns had played the political game successfully at the state level, by leaguing with Governor Simon Snyder and displacing Duane as Pennsylvania's preeminent printer; a more genteel Irish émigré, Edward Fox, thought that Binns controlled most of the state patronage under Snyder, and that Snyder could not get rid of him even if he wished to do so. With the war, Binns was making a bid for national influence and power, and accordingly asked Jonathan Roberts to speak to Rush about obtaining printing contracts from the federal government. He did not hesitate to request "that fair preference to which I think I am entitled"—a fairly blunt demand for compensation for supporting the Madison administration.[45]

From an ideological perspective, the War of 1812 was a Republican success, even though the egalitarian fantasies of men like Rush, Binns, and Rogers, in which American democracy triumphed due to its inherent self-worth, did not exactly come true. The United States commenced a war with a weak military, against an opponent far more capable than they imagined. From the outset of the war, a series of near disasters exposed the administration's inability to manage either the military or political side of the conflict, and by the end of 1814, the war was arguably beyond the control of the federal government altogether. American forces did finally penetrate extensively into Canada in the summer of 1813, but they never came close to taking control of Upper and Lower Canada, despite marching many miles and having many handfuls of troops. Then, in the summer of 1814, the United States found itself throwing up a hasty defense of Washington. Prior congressional refusal to provide for the capital's defense, coupled by administrative inefficiencies and the presumption that the British would choose not to attack Washington, made for a debacle. Massachusetts Republican Joseph Bradley Varnum's son wrote from the capital on May 9, 1814, to reassure his father that although "many persons in Washington feel somewhat alarmed for fear the city may be assail'd by the Enemy . . . I never have felt under very fearful apprehensions on that scene." He was overconfident. Throughout the summer, runaway slaves from Tidewater Virginia and Maryland helped the British navy expand its raids throughout the Chesapeake, setting the stage for the British attack on the American national capital, a pet object of British Rear Admiral George Cockburn. On August 24, the British defeated a poorly trained, but significantly larger American contingent at the Battle of Bladensburg, and then proceeded to enter and burn Washington unopposed.[46]

Americans withstood a British attack at the Battle of Baltimore a few weeks later, escaping complete defeat in the Chesapeake in the summer of 1814. But the war had hardly gone according to Republican fantasy. The image of Washington in flames makes it difficult to understand retrospective accounts of American "victory," which grew louder as the war receded into the past. As Federalists realized, however, those acts were not simply retrospective justifications of a failed war but part of an ongoing Republican campaign to control the American state and political culture.[47] This ideological contest had very real political stakes, both domestically and internationally: for thousands of Irishmen and other British subjects turned American citizens, the War of 1812 was an anti-imperial war of grand proportions. As one Irishman put it, "Ireland will be rescued from British bondage on the plains of Canada."[48] Ireland was not rescued, but the defense of American naturalization and the preservation of the United States as a political alternative to British rule were hardly meaningless to men like Binns and Duane. To fight and not lose absolutely—to maintain American sovereignty in the face of British power—was, much like during the Revolution, to win.

Race and Nation

But what did Republicans win? When they focused on British power and Federalist dissent, they portrayed themselves as victims, fighting to become free from "tory" plots to undermine American freedom. In reality, the War of 1812 was often a war of aggression, as the United States fought to defend and extend territorial sovereignty over Native American land and to preserve slaveholder power. For masters like Andrew Jackson, Wade Hampton, and the planters of Tidewater Virginia, these were practical questions about combating Native opponents and preventing slaves from escaping to the British. For Republicans like Richard Rush and other militants engaged in the war of ideas, they were ideological questions, often answered by a racialized nationalism that justified American violence and power.

Throughout the war, Republicans were fixated on the threat of Native American violence, on frontiers north and south. After Hull's defeat at Detroit, Rush worked himself into a frenzy in Washington, imagining that "2000 Indians may at this moment be using the scalping knife in our Western country!" Panic then provided the grounds for decisive and violent action: "To fight instantly and everywhere is our only resource; to fight like tigers! We are the scorn of the world otherwise. We must joyously shed our blood and theirs, and drink Hulls." In the winter of 1813 at Frenchtown, on the Raisin River in Michigan Territory, Rush's nightmare became a reality. Native warriors massacred a group of wounded American prisoners, first setting fire to the houses in which they were held, then killing and scalping those who sought to escape. Outrage quickly became motivating force, as Republicans condemned the British use of "savage" warriors, and called for vengeance. Duane's *Aurora* demanded a "war of extermination" to force Native Americans to "disappear from the borders of our extensive country."[49] Jefferson agreed, claiming that "this unfortunate race whom we have been taking so much pains to save and to civilize, have by their unexpected desertion and ferocious barbarities justified extermination, and now await our decision on their fate." In Ohio, the governor used the threat of Indian warfare as a recruiting device for the militia. "*Freemen of Ohio*—Your state is again invaded by the British and their savage allies," began a July 2, 1813, circular.[50] That fall, Americans achieved a symbolic victory over Indian resistance in the Northwest at the Battle of the Thames. In October 1813, American forces, composed mostly of Kentucky militiamen, killed the Shawnee warrior Tecumseh, who had spent years before the War of 1812 attempting to organize a pan-Indian resistance to American expansion.[51]

In the South, Jackson gave Duane the war he requested, in his fight against the Red Stick Creeks. Influenced by Tecumseh, the Red Sticks sought to check American expansion and indigenous assimilation to Euro-American cultural and economic practices, much like the Shawnees in the Northwest. The Red Sticks gained power among the Upper Creeks during the early years of the War of 1812, and sought military assistance from the Spanish in Florida. What began as an internal war among Upper and Lower Creeks became a war with the United States in July 1813, when militiamen from Mississippi attacked a Red Stick party returning from Spanish Florida with arms and supplies. The Red Sticks responded by attacking Fort Mims, forty miles north of Mobile, in late August, killing approximately 250 people who had taken refuge there. Outrage predictably followed, and Andrew Jackson, still recovering from a brawl with Thomas Hart Benton and his brother, took charge of the Tennessee militia and commenced a campaign of vengeance. In March 1814 at Tohopeka, or the Battle of Horseshoe Bend (in what at the time was the Mississippi Territory and is currently the state of Alabama), Jackson's men killed close to 900 people, and defeated the Red Stick resistance. Jackson then forced the Treaty of Fort Jackson on all the Creeks, including those who had remained allies of the United States, leading to the loss of half of Creek territory.[52]

The land secured by the Treaty of Fort Jackson included large tracts in southwest Georgia and central Alabama, which would allow for the further expansion of the cotton frontier in the Deep South, a clear indication of how Americans in the War of 1812 fought to protect their burgeoning slave society. The defense of slavery was likewise obvious along the eastern seaboard, where British troops raided towns in the Chesapeake in the summers of 1813 and 1814. Much as they had done during the Revolution, the British provided opportunity for slaves to escape their masters and the American republic. Roughly 3,400 enslaved people in the Chesapeake chose to do so by the end of the war and, as they had after the American Revolution, republican slaveholders cried foul and demanded compensation.[53]

The ideological politics of slavery within the United States, however, were far from transparent, particularly in the North. Jeffersonians, who viewed the War of 1812 as a struggle for democratic emancipation, were forced to come to terms with American slavery, since the institution was under attack by Federalists in Congress and by British troops and enslaved people on the ground. During the war, northern Republicans tended to view slaves as an internal threat that had to be controlled militarily and politically.

British attacks on the southern states were portrayed as the depredations of a particularly ruthless enemy, who leagued with African Americans to despoil the United States. John W. Taylor wrote with horror of the June 1813 British attack on Hampton, Virginia, telling his wife that "Admiral Cockburn (the same man or rather monster that burnt Frenchtown, Havre de Grace &c) delivered up the women without discrimination to the brutality of his sailors & soldiers who after gratifying their brutal passions treated them with savage barbarity & in some instances it is said compelled the slaves to go to bed with their mistresses."[54] Jonathan Roberts affirmed this story, which had arrived by post in Washington: "they violated the women," he said of the British sailors, and then "turned them over to the negroes when they had done with them." Outrage in the Republican press was pervasive, and generated demands for vengeance comparable to the appeals that followed Frenchtown and Fort Mims. *The Columbian*, the Clintonian paper from New York, claimed that Hampton was a national, not a partisan question: "This is no question of democracy or federalism. It has nothing to do with politics. It is the cause of humanity—of dishonored American females—there can be no hesitation. Justice must retaliate—*full, ample* and *complete.*"[55]

Binns and other editors ran the Hampton story in their papers as an example of "British Barbarities" (to borrow William Duane's heading), usually classifying slaves as the inept but violent pawns of British troops.[56] The story was repeated in order to mobilize vengeance against the British, rather than slaves, but it helped northern Republicans to sympathize with slaveholders, and to consider slaves their mutual enemies. A good example of this accord came in another story of female virtue besieged by black violence, which Binns copied from Thomas Ritchie's *Richmond Enquirer*. While her husband was away fighting the war, a "poor but respectable" wife from Hanover, Virginia, was accosted in the night by "a negro, a man, a slave of her neighbor Mr. Bootwright's!," who demanded to sleep with her. Afraid but resolute, she feigned submission, but demanded the man wash his feet before entering her bed. He agreed, and sat down to wash, at which point she grabbed an ax and split his skull in two. She then ran to her neighbor's to recount what had occurred, and he consoled her, admitting "that he was sorry to lose such a fellow, but, that so far from blaming her, he commended the *spirit* which she had exhibited in defence of her *virtue.*" In this gothic story, slaves were confirmed as both dangerous yet simpleminded enemies and the legitimate (and expendable) property of their masters.[57]

Of course, one only needed to read the runaway advertisements in the *Democratic Press* to understand the extent to which property rights in slaves were taken for granted by Binns and his readers. Sympathy for white wives and mothers helped racialize the war, while the accommodation of slavery protected the master's control over black women and children in bondage. This was obvious in a March 1813 advertisement offering $100 for Kesiah, who was "expected" to have "a young child at this time"; she was on the run from Virginia with her husband, Jacob. From the accompanying advertisement offering $100 for Jacob, listed by a different master, it appeared that husband and wife fled when Kesiah became pregnant or when Jacob was sold away from his wife or simply because they wished to live together and raise their child in relative freedom.[58] Their situation was far from unique, as thousands of slaves in the Tidewater ran away during the War of 1812, although most sought their freedom with the British navy rather than in Philadelphia. For many, a central motivation for flight, as in the case of Jacob and Kesiah, was to keep their families together, free from the threat of sale.[59]

While runaway slaves sought to reverse the natal alienation imposed by bondage—their inability to maintain filial ties and a sense of belonging on their own terms—Jeffersonians like Binns fought to protect their status as citizens, aliens transformed into civic persons by the republic's embrace. As the ideology of the war showed on countless occasions, their new status as Americans required a reciprocal accommodation of slavery, an institution that restrained slaves from claiming civic personhood. Aliens became citizens of a nation-state that confined slaves to perpetual alienation.[60]

The Return of the White Slaves

As had been true in the early days of Jeffersonian democracy, Republicans responded to these ideological contradictions by taking refuge in white emancipation. While northern Republicans identified black men as their enemies and advertised for the return of slaves, they continued to indict slavery as a horrible crime. But the slavery they feared and condemned was their own, personified in the figure of the impressed sailor, a man compelled to serve British masters.

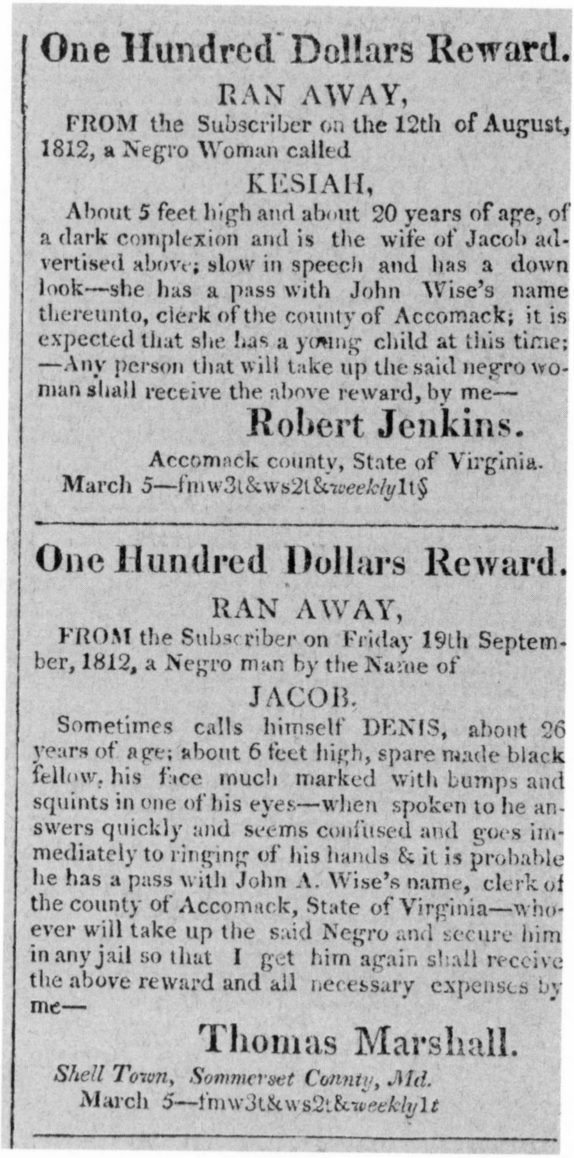

One Hundred Dollars Reward.

RAN AWAY,

FROM the Subscriber on the 12th of August, 1812, a Negro Woman called

KESIAH,

About 5 feet high and about 20 years of age, of a dark complexion and is the wife of Jacob advertised above; slow in speech and has a down look—she has a pass with John Wise's name thereunto, clerk of the county of Accomack; it is expected that she has a young child at this time; —Any person that will take up the said negro woman shall receive the above reward, by me—

Robert Jenkins.

Accomack county, State of Virginia.
March 5—fmw3t&ws2t&*weekly*1t§

One Hundred Dollars Reward.

RAN AWAY,

FROM the Subscriber on Friday 19th September, 1812, a Negro man by the Name of

JACOB.

Sometimes calls himself DENIS, about 26 years of age; about 6 feet high, spare made black fellow, his face much marked with bumps and squints in one of his eyes—when spoken to he answers quickly and seems confused and goes immediately to ringing of his hands & it is probable he has a pass with John A. Wise's name, clerk of the county of Accomack, State of Virginia—whoever will take up the said Negro and secure him in any jail so that I get him again shall receive the above reward and all necessary expenses by me—

Thomas Marshall.

Shell Town, Sommerset County, Md.
March 5—fmw3t&ws2t&*weekly*1t

Figure 8. Runaway advertisements for Kesiah and Jacob, *Democratic Press*, March 15, 1813. Courtesy of the American Antiquarian Society.

Impressment defined a central cause of the War of 1812 for immigrant radicals like Binns and Duane as well as for zealous young Republicans like Richard Rush. Throughout the Napoleonic Wars, the British turned to impressment to meet the needs of the wartime fleet, often preying on American merchantmen, as seamen found far more lucrative employment in the American mercantile trade than in the British navy. Moreover, American ports presented ample opportunity for British desertion, because Britons could easily blend into the local population, and it was fairly easy for seamen to obtain forged papers testifying to their American citizenship. Britain did not acknowledge voluntary expatriation, so even legitimately naturalized citizens, if they had been born in Britain, were treated as subjects of the Crown liable to impressment. To Americans, in contrast, impressment evoked a long history of struggle against British power. In the 1760s, opposition to impressment had influenced colonial resistance in port cities, building strong connections between sailor's rights and national independence. Post-independence, impressment disputes bolstered American conceptions of citizenship as voluntary allegiance and generated demands that the United States government protect the rights of its citizens. Depriving seamen of their bodily autonomy, impressment represented a direct assault on the very notion of the independent political subject, capable of deciding national allegiance for oneself.[61]

Republicans consciously invoked slavery to condemn British oppression of American seamen. In the years before the War of 1812, Binns's *Democratic Press* ran constant indictments of impressment, often copied from other Republican papers. In effect, he was a clearinghouse for a growing national consensus that America's struggle with Britain was a fight for emancipation. Binns, with his personal experience of British justice, was well suited to make such an argument; in March 1800, he had written to the duke of Portland from Gloucester prison, wondering how much longer he would remain "the bondslave" of the British state. In 1809, he reprinted the *Baltimore Evening Post*'s comparison of the "*negro stealer*" in the United States and the "*sailor stealer*" on the high seas. Both were villains, but the sailor stealer was far worse, because he robbed a "gallant, generous, and noble" man of his freedom. The comparison directed antislavery outrage away from American slavery and toward British power, while implying that the "negro" ("commonly estimated as a poor, debased creature, better in bondage than freedom") deserved neither liberty nor sympathy. "See the American citizen dragged into a slavery more horrid than that, which Afric's sons experience" said the

Democratic Press in January 1810, copying the *Essex Register*; in May 1810, Binns reprinted a claim out of Newburyport, Rhode Island, that "there are more than TEN THOUSAND Americans in slavery, on board the British men of war!!" In June, he ran deploring comments from *The Plebeian* that some Americans, rather than sympathizing with "our unhappy brethren who now experience the most abject slavery on board British ships of war," instead "scoffed at their miseries" and "applauded their tyrants." Federalists, in other words, true to their anti-democratic pretensions, endorsed the enslavement of white American men by British masters.[62]

Explicit comparisons to African slavery tended to reduce the complexity of impressment, which affected black seamen as well as white. Some impressed black sailors considered themselves Americans whose rights had been violated by Britain, but African American victims of British power were not presented as national martyrs in the way that white seamen were. During the public outrage over the attack on the *Chesapeake* in 1807, Republicans did defend two men of color, David Martin and William Ware, as citizens of the United States unjustly taken by the British. But neither they nor their fellow American captive John Strachan received as much attention as Jenkin Ratford, the British citizen taken from the *Chesapeake* and executed in Halifax, Nova Scotia, for desertion. As Martin, Ware, and Strachan languished in prison in Nova Scotia over the next few years, they faded from public attention (and in the case of Ware, who perished in 1809, from life), even while the Republican press continued to attack impressment as the chief crime of imperial Britain. Their relative neglect was partly due to the fact that Martin and Ware, as men of color, were unapt symbols of an aggrieved American nation for white Republicans.[63] To defend Martin and Ware was to admit that some black Americans had legitimate claims of belonging and rights worthy of respect. That in turn inevitably raised questions about the perpetual denial of civic personhood to enslaved people by American masters.

The impressed white sailor, by contrast, was an ideal metaphorical figure for Jeffersonians, since he allowed northern men to appropriate the concept of slavery to serve their own ideological ends. Like many Republican printers, William Duane prefaced his stories about impressment with the ominous number "6,257" listed in bold typeface without comment. It was an estimate from a report by Secretary of State James Monroe of the total number of American citizens impressed since 1803. He also told harrowing personal stories, like that of John Clark, who, Duane reported, was "stolen" by the British in 1803, and returned to his home in Portland, Maine, in 1812 "after NINE *long years of slavery* on board a British man of war!!"[64] During the War of 1812, the ideological appropriation of slavery was more convoluted than ever before, since the United States fought both to liberate impressed sailors and to protect the rights and interests of American slaveholders. These ironies did not prevent leading Republicans like Matthew Carey from indicting the suffering of the "American slaves," by whom he meant American sailors, "stolen by violence and rapine from their families, and friends, and freedom, and beloved country, to fight the battles of their enslavers."[65]

The argument that impressment constituted slavery was endorsed by Republicans in the Madison administration. During a fourth of July oration in the House of Representatives in 1812, Richard Rush argued that impressment was the chief American grievance against Britain and that "the only parallel to it is to be found in the African slave trade." Indeed, he went on to say, in many respects "it is worse than the slavery of the African." In September, 1812, Jonathan Russell, American diplomat in London, repeated the impressment/slavery comparison in a complaint to the British foreign minister, Lord Castlereagh, in which he claimed that impressment was worse than slavery precisely because American seamen were free prior to impressment, whereas "the negro was purchased, already bereft of his liberty." Monroe and Madison rushed to publish Russell's claims in a pamphlet, effectively endorsing contentions that impressed seamen suffered far more than chattel slaves. The constant invocation of this analogy intended to establish the United States as a land of freedom—indeed, of emancipation—despite the obvious presence and power of American slavery during the War of 1812.[66]

Even as Americans fought to maintain control over their slaves, they sought to rescue their countrymen from British bondage and liberate the oppressed sailors and soldiers of the British military. In 1809, the *Maryland Republican* decried the "unremitting and interminable tyranny" aboard British ships; ordinary sailors, the paper claimed, "would seek the earliest opportunity for emancipation" when docked in the United States, "this land of liberty, this asylum for the oppressed." John O'Rourke, the self-appointed "President of the Society for Encouraging Deluded British Subjects to become Independent Citizens of the United States," appeared to agree. Writing in Binns's *Democratic Press* in June 1813, he invited British soldiers and sailors to abandon their masters and join "the only country upon earth which belongs to *the People.*" In a letter to Jonathan Roberts at the outset of the war, one Isaac Anderson, a veteran of the Revolution, made a more pragmatic suggestion: President Madison should offer 100 acres of land "in the now British

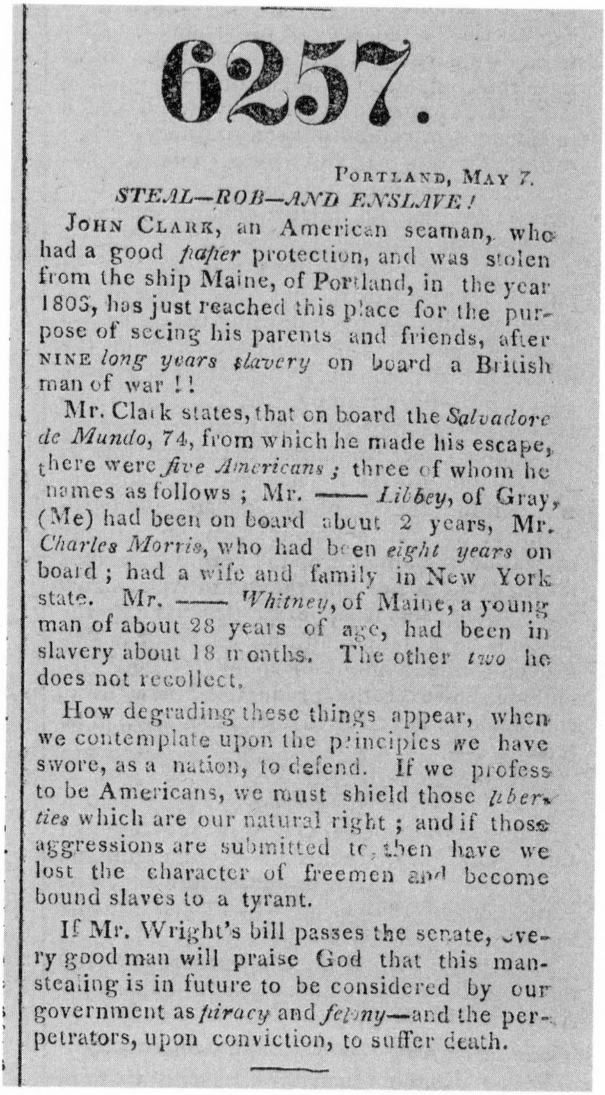

6257.

PORTLAND, MAY 7.

STEAL—ROB—AND ENSLAVE !

JOHN CLARK, an American seaman, who had a good *paper* protection, and was stolen from the ship Maine, of Portland, in the year 1805, has just reached this place for the purpose of seeing his parents and friends, after NINE *long years slavery* on board a British man of war !!

Mr. Clark states, that on board the *Salvadore de Mundo*, 74, from which he made his escape, there were *five Americans ;* three of whom he names as follows ; Mr. —— *Libbey,* of Gray, (Me) had been on board about 2 years, Mr. *Charles Morris,* who had been *eight years* on board ; had a wife and family in New York state. Mr. —— *Whitney,* of Maine, a young man of about 28 years of age, had been in slavery about 18 months. The other *two* he does not recollect.

How degrading these things appear, when we contemplate upon the principles we have swore, as a nation, to defend. If we profess to be Americans, we must shield those *liberties* which are our natural right ; and if those aggressions are submitted to, then have we lost the character of freemen and become bound slaves to a tyrant.

If Mr. Wright's bill passes the senate, every good man will praise God that this man-stealing is in future to be considered by our government as *piracy* and *felony*—and the perpetrators, upon conviction, to suffer death.

Figure 9. Article on impressed sailor John Clark, *Weekly Aurora*, May 19, 1812. Courtesy of the American Antiquarian Society.

territory" (presumably, the Canadian provinces) to any British soldier who would desert and "come over to our army." Doing so would not only make short work of the war, it would liberate subjects of monarchical oppression. John O'Rourke echoed the comparison between impressment and slavery in his plans for bringing freedom to "deluded British subjects." He made a particular appeal to the Irish, oppressed by Britain at home, and called for the emancipation of British seamen and soldiers: "Men resolved to be free cannot be kept in Slavery: Bring in the Ships in which you are Slaves; come by Regiments, Companies, or single-files." Such schemes were not entirely fanciful, as desertion did become a problem for the British during the course of the war, just as it had long been a problem for the British navy. For many men, desertion was driven by the greater degree of material comfort to be found in the United States; however, some deserters were clearly influenced by republican ideals, like Joseph Willcocks, the Canadian printer who crossed to American lines during the war, took up arms on behalf of the republic, and was killed in the fall of 1814 during the siege of Fort Erie.[67]

Yet throughout the war, American slaves found freedom by fleeing the republic, crossing to British lines in the Chesapeake and joining British marines and Seminole Indians in Spanish Florida. They thus allied themselves (in the eyes of volitional Americans like Binns) with an inveterate enemy to democracy. Republicans had little sympathy for such fugitives, as they built a culture of nationalism that condemned the rebellious slave to death, political and actual. In the original version of Francis Scott Key's "Star-Spangled Banner," widely printed in the American press after the Battle of Baltimore, the third verse spoke to this ideological vision, in which the free republic triumphed over its insubordinate bondsmen: "No refuge could save the hireling and slave / From the terror of flight, or the gloom of the grave."[68] A refuge for immigrants and deserters, the United States offered no refuge—no home, no sense of belonging, no civic standing—to the slave.

Race, Slavery, Union

There would also be less and less of a place for free African Americans in this nationalist vision as well, despite the fact that they helped to defend the United States throughout the war on sea and land. Officially, no African Americans were allowed to serve in the federal army, which weakened

American military efforts, but black Americans did help build military forti-
fications in Philadelphia, New York, and at the Battle of Baltimore. Addition-
ally, Andrew Jackson enlisted black men to aid in the defense of New Orleans.
Toward the end of the war, New York state likewise authorized free blacks
and slaves to serve in the militia, but peace came before the legislation could
take effect.[69] Free African Americans could legally enlist in the navy after
March 1813, however, and they composed above 10 percent of American seamen for the rest of the conflict. At the end of the war, close to 1,000 African
American seamen, alongside 5,000 of their white counterparts, were confined in the bleak Dartmoor prison in Devonshire.[70] They were not released
until April 1815, weeks after a riot in which guards killed seven prisoners.

   In a Fourth of July address likely given that summer, John W. Taylor denounced the violence at Dartmoor as the latest event in a long train of British
oppression. He appealed to his audience to

> examine the conduct of the british government & british officers to-
> wards this country for 40 years past from the month of April 1775
> when our fellow citizens were fired upon & murdered by British sol-
> diers at Lexington until the month of April 1815 when our unarmed &
> unoffending fellow citizens were wantonly fired upon, bayoneted &
> massacred by brutal soldiers at Dartmoor prison & thank God that
> you are not British subjects.

No doubt the citizens of Saratoga were thankful, but were they prepared to
accept free African Americans as their "fellow citizens"? In Dartmoor, white
Americans were unwilling to accept blacks as their equal prisoners, and they
demanded racially exclusive quarters within the prison. In the United States,
Taylor and other northern Republicans would soon confront the question of
black citizenship during the Missouri Crisis, as southerners pressed to formally exclude all African Americans from the body politic. In those debates,
some Northerners pointed to African American military service to prove
that free blacks had legitimate claims to national belonging. But the racial
rhetoric of the War of 1812, like the formal and informal racial proscriptions
in the northern states, suggested otherwise. Defining slaves and Native
Americans as enemies to the republic presented a whitened image of a nation
that was multiracial in fact, while the service of African Americans was often
forgotten, when it was not simply mocked.[71]

   Among Taylor's surviving papers is a manuscript copy of a song titled "The

Siege of Plattsburgh" (later known as "Backside Albany"), which David Waldstre-icher describes as the "first popular blackface song" in the United States. The song recounts, in black dialect, the American victory at the Battle of Plattsburgh on Lake Champlain, which repelled a British attempt to invade northern Vermont and New York in September 1814. The blackface narrator celebrates the American triumph, but the implicit ridicule built into the performance at the same time excludes him from embracing patriotism on equal terms. As Waldstreicher sug-gests, the song can be seen as a complex response to the active presence of free African Americans in the United States and their participation in the War of 1812, where they aided in naval victories at sea and on Lake Erie. Instead of being sub-ject to simple suppression or neglect, in "The Siege of Plattsburgh" blackness takes center stage, but as personified by whites under the veil of ridicule. In the context of the 1814 Chesapeake campaign, the song provides a reassuring sense of the place of African Americans in the American republic, as innocuous perform-ers rather than rebellious slaves. Whites hearing the song presumably both laughed at the singer and confirmed their sense of triumph in the war. Such com-placency obscured the very real challenge that free African Americans and run-away slaves presented to the emancipatory vision of the War of 1812.[72]

   Some Republicans did advocate black participation in the war, such as William Duane and Secretary of War John Armstrong. When Duane de-scribed the benefit of black troops in an August, 1814 letter to Jefferson, how-ever, he defined African Americans as racial subordinates rather than as oppressed people who deserved emancipation. Republicans called for wel-coming British deserters into the United States but few, it seems, could envi-sion African Americans as equal partners in the war and American nationalism. Duane believed that "the American born blacks," despite slav-ery, "feel a sentiment of patriotism and attachment to the U.S.," not because they made an elective decision to commit to the United States, but because they simply did not know any better. They were no worse off than they would have been in Africa, and there were no "African traditions" that could inspire them to imagine a different condition. "Slavery," in fact, was "congenial to the habits of thinking and to the condition of the actual Africans and their im-mediate descendants." "Their ideas of liberty like all other ideas are derived from association," Duane claimed with confidence,

   And apt as they are frequently to desire to imitate the whites, very few
   of them ever rise to [so] much above their condition as [to] feel the
   sentiment of equality of rights in the dissimilarity of colors. I have

known Africans of highly cultivated minds, I never found but one
who was not content to be an external imitator of the manners and
habits of white men.

This was little more than Jefferson's theory of the African mind in the *Notes
on Virginia*. As an added benefit, Duane was certain that black troops would
not only save white lives, but that they would be "the best force by which the
refractory of their own color"—those who despite Duane's theorizing sought
freedom by rebellion and escape—"could be kept in subjection."[73]

On the spectrum of white opinion, Duane's thoughts were hardly the
most racist, as most southern Republicans could not imagine the prospect of
blacks in arms.[74] But his framing of African American enlistment as a project
meant to protect the United States, and to protect the southern states from
slave revolt, indicated the extent to which Duane, like many wartime Republicans, took the defense of American slavery very much for granted. Restraining the freedom of slaves to escape was inseparable from the Republican
vision of the emancipatory War of 1812. As historian Matthew Mason notes,
Americans did capture actual slaves on one occasion, bound to British soldiers. Instead of liberating them from British tyranny, they confiscated them
"for the use of the United States."[75]

An 1814 Pennsylvania legal case, reported in the weekly edition of Duane's
Aurora General Advertiser, likewise demonstrated the toleration of slavery at
the heart of the American union. The case pitted Langdon Cheves, a South
Carolina Republican representative and leading war hawk, against his slave
Lewis. During the congressional recess of 1813, Cheves remained in the North
with his family in Germantown, Pennsylvania—for longer than six months,
the allowed time to "sojourn" with one's slave in the state under the 1780 abolition act. During that time, Lewis apparently decided he preferred life in
Pennsylvania, but without his master. Perhaps he had come into contact with
free African Americans; perhaps he had read the *Democratic Press* and decided that it was true that men who resolved to become free could not be kept
in slavery; perhaps he was aware that under Pennsylvania law, slaves remaining in the state longer than six months would be emancipated. He was certainly not alone in perceiving opportunities for freedom in Pennsylvania.
Lewis ran away in December 1813 and was captured in Philadelphia, where an
alderman jailed him based on a deposition Cheves swore to in Washington.
The alderman argued that as Cheves was officially a congressman in 1813, he
was exempt from the 1780 law, which made allowances for "members of

Congress." In addition, as the alderman explained, the war made it difficult for Cheves to travel home, thus making the exemption all the more warranted. The case was then brought to the state supreme court through a writ of habeas corpus. Here too the justices ruled conservatively, explaining that Cheve's exemption from the six-month limit still applied, even though the federal Congress no longer sat in Philadelphia. The justices adopted an expansive reading of the exemption, lest they subject slaveholders to "great inconvenience." Ultimately, said Chief Justice William Tilghman, "We all know that our southern brethren are very jealous of their rights on the subject of slaves, and that their union with the other states could never have been cemented without yielding to their demands on this point; nor is it conceivable that the legislature of Pennsylvania could have intended to make a law, the probable consequence of which would have been, the banishment of congress from the state." Tilghman was a conservative Federalist (originally from Maryland, where he continued to hold slaves) who had previously established a restrictive interpretation of Pennsylvania's gradual abolition law, so his ruling was not surprising.[76] Yet such arguments in favor of partiality toward slaveholders, which had circulated since the ratification of the Constitution, acquired new force during and after the War of 1812. Republican nationalism meant protection of slavery, as a necessary price of Union.

The most popular version of this argument came from moderate Philadelphia Republican Matthew Carey. In the fall of 1814, he published *The Olive Branch*, as well as a smaller pamphlet titled *A Calm Address to the Eastern States on the Subject of the Representation of Slaves*, which was included in future versions of the phenomenally successful *Olive Branch*. A plea for sectional and partisan harmony, *The Olive Branch* criticized past errors in Republican foreign policy, but focused its ire on New England Federalism. Carey believed there was a concerted effort underway to "effect a dissolution of the union." And the union was sacrosanct. Instead of a simple contract between regional parties, Carey argued in his *Calm Address*, the union was founded by "the noblest instrument ever executed by human wisdom": the United States Constitution.[77] In response to Federalist agitation against the three-fifths clause, Carey went to great lengths to prove that the "Eastern" or New England states had more than their fair share of representation at the national level, and therefore that the three-fifths clause provided no unjust advantage to the South. And he tried to demonstrate the great benefits that New England merchants received by being members of the Union, and how much they would lose without access to the raw materials and markets of the

South. *The Olive Branch* foreshadowed Carey's conservative nationalism in the 1820s, as he tried to incorporate slavery into a national vision for economic development. In the end, Carey did not believe that slavery or its institutional protection provided cause to question the Union, or its fundamental virtue.[78]

As the case of Lewis and Langdon Cheves suggests, the wartime union promulgated by Republicans offered little refuge for African American slaves other than bondage. Duane printed the record of Lewis's case in the *Aurora*, but without comment. He knew well that his "southern brethren are very jealous of their rights on the subject of slaves"; on more than one occasion he had indicted that jealousy as the height of antidemocratic behavior, fit only for a "miserable misanthrope" like John Randolph. Thomas J. Rogers, the Irish American printer from Easton, Pennsylvania, was likewise aware of the oppressive nature of slavery. In 1811, he wrote proudly to Jonathan Roberts to describe how he helped liberate six African American children from slave traders who were transporting them from New Jersey through Pennsylvania en route to sale in Kentucky. "In the name of heaven will not something be done to prevent the transportation of slaves from one state to another?" asked Rogers. He believed "the legislature of Pennsylvania ought to interfere and prevent this abominable traffic."[79] But during the furor of the war, these zealous democrats, along with Binns, Rush, and so many others, assaulted British enslavement of white sailors on the high seas and found their heroes in stories of virtuous resistance to rule by aristocrats and kings. Republicans invited the white slaves of Britain to seek freedom in America, while they attempted to keep the black slaves of the South from finding refuge in Pennsylvania or among the British.

The war encouraged racial proscription of the terms of civic membership, especially when white Republicans confronted Indian warfare on the frontier. In the same letter in which Rogers described his liberation of kidnapped African American children, he wrote of his ambitious hopes for conquering Canada. "Every day I think there appears greater necessity for energy in the government," he told Roberts, "and a force adequate to extirpate the savages, and to take Canada from the British; for there is no doubt but the British have set the Indians on." In the first year of the war, John Binns wrote to Roberts to demand a national militia law to better protect the nation, which was beset by enemies: "our Western States invaded by savages, our Southern states populated in alarming extent by slaves and our Eastern states the abode of disaffection." Violence on the frontier was associated with the violence of

Federalist opposition and the violence of slave rebellion, real and imagined. An expansive republic, at war on behalf of volitional belonging, was also a constrictive state, as vengeance cut deeper lines of racial exclusion.[80]

In the fall of 1813, hoping to bar runaways from his state, Philadelphia Republican merchant Jacob Mitchell proposed legislation in the Pennsylvania Assembly to compel all African Americans in the state to register themselves and carry passes proving their freedom. Jacob Mitchell's proposal did not succeed, but elsewhere in the North, wartime politics led to restrictions on African American freedom. In New York, Federalists controlled the state assembly through 1813, aided in part by African American votes, which could prove decisive in New York City elections. In the spring of 1814, in the face of recent losses on the New York frontier at Buffalo and Lewiston, Republicans ran an aggressively pro-war campaign, emphasizing the horrors of Indian warfare and the need to strike back against the British. They regained control of both houses of the New York Legislature, and soon passed a law that would compel all African Americans in New York City to obtain a certificate proving their status as free persons should they wish to vote at elections. Tightening procedures put in place by an 1811 law, the 1814 legislation sought to place additional institutional obstacles in the path of black voters. In their moment of wartime triumph, Republicans anticipated the more discriminatory restrictions on black suffrage enacted at the New York Constitutional Convention in 1821.[81]

The third verse of Francis Scott Key's original version of "The Star-Spangled Banner" opens by asking "And where is that band who so vauntingly swore / That the havoc of war and the battle's confusion / A home and a country should leave us no more?" They are thankfully dead and gone, claims the song, their "foul footsteps' pollution" washed away by their blood. Through the destruction of its enemies, the "home of the brave" has been preserved. Given the racial violence of the war and attempts at racial proscription in the North, free African Americans might well have wondered if they had any place in that American home. Mitchell's 1813 proposal for black registration in Pennsylvania prompted James Forten to write his "Letters from a Man of Colour," appealing to Pennsylvanians not to infringe on the equal rights of African Americans. Forten began by quoting the Declaration of Independence, and argued that the original drafters of the revolutionary Constitution of Pennsylvania did not intend to constrain equality by race. Yet at the same time, he was aware that American patriotism had a darker side, obvious on the Fourth of July, when "black people . . . dare not be seen after twelve o'clock in the day," lest they be beaten by drunken white celebrants. Having fought for American independence during the Revolution, Forten must have found such public racism all the more galling.[82] The War of 1812, fought in the name of democracy and volitional citizenship, extended the promise of the Declaration and American nationalism for men like Binns and Duane, but threatened to deny freedom to men like Forten. As a war fought to protect and expand the interests of slaveholders, and to protect and expand the national dominance of the Republican party, it limited democratic challenges to slavery, while wartime nationalism endorsed racial fears and racist constraints in the North.

The War of 1812 helped codify a sense of national identity that proved of great benefit to American slavery. By the end of the war, the Federalist challenge to slavery lost most of its power, as the Hartford Convention was the subject of satire throughout the nation. The Battle of New Orleans confirmed American control over the Southwest, and propelled Andrew Jackson to national prominence. The blackface rendering of "The Siege of Plattsburgh" effaced the free black presence in America with laughter, and the Pennsylvania courts declared their commitment to protect the property rights of slaveholders. Most important, Republicans like Binns, Duane, and Rush had won a major ideological war in the North. Republicans did not win many battles along the Canadian border, but they clearly emerged victorious in a more intricate campaign, one fought to defeat Federalism, suppress Republican dissidence, and convince themselves that civic life and democratic freedom could flourish amid the despotism and social death of slavery. Those transactions defined the home and the country, to modify Francis Scott Key, that Republicans built during the War of 1812.

CHAPTER 6

Democracy in Crisis

The War of 1812 not only produced the eventual national anthem of the United States, it indirectly led to the creation of one of the best-known images in American national iconography: John Trumbull's painting of the presentation of the Declaration of Independence to the Continental Congress. Commissioned in 1817, *The Declaration of Independence* was delivered to Washington in 1819. In the same year, Congress returned from temporary quarters to the Capitol, which had been under repair since the British invaded and torched Washington in 1814. The painting would eventually hang in the Capitol Rotunda, alongside three other works by Trumbull portraying the revolutionary history of the United States in epic terms.[1]

In many ways, the hanging of this painting in a rebuilt Capitol captures the nationalist achievement of the War of 1812. Burned by British invaders, the restored Capitol symbolized the persistence of the republic, while Trumbull's Declaration painting celebrated the nation's mythical founding moment. Jefferson's prominent place in the painting, offering the Declaration with both hands, must have been especially resonant for those Republicans whose lives had been shaped by the election of 1800 and who constantly invoked the Declaration as the source of their political ideals. While the painting was on display in Philadelphia in January 1819, John Binns's *Democratic Press* printed a celebratory account of Trumbull's depiction of so many great men, "men destined to arrest the powerful arms of *Tyranny* and *Superstition*, and to proclaim to the universe the true principles of civil and religious liberty."[2]

Binns had material reasons to celebrate Trumbull's painting. Since 1816 he had been working on an ornate print copy of the Declaration, adorned by engravings of Jefferson, Washington, John Hancock, the seals of the original thirteen states, and facsimiles of the original signatures on the document.

Figure 10. John Trumbull, *The Declaration of Independence* (1818). U.S.
Capitol Building, Washington, D.C.

Released to widespread acclaim in the fall of 1819, the print, Binns later
claimed, offered to the public "the first *correct* copy ever printed or published
of this masterly assertion of the rights of men and of nations to the right of
self-government." It apparently sold quite well, distressing John Trumbull,
who struggled to sell engravings based on his oil painting.[3]

Not all postwar images were so triumphalist. A lesser-known artistic rendering of the United States confronted the persistence of slavery in the republic, a problem suppressed or ignored in nationalist iconography. The
frontispiece to Jesse Torrey's 1817 pamphlet *A Portraiture of Domestic Slavery*
presented an image of America in ruins, depicting the Capitol in flames after
the British invasion of Washington in 1814. Composed by two European immigrants, the painter Alexander Rider and the engraver Alexander Lawson,
the frontispiece represented Torrey's experience of visiting Washington in
December 1815. En route to attend the opening of the new session of Congress, he encountered a coffle of slaves on a forced march through the city's

Figure 11. John Binns, *Declaration of Independence* (Philadelphia: John Binns, 1819). Courtesy of Library of Congress, Prints and Photographs Division.

Figure 12. Frontispiece from Jesse Torrey, *A Portraiture of Domestic Slavery in the United States* (Philadelphia: John Bioren, 1817). Courtesy of Library Company of Philadelphia.

streets, bound for sale in Georgia. Witnessing human beings bound by "*iron chains*" for the first time, Torrey was overwhelmed. He followed the slaves until he stood "just opposite the old capitol (then in a state of ruins from the conflagration by the British army)." The frontispiece dramatized this agonizing moment, conflating it with the immediate aftermath of the August 1814 attack on Washington. The Capitol, still smoldering, dominates the scene, the slaves bound for sale march past in the right foreground, while Torrey (or a generic witness) stands between the two, arms outstretched. Meanwhile, two angelic figures look down from heaven, as if to indicate divine judgment. Torrey wondered if God had not allowed the burning of Washington as a sign of "displeasure at the conduct of his Columbian children," who lived such contradictory and hypocritical lives, worshipping freedom while they oppressed slaves.[4]

The contrast between Trumbull's triumphant image of the origins of the United States and Torrey's point to an ongoing conflict between nationalism and slavery in the post-War of 1812 United States. That conflict was most acute for the northern acolytes of Jeffersonian democracy. Awash in Republican nationalism, northern Republicans found it impossible to suppress the problem of slavery.[5] As Trumbull's painting made its way toward Washington in 1819, northern Republicans began what turned out to be a three-year debate over the admission of Missouri to the United States. Throughout that extended conflict, northern Republicans alternated between Trumbull's image of the United States and Torrey's: a nation conceived in liberty and a nation damned by slavery. As irreconcilable as those visions were, northerners attempted to maintain them alongside each other, as they condemned slavery by appealing to the Declaration of Independence. They wanted to acknowledge the reality of Torrey's United States while protecting its idealist origins as depicted by Trumbull.

Traditionally seen as the opening act in the long antebellum conflict over slavery in the United States, the Missouri Crisis also marked the culmination of sectional conflict over slavery during the Jeffersonian era. For northern Republicans, the Crisis was a referendum on Jeffersonian democracy, as they found themselves confronting, with more clarity than ever before, some of the central dilemmas of their ideological and partisan past. How would they respond to the power of slaveholders in their political coalition, especially when it came to making national-level, democratic decisions about slavery? Would they defend universalist conceptions of citizenship and democracy on behalf of free African Americans or would they continue to draw racial lines around democratic freedom? Would they continue to tolerate southern bondage in defense of their own freedom?

Northern Republicans answered these questions ambivalently, leaving a complicated legacy for the antebellum period. Their resistance to slavery extension foreshadowed the moderate antislavery politics of a very different Republican party in the 1850s. Yet they retained many of the key symbols and concepts of Jeffersonian politics, and they rarely questioned the relationship between slavery and democracy that had allowed southern bondage to expand alongside northern freedom in the early republic. And their militant opposition to southerners on the question of slavery expansion weakened considerably when it came to the question of civic rights and standing for free African Americans. Above all, northerners remained committed to the American nation, which they now defined as foundationally opposed to slavery. This reflected the legacy of wartime nationalism, which few Jeffersonians were inclined to question. But it was unstable ground from which to contest slaveholder power, since the United States had long enabled the expansion of slavery, through institutional protection and territorial conquest. That remained true well after the Missouri Crisis, regardless what the Declaration of Independence did or did not say about human freedom.

In the end, the Jeffersonian synthesis between northern freedom and southern power proved resilient in the face of sectional crisis. The Democratic-Republican coalition fractured in the 1820s, but it soon reformed in a new guise under the iconic leadership of Andrew Jackson. The Missouri Crisis indicated the potential influence of antislavery nationalism, but it also confirmed the ongoing political power of slaveholders in the American nation-state. Thus in some respects it was a crisis of meaning as much as a crisis of policy. As northerners and southerners fought over the expansion of slavery and the admission of Missouri, a more obscure conflict took place over the nature of the Jeffersonian coalition, and the legacy of past reconciliations between freedom and slavery. In attempting to articulate a foundational antislavery nationalism, northerners were struggling not only with slaveholders in the American Congress, but also with themselves.

Persistence of Nationalism

Northern nationalism did not fade away after the War of 1812. In some respects, it grew stronger, as Republicans focused on developing the country they had fought to defend. Joseph Story of Massachusetts typified this strain of Republicanism, anticipating the ethos of antebellum Whigs. "Never was there a more glorious opportunity for the Republican party to place themselves permanently in power," he wrote in the immediate aftermath of the war, outlining a host of new national initiatives, from a military academy to a national bank. "Let us extend the national authority over the whole extent of power given by the Constitution. . . . Let us prevent the possibility of a division, by creating great national interests which shall bind us in an indissoluble chain." Over time, Story's developmental vision for the United States would be primarily identified with the Northeast and especially with New England; opponents argued that such ambitious plans for national development were little more than refurbished Federalism. There was some truth to those charges: Story, for example, reconciled with the New England Federalists he opposed during the War of 1812, helping build a "sectional nationalism" in which New England redeemed itself from the stigma of the Hartford Convention and became the voice of union.[6] But in its genesis, Story's vision was shared across the United States. South Carolinian John C. Calhoun's plans for postwar America, for example, were far bolder. As many scholars have argued, the institutional crises of the war helped temper older Republican objections to state-building. In 1816, Congress voted to establish a national bank and a tariff with considerable southern support. Congress likewise passed Calhoun's Bonus Bill to fund internal improvements, but here a departing President Madison drew the line, claiming lack of constitutional authority. Likewise, the 14th Congress's attempt to create a salaried national legislature led to rebuke at the polls, as close to two-thirds of the House failed to win re-election in the fall of 1816. While these setbacks indicated new discord over Republican state-building, the nationalist message of the war remained compelling.[7]

Ongoing northern Republican support for the wartime nation was obvious in the congressional debates over the first Seminole War, a conflict with direct roots in the War of 1812. During and after the war, Spanish Florida contained a diverse set of opponents of American sovereignty. In East Florida, Georgians and American soldiers fought a two-year border conflict with the Seminoles and Spanish from March 1812 to 1814. In the summer of 1814, the British sought to establish a guerrilla force of Indians and fugitive slaves in West Florida for a possible attack on the United States. Florida remained in Spanish control after the war and served as a refuge for runaway slaves and Native Americans who opposed the United States. Many Red Stick Creeks had fled to Florida after the Battle of Tohopeka, where they joined bands of Seminoles. Their war with the United States was far from over. Nor was the war over for Andrew Jackson, who had fought in Florida during the War of 1812 as well. He attacked Pensacola in November 1814 before moving west to defend New Orleans. These multiple conflicts continued to simmer after the end of the War of 1812, while American interest in seizing Spanish Florida only grew stronger.[8]

In the summer of 1816, Americans attacked the "Negro Fort" on the Apalachicola River, which had been constructed by the British during the war and passed into control of a community of fugitive slaves after the conflict. On July 27, American and friendly Creek forces destroyed the fort by firing a heated cannonball into the fort's powder magazine, causing an explosion that killed close to 270 people. But resistance in Florida persisted, and in 1817 the Seminoles became involved in a cross-border conflict with Georgia. In November 1817, the Seminoles attacked an American ship on the Apalachicola, killing over forty people. In response, the federal government authorized an invasion of Florida to suppress Indian resistance. In March 1818 Andrew Jackson entered Florida with 2,000 men, bent not simply on suppressing the Seminoles, but on taking possession of Florida. When Jackson briefly seized control of the Spanish outposts St. Mark's and Pensacola, he provoked a diplomatic crisis with Spain; when he oversaw the execution of two British subjects, the trader Alexander Arbuthnot and the ex-marine Robert Ambrister, he provoked a crisis with Britain as well.[9]

In its genesis, prosecution, and justification, the Seminole War was an extension of the War of 1812. The Creeks and Seminoles in Florida protested the punitive 1814 Treaty of Fort Jackson, which ceded large amounts of Creek territory in southern Georgia to the United States. The Florida Creeks, with the assistance of Arbuthnot, argued that per the Treaty of Ghent, which ended the War of 1812, they should regain control of lands they held before the war in 1811. Jackson and many Americans, in contrast, viewed the Creeks, Seminoles, and fugitives in Florida as a threat to American sovereignty aided by British power. In particular, they argued that Florida provided a haven for runaway slaves from Georgia. Jackson's 1818 campaign was thus fought in the interests of slaveholders, which were inseparable from American interests along the southern border. But unlike the reaction to Jackson's defense of New Orleans in 1815, the Seminole War was not greeted with universal acclaim by the American public. By 1818, many leading political figures viewed Jackson's popular appeal as a threat, and some Republicans in the administration and Congress saw his Florida campaign as an unconstitutional seizure of military and political power. In January 1819, the House Committee on Military Affairs submitted a resolution disapproving of the execution of Arbuthnot and Ambrister. In the subsequent debate, Henry Clay and other southern Republicans, hoping to embarrass President James Monroe or Jackson or both together, openly condemned the general's behavior.[10]

In contrast, northern Republicans were among Jackson's strongest supporters. While the South divided, northern Jeffersonians, especially from Pennsylvania and New York, unified in approbation of General Jackson. Although they tried to answer the constitutional arguments of Jackson's critics, his defenders mostly relied on arguments that had been well honed by northern Republicans during the War of 1812: Indian enemies who threatened America had to be killed and anyone who aided such "savages" merited death as well. In his defense of Jackson, John Holmes of the District of Maine was so overcome with emotion that he imagined a "female form" speaking to him in a "distant wilderness." After recounting how she and her family had died horrific deaths at the hands of Indians, she pleaded to Holmes (and Holmes, in her voice, pleaded to Congress) that America "punish, with instant death, every instigator of Indian barbarity, wherever he may be found." James Tallmadge of New York, soon to be Holmes's opponent in the conflict over Missouri, shared Holmes's admiration for Jackson and his desire for vengeance. Reminding the House that Jackson had found "three hundred dried and fifty fresh scalps" at a Seminole village, he reproved the general's skeptics for their want of patriotism. "Sir you are an American! Go, count the bleeding scalps of your murdered countrymen, of all ages and sexes, found by General Jackson; and then return, and tell to this House if this Seminole war was, on the part of your country, an offensive war!" The intimate connection between violence and justified vengeance, which had played such a powerful role in the War of 1812, was once again brought forth as the defining experience of the nation. Tallmadge made a more explicit connection to Anglophobia than Holmes, explaining that a Red Stick Creek leader whom Jackson executed, Hillis Hadjo (referred to as "Hillishajo" in Congress and also known as Josiah Francis), had traveled to England "and while there was commissioned *Brigadier General*. . . . Therefore General Jackson did not hang an Indian. He hung a British Brigadier General. I honor him for it." Should Britain complain of Jackson's actions, Tallmadge thought the matter should be "handed over for adjustment to our naval heroes; those gallant sons . . . who have held their steady march upon the mountain wave." In other words, Tallmadge, like Jackson, would be happy to go to war again to defend American expansion and territorial sovereignty.[11]

Tallmadge's defiant patriotism was influenced in part by his father, James Tallmadge, Sr., who wrote to his son on January 7, two weeks before his speech in the House. Jackson's opponents, he told his son, "were all the old Tories and some other who have lost sight of the fifty fresh scalps and two or three hundred that had got partly dry . . . I have no doubt General Jackson had a right to execute Arbuthnot and Ambresty by all laws both human and divine, while the blood of innocent women and children cries aloud for vengeance." Finally, said his father, "you must not lose sight that you are legislating for a great nation whose decisions may be a president for ages to come." (His rendering of "precedent" turned out to be apt.) The younger James took his father's injunctions to heart, and offered Congress a straightforward proposition: if you were a true American, you would not indict Jackson. Most northern Republicans agreed, voting by large majorities to defend Jackson's execution of Arbuthnot and Ambrister and his seizure of Pensacola.[12] John Quincy Adams, Monroe's secretary of state, was Jackson's chief defender in the cabinet, and he used the Florida incident as leverage to force Spain to sign the Transcontinental Treaty in 1819. Finally ratified in 1821, the treaty ceded Florida to the United States and drew a meandering east-west line to the Pacific Ocean, confirming American power over the Louisiana Purchase and joint control with Great Britain of the Oregon Territory. It was a dramatic expression of the territorial sovereignty gained during the War of 1812, and of Adams's conviction the "proper dominion" of the United States was "the continent of North America."[13]

Sectional Strains

The northern defense of Jackson implied some toleration of the expansion and consolidation of slavery in the Southeast and the Southwest. But northerners proved unwilling to tolerate slavery everywhere, and soon found themselves in open conflict with the South over the expansion of slavery to Missouri. The Missouri Crisis of 1819–1821 brought forth two contrasting visions of the United States, each with deep roots in Jeffersonian political culture. Northerners imagined they lived in a nation that contained slavery, but had no fundamental ties to the institution, and they hoped federal power would check its western advance. Southerners, in contrast, believed they lived in a nation in which slavery benefited from American power while being protected from excessive federal interference. They defended their right to control slavery on their own terms.

There were signs of a looming conflict over Missouri early in the second session of the 15th Congress. In November 1818, James Tallmadge challenged the admission of the new state of Illinois, on the grounds that its constitution did not go far enough to conform to the terms of the Northwest Ordinance and prevent slavery. A fairly rancorous debate saw southerners and Ohio's William Henry Harrison defend the rights of individual states to regulate their own internal affairs, including the institution of slavery. That defense of states' rights would be the dominant southern position during the Missouri debates. In contrast, Tallmadge believed it was the duty of Congress "scrupulously to guard against slavery's passing into a territory where they have the power to prevent its entrance." He was very much in the minority, as the House voted 117-34 to admit Illinois under its extant constitution, leaving the status of slavery, as Harrison wished, to local decision. For the next five years, freedom in Illinois would remain a fragile proposition, and it took a concerted campaign by

ex-Virginian Edward Coles to block full imposition of slavery in 1824. As it
was, a limited form of slavery existed in Illinois until the 1840s.[14]

Missouri was not governed by the Northwest Ordinance, since it was acquired as part of the Louisiana Purchase in 1804. Although Congress never
explicitly sanctioned slavery in Missouri, it never disallowed it either. Brief
attempts to restrict slavery during the territorial stage (including a proposal
by Pennsylvania Republican Jonathan Roberts) failed to gain any traction in
the House. Left to "local law and territorial statute," as historian John Craig
Hammond explains, slavery grew consistently in the area that would become
the state of Missouri, especially after the War of 1812. The 1820 census counted
over 10,000 slaves in the Missouri Territory, close to one-sixth of the total
population. Thus when Missourians applied for statehood in November 1818,
slavery was an important part of the local economy and slaveholders were
determined to maintain the institution.[15]

As in debates over the Orleans Territory of the Louisiana Purchase in
1804, southern congressmen defended slavery expansion during the Missouri Crisis by arguing that the diffusion of the slave population would be a
prelude to eventual emancipation. But by 1819 it was obvious that geographical expansion had done nothing to limit slavery's growth. The slave population of the United States, which stood at 700,000 in 1790, reached over 1.5
million in 1820, as slaveholders pushed into new territory west of the Appalachians. Congress had voted to admit the states of Mississippi (1817) and Alabama (1819), as they had Louisiana (1811), into the Union with slavery intact,
and with very little protest.[16] Combined with the relative decline of northern
slavery since 1800, that meant that an institution that was geographically
widespread in 1790 had become both more deeply entrenched in the United
States but also more confined to the South.

While northerners tolerated the accession of new slaveholding states in
the Southwest, other developments indicated that they were growing uneasy
with the expanding power of slavery in the postwar years. In the first place,
many northerners objected to the persistence of the now illegal international
slave trade. After the War of 1812, Congress received memorials and petitions
against illegal traders, leading to new legislation to constrain the trade in
1818, 1819, and 1820. In the Missouri debates, multiple congressmen argued
that the expansion of slavery would create an open market for additional illegal imports.[17] The domestic slave trade was very much a subject of attention
in the years before 1819 as well, as it had grown significantly since the official
closing of the international trade in 1808. Alexandria, Virginia, just outside

Washington, would soon become a principal depot in the domestic trade, and slave coffles frequently passed through the capital en route to forced migration to the southwest. Some southerners spoke out against the domestic trade as well. In 1816, John Randolph, one of the foremost opponents of slavery restriction in Missouri in 1820, attacked the domestic trade in Congress, and headed a committee to investigate slave trafficking in the capital. Jesse Torrey's *Portraiture of Domestic Slavery*, based in part on the committee's findings, denounced the domestic trade through harrowing stories of slaves who chose suicide rather than forced migration and sale.[18] Torrey was even more incensed by the practice of kidnapping of free blacks in order to sell them through the domestic trade. Kidnapping enslaved "men, women, and children, whose freedom and moral rights are guaranteed by our national and state constitutions."[19] Many northerners apparently agreed. Antislavery groups condemned kidnapping, northern states passed laws to protect free blacks from illegal capture, and petitioners appealed to Congress for federal legislation to supplement state protections.[20]

Congressmen had attacked the domestic trade before the War of 1812, but the agitation of the postwar years and the Missouri debates confirmed the trade as a new symbol of slavery's inhumanity, entirely American in origin. The domestic trade was clearly on the minds of northern Republicans during the Missouri debates, as more than one member indicted the practices of family separation and forced sale in their attacks on slavery expansion.[21] James Tallmadge decried the fact that while Congress fought over Missouri, a slave trader had "passed by the door of your Capitol, on his way to the West, driving before him about fifteen of these wretched victims of his power."[22] Soon after the House "shamefully concurred" to the admission of a slaveholding Missouri, Pennsylvania Republican William Darlington recorded an advertisement for a slave sale from the *Richmond Enquirer* in his journal, "as a matter of curiosity, disgraceful to our republic." A woman offered for sale was billed as an advantageous purchase because she was likely to give birth to a child within the month. Outraged, Darlington could not understand how unborn children could be sold at auction "in a country which has solemnly declared that 'all men are created equal' &c! What dreadful vengeance may we not expect to be in preparation for such shameless conduct?" Such exclamations echoed longstanding laments about the hypocrisy of the United States. However, during the Missouri Crisis Republicans like Darlington did not simply complain. They attempted to constrain the expansion of slavery and the power of slaveholders in the United States.[23]

While Virginians like John Randolph also opposed slave trading, they continued to see slavery itself as an institution that should be controlled by masters. Northerners saw the domestic trade as an inherent incident of slavery, driven by the institution's expansion. To end it would require the restriction of slavery, beginning with Missouri. Randolph, meanwhile, would brook no interference in a slaveholder's property rights. This pointed to the ongoing secondary importance of the morality of slavery in sectional conflict over the institution. Northerners voiced countless ethical objections to slavery during the Missouri debates, and on ethical terms alone, they appeared to have common ground with those southerners who continued to consider slavery a moral evil. But as in the slave trade debates of 1807, the morality of slavery was not the fundamental issue at stake. Instead, the Missouri Crisis turned on the question of national democratic control of slavery, on whether non-slaveholding northerners in the federal government could exercise power over slavery and the rights of slaveholders. On this point Virginians had grown more conservative, particularly in the Tidewater. Throughout the War of 1812, they had suffered repeated attacks by the British and saw over 3,000 slaves flee to British warships in the Chesapeake. The federal government had been unable to protect the region during the war, and widespread slave flight persuaded most masters to take a harder line in defense of their prerogatives. In addition, states' rights Virginians opposed the nationalist agenda of the postwar years, particularly as expressed by John Marshall's Supreme Court in the case of *McCulloch v. Maryland*, decided in March 1819. Fear of a stronger federal government merged with the defense of slaveholder prerogatives in the minds of many Virginians, who viewed the prospect of slavery restriction in Missouri as a challenge to both state and southern rights.[24]

Conflict over fugitive slaves and the kidnapping of free blacks also revealed fundamental differences between northern and southern perceptions of slavery. In January 1818, southerners sought to obtain a stronger fugitive slave bill, and northern members resisted them, on grounds that the bill would curtail the rights of free black people in their states. Slaveholders wanted greater federal power to protect their property rights, while northerners sought to protect state prerogatives and the liberty of free African Americans. For northerners who recalled this dispute during the Missouri Crisis, southern appeals to states' rights in order to protect Missouri slaveholders from federal interference must have seemed hypocritical. Like the domestic trade and kidnapping of free blacks, southern demands regarding fugitive slaves demonstrated that slaveholders aggressively sought national power to protect their interests in human property. The 1818 bill, submitted by Virginia Representative James Pindall, would have severely limited a presumed fugitive's access to legal protection. A fugitive's status could be determined in the slave states, and on request to any state or federal judge, or justice of the peace, in the state where a fugitive resided, the claimed slave was to be arrested, identified (an affidavit from a southern jurisdiction would suffice), and returned to slavery. In addition, the bill limited the ability of northern officials to interfere in the process of rendition. It was, according to legal historian Thomas Morris, "a clear and complete statement of the proslavery viewpoint."[25]

Northern opponents struggled to contain their outrage, instigated not only by excessive southern demands, but also by ongoing reports of the kidnapping of free African Americans from their states. Arthur Livermore of New Hampshire, later a powerful advocate of restriction in Missouri, protested that the bill would endanger "the liberty of any colored man carried there [to a slave state], and charged with being a fugitive"; Connecticut Federalist Thomas Scott Williams joined him in opposition, declaring that the rights of free people of color should not be impaired to benefit slaveholders. At first, northern members did not have enough votes in the House to block the bill, in part because some northerners voted with the South. In that respect, the debate foreshadowed the "doughface" behavior of Republicans Henry Baldwin of Pennsylvania and John Holmes of Maine (at the time part of Massachusetts) as well as Federalists Henry Storrs of New York and Jonathan Mason of Massachusetts, all of whom voted for the southern fugitive bill and would later vote against restriction in Missouri. In the Senate, northerners likewise failed to modify the major pro-southern portions of the bill. However, when the bill returned to the House at the end of the session, northerners now had enough votes to forestall consideration, and it never became law.[26]

In contrast to these bitter sectional disputes over slavery, the formation of the American Colonization Society (ACS) in December 1816 suggested that reformers and national political elites might join to support a program of gradual abolition accompanied by the colonization of free African Americans outside the United States. The ACS attracted moderate antislavery figures form the North like Jesse Torrey, who hated slaveholding but could not imagine a post-abolition interracial United States, as well as upper South paternalists, like Virginia's John Randolph. In his *Portraiture of Domestic Slavery* Torrey proposed a form of colonization (within the United States) and included a report on the founding meeting of the ACS. Supporters of the

ACS did achieve some real antislavery victories in Congress, particularly when it came to the international slave trade. In 1819, when the ACS obtained federal funding, Congress revised the objectionable provision of the 1807 law leaving slaves captured through interdiction to the disposition of the individual states, and thus to likely sale into slavery. Now, such slaves would be returned to Africa. In 1820, Virginian Charles Fenton Mercer, a principal founder of the ACS, fought successfully to punish slave trading with death, the exact penalty that southerners had resisted in 1807.[27]

But whatever promise for white national unity that the ACS held was short-lived. By the 1820s, lower South slaveholders grew wary of the ACS, which they viewed as a threatening external force, backed by the federal government, that might interfere in the southern control of slavery. Well before then, free African Americans in the North had publicly opposed colonization, most dramatically at a mass meeting in Philadelphia on January 15, 1817. Although Torrey gave apparent support to colonization in *Portraiture on Domestic Slavery*, he also included a telling note recording a conversation with two black women, one of whom "expressed great repugnance" at going to Africa. As her counterpart bitingly noted, "if they (the Americans) did not want us, they had no need to have brought us away; after they've brought us here and made us work hard, and *disfigured the colour*, I don't think it would be fair to send us back again." Black opposition proved pivotal in persuading antislavery white northerners to reject colonization as well.[28]

By the end of the Missouri Crisis, furthermore, many antislavery northerners who might have embraced colonization became convinced that southerners had no real interest in ending slavery, given their fierce defense of Missouri's right to enter the Union as a slaveholding state.[29] Colonizationists, some of whom maintained antislavery commitments, did persist in the North and South after the Missouri Crisis. But in many respects the only national unifying sentiment attached to colonization after 1820 was hostility toward free African Americans. As the final round of Missouri debates indicated, racist unionism was a potent force that could connect white Americans from the Northeast to the lower South. Moderate antislavery politics, on the other hand, most definitely could not.

On April 3, 1818, shortly before the final vote on the fugitive bill, John Scott, the territorial delegate from Missouri, reported a bill that would allow Missouri to draft a state constitution and be admitted into the Union. The following day, Livermore of New Hampshire proposed a constitutional amendment to outlaw slavery in any new state "hereafter admitted into the Union." There was no debate, and the proposal was summarily rejected, but it was yet another sign of growing discord over slavery.[30] The constant and diverse conflicts over slavery after the War of 1812 ensured that the Missouri Crisis would not be of short duration. The Crisis evoked prewar slavery debates as well, especially the conflicts over the international slave trade during Jefferson's presidency. From 1819 to 1821, Congress confronted not only the problem of slavery expansion but also the more fundamental problem, which cut to the heart of the Jeffersonian alliance, of who should rule over slavery. As in previous debates, southerners demanded that non-slaveholders tolerate the coercive authority of slaveholding, while refraining from any attempt to control it.

In the midst of his attack on the domestic slave trade in 1816, John Randolph reminded the House that during the debates over ending the international trade in 1807, he had opposed any limitation on a master's rights to transport his slaves. He had been so defiant, he explained, because the 1807 law "professed a principle against which it was the duty of every man of the southern or slaveholding States to set his face; for it assumed a prerogative to interfere in the right of property between the master and his slave."[31] The Missouri controversy would revisit the conflict between slaveholder power and national democratic governance and Randolph would return to Congress as the voice of southern dissent. Compared to the legislative conflict over ending the international trade, the Missouri Crisis was far more explosive, as it catalyzed sustained sectional and antislavery sentiment outside Congress. Yet in many ways it simply restated the central dilemma of Jeffersonian democracy, the conflict between slaveholder power and democratic governance. That conflict was more severe in 1819–1821 in part because northerners had increased their challenges to slavery after the War of 1812. But it was also more severe because northern Jeffersonians had amplified their nationalist sentiments during the war by identifying the defense of the United States with the defense of the Republican coalition. In other words, the Jeffersonian conflict between slavery and democracy had now become foundational, a problem not simply for the Democratic-Republican coalition, but for the very idea of the United States.

Missouri

On February 13, 1819, James Tallmadge, a defiant nationalist during the Seminole debates, introduced an antislavery amendment to a House bill authorizing Missouri to become a state. Tallmadge's amendment prohibited the "further introduction of slavery or involuntary servitude" in Missouri, and required that the new state adopt a policy of gradual emancipation, freeing all children born into slavery by age twenty-five. Although debate about the Tallmadge amendment focused primarily on its future implications, it was not simply prospective in intent: Tallmadge sought to dismantle the existing institution of slavery in the Missouri Territory.

Tallmadge had a very rough term in Washington. For much of the early part of the session, he suffered a "constant diarear," according to his mother, so afflicting that it was "with the utmost difficulty for him to get threw speaking." Shortly after his defense of Jackson's conduct during the Seminole War, his young son died, and Tallmadge returned home to New York.[32] He came back to Washington just in time to offer his amendment to the Missouri statehood bill, on February 13, 1819. That was a Friday, and debate began in earnest the following Monday, with John W. Taylor, Tallmadge's New York colleague, taking the floor. Taylor, a confirmed wartime nationalist, had voted with Tallmadge against censuring Jackson for the execution of Arbuthnot and Ambrister, but he had also joined the minority opposition to the admission of Illinois. In a blunt speech, Taylor presented the conflict over Missouri as a conflict between free labor and slave societies. He argued that the South did not respect labor, that rich slaveholders controlled local politics in their states, and that southerners would not allow "a laboring man, however well educated" to represent them in Washington. Although Taylor at one point asked southern representatives to live up to their professed antislavery principles, and join him in the fight for restriction, most of his argument was openly sectional. Free labor and the northern states were better—more free, more productive, and more democratic than the South. Missouri should therefore become a second Pennsylvania, rather than an imitation of Maryland.[33]

Taylor's sectional comparisons also emphasized race, as he contrasted the "neat, blooming, animated, rosy-cheeked peasantry" of Pennsylvanian with the "squalid, slow-motioned, black population" of Maryland. Such language accorded with Taylor's strong commitments to white settler expansion. During the War of 1812, he spoke of his desire to secure settlers "from the tomahawk of the savage Indian stimulated by the jealousy & hatred of the more savage Briton." Similar sentiments no doubt informed his support for Andrew Jackson's violent suppression of the Seminoles. Northerners like Taylor did not question the propriety of national expansion. When they imagined the future of an antislavery Missouri, they likely pictured families like their own taking up residence in the state. Indeed, Taylor reputedly expressed a wish that his relatives might settle in a Missouri free from slavery, to the disgust of the territorial delegate John Scott.[34] In this respect, Republicans like Taylor were different from early Federalist opponents of slavery expansion, who often questioned the benefits of expansion itself. Taylor and Tallmadge wanted to build a settler empire in North America, but they wanted to build it on their own terms. The decision of whether to allow slavery in Missouri was a decision for posterity, claimed Taylor, "exerting its influence for centuries to come over the population of half our continent." When Tallmadge rose in support of his own amendment, he was more explicit, inviting Congress to "look down the long vista of futurity" at the "extended empire over which your republican Government is now called to bear sway." An empire of free farmers, owning their own lands, from the Atlantic to the Pacific, would be "without a parallel" in the world; an empire of slavery would be an unparalleled abomination. He wished to see the "prohibition of slavery . . . extended from the Mississippi river to the Pacific ocean."[35]

Obviously, far more was at stake in these debates than whether slavery should be allowed in Missouri. Republicans believed they were fighting for the future destiny of the United States. They also believed they were contending over the foundational principles of the American union. Timothy Fuller, Republican of Massachusetts, based his national antislavery vision on the Declaration and the Constitution. Article IV, Section 4, of the Constitution, he argued, "expressly makes a republican form of government in the several states a fundamental principle, to be preserved under the sacred guarantee of the National Legislature." Furthermore, the Declaration of Independence, with its commitment to equality and natural rights, "defines the principle on which our National and State Constitutions are all professedly founded." If Congress decided to admit slavery into a new state, Fuller concluded, "we violate the Constitution." Tallmadge agreed, and contended that upholding the Declaration to the letter was a matter of national honor. He had made a similar case in the debate over the Illinois Constitution, warning that English writers mocked America as a hypocrite, "holding in one hand the Declaration of Independence, and with the other brandishing a whip over our affrighted slaves."[36] These nationalist arguments persuaded northerners in the House to back the restriction of slavery, despite bitter responses from southern members and Missouri delegate John Sott. On February 16, the first part of the Tallmadge amendment, to restrict slavery in Missouri, passed 87-76;

the second part, to enact gradual emancipation, passed 82-78. Each vote was divided on sectional lines. But in the Senate, five northerners, including the two Illinois senators (both southern born and both slaveholders) voted with a unanimous South to strike out the Tallmadge amendment. The House would not agree to the Senate bill, and Congress adjourned without a decision on admission of Missouri.[37]

In the same session, northerners in the House lost a related attempt to block the extension of slavery to the Territory of Arkansas and gradually emancipate the children of slaves already there. (Arkansas had been carved out of the Missouri Territory when Missouri applied for statehood.) But the close votes in this debate suggested the strength of the northern opposition.[38] Unlike earlier debates over slavery, the Missouri issue catalyzed sustained conflict. Because the 15th Congress left the issue unresolved, everyone knew that the Missouri question would return at the beginning of the 16th Congress the following fall. The corresponding uproar among the northern public, which began in the summer of 1819 and escalated until the new Congress sat the following November, only encouraged northern members to remain committed to restriction.[39] By the fall of 1819, the issue was constantly addressed at public meetings, in newspapers, and in northern state legislatures, ensuring that the second round of debates on the Missouri question would dominate the first session of the 16th Congress.

Tallmadge did not return to Washington the next winter, but he kept in touch with his colleague John W. Taylor, who renewed the fight for slavery restriction on January 26, 1820. Unlike the relative brevity of the debates the previous year, in 1820 congressmen spoke at great length on the Missouri question. They seemed inclined to justify one member's portrait of an inflated congressman, bursting with the desire to speak.

Although often repetitive, the extensive record of debate in the 16th Congress provides a more thorough view of the northern position on Missouri, and an invigorated northern sectional consciousness that threatened to undermine the Republican alliance. Like Tallmadge and Fuller in the winter of 1819, northerners in the 16th Congress rested their ultimate case against the expansion of slavery on the fundamental precepts of the Declaration of Independence and the U.S. Constitution. The Declaration's invocation of the equal rights of all men was quoted multiple times, and numerous Republicans likewise attempted to prove by artful logic that the Constitution intended to prevent the extension of slavery. Some claimed it went much farther, and intended to promote slavery's abolition. As historians Major

Figure 13. Henry Meigs, sketch of inflated congressman, from Henry Meigs to Josiah Meigs, November 14, 1819. Meigs Papers, New-York Historical Society. Courtesy of the New-York Historical Society.

Wilson and, more recently, Sean Wilentz have argued, such arguments anticipated the Free Soil and Republican antislavery position of the 1840s and 1850s.[40] Like Abraham Lincoln, northern Jeffersonians claimed that they would not interfere with slavery where it already existed, that they only wanted to check the advance of slavery beyond the original limits of the United States. But they also insisted that the United States was founded on principles of freedom. The Declaration of Independence and the Constitution, they believed, gave them the right and duty to restrict expansion of slavery to Missouri.

So too, claimed northerners, did the tenets of Jeffersonian democracy. When southerners and their northern supporters tried to suggest that restriction was either a Federalist plot or the opening gambit of a DeWitt Clinton presidential campaign in 1820, northern Republicans rebuked them in hostile terms. They claimed the Jeffersonian legacy for themselves, and for their attempt to restrict slavery in Missouri. William Darlington opined at length on his lifelong commitment to the Democratic-Republican party and the deep loyalty of Pennsylvania to the Republican cause. "I have always been taught to believe," he said, "that it was no part of republicanism to authorize, or even to connive at slavery, in the formation of governments, where it could possibly be prevented." Republican William Plumer, Jr., of New Hampshire, son of a Federalist turned Jeffersonian, was equally defiant, and claimed that everyone knew that the movement for restriction "originated with Republicans; that it is supported by Republicans throughout the free States; and that the Federalists of the South are its warm opponents." He saw the conflict in more openly sectional terms than Darlington, but he too based his antislavery convictions on Republican nationalism. He was only fulfilling his duties to the Constitution and as a republican, he explained, since the defense of slavery was little more than "the very essence of kingly government—the doctrine of tyrants, in every age."[41]

Many Jeffersonians refused to countenance such arguments. While southern Republicans in Congress fought for the right to extend slavery westward, other Republicans evaded the challenge of restriction by describing the Missouri Crisis as a Federalist-Clintonian scheme to regain national power. Thomas Jefferson apparently convinced himself that the Federalists were behind the crisis, and cryptically warned John Taylor in February 1821 that "the northern bears seem bristling up to maintain the empire of force." In contrast to northern restrictionists, who believed the conflict over Missouri might begin the redemption of the United States from the tyranny of slavery, Jefferson believed the crisis threatened the destruction of the American republic because it imperiled the equality and freedom of the individual states. But in many respects, that assessment mistook the nature of the debate in Congress and it certainly mistook its instigators. Not Federalists but ardent Republican nationalists threatened a union that had given a relatively free hand to slaveholders and slaveholding states to regulate themselves.[42]

In Congress, Maine's John Holmes answered northern attacks on slaveholding by asserting that the movement for restriction was merely a Federalist-Clintonian "*hobby* [horse] . . . and that the head of the pony is directed towards the chair of the General Government." There was very little substance to Holmes's charge, but it did convince some northerners and was given substantial credence by the principal historian of the Missouri Crisis in the mid-twentieth century.[43] It was true that Federalists, especially Rufus King in the Senate and John Sergeant in the House, spoke strongly against the expansion of slavery, but there was no question that the Missouri Crisis was fomented by Republicans, who were the strongest advocates of restriction in 1819 and 1820. The Clintonian suggestion was somewhat more plausible, since both Tallmadge and Taylor had ties to Clinton, and the New Yorker represented the threat of northern political realignment in 1812. New York's jealousy of Virginia resurfaced after the war and in 1816 the Republicans of the New York Legislature recommended that the Jeffersonian congressional caucus nominate then Governor Daniel D. Tompkins for the presidency. They believed a New York president would help maintain Republican unity and suppress sectional criticism of Virginia as "arrogant, dictatorial, and assuming." "As a Republican & as a man," Tompkins reputedly "felt that the President ought no longer for the present to come from Virginia." On Tompkins's part, such sentiments were short-lived: he became vice president instead, and apparently worked with Monroe to achieve the Missouri Compromise and defeat northern restriction in 1820.[44]

Clinton, on the other hand, did use the opportunity presented by the Missouri Crisis to attack Martin Van Buren and the "Bucktail" Republicans, his rivals in New York state, and he opposed slavery expansion after being elected governor of New York in 1820. Yet there was no sustained Clinton campaign in 1820 or at any point thereafter. Even more so than in 1812, northern dissent in 1819 and 1820 was hardly contained or symbolized by the figure of DeWitt Clinton. Instead, the Missouri debates provided occasion for long-held northern resentments to resurface, grow in intensity, and fixate on a single demonstrable case of the antidemocratic power of the slaveholding South. Missouri provoked a widespread movement of sectional disaffection that threatened the Jeffersonian political order, as northerners seemed liable to revoke their prior toleration of slavery. Doing so would destabilize the cross-sectional bonds that had made Jeffersonian democracy so powerful since 1800. In other words, as John Quincy Adams argued, the Missouri controversy "revealed the basis for a new organization of parties."[45]

The North Against Slavery

As a young Jeffersonian, Joseph Story believed Virginia was "the most patriotic, disinterested and magnanimous state in the Union," and he at times signed his letters, "really at bottom a Virginian." He dreamed of living in "some southern clime, more congenial with my nature than the petty prejudices and sullen coolness of New England." But in 1820 Virginia hubris during the Missouri Crisis caused him to look northward. "We have foolishly suffered ourselves to be wheedled by Southern politicians," he told Edward Everett, but no longer: "It is high time that all honest and intelligent men of all parties in Massachusetts were united in the cause of our country."[46] A Republican nationalist during the War of 1812, Story now wished for northern unity in opposition to the South. He was really at bottom a New Englander.

Story's sectional sentiments were shared by a wide variety of political actors across the northern states during the Missouri Crisis. Hostility to slavery extension became, in the face of southern resistance in Congress, hostility to southern political power. The New York Manumission Society wrote a congratulatory note to John W. Taylor in the winter of 1819, emphasizing that the extension of slavery was "irreconcilable with the genius of our government and institutions" and that Taylor and Tallmadge had "elevated the character of the state of New York." This note was compiled with a response by Taylor and Tallmadge and Tallmadge's speech in favor of restriction in a pamphlet printed to publicize the antislavery cause. Isaac Ely, a member of the Manumission Society, wrote again in the fall of 1819 to commend Taylor's position on Missouri, and then once more in February 1820, at the height of congressional debate, to affirm that New Yorkers opposed the extension of slavery. "There is no party with us about it," he wrote; "opinion is unanimous." Salma Hale of New Hampshire, who had served in Congress with Taylor, felt similarly about sentiments in his state and saw "no necessity for compromise" with the South.[47]

Ely and Hale were invested in the Missouri question because they were, respectively, members of formal antislavery and partisan political organizations. But the Missouri Crisis affected ordinary citizens as well, who followed the debates and editorial comment in the partisan press, and participated in public meetings opposing slavery expansion. Taylor received a copy of resolutions from such a meeting in Oneida County, New York, requesting their congressional representatives to prevent expansion of slavery. One of Taylor's most intriguing correspondents presumably wrote from a jail cell in Virginia in August 1819. Josiah Goodall claimed that he had "been imprisoned eleven months above half the time chained hand & foot," for aiding in the escape of a fugitive slave. He was originally from Massachusetts and condemned the violence and tyranny of slavery in Virginia. He read the congressional reports of the Missouri debates in detail, and provided a deliberate refutation of arguments against restriction. Like Taylor, he felt that slavery disgraced labor and he warned that "if the Country west of the Mississippi is ruled by slaveholders, they will always keep the lead of you." "I insist on it," said Goodall, "the friends of freedom are without excuse if they now do not look to their own interest." Buffeted by such sentiments, Taylor introduced a new version of the Tallmadge amendment in the 16th Congress, spoke first on its behalf, and came to symbolize, for both northern and southern members, the political argument against slavery expansion.[48]

Pennsylvania Republicans likewise received militant letters in support of restriction. Thomas J. Rogers, the irate wartime nationalist and correspondent of Jonathan Roberts, had been appointed to the 15th Congress, where he voted for restriction, and reelected to the 16th, which was dominated by the Missouri debates. In January 1820, his constituent and friend John Hurter wrote that the Missouri conflict had "excited great freedom & interest" in Rogers's hometown of Easton. "We earnestly hope," said Hurter, "it will terminate in favour of freedom." It did not, but Rogers apparently took Hurter's words to heart, and voted for restriction in the first session of the 16th Congress.[49]

Hurter's sentiments were mild compared to a letter that Philadelphian William Jones, secretary of the navy from 1813 to 1814, sent to Jonathan Roberts, now sitting in the Senate. Like Tallmadge, Taylor, and initially, at least, Roberts himself, Jones's wartime nationalism did not suppress antislavery sentiment when it came to Missouri. On the eve of war in 1812, he expressed typical Jeffersonian aspirations for the looming conflict: "the national morals, habits and character will be purged from impurities, and established upon the firm and durable basis of a solid, real, independence." But now, in 1820, Jones believed the nation was threatened by slaveholders rather than by Great Britain. Declaring slavery a "violation of the laws of nature in the persons of any people whether black, white, or red," he saw the Missouri question as a conflict between "the free states" and the "slaveholding states." Slaveholders, he believed, "have interests and views of policy entirely at variance with the rights and best interests of the free states," including "the very obvious interest of breeding slaves for an insatiable market." Jones "perceived in many of the southern men . . . a spirit of sectional domination, confident in growing strength, bent upon its increase and claiming from its representatives an allegiance paramount to that which they owe the Federal compact." For Jones, as for many other northerners, antislavery principle became anti-southern political argument in the institutional context of the Missouri debates.[50]

Roberts initially found such arguments persuasive, perhaps in part because his wife Eliza, to whom he wrote constantly, likewise feared that "the Southern interest will preponderate. . . . If there is no restriction, in vain will

be the measures taken for putting an end to the slave trade, those poor crea-
tures will in defiance of law be torn from their family and homes, and indeed
our own country will not present a less horrible picture." In response, Roberts told her that "the slaveholding men are truly violent" and proclaimed
"abominable doctrines . . . they claim the right of holding slaves as a matter of
right." Such exchanges of sectional antislavery feeling helped northerners in
Congress define a committed defense of restriction. Earlier conflicts over
slavery had faded into the resurgence of national political competition and
corresponding Jeffersonian unity; this seemed far less likely given both the
depth and pervasiveness of northern bitterness during the Missouri Crisis.
Even after he had decided to endorse a compromise that would allow slavery
in Missouri, Roberts remained averse to the South. "My abhorrence of slavery is now fixed and absolute," he told his wife in April 1820, "& I cannot feel
toward slaveholders as formerly—I had believed they conceived it wrong
from their protestations—I have found them all illusion. They hold their
slaves as their most precious rights & it is impossible to overlook the vices the
aspect of it engenders."[51] Roberts had come face to face with slaveholder
power, with the notion that slaves were "rights" rather than oppressed men
and women. The starkness of that confrontation threatened the Jeffersonian
accord between North and South and the ability of Republican ideology to
accommodate the prerogatives of southern masters.

The fraying of the Jeffersonian coalition was perhaps most obvious in the
pages of the *Aurora*, the leading Democratic-Republican paper in the election of 1800. William Duane articulated a strong northern position, opposed
to any compromise on Missouri. He and his colleague Stephen Simpson, who
wrote under the pseudonym "Brutus," assailed the South and eventually
called for Republicans to abandon James Monroe in 1820 and build a new
antislavery party. As the *Aurora* declared on January 4, 1820, slavery was "re-
pugnant to the very nature of our government." Like many northern Republicans, Duane and Simpson often perceived the injustice of slavery in terms
of its effects on white people. In the winter of 1820, the *Aurora* repeatedly attacked Virginia, especially in a series on "Political Agriculture" that emphasized Duane's principal criticism of slavery: "the *degradation of the white
man.*" But Duane also revised his racist view of African Americans expressed
during the War of 1812, and now declared whites and blacks equal in nature,
under the law, and "in the eye of the creator." In the pressure of sectional conflict, Duane redeemed his egalitarian politics from racial constraint.[52]

The *Aurora* was very much versed in the antislavery nationalism that marked northern congressional speeches. "Will congress," asked Duane on February 24, "to gratify the cupidity and avarice of slave holders, violate all moral and divine laws. . . . Will they perpetuate and extend that cruel curse which the founders of the nation declared to be only tolerable because it was temporary and must be limited in its duration and extent?" More openly than most northern Republicans, however, Duane used nationalism for sectional ends. In a letter to Pennsylvania's congressional delegation, he declared: "you are representatives of a commonwealth, which would be one of the very first in this confederacy, if her citizens were but faithful to their [great] and obvious interests." He publicly shamed Henry Baldwin, the anti-restrictionist from Pittsburgh, claiming that his disrespect for his constituents' wishes brought republican government "into disrepute and disgrace." "NO COMPROMISE OR SURRENDER OF THE RIGHTS OF MAN!" exclaimed the *Aurora*, connecting the antislavery struggles of 1820 to the democratic struggles of 1800.[53] Only now, instead of building a coalition with slaveholders, Duane employed natural rights egalitarianism to oppose southern power.

While the *Aurora* had long lost the national influence it held in 1800, some southerners perceived Duane's course as a powerful threat to slavery. James M. Garnett, a Virginia congressman from 1805 to 1808 and a close friend of John Randolph's, described the *Aurora*'s criticisms as "a most violent libel against the whole Southern People, but especially of the Old Dominion," and sought to repel Duane in print. Garnett believed Duane was "designedly cooperating with the Abolitionists, who are playing the deep & desperate game, now going on for the whole country North & West of the Ohio & the Mississippi, Louisiana only excepted." If northerners like William Jones saw in Missouri the threat of an illicit, illiberal expansion of slavery and the slave trade, Garnett and other southerners feared an expanding northern free-labor empire that would undermine slavery and plantation agriculture.[54]

A burgeoning sectional self-consciousness encouraged the breakdown of partisan divisions in the North. Southerners at the time and some historians since have been inclined to see Federalist plotting in the Missouri conflict in part because Republicans began to adopt Federalist language, and expressed admiration for Federalist argument during the Missouri debates. William Darlington, who would tolerate no "insinuation" that Pennsylvania Republicans were influenced "by the spirit which erst displayed itself at Hartford," was also deeply moved by Federalist John Sergeant's defense of restriction in

Congress, calling it "the most splendidly argumentative speech . . . that I ever heard in my life." In the *Aurora*, Duane attacked the three-fifths clause and gave his approbation to an anti-Missouri pamphlet likely written by the Federalist Robert Walsh. In New England, reconciliation between Federalists and Republicans was obvious at a meeting in Boston on December 3, 1819, to oppose the extension of slavery to Missouri. John Gallison, Joseph Story's law student and, like Story, a decided Republican during the War of 1812, drafted the resolutions passed at the meeting, which appealed to the Northwest Ordinance to justify restricting slavery in Missouri; a subsequent memorial was addressed to Congress. Old Federalist ideas, particularly opposition to the three-fifths clause, were revised and given new legitimacy in the Boston memorial, as they were in congressional speeches. Such accord revived the limited fusion between Federalists and Republican dissidents before the War of 1812, when renegades like James Sloan likewise indicted the three-fifths clause and the political power of slaveholders.[55]

Instead of outright opposition to the clause, Republican restrictionists accepted its existence, as they did the existence of slavery, in the original states and territories of the Union at the time of the Constitution.[56] Thus John W. Taylor, on reintroducing the Tallmadge amendment to the 16th Congress, began by disavowing any intention to question the fundamental constitutional compromises with slavery: the three-fifths clause, fugitive slave rendition, and the obligation of northerners to assist in the suppression of slave rebellions. Compared to the Ely amendment of 1804 and Federalist attacks on the three-fifths clause through the War of 1812, this was a moderate position. On the other hand, when it came to the extension of the three-fifths clause to Missouri, Republicans now openly criticized slave representation instead of indicting Federalists for doing so. In a closing peroration, Taylor warned that the precedent of allowing slavery in Missouri might be used to acquire Florida, Cuba, and other Caribbean islands. "Are the millions of slaves inhabiting these countries too, to be incorporated into the Union and represented in Congress? Are the freemen of the old States to become the slaves of the representatives of foreign slaves?"[57] Taylor's jeremiad enlisted Federalist argument in an emerging defense of free soil.

No wonder, hearing such rhetoric, that Jefferson and other southerners assumed the Missouri Crisis must have been a Federalist plot to regain political supremacy. Jefferson overlooked the far greater danger, that Republicans had come to question their past ties to the South and to refashion old Federalist arguments as their own. As Joseph Story wrote to Edward Everett in May

1820, "there is really no difference in principle between the great body of the Republicans and Federalists in the East." In Story's case, such harmony reflected his growing conservatism. Yet the Missouri Crisis proved decisive in his turn toward sectionalism, as it did for a number of northern Republicans. William Plumer, Jr., of New Hampshire, who wanted Congress to know that restriction had been first and foremost a Republican measure, also explained that it was not ultimately a partisan issue at all. "The question," he explained, "is not between Federalists and Republicans, but between slaveholders and those who hold no slaves. It is a knowledge of this fact which has induced the free States, usually so much divided among themselves, to advance on this occasion with so much ardor and unanimity to the attainment of their object."[58]

Plumer, Jr., felt the Missouri question transcended partisanship; in the eyes of many northerners it also transcended the question of states' rights, which southerners like Jefferson turned to in order to defend the expansion of slavery. For northern restrictionists, the Missouri debates raised far larger and more fundamental questions about the nature of the United States and American democracy. As William Jones told Jonathan Roberts, "the institution of slavery is only maintained by brutal force." Its presence in the United States had been "secured by compact, extorted from the friends of Union as only less intolerable than anarchy." Jones could not believe that northerners would "submit to the extension of an evil which in its early progress must render their voice in the union entirely nugatory."[59] Slaveholder power, antidemocratic in principle, threatened to undermine northern freedom. Northern Republicans had made similar arguments in the past, but generally in episodic ways: in prior conflicts over slavery in Congress, or as marginal complaints in sectional contests focused on other issues, as in debates over the embargo and over the presidential election of 1812. During the Missouri Crisis, Northerners defined the nature of slaveholder power and its political consequences in much more precise terms. Doing so pointed toward a political alignment that would isolate slaveholding as a threat to northern freedom. While antislavery northerners still gestured toward Democratic-Republican ideals, in many respects they were attempting to reverse the course of Jeffersonian democracy for the past two decades, by forcing the problem of slavery to the center of national politics.

But the Missouri Crisis also revealed the capacity of the American political system to contain conflict over slavery, and that was in many ways a very old story. For over twenty years, Jeffersonian democracy had convinced white northern men to embrace the slaveholding republic of the United States and to tolerate the power masters wielded over their slaves. In Congress, meanwhile, southerners were by and large able to protect slaveholder power from northern interference. On most conflicts over slavery, northerners simply did not have the votes. That institutional limitation was obvious throughout the Missouri Crisis. Northerners prevailed in the House on the question of restriction in 1820, as they had in 1819, but they could not win in the Senate. Pro-southern Senators tied the admission of Maine, which was also seeking statehood from the 16th Congress, to the admission of Missouri. Jesse B. Thomas of Illinois, a southerner by birth and a consistent opponent of restriction, proposed the key provision of the eventual compromise: Missouri would be admitted with no restriction as to slavery but the institution would be excluded in the remainder of the Louisiana Purchase north of the latitude 36°30', the southern border of Missouri. The House initially refused the Senate's measures, but after a legislative deadlock, a conference composed of members from each house recommended that the House should abandon restriction, that the Senate should separate the admission of Missouri and Maine, and that the 36°30' line should be adopted. When forced to a final vote in the House on March 2, 1820 just enough northern members joined a solid South to ensure that Missouri was admitted with slavery intact. Directly following that vote, a much larger majority of the House decided to accept the 36°30' compromise. The opponents in this case were primarily southerners who objected to any restriction of slavery by the federal government.[60]

Northern advocates of compromise had many different motivations, but their behavior was hardly exceptional in the context of Jeffersonian democracy. For over two decades, the Republican coalition had tolerated a massive expansion of slavery. An elderly Jefferson attempted to perpetuate that toleration by opposing restriction and lending his support to John Holmes of Maine, a northern Republican who voted for admitting Missouri with slavery. Holmes defended his course in a circular letter to his constituents that he forwarded to Jefferson. In his now famous response written on April 22, 1820, Jefferson called the Missouri crisis a "fire bell in the night" and described the dilemma of slaveholders, like himself, who desired emancipation in theory but could not bear to live alongside emancipated black people as holding a "wolf by the ear." He promoted the "diffusion" of slavery to new states, claiming that it would make enslaved people "individually happier and proportionally facilitate the accomplishment of their emancipation." He also defended the right of states to decide the question of slavery for themselves. In closing, he grew plaintive, as he worried that the instigators of the

Missouri Crisis might destroy the United States in pursuit of the "abstract principle" of restricting slavery. "If they would but dispassionately weigh the blessings they will throw away against an abstract principle more likely to be effected by union than by scission," he told Holmes, "they would pause before they would perpetrate this act of suicide on themselves and of treason against the hopes of the world."[61] Of course, Jefferson's flattery and grand language, to the extent that they were intended to help Holmes stay the course, very much proved the opposite point—that scission, not union, would be essential for a cogent antislavery political movement. The history of the Democratic-Republican coalition demonstrated that ideological union between northerners and southerners routinely suppressed antislavery argument. In 1820, enough northerners continued to believe in the promises of Jeffersonian democracy to preserve that ideological union, and the expanding slave society that it embraced.

The North Against Restriction

Northerners who voted with the South were driven by various motives, often tied to local interests and partisan loyalty. For legislators from Maine, for example, the Missouri Crisis posed the very real possibility that they might not achieve statehood and independence from Massachusetts. But ideological commitments were just as influential in persuading northern men to side with the South. Many northerners agreed with Thomas Jefferson that the slaveholding United States embodied the "hopes of the world" and must be defended at all costs.

Although Pennsylvania Senator Jonathan Roberts had been a strong advocate of restriction at the start of the Missouri debates, so much so that Nathaniel Macon claimed he had "joind the Hartford men," he soon became a proponent of compromise, which he considered "the genius of our government." In a series of letters to his brother, he tried to rationalize his evolution from opponent to tolerator of slavery expansion. He could not stand New York Federalist Rufus King, the chief advocate of restriction in the Senate, and believed that the northern position on Missouri had been coopted by "ultra federalists," who sought to make DeWitt Clinton president in the fall of 1820. He remained equally suspicious of the South, describing Virginia as "the spoild child of the Union." Roberts convinced himself that he stood above the partisan and sectional fray, alongside Maryland's William Pinkney, previously his chief antagonist in the Senate. Together they were "ready to baffle the factions." Compromise, although unpopular, was politically necessary to preserve "the harmony & Union of these states." That union, Roberts finally decided, was not inherently opposed to slavery: "In the abstract I should say slavery is incompatible in a republican government. But constitutionally this cannot be made out. The foundation of our Union proves this is not a vital principle of it & the reasons which induced compromise ought ever to operate." Thus Roberts broke with the antislavery nationalism cultivated by northern Republicans, who thought restriction had a constitutional mandate, and decided the Union he had fought to defend during the war required compromise with slavery.[62]

Unlike Roberts, New York's Henry Meigs never supported restriction in Missouri, and apparently arrived in the 16th Congress prepared to vote against it; he spoke at length on the subject before John Taylor had introduced his amendment to end slavery in the new state. In part, Meigs's position was entirely partisan: he despised DeWitt Clinton and his canal, and he was close to Martin Van Buren, Clinton's chief opponent in New York. He had ties to the Monroe administration through his father, Josiah Meigs, the commissioner of the General Land Office, and his uncle, Return J. Meigs, the postmaster general, and he helped distribute federal patronage in the state of New York. But Meigs, like Roberts, explained his position on Missouri in ideological more than partisan terms. In his mind, Federalism had not passed away after the war, but remained as a potent political threat. He worried, he told his father, that the "Aristo Feds" would soon return and establish "a strong & stable Government, in which the Jemmy Hillhouses, Dwights, Otises, & Kings shall be Presidents & Senators, hereditary for life. When the orders of Society shall be exactly marked off & defined." Like many Jeffersonians, Meigs was a nationalist who loved Andrew Jackson and projected a continental future for the United States. He condemned Clinton for his "intrigues with Federalists in 1812 & his cold neglect of the deepest interests of his Country in that war." He believed in a limited government: he did not think he should legislate for the people of Missouri, and thus accepted the southern position that Missouri should be allowed to decide for itself whether it would admit slavery. This seemed a sincere conviction, reflecting both Meigs's relative lack of concern for human suffering, which he justified with a Panglossian faith, and his view that "Governments answer their ends when they put no obstacles in the way of Individual execution. No Government can contain science enough to direct." Yet he had ambitious plans for the unfettered United States, which he believed would one day expand across the North American continent and serve as an example to the world. "We are the instruments of God," Meigs believed, "to exhibit an improved grade of Human Government!"[63]

Meigs's northern opponents believed likewise, but saw restricting slavery as part of that ameliorative process. They would not forget his position during the Missouri Crisis, even though he tried to temper his vote against restriction with a grandiose proposal to emancipate all the slaves in the United States and colonize them in Africa, financed by western land sales.[64] Returning home from Congress in the summer of 1820, he found that "my Missouri vote deeply offended many of my political friends—my political enemies make a glorious use of it privately and publicly for my destruction." A year later, things had not improved: "every 19 out of 20 feel deeply my vote on that occasion, very many would have preferred Civil War. They feel their pride hurt by the supposed victory gained by the South." Meigs did not regret his vote, however, and took refuge in the Jeffersonian commitments that had caused him to side with the South in the first place: "There is no federalist who does not hate me, and as far as I can see with great propriety, for I have done & shall do every thing I can to prevent them from regaining that power which they will use for Aristocratic & finally Monarchical systems in this country."[65] Hatred of Federalists allowed Meigs to believe that his vote against restriction had struck a blow at a potential American monarchy. Put differently, it allowed him to believe that tolerating the expansion of slavery preserved his freedom.

Rhode Island Republican Jonathan Russell, who arrived in Congress just after the Missouri Crisis had concluded, made that transaction explicit in an unsent letter to one "Jarvis" in 1822. "As a republican of the old school," he began, "I greet you & cordially join with you in reprobating that cut-throat philanthropy that would exterminate the whites under the pretext of liberating the blacks & rivet the chains of the Republicans of the east with the same federal hammer which is hyperbolically brandished to break the negro fetters of the south."[66] If restriction of slavery was a mere Federalist plot, by implication, toleration of slavery expansion sustained Republican freedom. Similar negotiations had allowed antislavery Republicans to support Thomas Jefferson for the presidency and deflect northern Federalist criticism of the three-fifths clause. In 1800, however, the relationship between the Jeffersonian alliance and the expansion of slavery was far more opaque. With the greater clarity of the Missouri Crisis, it was harder to disguise the consequences of accommodating slaveholder power. Thus Henry Meigs's professed Republican commitments seemed bankrupt to many New Yorkers. Instead of an "instrument of God" serving the advancement of human government, he was simply an "advocate of slavery," as a New York broadside put it in 1820.[67]

Slaveholder Power

While Meigs justified his course by opposition to an imagined aristocratic threat, southerners in Congress defended their right to control slavery in openly antidemocratic terms. Southerners prevailed on Missouri, as they had on other slavery debates in the past, because of their high degree of unanimity when it came to the power of the states and slaveholders to control slavery. They had a contrasting vision of the United States from men like John Taylor, one which was arguably far more accurate than northern antislavery nationalism. They argued that the Constitution sanctioned slavery, and that Congress had repeatedly endorsed its expansion, not only within the limits of the original United States, but beyond, in the case of Louisiana. Southerners did attempt to reject restriction on federalism grounds, by arguing that as an independent state, Missouri must be allowed to decide the question of slavery for itself. But appeals to federalism were simply one tactic in a wide-ranging defense of slaveholder power.[68]

In the first round of debates over Missouri in 1819, for example, Philip P. Barbour of Virginia argued that Congress might have restricted slavery in Missouri when it was still a territory, but restricting slavery when Missouri was poised to enter the Union as a state would violate its equality with other states. But Barbour went on to say that the Northwest Ordinance "was utterly void" (because the states of the Northwest Territory had the sovereign right to make their own decisions about slavery) and he argued that prohibitions on slavery in Missouri would, "in effect, entirely shut out the whole Southern people." Arguments about the technicalities of federalism quickly led to much broader claims about the rights of slaveholders and the propriety of slavery expansion in general. A few days later, in a debate over the status of slavery in the new Arkansas territory, Louis McLane of Delaware argued that Congress could not restrict slavery even in the territorial phase, for the treaty of cession granting Louisiana to the United States promised to protect the property of the inhabitants and to accord them "the enjoyment of all the rights, advantages, and immunities of citizens of the United States." Those rights, McLane contended, included "the right to hold slaves" and "the right to decide whether they will or will not hold them." Although McLane claimed that he hoped the Louisiana Purchase might someday be divided between slave and free territory, he did not believe Congress currently had the power to restrict slavery under the Constitution. Masters had a right to keep their slave property without restraint until a state government of their choosing decided on whether or not to allow slaveholding. Such arguments demonstrated that many Southerners understood restriction not simply as a threat to the equal rights of the imminent state of Missouri, but as an implicit threat to the rights of all slaveholders. Masters could not tolerate restrictions on slavery expansion because they could not tolerate federal interference with their property rights in slaves.[69]

Neither McLane nor Barbour took a strong proslavery stance in ethical terms. Barbour opined about how masters felt "sympathies" for their slaves and McLane expressed his "abhorrence of slavery" and his hope that the dispersion of slaves to the West would lead to better treatment and perhaps emancipation. In the more extensive debates in the 16th Congress, Southerners once again expressed a similar mixture of paternalism and diffusionist fantasy, an indication that they were unprepared to mount a firm ethical defense of bondage. Most Southerners still admitted slavery to be an evil, and took different positions on why that evil should be allowed to expand to Missouri—because masters loved their slaves, much like their own family members, and should be allowed to take them to Missouri if they wanted to move there; because allowing the slave population to "diffuse" among a wider number of slaveholders would ensure better lives for their chattel; because diffusion would reduce the number of slaves in the East, thus lessening the chances of rebellion and making emancipation at some future date more possible (because masters would be less afraid to emancipate if they were surrounded by fewer black people). And in the meantime, noted one humanitarian, the slaves in the West would have more food. While some of these claims suggested the emergence of a paternalist defense of slaveholding, the variation and special pleading in southern argument also demonstrated a relative lack of consensus on the morality of slavery as an institution. Ultimately, however, southerners did not need to justify slavery in moral terms. They simply needed to justify their political right to control it.[70]

South Carolina's Charles Pinckney explained that the real issue at stake in the controversy, far more important than whether Missouri was admitted with slavery, was "keeping the Constitution inviolate." To him, that meant "keeping the hands of Congress from touching the question of slavery." Although Pinckney thought Africans suited for slavery by nature, he hardly needed racial theories to justify the simple proposition that slaveholders were not willing to cede control over an extremely valuable "species of property." As Alexander Smyth of Virginia contended, "the States who hold slaves cannot consent that any State shall surrender to this Government power over that description of property. Its value amounts to five hundred millions of dollars." As one southerner had warned the previous year, northern arguments appeared to challenge the property rights of all slaveholders, not only those in Missouri, which was all the more incendiary considering that there "might be slaves in the gallery listening to the debate." Such anxiety may have been hyperbolic, but it perfectly expressed the fundamental threat of the Missouri Crisis in southern eyes: that northerners might interfere with the deepest political relationship of slavery, the dominance of the master over the slave. Republicans like William Plumer, Jr., certainly indicated as much when they defined the lines of conflict as "between slaveholders and those who hold no slaves." In response, southerners insisted on a core political principle for most slaveholders: the right to be left alone to control their property as they saw fit.[71]

John Randolph, who had defined this position so clearly during the slave trade debates in 1807, did not serve in the Fifteenth Congress, and so missed the first round of debates over Missouri. But he returned to Congress in the winter of 1819–1820 to define it again, in a series of speeches that most northerners deemed incoherent. "Egotism, Virginia aristocracy, slave-scourging liberty, religion, literature, science, wit, fancy, generous feelings, and malignant passions constitute a chaos in his mind, from which nothing orderly can flow," wrote John Quincy Adams in his diary. William Darlington, listening to Randolph in the House, noted that he spent one day giving "a long, incoherent speech," and the next speaking "in a most rambling style." John Taylor told his wife that after spending the better part of two days speaking against restriction, Randolph "has fallen far short of public expectation & was mortified at his failure of success." Randolph, meanwhile, penned a series of desperate letters to his friend James M. Garnett in which his opposition to restriction in Missouri was intertwined with his own physical survival. Suffering a "raging fever" in the Washington winter, Randolph came to the House and "was delivered by forceps of the disjecta membra of a speech on the Missouri question, in attempting to finish which I was struck blind." He was on the "brink of the grave" and told Garnett, "you have probably received the last letter in my handwriting." Eleven days later, still among the living, Randolph dated his letter "from my Castle of Crazy." Despite fever and blindness, he "continued to attend the house, as a man would not ask a furlough before a general engagement." He left his bed to hear "Mr. King's <u>memorable</u> speech . . . In an hour afterwards I was seized with spasms that threatened dissolution. Nevertheless I crawled out on Tuesday the 15th." And he continued to crawl out, speaking for "four hours & a half" on February 22, 1820, while believing he was soon to die. "The vulture daily whets his beak for a repast on my liver & his talons are fixed in my very vitals." He longed to return home to Virginia, "to take the only chance of prolonging my <u>now</u>, I trust, not altogether useless life."[72] These comments amounted to a crazed rendering of a foundational southern principle: the defense of the slaveholder's power over slavery was the defense of the slaveholder's self.

Little wonder that in the midst of such ailments, real or imagined, Randolph's oratory suffered in point of clarity. But he still managed some choice insults, and Adams, despite judging his speeches disordered, counted him among the South's chief spokesmen, unmatched on the northern side. For Joseph Story, Randolph "let out the great secrets of Virginia, and blabbed that policy by which she has hitherto bullied us, and led us, and wheedled us, and governed us." While a small majority of southerners ultimately backed the compromise in its final form, accepting the 36°30' restriction on slavery in the rest of the Louisiana Purchase territory in exchange for the admission of slavery in Missouri, Randolph dissented, unwilling to accept any federal limits on slaveholder property rights. Speaking against the 36°30' line, he "made a furious attack upon all who advocated the compromise," recounted Joseph Story. "He said, 'the land is ours, (meaning Virginia's) and we will have it, and hold and use it as we (Virginians) please.' He abused all the Eastern States in the most bitter style; and intimated, in the most direct manner, that he would have nothing to do with them."[73]

For Republicans who had mocked the dissenter Randolph during the War of 1812 and looked beyond him to a new nationalism founded in alliance with Virginians like Madison and Monroe, his return to prominence must have been unsettling. For despite his rambling, Randolph certainly spoke for a broad majority of Virginians, seventeen of whom joined him in opposing the 36°30' provision of the Missouri Compromise. That Virginia Republicans were unwilling to compromise in a measure that most antislavery northerners viewed as a defeat suggests how opposed Republicans North and South truly were on the Missouri question. Randolph scorned the northern men who voted with the South, insulting them as cowards who were "scared of their own dough faces." The epithet, which soon stuck, suggested how little Randolph cared for the national ideological bonds that convinced men like Henry Meigs to vote against slavery restriction.[74]

Northern Dreams, American Realities

By the end of the second round of debates over the restriction of slavery in Missouri, Joseph Story, who had dreamed of becoming a Virginian as a young man, now decided that northerners had to rely on themselves and claim "the honors and the Constitution of the Union" as their "birthright." Story expressed a conservative variant of a widespread sentiment: in the face of southern resistance on the Missouri question, northerners had to seize national power on their own terms. Various attempts to do so proved how difficult this would be. In the fall of 1820, William Duane's *Aurora* ran numerous articles against the reelection of James Monroe, on the grounds that Monroe had orchestrated the Missouri Compromise and thus the extension of slavery. Mostly written by Stephen Simpson, under the pseudonym "Brutus," the *Aurora* essays were relentless. "He who votes for James Monroe, votes for slavery," said the *Aurora* on October 26, 1820. On November 1, Brutus called Monroe a "*slave president*" who had forced "the *slave bill of Missouri*" through Congress and recommended the election of DeWitt Clinton, "a foe to slavery," in his place. The following day the *Aurora* asked Pennsylvanians to look beyond partisan sentiment and "*record your vote against the curse of slavery.*"[75]

Duane, of course, was influenced as much by personal grievance as principle, as had been the case in almost every political fight he had ever engaged in. Stephen Simpson, meanwhile, was even more opposed to the national bank than he was to slavery, so his argument for an antislavery ticket was perhaps not entirely genuine.[76] These qualifications aside, the *Aurora* made a strong sectional case, one northerners like James Sloan had voiced in the past. And it was hardly unthinkable, given the sectional passions of 1819–1820, that northerners might attempt to run a candidate on a limited antislavery platform. In the Pennsylvania gubernatorial race of 1820, both Duane and Binns's *Democratic Press* had attacked the incumbent William Findlay for being a slaveholder. They successfully helped elect Joseph Hiester, who had voted against the extension of slavery to Missouri in Congress, in his place.[77]

In New York, Clintonians likewise used the Missouri issue to attack their opponents, the Bucktail followers of Martin Van Buren, in the 1820 gubernatorial race, which pitted DeWitt Clinton against Vice President Daniel D. Tompkins. A broadside titled *The Voice of Freedom* singled out Van Buren, Henry Meigs, Tompkins, and his brother Caleb, among other Republicans, as "advocates of slavery" and claimed that Clinton, in contrast, was a "champion of freedom."[78] Clinton narrowly won the gubernatorial race, and Tompkins's association with Monroe and the Missouri Compromise may have contributed to his defeat in the charged atmosphere of the spring of 1820.

But in other respects, 1820 electoral contests revealed the limitations of political antislavery in the North. While Clinton won the governorship, Republicans allied with Martin Van Buren (know as the Bucktails) maintained control of the legislature and thus the state's Council of Appointment, a major source of patronage power. With Clinton's capacity to deliver New York's electoral votes doubtful, any plans for his presidential candidacy quickly collapsed.[79] Monroe was reelected in a near unanimous electoral college vote. In Pennsylvania, while Binns was willing to use antislavery language to win power at the state level, he was not willing to forgo the alliance to Monroe and the Republican coalition that had brought him so much influence during the War of 1812. He condemned Duane's opposition to Monroe, arguing that "questions which vitally affect the rights and happiness of the human family" (like slavery) should not be "mixed up with party politics." Furthermore, Binns noted, every American president except John Adams had been a slaveholder, and they constituted a remarkable "succession of able, patriotic, and honest men." On Binns's urging, Republicans favorable to Monroe, including Nicholas Biddle, disrupted a public meeting that Duane had advertised to form an antislavery ticket. Slavery had an obvious presence in American public life, as four slaveholding presidents out of five suggested, but it could not, according to Binns, be confronted through politics.[80]

Binns did not simply try to suppress antislavery political action. He also argued for an American nationalism that embraced a progressive amelioration of slavery; as evidence of such antislavery improvement, Binns cited the escalating penalties Congress had imposed on Americans engaged in the international slave trade. Duane should have been familiar with such arguments, as he had made similar claims in support of Jefferson in 1800. As in 1800, such nationalist fictions suppressed any serious confrontation of the South. Now it was Duane's voice that was being drowned out, as Binns helped ensure that the presidency would remain in the hands of a Virginia slaveholder.[81]

While the *Aurora's* forthright sectional attacks proved to have limited purchase in the fall of 1820, more moderate northerners apparently believed that they could gain increased power within the Republican coalition after the Missouri Crisis. Outright opposition to the Missouri Compromise by John Randolph and other Virginians may have allowed some northerners to salvage a sense of achievement from the Missouri conflict. The 36°30' line, although offering very little of immediate value, did promise to block the extension of slavery in much of the rest of the Louisiana Purchase territory, which men like Randolph viewed as a threatening imposition on their property rights. John W. Taylor wrote to his wife in a resigned but optimistic tone: "we have gained all that was possible if not all that was desired . . . what we have gained is an ample recompense for all the time & labour it has cost us." Other northerners were far less sanguine: Salma Hale called the compromise a "disgraceful result" and Isaac Ely noted more diplomatically that it "has not met with the approbation of intelligent men of all descriptions." But both men took heart when Taylor, after multiple ballots, was elected speaker of the House in November 1820. They saw in his ascendancy the rise of northern power in national politics, and the genesis of a new national coalition opposed to slavery expansion. Clintonian Charles Haines exclaimed that "To the friends of Missouri & Slavery," Taylor's election "has been a thunderbolt!" Even to Taylor, it was something of a surprise, as he was certain prior to the election that "all the southern states oppose me because I moved the prohibition against slavery in Missouri."[82]

But events quickly proved how hollow Taylor's victory truly was. Throughout the session, Taylor presided diplomatically over the contentious final round of Missouri debates, winning the praise of southern members. Historian Robert Forbes suspects he may have been acting in concert with Henry Clay and James Monroe to stifle the more strident tones of northern dissent.[83] Such moderation gained him little. In the fall of 1821, he lost the speakership to defiant anti-restrictionist Philip P. Barbour of Virginia, who was supported by Martin Van Buren's New York Bucktail adherents. "The same New York party which opposed my election last spring have maintained against me the most inveterate hostility since the balloting commenced," wrote a disappointed Taylor to his wife Jane Taylor. "All Virginia—Federalists & Republicans, radicals and administration men—all united in Barbour's support. A majority of the New York members also voted for him & indeed for every man whose chance of success against me they thought the best." Many years later, a still embittered Taylor was even more harsh, and blamed his defeat principally on Van Buren. He was denied the speakership, claimed Taylor in 1845, because his "persevering efforts to add Missouri to the free states was a sin too heinous to be forgiven. The friends of slavery found their party strengthened by a new ally from N.Y. who now took his seat in the U.S. Senate. The northern man with southern principles or rather with selfish principles, after having ruined the political fortunes of De Witt Clinton under the mask of friendship, became his persecuting foe & waged war against all in N.Y. who refused to unite with him in the destruction of that great states-man."[84] So long as partisanship and self-interest trumped sectional accord, northern interests would be constrained in national politics, particularly when it came to slavery.

The 1821 battle for the speakership was a proxy for Van Buren's later call for a coalition between the "plain republicans of the North and the planters of the South," the alliance that led to the rise of Jacksonian democracy.[85] In New York, the Bucktails had fought throughout the fall of 1821 for a new state constitution that expanded democracy for ordinary white men, while bar-ring most African Americans from the suffrage. At the national level, Van Buren and the Bucktails leveraged their power to defeat Taylor, whom they associated with DeWitt Clinton, their political enemy at home. Local divi-sions thus thwarted northern unity at the national level. Even advocates of restriction could not come to terms: Rufus King, a bitter enemy of Clinton's and the leading northern advocate of restriction in the Senate, refused to support him in 1820. James Tallmadge, angry over state patronage matters, likewise turned against Clinton.[86] Ultimately, the Missouri Crisis demon-strated that northerners did not have a principle or cause that could sustain a sectional unity comparable to the South's unanimity in defending slaveholder power. John Quincy Adams may have believed the conflict over slavery ex-pansion "revealed the basis for a new organization of parties," but he also knew that "the slave men have indeed a deeper immediate stake in the issue than the partisans of freedom . . . whose only individual interest in this case arises from its bearing on the balance of political power between North and South."[87] Conflict over slavery provoked northerners to dream of sectional power, but that desire alone could not support a successful antislavery poli-tics. Meanwhile, the lack of sectional unity continued to limit northern influ-ence over slavery at the national level. That dilemma had no obvious solution in the early 1820s.

Northerners like Van Buren and John Holmes could define their political course in reference to a long legacy of political union between northern

democracy and southern slavery, a union that had produced remarkable benefits for Republicans since 1800. Traditionally, Van Buren has been seen as
heralding a new age of democratic politics or, in Richard Brown's classic interpretation, a new age of southern power.[88] But in many respects, Van Buren
was simply acting like a Jeffersonian. After the Missouri Crisis, any attempt
to keep the slavery question out of national politics was inevitably more explicit, but the reasons for doing so—to preserve the Union and to preserve a
political coalition that guaranteed democratic freedom for white
northerners—were hardly novel.

In contrast, northern opponents of slavery expansion struggled to find a
language and an ideal that could sustain them in a drawn-out contest for
political power. Throughout the Missouri Crisis, they attempted to define the
founding documents of the United States and its early political history as
fundamentally opposed to slavery, to ground their resistance in an idealized
American nation. But nationalism proved, in some respects, to be their chief
liability. The nation they imagined had never existed in reality, whereas the
slaveholding United States was a practical fact: it existed not in theory but in
time. And whereas northerners in 1819, 1820, and 1821 could not imagine
their way into another polity, nationalist sentiments had long proved their
capacity to attach white men to the United States, slavery and all; indeed,
such sentiments had helped make the slaveholding nation that northern restrictionists sought to dismantle.

James Johnson of Virginia was kind enough to point this out to his northern counterparts in a response to New Yorker Silas Wood. Wood, like other
northerners before him, had tried to contend that the Constitution's republican government clause inherently opposed slavery, since slavery was inherently antirepublican. Johnson felt no need to contend with Wood on abstract
grounds, and simply informed the House that "the gentleman is rather unfortunate in point of time; he has made his discovery too late; experience and
fact are both against him." Wood's argument for an antislavery constitutionalism, said Johnson, was "something like a discovery, at this day, that Homer
and Virgil were destitute of taste and talents for poetry. The question has long
since been settled by the unerring standard of taste—the concurring testimony of ages." From Johnson's perspective, it was poor form for northerners
to complain that the South was failing to live up to antislavery principles central to the nation's founding documents. Southerners had been clear about
where they stood on the national politics of slavery since the first federal-level
debates over the institution in 1790. They did not make radically new

arguments during the Missouri Crisis; they simply repeated the longstanding demand of slaveholders to be left alone to control slavery as they saw fit. Their federal government was at best agnostic on the moral question of slavery, it granted significant institutional protections to slaveholders, and it was ultimately powerless to restrain their prerogatives.[89]

Southerners were, however, mostly willing to cede the Declaration of Independence to northerners. In response to the constant invocation that "all men were created equal," they simply reminded northern Republicans that the Declaration did not establish the United States government, a position that had the advantage of being true. Some went further, like John Randolph, who reportedly "pronounced its doctrine of Equal Rights to be an absurd 'fanfaronade of metaphysical abstractions.'"[90] One might see Randolph as the vanguard of the antebellum southern retreat from the Declaration, and therefore declare an ideological victory for northern Jeffersonians in laying claim to an antislavery nationalism. But it was at best a symbolic one, allowing northern men to continue to believe in the antislavery potential of the United States, despite obvious evidence of the power of slaveholders in the American Congress, and the expansion of slavery under American rule. One of the more poignant moments in the Missouri debates came when John W. Taylor, after reading from the Declaration, asked of Jefferson and the committee that drafted it, "Did they lay the foundation of this infant Republic in fraud and hypocrisy? The supposition is incredible." Taylor then went on to cite Jefferson's "denunciation" of slavery in the *Notes on Virginia* as further proof of the antislavery intentions of the United States.[91] Such nationalist fictions were incredibly strained in the course of the Missouri Crisis, which tended to prove less that Taylor's supposition was incredible than that it was groundless, given the longstanding commitment of the United States to the protection and expansion of slavery. Taylor's incredulity, James Johnson might have said, simply occurred too late.

But there was a yet more complex rendering of what Johnson meant when he contended that northerners were "unfortunate in point of time." In attempting to argue that the idealist origins of the republic were unstained by slavery, northerners found themselves in a dilemma that was essentially historical. They wished to both check the advancing power of slavery in the United States while believing that the nation, in its truest sense, had never countenanced the institution in the first place. Yet in many respects, similar acts of idealism—in opposition to Federalism and Great Britain; in defense of northern aspirations for freedom—had formed the texture of Jeffersonian democracy and helped northerners reconcile with slavery from the 1790s onward. In a sense, that is what Johnson gestured to by appealing to "the unerring standard of taste": northerners had long been living in the midst of slavery without doubting that they also lived in the midst of republican freedom. They liked the poetry that was the United States.

There was thus something appropriate in allowing northerners to claim the Declaration for themselves: they retained a symbol of nationalism, recently commemorated in the John Trumbull painting that would eventually hang in the Capitol. Meanwhile, southerners retained power in the national government when it came to making decisions about slavery. In some respects, that state of affairs simply recapitulated the structure of Jeffersonian democracy. The Missouri Crisis exposed the tangled roots of the Republican compact between northern democracy and southern slavery, but northerners avoided any serious investigation into the ideological origins of their predicament. In an otherwise candid debate about the nature of slavery in the United States, the northern Republican case for restriction came to rest on promises of American purity and ameliorative potential. "Experience and fact," meanwhile, had revealed those national myths not as false renderings of a polity bound to slavery, but as crucial factors in tying northerners to the slaveholding republic in the first place.

This problem of historical consciousness stemmed from northern attachments to American nationalism. In many ways, nationalism and antislavery were contradictory impulses. The Declaration aided the ideological project of imagining an antislavery America, but it was not obvious in the winters of 1819, 1820, and 1821 that it aided the more practical objective of winning power in Congress, and thus turning the existing American nation-state against the ongoing expansion of slavery. Invoking the Declaration allowed northerners to overlook the toleration of slavery at the heart of Jeffersonian political culture, and the long relationship between their experience of freedom and southern bondage. Instead, they argued that freedom in America had always opposed slavery. In theory, such an argument threatened slaveholders in the United States. But in practice, it sanitized a Jeffersonian nationalism which had far more often condoned slavery. Thus the deeper Missouri Compromise was less about a geographical line than an ideological relationship between northern democracy and southern slavery. Under duress, white northern men continued to believe in the freedom they had won with Jefferson, as Republicans, and as Americans.

Democracy, Race, Nation

The relationship between democracy and slaveholder power fundamentally shaped political life in Jeffersonian America. Beginning in the 1790s, democrats in the North found multiple ways to accommodate slavery in order to justify their political alliance to the South, and those acts of accommodation constrained the universalist tendencies of northern egalitarian thought. Race played an important role in this process, as northerners sought solidarity with southern masters and suppressed claims to freedom by African Americans, free and enslaved. At the same time, the institutional politics of slavery produced periodic discord within the Jeffersonian coalition, as slaveholders aggressively defended their property rights and their power at the national level. In 1819 and 1820, the Missouri Crisis made it clear that there was no national consensus over the virtues of slavery. But the divisive sectional conflict over Missouri took place in a political context shaped by two decades of Jeffersonian democracy. Slaveholders were more powerful in 1820 than they had been in 1800, in part because northern Jeffersonians, despite their episodic misgivings about slaveholder power, had helped build a robust nationalism that managed to contain sectional dissent. In the end, northerners simply could not prevail in the Missouri debates. They did not have the institutional power in Congress and they could not overcome a long ideological history of tolerating slavery in defense of their own freedom and the virtues of the American nation-state.

The last phase of the Missouri Crisis, in the winter of 1820–1821, evoked this prior history of accommodation and conflict as well. However, instead of focusing on the expansion of slavery, the last round of debates focused on the question of race, as Congressmen debated the political status of free African Americans and their ability to claim rights under the U.S. Constitution. Although in many ways the conflict of 1820–1821 simply recast the sectional acrimony of the previous two sessions of Congress, it also introduced different problems and different resolutions. More so than ever before, northern Republicans had to confront the connection between two dominant antidemocratic elements in Jeffersonian political culture: the toleration of slaveholder power and the exclusion of all African Americans from equal political standing in the United States.

The Compromise of 1820 did not end debate on the new state of Missouri, due to be admitted to the Union the following year. Missouri had been authorized to draft a state constitution and was promised admission into the Union, but it had not yet been finally accepted as a new state. A committee in the House moved to admit Missouri on November 23, 1820, but debate immediately began over the nature of Missouri's state constitution. This final phase of the Missouri Crisis did not officially conclude until March 2, 1821. At various moments in the extensive Congressional debate, members from both sections believed the Missouri Compromise might not survive.

Missouri's constitution, submitted to the second session of the 16th Congress, established slavery but also required the new state legislature to pass a law barring free African Americans from entering the state. The third round of debates on Missouri thus focused not on slavery but on the status of free African Americans in the United States. A similar dialectic between a theoretically antislavery nationalism and the very real slaveholding nation governed this last crisis of 1820–1821, which exposed more deeply the contradictions in northern democratic thought. Now white northern Republicans had to contend on the terrain of race, where their sentiments had always been unstable. In response to Missouri's challenge and in the context of still heated sectional passions from the previous winter, some northerners returned to earlier universalist claims. Northerners claimed that exclusion of black migrants from Missouri conflicted with the privileges and immunities clause of the Constitution; since some African Americans were citizens in the northern states, Missouri was effectively denying them comity by denying them entry. On the one hand, this argument had clear roots in prior opposition to national-level racial restrictions on the rights and lives of free African Americans.[1] On the other hand, it was difficult for Republicans to mount a sincere defense of black citizenship, given a long and accelerating history of denying blacks equal political standing in the northern states. The end of the Missouri Crisis thus dramatized the tension between universalist and racist conceptions of the American polity among white northerners.

Behind that tension lay the yet more profound conflict between democracy and slaveholder power that had determined the Jeffersonian alliance from its inception. Resolving these contradictions proved impossible, as the practical and ideological constraints of Jeffersonian democracy ensured that northern opposition to Missouri's constitution, like the northern movement for restriction in 1819 and 1820, would not prevail in Congress. It did, however, prove possible to live with these contradictions and to praise the political union of the United States that produced them. A number of white northerners took this path, consciously choosing union with slaveholders over defense of black rights. Others left the Missouri Crisis in a state of resignation. Others continued to hope for the fruition of northern sectional power in the near future. All remained bound by the political and ideological legacy of two decades of Jeffersonian rule, which had sustained the intertwined expansion of slavery and democracy.

On November 14 and 20, 1820, John Binns's *Democratic Press* reported that Republican and DeWitt Clinton ally John Spencer had proposed resolutions in the New York legislature opposing the new Missouri Constitution. The resolutions objected to the establishment of slavery in the state and a clause that prohibited emancipation without the consent of slaveholders, a fairly transparent statement of antidemocratic political authority. But Spencer's chief objection was that the proposed ban on free black migration violated the privileges and immunities clause of the U.S. Constitution. New York and other states contained free black citizens, claimed Spencer, and in addition to other rights, blacks in New York possessed "the distinguishing characteristic of a citizen, the elective franchise." By the Missouri Constitution, "our citizens," said Spencer, were "denied the right of emigrating to Missouri. This was a palpable violation not only of the express terms of the Constitution of the United States, but of the great principle of our confederacy."[2] Much like the antislavery nationalists of the previous two years, Spencer articulated a vision of the United States fundamentally at odds with that of most slaveholders. In his America, free African Americans were citizens who possessed equal standing with all others.

Northern opponents of the Missouri Constitution advanced a similar position in Congress. Federalists were more prominent than northern Republicans in these debates; however, Republicans did speak against the Missouri Constitution, and they provided the bulk of the votes against the second Missouri compromise, in which Congress finally accepted the new state of Missouri. The compromise was made on the basis of a resolution that allowed Missouri into the Union but stipulated that the state's proposed restriction of black migration "shall never be construed to authorize" a law that would limit the "privileges and immunities" of any "citizen" of the United States. The new state legislature had to publicly agree to these terms.[3] But the terms themselves were lenient and evaded the main question raised by debate in Congress: were free African Americans citizens of the United States with rights worthy of protection?

A number of northern Federalists and Republicans in the House answered that question in the affirmative, by appealing to the Declaration of Independence, the privileges and immunities clause of the Constitution, and the facts on the ground. Free African Americans were citizens in many of the existing states, where they exercised fundamental political rights, including the right to own property and, in some states, to vote. Even where black political capacity was restricted, African Americans maintained a wide variety of basic rights alongside other citizens. Black citizens included men who had fought for the United States in the Revolution and the War of 1812; who had been impressed by the British; whose impressment was justly complained of, on the grounds that they were citizens of the United States; and who, according to Pennsylvania Federalist Joseph Hemphill, had elected men to the ratifying conventions of the Constitution, and thus clearly were embraced under the terms of that document. Indeed, added Republican William Eustis of Massachusetts, the Constitution said "We the People," not "We the *white* people"; if it had been openly restrictive on the grounds of race, the northern and middle states would not have ratified it.[4] This was not a new position: as was true of the Missouri debates in the winters of 1819 and 1820, northerners were simply restating more forcefully and extensively a conviction that they expressed on occasion in the past. While some southerners thought that northern men were simply using the disputed clause in the Missouri Constitution as a pretext to perpetuate the crisis of the previous winter, the record of debate suggests otherwise. Northerners, Republican and Federalist alike, mounted a clear and consistent defense of African American citizenship.

But their position was far from universally held in the North, especially among Jeffersonians. Republicans had repeatedly constrained their egalitarian and democratic convictions in order to accommodate American slavery, and doing so led many northerners to restrict or deny the civic standing of free African Americans. This legacy perhaps explains why Federalists in the House were more vocal than Republicans in defending black rights to citizenship. As speaker, John W. Taylor did not engage in debate, and men like William Darlington, William Plumer, Jr., Arthur Livermore, and Timothy

Fuller, leading advocates of restriction in the past session, did not address the
Missouri Constitution. In letters to his wife, Plumer, Jr., expressed frustration
that the Missouri question had returned, as it "kept us in a constant quarrel
to no purpose." The outcome of the last session left him resigned that Missourians were "destined to the curse of slavery, & they seem to desire it with
as much ardour as if it were the greatest of blessings."[5] Although he voted
against the second Missouri compromise, Plumer appeared willing to let
Missourians be cursed with slavery, and bar free African Americans from
entry along the way.

That free African Americans born in the United States had some claim to
citizenship was hard to deny based on existing common law, which acknowledged the principle of birthright citizenship. Southerners, in response, began
to invert the common law notion that being born free in a particular political
community established political belonging and thus the protection of certain
rights. Instead, they contended, one's status in a given community determined one's eligibility for citizenship. Like immigrant radicals in the Jeffersonian coalition, they too argued for citizenship by consent. But they
emphasized the consent of the existing community of citizens, without which
no outsider could claim political standing. Since African Americans did not
have equal rights to whites, it was obvious that whites did not accept them as
civic equals. And this, some southerners contended, had always been the
case. The Constitution may not have said, but it did in fact mean "We the
white people."[6]

As Louis McLane of Delaware argued, the people who colonized the land
that would become the United States were "essentially a white community. In
its origin the black population could have formed no part of it, and throughout its progress the invincible barrier to a mixture of white and black, and the
positive regulations of society, have perpetually excluded them. They could
not, therefore, upon the principles of the association, and in the nature of
things, be entitled to equal rights." Indeed, prohibitions on interracial marriage, claimed McLane, were the strongest evidence that white people intended to keep black people separate from themselves. That taboo, he
emphasized, "strengthens and sanctifies the moral feelings of society; it keeps
the black forever without its bosom, and perpetuates his discrimination." African Americans were "perpetual inhabitants" of the United States but they
were not, nor were they ever likely to be, American citizens.[7] In this story of
American political development, whiteness became the defining principle of
national belonging.

Southern congressmen who spoke in the last round of Missouri debates by and large agreed with McLane's position. They insisted, moreover, that white northerners agreed with it too, no matter what their representatives might argue in Congress. Southerners pointed out that blacks did not vote in Pennsylvania, that it was illegal for a black man to marry a white woman in Massachusetts, and that in Connecticut, whose constitution was "made but the other day," black men were explicitly excluded from the franchise. While a few southerners were willing to admit that some African Americans might be citizens, most argued that none were, nor were they ever intended to be. "Indians, free negroes, mulattoes, slaves!" exclaimed Virginia's Philip Barbour. "Tell men not that the Constitution, when it speaks of *We, the people*, means these." Fellow Virginians Alexander Smyth and John Floyd agreed. Smyth claimed that "nature seems to have made the negro a perpetual alien to the white man," and Floyd, who found the idea that blacks were a party to the Constitution an absurdity, said that the states could force free blacks into slavery at a moment's notice. Finally, South Carolina's Charles Pinckney claimed that he had drafted the privileges and immunities clause at the Constitutional Convention, and that he "perfectly knew that there did not then exist such a thing in the Union as a black or colored citizen, nor could I then have conceived it possible such a thing could ever have existed in it; nor, notwithstanding all that is said on the subject, do I now believe one does exist in it." He went on to add that the northern states had driven their black population away through "the most marked contempt," listing a litany of racist laws that, he contended, provided clear precedent for Missouri's attempt to exclude free blacks. For extra measure, he appealed to science, citing Jefferson and others to show that black people were unequal to whites by nature, and "were most probably intended to serve them." In effect, Pinckney was rehearsing Roger Taney's position in *Dred Scott v. Sanford*: black men had no rights white men were bound to respect, and the northern states had long demonstrated the truth of that proposition through their treatment of free African Americans.[8]

Pinckney and other southerners had ample evidence of northern racism to draw from and Jeffersonians furnished even more as the last phase of the Missouri Crisis unfolded. Beginning on November 25, Philadelphia Republican Tench Coxe set out to refute claims of black citizenship in a series of articles for John Binns's *Democratic Press*. The first number of Coxe's "Considerations Respecting the Helots of the United States," was published shortly after the *Press* reported John Spencer's resolutions against the

Missouri Constitution in the New York legislature. As if in rebuttal, Coxe cited a litany of racist restrictions on free blacks and then offered his own racial theories as to why Africans and African Americans were not "capable of genuine modern civilization." As Gary Nash has argued, Coxe's arguments marked a reversal from his early support of the Pennsylvania Abolition Society, foreshadowing the rise of a full-fledged white man's democracy in Philadelphia and throughout the North.[9]

In New York, Republicans did not just talk about black inequality, they imposed it. In August of 1821, the New York State Constitutional Convention would undermine John Spencer's argument that blacks possessed "the distinguishing characteristic of a citizen, the elective franchise," by barring all African Americans who did not own $250 worth of property from the vote, while widening access to the suffrage for white men. In some respects, the $250 qualification was a compromise measure, as New York Bucktail Republicans had tried to deny blacks the suffrage outright. In doing so, they sounded very much like their southern counterparts in Congress: they claimed that "the minds of the blacks are not competent to vote"; that existing social discrimination justified excluding blacks from equal political rights; and that blacks were already barred from the suffrage in most other states.[10] Opponents of racial exclusion in turn rephrased many of the arguments for equal citizenship voiced in the last round of Missouri debates, and some pointed directly to the recent conflict in Congress. As Federalist Peter Jay warned, the exclusion of African Americans contradicted New York's recent stand against the Missouri Constitution as well as the privileges and immunities clause of the United States Constitution. Like northerners in Congress, he defended the rights of African Americans in New York who were "born as free as ourselves"; he likewise deemed the idea of natural inferiority between black and white "completely refuted" and "universally exploded." If New York restricted access to suffrage based on race, Jay predicted, "you will hear a shout of triumph and a hiss of joy from the southern part of the union, which I confess will mortify me." In the end, Jay was no doubt mortified. Outright racial proscription did not pass, but a large majority agreed to the $250 qualification, including James Tallmadge, who had returned to New York in the spring of 1819. He thought the qualification "held out inducements to that unfortunate class of our population to become industrious and valuable members of the community." In contrast to his defiant attack on slavery at the outset of the Missouri Crisis, Tallmadge was willing to compromise when it came to equal rights for African Americans, despite the fact that he had apparently earned significant political support among black New Yorkers for his resistance to slavery expansion.[11]

In Congress, advocates of admitting Missouri outright stressed that union between whites in the United States should take precedence over the rights of black men. Charles Pinckney expressed surprise that northerners would threaten the Union, from which they derived so many political and economic benefits, "to give to a few free negroes and mulattoes the right to settle in Missouri contrary to the declared unanimous wish of the people of that State." Some northerners felt similarly, and used the Union as justification for their votes in support of the second Missouri Compromise. Jonathan Roberts, who supported the first Missouri Compromise in the spring of 1820, was in a panic the following fall, as the debate over Missouri's constitution began. "It is not improbable Missouri will be refused admission by the House at the present session," he wrote to his brother. "The South is alarmed and consternated. Indeed a crisis is arrived little less awful than that which resulted in the establishment of the federal constitution." Roberts hoped to stay the course and "ride out this storm." He wished that the Pennsylvania delegation might "harmonize" on the Missouri question and come to terms, for in the current state of things "what can be done must be accepted for what ought to be done." In other words, the slaveholding republic had to be saved.[12]

Roberts proposed a compromise measure in the Senate on February 16, 1821 that was similar to the version later adopted by Congress. It would have admitted Missouri with a stipulation that it amend its state constitution so that the ban on black migration did not infringe on the rights of "citizens," but it did not specify that the ban had to be eradicated altogether or that free African Americans were citizens whose rights demanded protection. Roberts's proposal did not pass but he did vote for the eventual compromise resolution, joining a substantial majority in the Senate.[13] In effect, he agreed with Charles Pinckney that the Union took precedence over the rights of free blacks.

In public, Roberts took the position of virtuous compromiser, but in private, he had little respect for African Americans. Over the past year, Roberts had been having trouble at home with a disobedient servant named Ned, apparently a black fugitive from Delaware whom Roberts had purchased in order to help him gain his freedom. Roberts expected labor in return for his assistance, and "kept the manumission as security" until Ned worked off his purchase price. Roberts was disappointed in his expectations, as he noted in his memoirs: "The black did but little good for us afterwards. He left us

before the money was paid, but eventually took up his manumission. This
transaction cur'd me from meddling with these people." In May 1820, responding to a series of complaints about Ned from his wife, Roberts declared
that "the African race seems formed for every kind of baseness—Neds wickedness is not from ignorance. It is a diabolical spirit at bottom." Given these
racist sentiments, it is hard to imagine Roberts ever providing strong support
for the rights of free African Americans.[14]

In contrast, he and other northerners were happy to support perpetual
union with slaveholders. Pennsylvania's Nicholas Biddle, observing the Missouri debates in Washington, felt that events had become desperate in
mid-February, when Roberts proposed his compromise measure in the Senate. He viewed compromise as a laudatory act and hoped to ensure that
Pennsylvania received due credit for the efforts of Roberts and his colleague
(and fellow compromiser) Walter Lowrie. Writing to Charles Jared Ingersoll,
Biddle emphasized the necessity of making Roberts's proposal "appear, as it
certainly is, a voluntary & magnanimous exertion on the part of Pennsylvania to interpose between the contending parties & to close a breach which
rash & violent spirits are daily widening." Biddle then asked Ingersoll to try to
ensure that the Republican press in Philadelphia would support the state's
senators "& come out distinctly in favor of what is emphatically a Pennsylvania measure." "A paragraph or two," he suggested, "expressive of favorable
sentiments towards Mr. Roberts's proposition would I think be decisive of its
fate & thus relieve the country from the [menace] of this miserable
controversy."[15]

Republican Samuel Southard of New Jersey, who also served in the Senate, was proud to say that he had compromised in favor of the Union. He
wrote a detailed pamphlet to justify his vote for the second Missouri Compromise. He took great pains to explain that he had never stood with "the
Slave-holding party" nor had he been "favorable to slavery." But he was happy
to say that he had voted for the compromise measure, as "the peace of the
Union seemed to be jeopardized, *by the question as it then stood, whether free
blacks and mulattoes should live in Missouri."*[16] The italics indicated Southard's disdain for black rights and agreement with southerners like Charles
Pinckney. How could the rights of "a few free negroes" compare to the paramount importance of the Union? Of course, to ask that question was already
to accept the legitimacy of a Union on Pinckney's terms—one that not only
incorporated racial exclusion, but did so in the interests of the slaveholding
class.

The conjunction of events at the end of the Missouri Crisis—the rise of the American Colonization Society to national prominence, black disfranchisement in the North, the robust defense of slaveholder rights in Congress, and Martin Van Buren's first attempts to form a new democratic coalition—suggests that 1821 marks the emergence of a self-consciously white republic. Northern congressmen may have hesitated to embrace Louis McLane's theory of the United States, but white Americans by and large did not. In many respects, the outcome of Jeffersonian democracy, whether one deems it logical or not, was an egalitarian community of white men who protected their own interests by accommodating slavery; doing so required, as southerners made clear, an investment in white supremacy.[17]

Yet there are reasons to resist such a strong conclusion, not least in the resistance to slavery and racial exclusion by northern Republicans and Federalists on the floor of Congress from 1819 to 1821. In the end, northern Republicans provided the large majority of the votes against the second Missouri Compromise, just as they had against the first. Equally important, northern Republican arguments during the Missouri Crisis, constrained as they were by American nationalism, employed universalist claims to oppose slavery and, in 1821, to defend the rights of black Americans. Such arguments evoked a prior history, in which Jeffersonians attacked Federalism as part of a radical, transatlantic Enlightenment project that sought to establish democracy as a universal good. The democratic commitments of the 1790s were not inherently confined by race or nation, and they allowed men like Abraham Bishop, William Duane, Thomas Branagan, and many others to indict slavery in the United States and the world.

In multiple cases, of course, those democratic commitments were soon deeply compromised on behalf of a slaveholding republic. But it is important to acknowledge the difference between a democratic culture that was formed by slavery and white supremacy from the outset—an American freedom that was created by American slavery, in other words—and a democratic culture that had far more complex origins but came to embrace slaveholder power and white supremacy on the narrow terms of American nationalism. Doing so better accounts for American democracy's diverse roots, which extended far beyond the minds of Virginian slaveholders like Thomas Jefferson. It also better accounts for the political problem of slavery in a democratizing society. Rather than an institution that was taken for granted, that, to modify John Randolph of Virginia, Americans were simply born into, slavery was instead subject to ongoing political negotiation. It required acts of

accommodation and toleration. And those acts made all free Americans, especially the white male electorate, responsible for slavery. "He who allows
oppression shares the crime," said Thomas Branagan in his *Penitential Tyrant*,
employing a phrase that the Federalist *Columbian Centinel* echoed in the
midst of the Missouri Crisis.[18] It was an apt description of the predicament
faced by northern democrats, whose political freedom was not simply defined against slavery, but also helped to sustain the coercive power of
slaveholders.

In other words, while democracy did not originate in slavery, northern
democratization was by no means an exceptional aspect of Jeffersonian America that remained relatively separate from and foundationally hostile to the
expansion of southern bondage. Instead, democratic culture became deeply
entangled with slavery, through the institutional politics of the Jeffersonian
coalition and the ideological politics of northern freedom. Decades of tolerating slavery's antidemocratic authority while celebrating democratic freedom
had produced two dominant forms of American nationalism: a racial unionism that rejected African Americans as incapable of full political belonging in
the United States, and a more generic patriotism that made accommodating
slavery the necessary price of union. The strength of these ideological forma-
tions was most obvious in moments of crisis, as during the War of 1812 and
congressional conflict over Missouri, when white northerners used their
voices and their votes to defend the slaveholding republic as it was.

But the democratic encounter with slavery also produced constant discord. The very fact that slavery required ongoing political accommodation
ensured that it would be subject to ongoing contestation. Slaveholders were
well aware of that dilemma, which is why they so fiercely defended the autonomy of masters from democratic rule. Slaveholder power, albeit in a very different way from democratic universalism, had likewise never been contained
by race. Slaveholders did not advance the cause of white supremacy simply to
win friends in the North; they did so in order to maintain their control over
slavery. They needed to be sure that white non-slaveholders would not defend the rights of "a few free negroes and mulattoes" because doing so might
threaten the institution of slavery—in the short term by impairing the ability
of Missouri to become a slaveholding state; in the long term by opening the
door to the recognition of emancipated and runaway slaves as members of
the political community with equal standing to their masters. Invocations of
a beloved white community, bound together by mutual consent never to
marry black people, were attempts to protect the political authority that

made slavery possible. When slaveholding claims to power emerged from the ideological veil of whiteness, however, they repeatedly fractured the very real community of white men in Congress and in the Jeffersonian coalition.[19]

Thus as much as the end of the Missouri Crisis pointed to a new era of white supremacy and the suppression of antislavery politics, it also outlined two of the main ways in which slavery would be contested throughout the antebellum period: by attempting to limit its expansion and legal authority and by acknowledging the rights of free African Americans and, increasingly, fugitive slaves to basic legal protection. Both struggles were connected to a long-term political fight against slaveholder power in the American political system, one that divided antebellum abolitionists between those who thought that system was fundamentally corrupt and those who thought it might be reformed. But the opposing sides of this debate ultimately had the same goal: to undermine the legitimacy and power of slaveholders in the United States. In making that case, antislavery activists repeatedly turned to the words and actions of slaveholders themselves, who wantonly displayed their antidemocratic authority when under threat.[20]

Many of the men involved in the antebellum struggle against slavery invoked the name of Thomas Jefferson or at the very least paid some homage to the Declaration of Independence in order to justify their cause. Some reached directly back to the northern version of Jeffersonian democracy. A few Republicans, still alive in the 1850s, republished their antislavery arguments from many years ago; others communicated with a new generation of antislavery activists.[21] But in many respects, these links to the past obscured the fact that abolitionists and antislavery politicians were struggling against a central feature of Jeffersonian politics: the toleration of slavery and slaveholders by non-slaveholding northern democrats. That toleration had infected every aspect of political life in the North, including the democratic and nationalist ideals to which a later generation appealed in order to oppose slavery. As Frederick Douglass put it on returning to the United States from England in 1847, "slavery is everywhere."[22]

Such a claim was based less on Douglass's experience of bondage than on his experience of a treacherous freedom. For Douglass, as for other African Americans in the northern states, the ubiquity of slavery was not a metaphysical condition. Constitutional and political accommodations of mastery threatened fugitives with reenslavement, while racism and the threat of kidnapping undermined liberty for free black northerners. Douglass understood the reach of slaveholder power in a profound way, and he therefore knew how important it was to persuade nonslaveholders to reject the legitimacy of mastery. His very life, in many respects, depended upon it.

In 1845, after publishing the first edition of his narrative, Douglass traveled to "monarchical England" in order to escape from "republican slavery" and to agitate for abolition. In speeches across Britain, Douglass denounced American slaveholders in no uncertain terms. He also spoke at length about the role of the northern states in sustaining mastery. "If they are not actual slaveholders," said Douglass, "they stand around the slave system and support it." Northern whites might pretend to oppose slavery, but by promising to return fugitives and by treating free blacks with "deadly hate and deep prejudice," they effectively promised enslaved people that they would find no refuge within the United States. Thus Douglass described himself as "an outlaw in the land of my birth." Northern disregard for black freedom effectively fulfilled the claims of slaveholders during the Missouri Crisis, when southerners had insisted that black people could never be equal citizens of the United States.[23]

The indifference and contempt that Douglass faced in the 1840s grew out of a long political history of tolerating the authority of slaveholders. American democracy had been deeply shaped by complex ties between individual political subjects and the institution of slavery, as white men claimed membership in a slaveholding nation. Emancipation demanded overcoming that ideological history, in order to convince northerners to refuse to sanction slaveholder power. That struggle, Douglass argued, required international allies, as slavery was so deeply woven into American institutions. But it was inevitably a struggle for the hearts and minds of nonslaveholders in the United States. In other words, as Douglass pointed out on returning from England, it was a struggle that had to occur on the terrain of conscience.

Skeptics had doubted the efficacy of Douglass's British tour, he told a New York audience in May of 1847. "Have you not irritated, have you not annoyed your American friends, and the American people," his detractors wondered, "rather than done them good?" "We have irritated them," Douglass readily admitted, because "they deserve to be irritated. I am anxious to irritate the American people on this question." The problem of slavery, he continued, was one of those "cases which demand irritation, and counter irritation. The conscience of the American public needs this irritation. And I would *blister it all over, from centre to circumference*, until it gives signs of a purer and better life than it is now manifesting to the world."[24]

As Douglass knew firsthand, the need for irritation did not decline after the formal end of slavery. The reconciliation between democratic freedom and oppression, a lasting legacy of Jeffersonian politics, persisted well after the Civil War, as the Democratic party and white supremacy helped to shape a postbellum consensus that retained many aspects of the old order. Antidemocratic authority survived the end of slavery and dramatic attempts to fundamentally revise the political order of the United States. So too did toleration of coercive power in the name of race and nation.[25]

As the Missouri Crisis suggested, the greatest obstacle to overthrowing slavery was neither tactical nor ideological but historical. White Americans had to be persuaded not only to oppose slaveholder power, but also to come to terms with a long legacy of accommodating mastery. That legacy, insofar as it was woven into political identity and the very experience of freedom for white northerners—woven into not only acts of prejudice but acts of idealism—was incredibly hard to confront. And it remains hard to confront in a contemporary United States sustained by new compromises between freedom and power.

Coming to terms with slavery's past, whether in the 1860s or the 1960s or in decades to come, demands a political language unbound by the constraints of nationalism and self-aggrandizement so central to Jeffersonian democracy; it demands political institutions unbound from the constraints of antidemocratic power. And perhaps most critically of all, it demands a political subjectivity willing to place the oppression of others before the freedom of the self; to believe, in the first place, that freedom has often been inseparable from slavery. In other words, confronting slavery has long required not only a democratic politics but a democratic conscience.

ABBREVIATIONS

AAS: American Antiquarian Society
AC: *Annals of Congress*
AHMC: American Historical Manuscript Collection, New-York Historical Society
AHR: *American Historical Review*
AMLC: American Memory Collection, Library of Congress
ANB: *American National Biography*, online edition
HL: Huntington Library
HSP: Historical Society of Pennsylvania
JAH: *Journal of American History*
JER: *Journal of the Early Republic*
JSH: *Journal of Southern History*
LC: Library of Congress
MCNY: Museum of the City of New York
MHS: Massachusetts Historical Society
NEQ: *New England Quarterly*
NYHS: New-York Historical Society
PMHB: *Pennsylvania Magazine of History and Biography*
PTJ: *The Papers of Thomas Jefferson*, ed. Julian P. Boyd, Barbara B. Oberg, et al. (Princeton, N.J.: Princeton University Press).
RDU: Rubenstein Library, Duke University
WMQ: *William and Mary Quarterly*

NOTES

Introduction: North of Jefferson

1. Jefferson to John Wayles Eppes, June 30, 1820, in *Thomas Jefferson's Farm Book*, ed. Morris Betts (Princeton, N.J.: Princeton University Press, 1953), 45–46.

2. Orlando Patterson provides a more general rendering of this problem: "If the master sought to exclude as far as possible all other claims and powers in his slave, it nevertheless remains true that he needed both the recognition and the support of nonslave members of his community for his assumption of sovereign power over another person. An isolated master faced grave risks. Plato, who knew what he was talking about on this issue, shrewdly pointed out that a slave owner within his community had nothing to fear from his slaves because the entire state was ready to defend each individual citizen. But if he and his immediate family with more than fifty slaves were transported to the middle of a desert where no freeman could come to his defense, that citizen would be in great fear for his own life and that of members of his family, and he would try to ingratiate himself with the slaves by making promises and offers of freedom." Orlando Patterson, *Slavery and Social Death: A Comparative Study* (Cambridge, Mass.: Harvard University Press, 1982), 35. My characterization of mastership is based on Steven Hahn, *A Nation Under Our Feet: Black Political Struggles in the Rural South from Slavery to the Great Migration* (Cambridge, Mass.: Harvard University Press, 2003), 16–17, and Walter Johnson, *River of Dark Dreams: Slavery and Empire in the Cotton Kingdom* (Cambridge, Mass.: Harvard University Press, 2013), 151–75. On the economic significance of slaveholder property rights, see James Huston, *Calculating the Value of the Union: Slavery, Property Rights, and the Economic Origins of the Civil War* (Chapel Hill: University of North Carolina Press, 2003); Gavin Wright, *Slavery and American Economic Development* (Baton Rouge: Louisiana State University Press, 2006); Robin L. Einhorn, "Slavery," *Enterprise and Society* 9 (September 2008): 491–506.

3. On Jeffersonians and the rise of middling men: Paul Goodman, *The Democratic-Republicans of Massachusetts* (Cambridge, Mass.: Harvard University Press, 1964); Alfred Young, *The Democratic-Republicans of New York* (Chapel Hill: University of North Carolina Press, 1967); Gordon Wood, *The Radicalism of the American Revolution* (New York: Vintage, 1993); Wood, *Empire of Liberty: A History of the Early Republic, 1789–1815* (New York: Oxford University Press, 2009); Alan Taylor, *William Cooper's Town: Power and Persuasion on the Early American Frontier* (New York: Vintage, 1996). On immigrant radicals and Jeffersonian democracy: Richard Twomey, *Jacobins and Jeffersonians: Anglo-American Radicalism in the United States* (New York: Garland, 1989); Michael Durey, *Transatlantic Radicals and the Early American Republic* (Lawrence: University Press of Kansas, 1997); David Wilson, *United Irishmen, United States: Immigrant Radicals in the Early Republic* (Ithaca, N.Y.: Cornell University Press, 1998);

Alan Taylor, *The Civil War of 1812: American Citizens, British Subjects, Irish Rebels, and Indian Allies* (New York: Knopf, 2010); Seth Cotlar, *Tom Paine's America: The Rise and Fall of Transatlantic Radicalism in the Early Republic* (Charlottesville: University of Virginia Press, 2011).

4. Recent scholarship has firmly established the advent of democracy in the early national period, and has turned attention away from political elites to the men who built democratic institutions and political culture. See Simon P. Newman, *Parades and Politics of the Street: Festive Culture in the Early American Republic* (Philadelphia: University of Pennsylvania Press, 1997); David Waldstreicher, *In the Midst of Perpetual Fetes: The Making of American Nationalism, 1776–1820* (Chapel Hill: University of North Carolina Press, 1997); Jeffrey L. Pasley, *"The Tyranny of Printers": Newspaper Politics in the Early American Republic* (Charlottesville: University of Virginia Press, 2001); Jeffrey L. Pasley, Andrew W. Robertson, and David Waldstreicher, eds., *Beyond the Founders: New Approaches to the Political History of the Early American Republic* (Chapel Hill: University of North Carolina Press, 2004); Jeffrey L. Pasley, *The First Presidential Contest: 1796 and the Founding of American Democracy* (Lawrence: University Press of Kansas, 2013); and the essays in the Summer 2013 issue of the *Journal of the Early Republic* on the electoral data collected by Philip Lampi, especially Donald Ratcliffe, "The Right to Vote and the Rise of Democracy, 1787–1828," *JER* 33, 2 (Summer 2013): 219–54.

5. There is a vast literature on women, politics, and male power in the early national period. The best recent overview is Rosemarie Zagarri, *Revolutionary Backlash: Women and Politics in the Early American Republic* (Philadelphia: University of Pennsylvania Press, 2007). I try to examine some of the men in this book in terms of gendered power in Padraig Riley, "The Lonely Congressmen: Gender and Politics in Early Washington, D.C.," *JER* 34, 2 (Summer 2014), 243–73. On the impact of race, see Joanne Pope Melish, *Disowning Slavery: Gradual Emancipation and "Race" in New England, 1780–1860* (Ithaca: Cornell University Press, 1998); James Brewer Stewart, "The Emergence of Racial Modernity and the Rise of the White North, 1790–1840," *JER* 18, 2 (Summer 1998): 181–217; Stewart, "Modernizing 'Difference': The Political Meanings of Color in the Free States, 1776–1840" *JER* 19, 4 (Winter 1999): 691–712; John Wood Sweet, *Bodies Politic: Negotiating Race in the American North, 1730–1830* (Baltimore: Johns Hopkins University Press, 2003). On the influence of race and gender on citizenship and American national identity see Judith N. Shklar, *American Citizenship: The Quest for Inclusion* (Cambridge, Mass.: Harvard University Press, 1991); Rogers Smith, *Civic Ideals: Conflicting Visions of Citizenship in U.S. History* (New Haven, Conn.: Yale University Press, 1997); Barbara Welke, *Law and the Borders of Belonging in the Long Nineteenth Century United States* (Cambridge: Cambridge University Press, 2010); Carroll Smith-Rosenberg, *This Violent Empire: The Birth of an American National Identity* (Chapel Hill, NC: UNC Press, 2010)

6. For a broader argument against "latent virtue," see Robin Blackburn, *The American Crucible: Slavery, Emancipation, and Human Rights* (London: Verso, 2011), 26.

7. Wood, *Radicalism of the American Revolution* and *Empire of Liberty*; see also Joyce Appleby, *Capitalism and a New Social Order: The Republican Vision of the 1790s* (New York: New York University Press, 1984). Other early national surveys that minimize slavery's impact include Stanley Elkins and Eric McKitrick, *The Age of Federalism* (New York: Oxford University Press, 1993).

8. Richard Hildreth, *The History of the United States of America: From the Adoption of the Federal Constitution to the Sixteenth Congress* (New York: Harper, 1851); Hildreth, *Despotism in America: An Inquiry into the Nature, Results, and Legal Basis of the Slave-Holding System in the United States* (Boston: Jewett, 1854); Henry Wilson, *History of the Rise and Fall of the Slave Power*

in America (Boston: Houghton Mifflin, 1872–1877); Hermann von Holst, *The Constitutional and Political History of the United States*, vol. 1, trans. John J. Lalor and Alfred B. Mason (Chicago: Callaghan, 1877); Henry Adams, *The History of the United States of America, 1801–1817* (New York: Scribner's, 1889–1891); Charles Beard, *Economic Origins of Jeffersonian Democracy* (New York: Macmillan, 1915).

9. The key titles among Claude Bowers's many works are *Jefferson and Hamilton: The Struggle for Democracy in America* (Boston: Houghton Mifflin, 1925); *Jefferson in Power: The Death Struggle of the Federalists* (Boston: Houghton Mifflin, 1936); *The Tragic Era: The Revolution After Lincoln* (Cambridge, Mass.: Riverside Press, 1929).

10. W. E. B. Du Bois, *The Suppression of the Atlantic Slave Trade to the United States of America, 1638–1870* (New York: Longman's, 1896); Du Bois, *Black Reconstruction: An Essay Towards a History of the Part Which Black Folk Played in America, 1860–1880* (New York: Harcourt Brace, 1935).

11. Staughton Lynd, "The Abolitionist Critique of the United States Constitution," in *The Antislavery Vanguard: New Essays on the Abolitionists*, ed. Martin Duberman (Princeton, N.J.: Princeton University Press, 1965), 209–39; Lynd, *Class Conflict, Slavery, and the United States Constitution* (Indianapolis: Bobbs-Merrill, 1967); Donald Robinson, *Slavery in the Structure of American Politics* (New York: Harcourt Brace, 1970); Duncan Macleod, *Slavery, Race, and the American Revolution* (Cambridge: Cambridge University Press, 1974); David Brion Davis, *The Problem of Slavery in the Age of Revolution, 1770–1823* (Ithaca, N.Y.: Cornell University Press, 1975); Robin Blackburn, *The Overthrow of Colonial Slavery, 1776–1848* (London: Verso, 1988)

12. The paradigm of republicanism was inspired by the related work of Bernard Bailyn, *The Ideological Origins of the American Revolution* (Cambridge, Mass.: Harvard University Press, 1967); Gordon Wood, *The Creation of the American Republic, 1776–1787* (Chapel Hill: University of North Carolina Press, 1969); J. G. A. Pocock, *The Machiavellian Moment: Florentine Political Thought and the Atlantic Republican Revolution* (Princeton, N.J.: Princeton University Press, 1975). See especially Daniel T. Rodgers, "Republicanism: The Career of a Concept," *Journal of American History* 79, 1 (June 1992): 11–38. Key works on Jeffersonian politics were Lance Banning, *The Jeffersonian Persuasion: Evolution of a Party Ideology* (Ithaca, N.Y.: Cornell University Press, 1978) and Drew McCoy, *The Elusive Republic: Political Economy in Jeffersonian America* (Chapel Hill: University of North Carolina Press, 1980).

13. On the institutional power of slavery see the varying accounts in Leonard L. Richards, *The Slave Power: The Free North and Southern Domination* (Baton Rouge: LSU Press, 2000); Don E. Fehrenbacher, *The Slaveholding Republic: An Account of the United States Government's Relations to Slavery* (New York: Oxford University Press, 2001); Paul Finkelman, *An Imperfection Union: Slavery, Federalism, and Comity* (Chapel Hill: University of North Carolina Press, 1981); Finkelman, *Slavery and the Founders: Race and Liberty in the Age of Jefferson* (Armonk, N.Y.: M.E. Sharpe, 2001); Mark Graber, *Dred Scott and the Problem of Constitutional Evil* (Cambridge: Cambridge University Press, 2006); Robin L. Einhorn, *American Taxation, American Slavery* (Chicago: University of Chicago Press, 2006); David Waldstreicher, *Slavery's Constitution: From Revolution to Ratification* (New York: Hill and Wang, 2009); George Van Cleve, *A Slaveholder's Union: Slavery, Politics, and the Constitution in the Early American Republic* (Chicago: University of Chicago Press, 2010); David F. Ericson, *Slavery in the American Republic: Developing the Federal Government, 1791–1861* (Lawrence: University Press of Kansas, 2011). See also Waldstreicher's critical review of Van Cleve, "Too Big to Fail, So Blame the Critics—Early Republic Style," *Reviews in American History* 40 (2012): 52–56.

14. See especially François Furstenberg, "Beyond Freedom and Slavery: Autonomy, Virtue, and Resistance in Early American Political Discourse," *JAH* 89, 4 (March 2003): 1295–1330; Furstenberg, *In the Name of the Father: Washington's Legacy, Slavery, and the Making of a Nation* (New York: Penguin, 2006); David Waldstreicher, *Runaway America: Benjamin Franklin, Slavery, and the American Revolution* (New York: Hill and Wang, 2004).

15. Richard Newman, *The Transformation of American Abolitionism: Fighting Slavery in the Early Republic* (Chapel Hill: University of North Carolina Press, 2002); Matthew Mason, *Slavery and Politics in the Early American Republic* (Chapel Hill: University of North Carolina Press, 2006); David N. Gellman, *Emancipating New York: The Politics of Slavery and Freedom, 1777–1827* (Baton Rouge: Louisiana State University Press, 2006); John Craig Hammond, *Slavery, Freedom, and Expansion in the Early American West* (Charlottesville: University of Virginia Press, 2007); John Craig Hammond and Matthew Mason, eds., *Contesting Slavery: The Politics of Bondage and Freedom in the New American Nation* (Charlottesville: University of Virginia Press, 2011); Paul J. Polgar, "Standard Bearers of Liberty and Equality: Reinterpreting the Origins of American Abolitionism," Ph.D. dissertation, City University of New York, 2013; Nicholas Wood, "Considerations of Humanity and Expediency: The Slave Trades and African Colonization in the Early National Antislavery Movement," Ph.D. dissertation, University of Virginia, 2013.

16. Linda Kerber, *Federalists in Dissent: Imagery and Ideology in Jeffersonian America* (Ithaca, N.Y.: Cornell University Press, 1970); Paul Finkelman, "The Problem of Slavery in the Age of Federalism," in *Federalists Reconsidered*, ed. Doron Ben-Atar and Barbara Oberg (Charlottesville: University of Virginia Press, 1998); Matthew Mason, "'Nothing Is Better Calculated to Excite Divisions': Federalist Agitation Against Slave Representation During the War of 1812," *NEQ* 75, 4 (December 2002): 531–61; Mason, *Slavery and Politics*; Mason, "Federalists, Abolitionists, and the Problem of Influence," *American Nineteenth Century History* 10, 1 (March 2009): 1–27; Garry Wills, *Negro President: Jefferson and the Slave Power* (Boston: Houghton Mifflin, 2003); Rachel Hope Cleves, *The Reign of Terror in America: Visions of Violence from Anti-Jacobinism to Antislavery* (Cambridge: Cambridge University Press, 2009).

17. For overall positive accounts of Jeffersonian antislavery, see especially Sean Wilentz, *The Rise of American Democracy: Jefferson to Lincoln* (New York: Norton, 2005); Wilentz, "Jeffersonian Democracy and the Origins of Political Antislavery in the United States: The Missouri Crisis Revisited," *Journal of the Historical Society* 4, 3 (September 2004): 375–401; and Wilentz's critical review of Garry Wills, "The Details of Greatness," *New Republic* 230, 11 (March 29, 2004): 27–35. For accounts emphasizing white supremacy, see Noel Ignatiev, *How the Irish Became White* (New York: Routledge, 1995), which interprets the Jeffersonian printer John Binns as a proto-Jacksonian, and Smith, *Civic Ideals*, 165–96.

18. On the expansion of slavery, see Adam Rothman, *Slave Country: American Expansion and the Origins of the Deep South* (Cambridge, Mass.: Harvard University Press, 2005); Brian Schoen, *The Fragile Fabric of Union: Cotton, Federal Politics, and the Global Origins of the Civil War* (Baltimore: Johns Hopkins University Press, 2009); Johnson, *River of Dark Dreams*; Edward Baptist, *The Half Has Never Been Told: Slavery and the Making of American Capitalism* (New York: Basic Books, 2014). John Craig Hammond questions an exceptionalist focus on expansion driven by the American nation-state in *Slavery, Freedom and Expansion in the Early American West* (Charlottesville: University of Virginia Press, 2007) and "Slavery, Settlement, and Empire: The Expansion and Growth of Slavery in the Interior of the North American Continent, 1770–1820," *JER* 32, 2 (Summer 2012): 175–206. On the consolidation of the southern defense of slavery, see Lacy K. Ford, "Reconfiguring the Old South: 'Solving' the Problem of

Slavery, 1787–1838," *JAH* 95, 1 (June 2008): 95–122 and *Deliver us From Evil: The Slavery Question in the Old South* (New York: Oxford, 2009).

19. Robert Pierce Forbes, *The Missouri Compromise and Its Aftermath: Slavery and the Meaning of America* (Chapel Hill: University of North Carolina Press 2007); Richard Brown, "The Missouri Crisis, Slavery, and the Politics of Jacksonianism," *South Atlantic Quarterly* 65 (Winter 1966): 55–72.

20. Frederick Douglass, "Farewell Speech to the British People" and "The Right to Criticize American Institutions" in *Frederick Douglass: Selected Speeches and Writings* ed. Philip S. Foner and Yuval Taylor (Chicago: Lawrence Hill Books, 1999), quotes at 58, 77.

21. David W. Blight, *Race and Reunion: The Civil War in American Memory* (Cambridge, Mass.: Harvard University Press, 2001). Ira Katzneslon, *When Affirmative Action Was White: An Untold History of Racial Inequality in Twentieth-Century America* (New York: Norton, 2005) and *Fear Itself: The New Deal and the Origins of Our Time* (New York: Liveright, 2013).

Chapter 1. The Emancipation of New England

1. Thomas Jefferson to Elbridge Gerry, March 29, 1801, Jefferson Papers, AMLC.

2. Donald Ratcliffe, "The Right to Vote and the Rise of Democracy, 1787–1828," *JER* 33, 2 (Summer 2013): 219–54; Chilton Williamson, *American Suffrage: From Property to Democracy* (Princeton, N.J.: Princeton University Press, 1960), 164–72; Harlow Sheidley, "'Preserving the Old Fabrick': The Massachusetts Conservative Elite and the Constitutional Convention of 1820–1821," *Proceedings of the Massachusetts Historical Society* 3rd ser. 103 (1991): 114–37; Harlow Sheidley, *Sectional Nationalism: Massachusetts Conservative Leaders and the Transformation of America, 1815–1836* (Boston: Northeastern University Press, 1998). For Federalist political culture, see David Hackett Fischer, *The Revolution of American Conservatism: The Federalist Party in the Era of Jeffersonian Democracy* (Chicago: University of Chicago Press, 1965); Linda Kerber, *Federalists in Dissent; Imagery and Ideology in Jeffersonian America* (Ithaca, N.Y.: Cornell University Press, 1970); James Banner, *To the Hartford Convention: The Federalists and the Origin of Party Politics in Massachusetts, 1789–1815* (New York: Knopf, 1970); Alan Taylor, *William Cooper's Town: Power and Persuasion on the Early American Frontier* (New York: Vintage, 1996); Doron Ben-Atar and Barbara B. Oberg, eds., *Federalists Reconsidered* (Charlottesville: University of Virginia Press, 1998); Seth Cotlar, "The Federalists' Transatlantic Cultural Offensive of 1798 and the Moderation of American Democratic Discourse," in *Beyond the Founders: New Approaches to the Political History of the Early American Republic*, ed. Jeffrey L. Pasley, Andrew W. Robertson, and David Waldstreicher (Chapel Hill: University of North Carolina Press, 2004), 274–99; Rachel Hope Cleves, *The Reign of Terror in America: Visions of Violence from Anti-Jacobinism to Antislavery* (Cambridge: Cambridge University Press, 2009); Seth Cotlar, *Tom Paine's America: The Rise and Fall of Transatlantic Radicalism in the Early Republic* (Charlottesville: University of Virginia Press, 2011), 82–114.

3. Henry Dearborn of Massachusetts as secretary of war, Levi Lincoln of Massachusetts as attorney general, Gideon Granger of Connecticut as postmaster general. Richard E. Ellis, *The Jeffersonian Crisis: Courts and Politics in the Young Republic* (New York: Oxford University Press, 1971), 30–31. For Jeffersonian politics in New England, see Jeffrey Pasley, *"The Tyranny of Printers": Newspaper Politics in the Early American Republic* (Charlottesville: University of Virginia Press, 2001); Paul Goodman, *The Democratic-Republicans of Massachusetts* (Cambridge, Mass.: Harvard University Press, 1964); Nobel Cunningham, *The Jeffersonian Republicans in Power: Party Operations, 1801–1809* (Chapel Hill: University of North Carolina Press, 1963),

125–47; Richard Purcell, *Connecticut in Transition, 1775–1818* (Washington, D.C.: American Historical Association, 1918).

4. See David Waldstreicher, *Runaway America: Benjamin Franklin, Slavery, and the American Revolution* (New York: Hill and Wang, 2004), 175–224 and Patricia Bradley, *Slavery, Propaganda, and the American Revolution* (Jackson: University Press of Mississippi, 1998).

5. David Brion Davis, *The Problem of Slavery in the Age of Revolution, 1770–1823* (Ithaca, N.Y.: Cornell University Press, 1975); Christopher Brown, *Moral Capital: Foundations of British Abolitionism* (Chapel Hill: University of North Carolina Press, 2006)

6. The 1800 Census counted slaves in only two New England states: Connecticut (951, .38 percent of the population) and Rhode Island (380 slaves, .55 percent). Both states had seen significant declines in their slave population since 1790 (Connecticut: 2,648 slaves, 1.11 percent of the population; Rhode Island, 958 slaves; 1.39 percent). In contrast, absolute numbers of slaves remained relatively constant in New York and New Jersey between 1790 and 1800.

7. Stephen Innes, *Creating the Commonwealth: The Economic Culture of Puritan New England* (New York: Norton, 1995), chap. 7; Jay Coughtry, *The Notorious Triangle: Rhode Island and the African Slave Trade, 1700–1807* (Philadelphia: Temple University Press, 1981); Joanne Pope Melish, *Disowning Slavery: Gradual Emancipation and "Race" in New England, 1780–1860* (Ithaca, N.Y.: Cornell University Press, 1998); John Wood Sweet, *Bodies Politic: Negotiating Race in the American North, 1730–1830* (Baltimore: Johns Hopkins University Press, 2003); Bernard Bailyn, *The Ideological Origins of the American Revolution* (Cambridge, Mass.: Harvard University Press, 1967), 232–46; Arthur Zilversmit, *The First Emancipation: The Abolition of Slavery in the North* (Chicago: University of Chicago Press, 1967), 124; Matthew Mason, *Slavery and Politics in the Early American Republic* (Chapel Hill: University of North Carolina Press, 2006), 27; James D. Essig, *The Bonds of Wickedness: American Evangelicals Against Slavery, 1770–1808* (Philadelphia: Temple University Press, 1982), chap. 5.

8. Jefferson to Madison, September 17, 1800, Jefferson Papers, AMLC. For biographies of Lincoln, see William Lincoln, *History of Worcester, Massachusetts* (Worcester: C. Hersey, 1862) 193-197, Marvin Petroelje, "Levi Lincoln, Sr., Jeffersonian Republican of Massachusetts" (Ph.D. dissertation, Michigan State University, 1969); Paul David Nelson, "Lincoln, Levi," *ANB*

9. Arguing on behalf of James Somerset in 1772, William Davy supposedly claimed that "[A]ny slave being once in England, the very air made him a free man" while Francis Hargrave described England as "a soil whose air is deemed too pure for slaves to breathe in it." Both men referred to *Cartwright's Case* (ca. 1569), where this description of English air as "too pure" for slavery seems to have originated. See George William Van Cleve, "*Somerset's Case* and Its Antecedents in Imperial Perspective," *Law and History Review* 24, 3 (Fall 2006), 601–645; 627 on Davy and 614 on *Cartwright*; Hargrave in *Somerset v. Stewart* (1772) 1 Lofft 3. Brief of Levi Lincoln in the Slave Case Tried 1781," *Massachusetts Historical Society Collections* 5th ser. 3 (1877): 438–42.

10. *Somerset* occurred when Charles Stewart sought to force his slave James Somerset, who had been purchased in Virginia and traveled with his master to England by way of Massachusetts, onto a ship bound for Jamaica, where Somerset would be sold. In its narrowest terms, the *Somerset* decision simply ruled that Stewart could not forcibly compel Somerset to leave England; Somerset (and presumably any slave) could appeal to the court on a writ of habeas corpus against the use of such coercion. Thus, in its narrowest terms, the decision was quite limited. But the implications of *Somerset* were far reaching, threatening the status of slave property throughout the empire. Effectively, Mansfield ruled that slavery could exist only by positive law, and

thus a slave in one jurisdiction might be able to seek freedom in another, where there was no positive law upholding slavery. This created a conflict of laws between England and slaveholding colonies, and potentially between separate colonies (with different positive laws regarding slavery) as well. In its broadest sense, *Somerset* allowed lawyers to invoke a natural law of freedom against the positive law of slavery. In both respects, *Somerset* had a significant influence on American antislavery legal and political argument. See William M. Wiecek, "Lord Mansfield and the Legitimacy of Slavery in the Anglo-American World," *University of Chicago Law Review* 42, 1 (Autumn 1974): 86–146; William M. Wiecek, *The Sources of Antislavery Constitutionalism in America, 1760–1848* (Ithaca, N.Y.: Cornell University Press, 1977), 20–39; Van Cleve, "*Somerset's Case* and Its Antecedents"; George William Van Cleve, *A Slaveholder's Union: Slavery, Politics, and the Constitution in the Early American Republic* (Chicago: University of Chicago Press, 2010), 31–34; David Waldstreicher, *Slavery's Constitution: From Revolution to Ratification* (New York: Hill and Wang, 2009), 21–56; Justin B. Dyer, *Natural Law and the Antislavery Constitutional Tradition* (Cambridge: Cambridge University Press, 2012), 37–73.

11. On the Quock Walker cases see John D. Cushing, "The Cushing Court and the Abolition of Slavery in Massachusetts: More Notes on the 'Quock Walker Case'" *American Journal of Legal History* 5, 2 (April 1961): 118–44; William O'Brien, S.J., "Did the Jennison Case Outlaw Slavery in Massachusetts?" *WMQ* 3rd ser. 17, 2 (April 1960): 219–41; Arthur Zilversmit, "Quok Walker, Mumbet, and the Abolition of Slavery in Massachusetts" *WMQ* 3rd ser. 25, 4 (October 1968): 614–24; Zilversmit, *The First Emancipation*, 113–15; Robert M. Spector, "The Quock Walker Cases (1781–1783): Slavery, Its Abolition, and Negro Citizenship in Early Massachusetts," *Journal of Negro History* 53, 1 (January 1968): 12–32; Robert Cover, *Justice Accused: Antislavery and the Judicial Process* (New Haven, Conn.: Yale University Press, 1975), 43–50; Thea K. Hunter, "Publishing Freedom, Winning Arguments: Natural Rights and Massachusetts Freedom Cases, 1772–1836," Ph.D. dissertation, Columbia University, 2005, chap. 3; Margot Minardi, *Making Slavery History: Abolitionism and the Politics of Memory in Massachusetts* (New York: Oxford, 2010), 17–19. The 1783 case of *Commonwealth v. Jennison* was a criminal case against Jennison for assault. In the Superior Court, Chief Justice William Cushing delivered a charge to the jury stating more explicitly than Lincoln had in 1781 that the Massachusetts Constitution of 1780 was an anti-slavery document.

12. James Madison to Levi Lincoln, October 20 1810, *Papers of James Madison Digital Edition*, ed. J. C. A. Stagg; extract of letter from Ebenezer Seaver to Levi Lincoln, November, 1810, Madison Papers, AMLC; Ebenezer Seaver to Levi Lincoln, January 3, 1811; Caesar A. Rodney to Levi Lincoln, January 11, 1811 Lincoln Family Papers, AAS; see also Jefferson to Gallatin, September 27 1810, Jefferson to Madison, October 15 1810, Jefferson Papers, AMLC; and Morgan D. Dowd, "Justice Joseph Story and the Politics of Appointment," *American Journal of Legal History* 9, 4 (October 1965), 265–85.

13. For Lincoln's refusal of the appointment, see Lincoln to Madison, November 27, 1810, January 20, 1811, Madison Papers, AMLC. Van Cleve, *A Slaveholder's Union*; Paul Finkelman, *An Imperfect Union: Slavery, Federalism, and Comity* (Chapel Hill: University of North Carolina Press, 1981), chaps. 1–3; Emily Blanck, "Seventeen Eighty-Three: The Turning Point in the Law of Slavery and Freedom in Massachusetts," *New England Quarterly* 75, 1 (March 2002): 24–51. As Blanck notes, the Supreme Judicial Court also refused to enlist state power to aid in rendition of fugitive slaves.

14. Goodman, *Democratic-Republicans of Massachusetts*, 73–78.

15. *The Virginia Chronicle* . . . (Norfolk, Va.: Prentis and Baxter, 1790), 21. On Leland, see Lyman Butterfield, "Elder John Leland, Jeffersonian Itinerant," *Proceedings of the American*

Antiquarian Society 62, pt. 2 (1952): 155–242; Nathan O. Hatch, *The Democratization of American Christianity* (New Haven, Conn.: Yale University Press, 1989), 93–101; Jeffrey Pasley, "The Cheese and the Words: Popular Political Culture and Participatory Democracy in the Early American Republic," in *Beyond the Founders: New Approaches to the Political History of the Early American Republic*, ed. Jeffrey L. Pasley, Andrew Robertson, and David Waldstreicher (Chapel Hill: University of North Carolina Press, 2004). A short autobiography and biography, along with many of Leland's speeches, pamphlets, and sermons, can be found in *The Writings of the Late Elder John Leland*, ed. L. F. Greene (New York: G.W. Wood, 1845).

16. For the evangelicals in Virginia, see Wesley M. Gewher, *The Great Awakening in Virginia, 1740–1790* (Gloucester, Mass.: Peter Smith, 1965 [1930]), 116; Thomas E. Buckley, S.J., *Church and State in Revolutionary Virginia, 1776–1787* (Charlottesville: University of Virginia Press, 1977) and *Establishing Religious Freedom: Jefferson's Statute in Virginia* (Charlottesville: University of Virginia Press, 2013); Rhys Isaac, *The Transformation of Virginia, 1740–1790* (Chapel Hill: University of North Carolina Press, 1982). On Leland and Madison, see "Madison's Election to the First Federal Congress, October 1788–February 1789," *Papers of James Madison Digital Edition*. Leland called Jefferson his hero in *A Blow at the Root, Being a Fashionable Feast-Day Sermon, Delivered at Cheshire April 9th 1801* (New London, Conn.: Joseph Huntington for Charles Holt, 1801), 32.

17. *The Rights of Conscience Inalienable* . . . (New London, Conn.: T. Green & Son, 1791), 7, 17; Brandon O'Brien, "From Soul Liberty to Self-Reliance: John Leland and the Evangelical Origins of Radical Individualism," *American Baptist Quarterly* 27, 2 (Summer 2008): 136–50; Staughton Lynd, *Intellectual Origins of American Radicalism* (New York: Pantheon, 1968), chap. 1. On Baptists and Republicans in New England, see Goodman, *Democratic-Republicans of Massachusetts*, 86–87, 94; Banner, *To the Hartford Convention*, 208–15; Purcell, *Connecticut in Transition*, 66–81, 92–97; and especially William McLoughlin, *New England Dissent: The Baptists and the Separation of Church and State* (Cambridge, Mass.: Harvard University Press, 1971), 2 vols. McLoughlin views Leland as an eccentric among New England Baptists (2: 929), and while he notes multiple points of alliance between evangelicals and the Republican cause, he also depicts significant differences. Many evangelicals were skeptical of deists within the Republican movement, while many Massachusetts Unitarian Republicans were skeptical of Baptists and were not, like Leland, firm advocates of disestablishment. And in many ways, as McLoughlin argues, the majority of Republicans were in favor of "establishing" a religion—Protestantism. They simply disagreed about whether or not to use state taxation to support Protestant denominations (see 1: 594). But these caveats aside, there was no doubt that resistance to Federalist clergy and the Federalist suppression of "conscience," especially in Connecticut, became a unifying cause among Republicans.

18. Leland, *A Blow at the Root*, 32; *The Virginia Chronicle* . . . (Norfolk, Va.: Prentis and Baxter, 1790), quotes at 10, 11, 8, 10, 11; *Letter of Valediction on Leaving Virginia, in 1791* is printed as an addition to *The Yankee Spy* . . . (Boston: Asplund, 1794). For the 1789 Baptist General Committee meeting, see Essig, *The Bonds of Wickedness*, 68, and Greene, ed., *Writings*, 51. Leland decried Christian injustice toward Native Americans as well. "Because the nation of Israel had a divine grant of the land of Canaan, and orders to enslave the heathen, some suppose Christians have an equal right to take away the land of the Indians, and make slaves of the negroes. Wretched religion, that pleads for cruelty and injustice" (*Virginia Chronicle*, 37).

19. Tim Matthewson, "Abraham Bishop, 'The Rights of Black Men,' and the American Reaction to the Haitian Revolution," *Journal of Negro History* 67, 2 (Summer 1982): 148–54, 150. Bishop's essays originally appeared in *The Argus* (Boston), under the pseudonym J. P. Martin, on

November 22, 25, and December 2, 1791. The quote is from the November 22 issue. See also Ashli White, *Encountering Revolution: Haiti and the Making of the Early Republic* (Baltimore: Johns Hopkins University Press, 2010), 134–36.

20. Matthewson, "Abraham Bishop," 151, reprinting *The Argus*, November 25, 1791.

21. Laurent DuBois, *Avengers of the New World: The Story of the Haitian Revolution* (Cambridge, Mass.: Harvard University Press, 2004), 163–70; Jeremy Popkin, *"You Are All Free": The Haitian Revolution and the Abolition of Slavery* (Cambridge: Cambridge University Press, 2010) 289–326; Robin Blackburn, *The American Crucible: Slavery, Emancipation, and Human Rights* (London: Verso, 2011), 238–39; Cotlar, *Tom Paine's America*, 55–67.

22. On Lyon, see *AC*, 5th Cong., 2nd Sess., 656–70; Ronald Lettieri, "Bacon, John," *ANB*; Bacon in *AC*, 7th Cong., 2nd Sess., 467–69.

23. *Independent Chronicle* March 2–March 5, 1801. The author of this piece, a paean to independent farmers titled "For the Chronicle," qualified his antislavery argument by noting that "the slave of another state is considered as the property of his owner—and it is only by time, by prudence and extreme moderation that this evil can be corrected." Melish, *Disowning Slavery*; but see also Minardi, *Making Slavery History*, 34–42, for the antislavery potential of narratives of a "free" New England.

24. Spector, "The Quock Walker Cases," 29–31; John P. Kaminski, ed., *A Necessary Evil? Slavery and the Debate over the Constitution* (Madison, Wis.: Madison House, 1995), 67–114; John Craig Hammond, "'We are to be reduced to the level of slaves': Planters, Taxes, Aristocrats, and Massachusetts Antifederalists, 1787–1788," *Historical Journal of Massachusetts* (Summer 2003); Robin Einhorn, "Patrick Henry's Case Against the Constitution: The Structural Problem with Slavery," *JER* 22, 4 (Winter 2002): 549–73

25. Joseph Bradley Varnum to George Washington Varnum, December 8, 1797, Huntington Manuscripts 4761, HL

26. Samuel Morse to Ephraim Kirby, July 2, 1800, Ephraim Kirby Papers, RDU; on Morse see Pasley, *"Tyranny of Printers"*, 162–64; Torringford toast in *American Mercury*, March 19, 1801.

27. *Independent Chronicle*, July 3–7 1800. Edward Rushton was identified as the author of this poem, which he titled "American Independency," in Rushton, *Poems* (London: T. Ostell, 1806). The poem appears to have first made an appearance in the United States, under the title "Stanzas on the Anniversary of the American Revolution" via the pamphlet *Liberty Scraps* (Liverpool, s.n., 1794), which contained a number of poems sympathetic to the French Revolution and critical of slavery. No author was noted in that publication. The poem was reprinted in a number of American papers in 1795, also without an author. See, e.g., *Independent Gazetteer* (Philadelphia) July 11, 1795 and *Columbian Centinel* October 14, 1795 (which acknowledged *Liberty Scraps*). In 1800 the *Chronicle* retitled the poem as "On the Fourth of July" and acknowledged neither Rushton nor *Liberty Scraps*. Rushton was acknowledged as the author of the poem in the Liverpool *Time-Piece* of July 3, 1797, and at least one American paper published the poem with attribution to Rushton before the release of *Poems* in 1806 (*Rhode-Island Republican*, December 26, 1801; my gratitude to Paul Baines of Liverpool University for this information). By 1807, presumably because of the publication of *Poems* in 1806, American papers now regularly identified Rushton as the author. See *City Gazette and Daily Advertiser* (Charleston), August 22, 1807 and *The Balance and Columbian Repository*, September 8, 1807. For more on Rushton, see Paul Baines, ed., *The Collected Writings of Edward Rushton* (Liverpool: Liverpool University Press, 2014) and Franca Dellarosa, *Talking Revolution: Edward Rushton's Rebellious Poetics, 1782–1814* (Liverpool: Liverpool University Press, 2014). For more examples of

Republican antislavery, see Cotlar, *Tom Paine's America*, 49–81; Douglas Bradburn, *The Citizen-ship Revolution: Politics and the Creation of the American Union 1774–1804* (Charlottesville: University of Virginia Press, 2009), 107–9, 186–87.

28. *AC*, 4th Cong., 2nd Sess., 2015–24.

29. Abraham Bishop, *Connecticut Republicanism: An Oration on the Extent and Power of Political Delusion* (Philadelphia: Matthew Carey, 1800), 6. For biographies of Bishop, see David Waldstreicher and Stephen R. Grossbart, "Abraham Bishop's Vocation; or, the Mediation of Jeffersonian Politics," *JER* 18, 4 (Winter 1998): 617–57; Grossbart, "Abraham Bishop: Teacher, Lawyer, Orator, Politician," in *The Human Tradition in Antebellum America*, ed. Michael Morrison (Wilmington, Del.: Scholarly Resources, 2000), 1–17; and Franklin B. Dexter, "Abraham Bishop and His Writings," *Proceedings of the Massachusetts Historical Society* 2nd ser. 19 (March 1905): 190–99. For descriptions of the Phi Beta Kappa episode see Bishop, *Oration Delivered in Wallingford . . .* (New Haven, Conn.: William W. Morse, 1801), appendix; Grossbart and Waldstreicher, "Abraham Bishop's Vocation," 635–36; Grossbart, "Abraham Bishop," 1–3; Marta Wagner, "The American Scholar in the Early National Period: The Changing Context of College Education, 1782–1837," Ph.D. dissertation, Yale University, 1983, 1–10. The figure 1,500 was Bishop's estimate of the crowd.

30. Bishop, *Connecticut Republicanism*, 6; Samuel Morse to Ephraim Kirby, July 2, 1800; Philo Murray to Kirby, September 21, 1801, Kirby Papers; Pasley, *"Tyranny of Printers"*, 162–66.

31. Bishop, *Connecticut Republicanism*, 66, 68, 6.

32. Bishop, *Connecticut Republicanism*, 19; Bishop, *Oration in Wallingford*, 105, 107; Bishop, *Proofs of a Conspiracy Against Christianity and the Government of the United States* (Hartford, Conn.: Babcock, 1802), 42.

33. For Bishop's "modern" understanding of culture, see Gordon Wood, *The Radicalism of the American Revolution* (New York: Vintage, 1993), 271. "Autonomy" had other liabilities, as François Furstenberg had shown. It led many early national Americans to view slavery as a condition one could accept, and therefore deserve, through failure to resist. See Furstenberg, "Beyond Freedom and Slavery: Autonomy, Virtue, and Resistance in Early American Political Discourse," *JAH* 89, 4 (March 2003); Furstenberg, *In the Name of the Father: Washington's Legacy, Slavery, and the Making of a Nation* (New York: Penguin, 2006), 187–222. Bishop explicitly adopted this conception of slavery in a later essay, although he did not apply it specifically to slavery in the United States: "A man, born free and who tamely submits to slavery, is unspeakably contemptible" (*Proofs of a Conspiracy*, 122–23).

34. Grossbart, "Abraham Bishop," 14; Bayard in *AC*, 5th Cong., 2nd Sess., 1229, as cited in Donald Robinson, *Slavery in the Structure of American Politics, 1765–1820* (New York: Harcourt Brace, 1971), 388.

35. "A Plain Fact," *Mercury and New-England Palladium*, January 20, 1801.

36. Fessenden as cited in Kerber, *Federalists in Dissent*, 52; John Quincy Adams in Linda K. Kerber and Walter John Morris, "Politics and Literature: The Adams Family and the Port Folio," *WMQ* 3rd ser. 23, 3 (Jul. 1966): 450–76, 457. See also Pasley, *"Tyranny of Printers"*, 256–57.

37. For relatively dismissive views of Federalist antislavery, see Sean Wilentz, *The Rise of American Democracy: Jefferson to Lincoln* (New York: Norton, 2005), 162; Wilentz, "The Details of Greatness: American Historians Versus American Founders," *New Republic* 230 (March 29, 2004); John Kyle Day, "The Federalist Press and Slavery in the Age of Jefferson," *The Historian: A Journal of History* 65 (2003). For more positive evaluations, see Garry Wills, *Negro President: Jefferson and the Slave Power* (Boston: Houghton Mifflin, 2003); Paul Finkelman, "The Problem

of Slavery in the Age of Federalism," *Federalists Reconsidered*, ed. Doron Ben-Atar and Barbara Oberg (Charlottesville: University of Virginia Press, 1998); Anthony Iaccarino, "Virginia and the National Contest Over Slavery in the Early Republic, 1780–1833," Ph.D. dissertation, University of California, Los Angeles, 1999, 100–102; Rachel Hope Cleves, "'Hurtful to the State': The Political Morality of Federalist Antislavery," *Contesting Slavery: The Politics of Bondage and Freedom in the New American Nation* (Charlottesville: University of Virginia Press, 2011), 207–26; Cleves, *The Reign of Terror in America*, chap. 3; and Linda Kerber's classic portrait in *Federalists in Dissent*. For Federalist aspersion of slaves, see, e.g., *Columbian Centinel*, January 3, 1800; for Federalist association of slave rebellions with Jacobin influence, see *Massachusetts Mercury*, September 30, 1800; *Columbian Centinel*, October 1, 1800.

38. Lincoln to Jefferson, June 28, 1802 ("that difficult part of the country"); Jefferson to Lincoln, July 11, 1801 ("sap the republic by fraud"); Lincoln to Jefferson, October 29, 1802 ("never be countenanced"); Jefferson to Lincoln, October 25, 1802 ("abyss"); Jefferson Papers, AMLC; on the *Aegis* and the "Farmer's letters" see Lincoln to Jefferson September 16, 1801, ibid.; see also Pasley, *"Tyranny of Printers"*, 203–15.

39. Levi Lincoln, *A Farmer's Letters to the People* (Salem, Mass., 1802), 13, 67, 70, 51. The letters began running in Worcester's *Massachusetts Spy* on August 19, 1801; later numbers were published in the *Aegis*. The *Palladium* first ran as a continuation of the *Massachusetts Mercury*, under the title *The Mercury and New-England Palladium* (beginning January 2, 1801); in 1803 it was renamed *New-England Palladium*.

40. *National Aegis*, March 24, February 24, 1802.

41. Nahum Mitchell to K. Whitman, January 19, 1804, Nahum Mitchell Papers, MHS.

42. *The Writings of John Quincy Adams*, ed. Worthington C. Ford (New York: Macmillan, 1914), 3: 70. The "Publius" articles appeared in *The Repertory* in October and November 1804. Leonard Richards, *The Slave Power: The Free North and Southern Domination* (Baton Rouge: Louisiana State University Press, 2000), 43–45; Albert F. Simpson, "The Political Significance of Slave Representation, 1787–1821," *Journal of Southern History* 7, 3 (August 1941): 315–42.

43. Elbridge Gerry to Thomas Jefferson October 27, 1803, Jefferson Papers, AMLC. Gerry likely referred to Connecticut, New Hampshire, and Massachusetts. *Independent Chronicle*, January 17, 24, 31, February 14, 1805; see also February 28, April 18, 1805 for more commentary.

44. *The Writings of John Quincy Adams*, 3: 70–73.

45. *AC*, 4th Cong., 2nd Sess., 2021.

46. *The Mercury and New-England Palladium*, March 31, 1801; October 20, 1801; November 19, 1802.

47. Webster to Rush, December 15, 1800, Henry R. Warfel ed., *Letters* (New York: Library Publishers, 1953), 227–28; Fischer, *Revolution of American Conservatism*, 24; Samuel Morse to Ephraim Kirby, July 2, 1800, Kirby Papers, RDU. For this more sympathetic view of Federalism, see Kerber, *Federalists in Dissent* and especially Cleves, *The Reign of Terror in America*.

48. Pasley, *"Tyranny of Printers"*, 142.

49. Republicans in Massachusetts benefited significantly from Jefferson's rise to the presidency when one looks at congressional representation. In the last two Congresses before Jefferson's election, they held only 3 of 14 seats. But in the 7th Congress, which sat in 1801, they held 6 of 14 seats; in the 8th, 7 of 17, in the 9th, 10 of 17, in the 10th, 11 of 17. They dropped to 8 of 17 in the 11th and 9 of 17 in the 12th, before declining abruptly after the onset of the War of 1812: 4 of 20 seats in the 13th Congress (1813–1815); 2 of 20 in the 14th. After that sharp decline, however, they regained their Jeffersonian era numbers. Vermont, Rhode Island, and New Hampshire followed a similar

pattern: Republicans became competitive during Jefferson's presidency, Federalists made significant gains after the embargo of 1807 and during the war, but Republicans rebounded after 1815. The exception was Connecticut, whose congressional contingent was dominated by Federalists until the 16th Congress of 1819–1820. See Kenneth C. Martis, *The Historical Atlas of Political Parties in the United States Congress, 1789–1989* (New York: Macmillan, 1989).

50. Cheshire also voted for the Republican gubernatorial candidate in Massachusetts by similar margins in every election from 1800 to 1808. See Butterfield, "Elder John Leland," 215–16.

51. See *Philadelphia Aurora*, August 8, 1801, copying an article from the *Rhode Island Impartial Observer*. See also Butterfield, "Elder John Leland," 219–23 for other examples. Jeffrey Pasley argues that the sobriquet "mammoth" was initially coined as a Federalist insult, a mockery of Jefferson's penchant for "mammoth" fossils, but appropriated by Republicans who went on to produce other mammoth foodstuffs (Pasley, "The Cheese and the Words," 33).

52. Jefferson to Thomas Mann Randolph, January 1, 1802, Jefferson to Danbury Baptist Association January 1, 1802, Jefferson Papers, AMLC; Butterfield, "Elder John Leland," 223; Daniel L. Dreisbach, "Mr. Jefferson, a Mammoth Cheese, and the 'Wall of Separation Between Church and State': A Bicentennial Commemoration," *Journal of Church and State* 43, 4 (Autumn 2001): 725–46.

53. *Life, Journals, and Correspondence of Reverend Manasseh Cutler*, ed. William Parker Cutler and Julia Perkins Cutler (Cincinnati: Robert Clarke, 1888), 2: 55, 58–59, 66–67; William Plumer, *William Plumer's Memorandum of Proceedings in the United States Senate, 1803–1807*, ed. Everett Somerville Brown (New York: Macmillan, 1923), 213. The dinner took place on December 3, 1804. The company was composed chiefly of Federalists, so the cheese was likely intended to provoke. Samuel Taggart to John Taylor, December 3, 1804, "Letters of Samuel Taggart . . . Part One," *Proceedings of the American Antiquarian Society* 33 pt. 1 (April 1923), 140.

54. See Butterfield, "Elder John Leland" 224, for the address. Pasley, "The Cheese and the Words," 35.

55. Lucia Stanton, "A Well-Ordered Household: Domestic Servants in Jefferson's White House" *White House History* 17 (2006): 5–23; Stanton, "'Those Who Labor for My Happiness': Thomas Jefferson's Family and the Transformation of American Politics," in *Jeffersonian Legacies*, ed. Peter S. Onuf (Charlottesville: University of Virginia Press, 1993), 147–80.

56. "Articles of Merchandise" referred to the fact that all citizens in Massachusetts were still compelled to pay a tax to support the Congregational ministry. Legally, dissenters could attempt to reclaim their share of the tax and apply it to their own churches. Tax exemption for dissenters was made easier under an 1811 law, but Republicans did not achieve complete disestablishment for another two decades. William McLoughlin contends that well before disestablishment in Massachusetts, only Congregationalists or nonadherents were being taxed, but men like Leland were indignant at the very idea of religious establishment. See Goodman, *Democratic-Republicans of Massachusetts*, 87–88, 164–65; McLoughlin, *New England Dissent*, 1: 684; Leland, *An Oration Delivered at Cheshire, Massachusetts* (Hudson, N.Y.: Charles Holt, 1802), 14–15.

57. *American Mercury*, March 19, 1801. On the celebration at Wallingford, see David Waldstreicher, *In the Midst of Perpetual Fetes: The Making of American Nationalism, 1776–1820* (Chapel Hill: University of North Carolina Press, 1997), 244–45; Waldstreicher and Grossbart, "Abraham Bishop's Vocation," 646–49; Grossbart, "Abraham Bishop," 11.

58. Abraham Bishop, *Oration in Wallingford . . .* (New Haven, Conn.: William Morse, 1801), iv, 29, 22. Bishop extended his attack on religious establishment in New England the following year, in *Proofs of a Conspiracy Against Christianity and the Government of the United States . . .* (Hartford, Conn.: John Babcock, 1802).

59. Bishop, *Oration in Wallingford*, iv, 96–97.

60. *American Mercury*, March 19, 1801.

61. Abraham Bishop, "The Porpoises of Connecticut," No. 7, *American Mercury*, February 24, 1803, as cited in Waldstreicher and Grossbart, "Abraham Bishop's Vocation," 648; Bishop, *Proofs of a Conspiracy*, 165. John Leland simply misunderstood the three-fifths clause: in his mind, it was a sign that the federal government, more benevolent than some southern state governments, at least recognized the slave was "three-fifths of a man" (Leland, *Writings*, 96). Connecticut retained a forty-shilling freehold requirement for the suffrage until the Republicans modified it in the new state constitution of 1818, allowing all white men who had a $7 freehold, paid taxes or served in the militia access to the vote. Yet the earlier property requirement often appears to have gone unenforced, especially in highly partisan elections. See Ratcliffe, "The Right to Vote," 226, 242–44.

62. *Independent Chronicle*, March 2–5, 9–12, 1801.

63. *Independent Chronicle*, February 23–26, 1801; *Columbian Centinel*, December 27, 1800; see also December 24, 1800, and January 3, 1801, for other examples.

64. Bishop, *An Oration at Wallingford*, 50, iii–iv.

Chapter 2. Philadelphia, Crossroads of Democracy

1. "Thomas Paine, to the People of England," *Aurora General Advertiser*, March 6, 1804.

2. Jefferson to Henry Remsen, October 14, 1799; Jefferson to Stevens Thomson Mason, October 27, 1799; Jefferson to Charles Pinckney, October 29, 1799, *PTJ*, vol. 31, 211, 223, 226–28.

3. Clay as cited by Pennsylvania's John Sergeant, *AC*, 16th Cong., 1st Sess., 1174.

4. On the PAS, see Gary Nash and Jean Soderlund, *Freedom by Degrees: Emancipation in Pennsylvania and Its Aftermath* (New York: Oxford University Press, 1991); Richard S. Newman, *The Transformation of American Abolitionism: Fighting Slavery in the Early Republic* (Chapel Hill: University of North Carolina Press, 2002). On Washington's slaves, see Don E. Fehrenbacher, *The Slaveholding Republic: An Account of the United States Government's Relations to Slavery* (New York: Oxford University Press, 2001), 59, 205–6; on cross-border tensions, see Stanley Harrold, *Border War: Fighting over Slavery Before the Civil War* (Chapel Hill: University of North Carolina Press, 2010), 17–34.

5. On African Americans and race in Pennsylvania, see Edward Raymond Turner, *The Negro in Pennsylvania: Slavery, Servitude, Freedom* (Washington, D.C.: AHA, 1911); Gary Nash, *Forging Freedom: The Formation of Philadelphia's Black Community, 1720–1840* (Cambridge, Mass.: Harvard University Press, 1988); Julie Winch, *Philadelphia's Black Elite: Activism, Accommodation, and the Struggle for Autonomy, 1787–1848* (Philadelphia: Temple University Press, 1993); Winch, *A Gentleman of Color: The Life of James Forten* (New York: Oxford University Press, 2003); Samuel Otter, *Philadelphia Stories: America's Literature of Race and Freedom* (New York: Oxford University Press, 2010). On the unfinished nature of the first emancipation, see Steven Hahn, *The Political Worlds of Slavery and Freedom* (Cambridge, Mass.: Harvard University Press, 2009), 1–54.

6. On the concept of political "standing," see Judith N. Shklar, *American Citizenship: The Quest for Inclusion* (Cambridge, Mass.: Harvard University Press, 1991).

7. Eric Foner, *Tom Paine and Revolutionary America* (New York: Oxford University Press, 1976)

8. There is considerable confusion about Duane's birthplace. Most sources claim Duane was born in colonial New York, which Duane asserted in U.S. federal court in 1801. However, his own counsel admitted on that occasion, "the only proof of the place of his birth arose from his

own declarations to some of the witnesses." See *Hollingsworth v. Duane*, 12 Fed. Cas. No. 6,615. More recently, historian Nigel Little has discovered an East India Company record that lists Duane's birthplace as St. John's, Newfoundland. See Little, *Transoceanic Radical: William Duane, National Identity, and Empire, 1760–1835* (London: Pickering and Chatto, 2008), 18, 63, 88.

9. Studies of Duane include the excellent work of Kim Phillips, "William Duane, Revolutionary Editor," Ph.D. dissertation, University of California, Berkeley, 1968, reprinted with same pagination as *William Duane, Radical Journalist in the Age of Jefferson* (New York: Garland, 1989); Jeffrey Pasley, *"The Tyranny of Printers": Newspaper Politics in the Early American Republic* (Charlottesville: University of Virginia Press, 2001); Andrew Shankman, *Crucible of American Democracy: The Struggle to Fuse Egalitarianism and Capitalism in Jeffersonian Pennsylvania* (Lawrence: University Press of Kansas, 2004); Little, *Transoceanic Radical*. For Duane's parting editorial, see Phillips, "William Duane," 31.)

10. *Aurora General Advertiser*, December 21, 1799

11. On Bache, see Jeffery A. Smith, *Franklin and Bache: Envisioning the Enlightened Republic* (New York: Oxford University Press, 1990) and James Tagg, *Benjamin Franklin Bache and the Philadelphia Aurora* (Philadelphia: University of Pennsylvania Press, 1991). On the transatlantic character of Jeffersonian democracy, see Richard Twomey, *Jacobins and Jeffersonians: Anglo-American Radicalism in the United States* (New York: Garland, 1989); Michael Durey, *Transatlantic Radicals and the Early American Republic* (Lawrence: University Press of Kansas, 1997); David Wilson, *United Irishmen, United States: Immigrant Radicals in the Early Republic* (Ithaca, N.Y.: Cornell University Press, 1998); Alan Taylor, *The Civil War of 1812: American Citizens, British Subjects, Irish Rebels, and Indian Allies* (New York: Knopf, 2010); Seth Cotlar, *Tom Paine's America: The Rise and Fall Transatlantic Radicalism in the Early Republic* (Charlottesville: University of Virginia Press, 2011).

12. Jasper Dwight [William Duane], *A Letter to George Washington, President of the United States . . .* (Philadelphia, s.n., 1796), 26, 47–48

13. Edward Rushton, *Expostulatory Letter to George Washington, of Mount Vernon, in Virginia . . .* (Lexington, Ky.: John Bradford, 1797), 6.

14. Henry Adams, *The Life of Albert Gallatin* (Philadelphia: Lippincott, 1879), 86; AC, 5th Cong., 2nd Sess., 656–70; AC, 6th Cong., 1st Sess., 229–45.

15. AC, 5th Cong., 2nd Sess., 660. On Pennsylvania's accommodation of slavery, see Paul Finkelman, *An Imperfect Union: Slavery, Federalism, and Comity* (Chapel Hill: University of North Carolina Press, 1981), 46–69.

16. AC, 4th Cong. 2nd Sess., 1733, 2019. Gallatin also supported anti-kidnapping measures and he introduced the petition that eventually led to the December 1796 debate. See AC 4th Cong., 1st Sess., 1025. For a detailed overview of these debates, see Nicholas P. Wood, "Considerations of Humanity and Expediency: The Slave Trades and African Colonization in the Early National Antislavery Movement," Ph.D. Dissertation, University of Virginia, 2013, 129–144.

17. AC, 5th Cong., 2nd Sess., 659 (Rutledge); AC, 4th Cong., 2nd Sess., 2021 (Smith). For a federalist interpretation of these early slavery conflicts, see Douglas Bradburn, *The Citizenship Revolution: Politics and the Creation of the American Union 1774–1804* (Charlottesville: University of Virginia Press, 2009), 248–56.

18. AC, 5th Cong., 2nd Sess., 1306–12 (Thatcher); 1567 (Harper); John Craig Hammond, *Slavery, Freedom and Expansion in the Early American West* (Charlottesville: University of Virginia Press, 2007), 22–27; Bradburn, *The Citizenship Revolution*, 163.

19. James Sloan, *An Address, Delivered at a Meeting of the Democratic Association* (Trenton,

N.J.: 1801), 18; Bruce Bendler, "James Sloan: Renegade or True Republican?" *New Jersey History* 125, 1 (2010): 1–19; *AC*, 8th Cong., 2nd Sess., 995–96.

20. "John Smilie," in *Irish Immigrants in the Land of Canaan: Letters and Memoirs from Colonial and Revolutionary America*, ed. Kerby A. Miller et al. (New York: Oxford University Press, 2003), 90–94; on Findley, see John Caldwell, *William Findley from West of the Mountains: A Politician in Pennsylvania* (Gig Harbor, Wash.: Red Apple, 2000). Gordon Wood has told the tale of William Findley and the rise of American democracy in "Interests and Disinterestedness in the Making of the Constitution," in *Beyond Confederation: Origins of the Constitution and American National Identity*, ed. Richard Beeman, Stephen Botein, and Edward Carter III (Chapel Hill: University of North Carolina Press, 1987); *The Radicalism of the American Revolution* (New York: Vintage, 1993), 256–59; *Empire of Liberty: A History of the Early Republic, 1789–1815* (New York: Oxford University Press, 2009), 217–22; and *The Idea of America: Reflections on the Birth of the United States* (New York: Penguin, 2011), 150–62.

21. On Sloan's mercantile activities, see Bendler, "James Sloan," 3. Samuel Taggart to John Taylor, November 17, 1804, "Letters of Samuel Taggart . . . Part One," *Proceedings of the American Antiquarian Society* 33, pt. 1 (April 1923): 133–34; *Newburyport Herald*, April 18, 1806.

22. *AC*, 6th Cong., 1st Sess., 229–31.

23. Abraham Bishop, *Connecticut Republicanism: An Oration on the Extent and Power of Political Delusion* (Philadelphia: Matthew Carey, 1800), 6; Lucas in *AC*, 8th Cong., 1st Sess., 1009.

24. Branagan's autobiography is printed in *The Penitential Tyrant; Or, Slave Trader Reformed* (New York: Samuel Wood, 1807), 1–38, 19. Studies of Branagan include Lewis Leary, "Thomas Branagan: Republican Rhetoric and Romanticism in America," *PMHB* 77 (1953): 332–52; Vivien Sanlund, "'To Arouse and Awaken the American People': The Ideas and Strategies of the Gradual Abolitionists, 1800–1850," Ph.D. dissertation, Emory University, 1995; Beverly Tomek, "From Motives of Generosity, as well as Self-Preservation': Thomas Branagan, Colonization, and the Gradual Emancipation Movement," *American Nineteenth Century History* 6, 2 (2005): 121–47; and Christopher Phillips, "Epic, Anti-Eloquence, and Abolitionism: Thomas Branagan's *Avenia* and *The Penitential Tyrant*," *Early American Literature* 44, 3 (2009): 605–37.

25. Thomas Branagan, *Political and Theological Disquisitions on the Signs of the Times* (Trenton, N.J., 1807), 29. For a reading of Branagan as an anti-Jacobin, see Rachel Hope Cleves, *The Reign of Terror in America: Visions of Violence from Anti-Jacobinism to Antislavery* (Cambridge: Cambridge University Press, 2009). On Lay, see David Waldstreicher, *Runaway America: Benjamin Franklin, Slavery, and the American Revolution* (New York: Hill and Wang, 2004), 80–82; David Brion Davis, *The Problem of Slavery in Western Culture* (Ithaca, N.Y.: Cornell University Press, 1966), 320–25.

26. Branagan, *The Penitential Tyrant*, 130.

27. This reading of Branagan and the intersubjective dimension of conscience has been influenced by Thomas Haskell's classic essay, "Capitalism and the Origins of the Humanitarian Sensibility," and the subsequent debate between Haskell, David Brion Davis, and John Ashworth. In contrast to Haskell, I argue that for men like Branagan, democracy as well as capitalism framed the ethical relationship between self and other. And in the context of American democracy, the relationship to distant oppressors, as well as distant "suffering strangers," posed a significant ethical problem. See Thomas Bender, ed., *The Antislavery Debate: Capitalism and Abolitionism as a Problem in Historical Interpretation* (Berkeley: University of California Press, 1992).

28. Thomas Branagan, *Serious Remonstrances, Addressed to Citizens of the Northern States* (Philadelphia: Thomas Stiles, 1805), v-vi; Branagan, *The Penitential Tyrant*, 143. On this point, see Phillips, "Epic, Anti-Eloquence, and Abolitionism."

29. The title page of the 1805 edition of *Avenia* explained that the pamphlet was "printed for Silas Engles . . . and Samuel Wood." See Thomas Branagan, *Avenia: Or, a Tragical Poem, on the Oppression of the Human Species and Infringement of the Rights of Man* (Philadelphia: S. Engles, 1805). The *Penitential Tyrant* was first published in Philadelphia in 1805 by Branagan as a much shorter work. Throughout this chapter, I use the 1807 edition of *Penitential Tyrant* published by Wood, cited in full above, and the 1805 edition of *Avenia*.

30. Thomas Branagan, *Avenia* (Philadelphia: J Cline, 1810). For his antebellum writings, see Thomas Branagan, *The Guardian Genius of the Federal Union . . .* (New York: Thomas Branagan, 1839) and an excerpt from that publication in *The Legion of Liberty and the Force of Truth* (New York: American Antislavery Society, 1842).

31. The *Penitential Tyrant*, iv; xi-xii; on the frontispiece see also Jenna M. Gibbs, *Performing the Temple of Liberty: Slavery, Theater, and Popular Culture in London and Philadelphia, 1760–1850* (Baltimore: Johns Hopkins University Press, 2014), 31–33. The lines on oppression were likely borrowed from Erasmus Darwin's 1791 *The Botanic Garden*, which accosts "YE BANDS OF SENATORS! whose suffrage sways / Britannia's realms . . ." and demands that they accept responsibility for African slavery. Personifying "CONSCIENCE," Darwin implores, "*Hear him, ye Senates! hear this truth sublime, / 'He, who allows Oppression, shares the crime.'*" Erasmus Darwin, *The Botanic Garden* (New York: T.& J. Swords, 1798), 89–90.

32. Thomas Branagan, *A Preliminary Essay on the Oppression of the Exiled Sons of Africa* (Philadelphia, 1804), 93–116; quote on 94.

33. Branagan was moved by the story of Quashi (Furstenberg's quintessential example of the "virtuous slave"), a slave who killed himself in melodramatic fashion rather than submit to unmerited punishment by his master. For Branagan, Quashi demonstrated that "Africans possess the same specific nature with ourselves . . . that they, no less than we, are capable of gratitude and resentment, friendship and honor" (*Preliminary Essay*, 112); François Furstenberg, *In the Name of the Father: Washington's Legacy, Slavery, and the Making of a Nation* (New York: Penguin, 2006), 202–4.

34. *Avenia*, 164–72.

35. Branagan, *Penitential Tyrant*, 130, 227–28.

36. Branagan, *Penitential Tyrant*, 230.

37. Thomas Branagan, *The Beauties of Philanthropy . . .* (New York: G.J. Loomis, 1839), 10. Branagan was referencing John 3:17.

38. Branagan, *Serious Remonstrances*, 112–15, 111.

39. See Branagan, *Serious Remonstrances*, 68–82 for examples of racist imagery. For Branagan's connection to Forten, Jones, and Allen, see *Preliminary Essay*, 284; *Avenia*, 310.

40. Branagan, *Serious Remonstrances*, 70–71.

41. Nash, *Forging Freedom*, 177–82; Gary Nash, *The Forgotten Fifth: African Americans in the Age of Revolution* (Cambridge, Mass.: Harvard University Press, 2006), 141–42; Nash, "Race and Citizenship in the Early Republic," in *Antislavery and Abolition in Philadelphia: Emancipation and the Long Struggle for Racial Justice in the City of Brotherly Love*, ed. Richard Newman and James Mueller (Baton Rouge: Louisiana State University Press, 2011), 90–117; Julie Winch, *A Gentleman of Color: The Life of James Forten* (New York: Oxford University Press, 2003), 169–74; James Forten, "Letters From a Man of Colour," in *Early American Abolitionists: A Collection of*

Antislavery Writings, ed. James G. Basker (New York: Gilder Lehrman, 2005); Nicholas B. Wainwright, ed., "The Diary of Samuel Breck," *PMHB* 102, 4 (October, 1976), 505.

42. Branagan, *Serious Remonstrances*, 79.

43. Key works on whiteness include Alexander Saxton, *The Rise and Fall of the White Republic: Class Politics and Mass Culture in Nineteenth Century America* (London: Verso, 1990); David Roediger, *The Wages of Whiteness: Race and the Making of the American Working Class* (London: Verso, 1991); Noel Ignatiev, *How the Irish Became White* (New York: Routledge, 1995); Theodore Allen, *The Invention of the White Race* (London: Verso, 1994); Matthew Frye Jacobson, *Whiteness of a Different Color: European Immigrants and the Alchemy of Race* (Cambridge, Mass.: Harvard University Press, 1998). For two critical reviews, see Eric Arnesen, "Whiteness and the Historians' Imagination," *International Labor and Working-Class History* 60 (Fall 2001): 3–32 and Peter Kolchin, "Whiteness Studies: The New History of Race in America," *JAH* 89, 1 (June 2002): 154–73.

44. James Morton Smith, *Freedom's Fetters: The Alien and Sedition Laws and American Civil Liberties* (Ithaca, N.Y.: Cornell University Press, 1956), 33–34, 47–49, 61–62, 94–95.

45. Smith, *Freedom's Fetters*, 277–306; Shankman, *Crucible of American Democracy*, 70; Pasley, *"Tyranny of Printers"*, 176–95; Phillips, "William Duane," 54–91; quote from 75, citing *Gazette of the United States* May 16, 1799; Douglas Bradburn, "A Clamor in the Public Mind: Opposition to the Alien and Sedition Acts," *WMQ* 65, 3 (July 2008): 565–600 and Bradburn, *The Citizenship Revolution*, 168–205. Duane was eventually jailed for thirty days, in May of 1801, for contempt of court in a separate case, in which merchant Levi Hollingsworth sued him for libel (see Phillips, "William Duane," 124–30). Duane criticized McPherson's Blues and other militia companies for their role in suppressing Fries Rebellion in spring 1799. On Fries' Rebellion, see Terry Bouton, *Taming Democracy: "The People," the Founders, and the Troubled Ending of the American Revolution* (New York: Oxford University Press, 2007), 244–57.

46. On Republican persistence in the face of the Sedition Act see Pasley, *"Tyranny of Printers"*, 105–31. On Cooper, see Phillips, "William Duane," 91. *Aurora General Advertiser*, December 23, 1806; John Binns, *Recollections of the Life of John Binns* (Philadelphia: Binns and Parry and M'Millan, 1854), 197; Duane to Jefferson, October 19, 1824, Jefferson Papers, LC, as cited in Phillips, "William Duane," 589.

47. In the Hollingsworth case cited above. The case was an action for libel in federal circuit court. The court had jurisdiction based on the premise that Hollingsworth, a citizen, had been defamed by Duane, an alien. Duane biographer Kim Phillips believes the case was brought in order to legally declare Duane an alien. Duane's counsel Alexander Dallas attempted to argue that Duane was an American citizen by virtue of his birth in the colony of New York in 1760. Federalist justice William Tilghman, in a charge to the jury, argued that Duane was born a British subject and that even if he did somehow have a right to American citizenship, he clearly had not taken it up when he became an adult, since he continued to live for over a decade "within the British dominions." The jury was convinced and decided that Duane was "an alien and subject of the King of Great Britain." Phillips, "William Duane," 125–26, 206; *Hollingsworth v. Duane* (1801), 12 Fed. Cos. no. 6,615. Holly Brewer, *By Birth or Consent: Children, Law, and the Anglo-American Revolution in Authority* (Chapel Hill: University of North Carolina Press, 2005), 136. Little, in *Transoceanic Radical*, argues that, based on East India Company records, Duane was born in Newfoundland. No one seems to have had that information in 1801, although there was some suspicion in the Hollingsworth case that Duane might have been born in French Canada rather than the colony of New York.

48. *Aurora General Advertiser*, July 7, 1801. See also Bradburn, *The Citizenship Revolution*, 206–34, on the emergence of the "hyphenated citizen."

49. *The Tickler*, September 16, 1807 ("purely American"), October 7, 1807 (Duane and "imported patriots.") See October 28, 1807, for mockery of one Paddy, "a young scion 'from the land of *potatoes*.'" See also Phillips, "William Duane," 196–97, 232–33. "Scum of Europe" modified Richard III's speech to his army in Act V, Scene III. On Helmbold, see George Helmbold to Thomas Jefferson, April 3, 1801, *PTJ*, vol. 33, 529–30; *The Tickler*, October 12, 1807, in which Helmbold details his previous work for the *Aurora*; and David E. E. Sloane, "The Comic Writers of Philadelphia: George Helmbold's 'The Tickler,' Joseph C. Neal's 'City Worthies,' and the Beginning of Modern Periodical Humor in America," *Victorian Periodicals Review* 28, 3 (Fall 1995), 186–98.

50. Phillips, "William Duane," 191–234. See also Kim Phillips, "William Duane, Philadelphia's Democratic Republicans, and the Origins of Modern Politics," *PMHB* 101, 3 (July 1977): 365–87.

51. "trampled to death": Binns, *Recollections*, 56. Binns claims he chaired the October 26 meeting (53–54); Little, *Transoceanic Radical*, 109, has Duane as a chairman as well; Phillips, "William Duane," 40–46, discusses Duane's involvement in the November 12 meeting.

52. Binns, *Recollections*, 40–140, quotes at 83; Wilson, *United Irishmen, United States*, 26–31.

53. James H. Kettner, *The Development of American Citizenship, 1608–1870* (Chapel Hill: University of North Carolina Press, 1978); Brewer, *By Birth or Consent*; Binns, *Recollections*, 173.

54. Jefferson to Priestley, March 21, 1801, *PTJ*, vol. 33, 393–95. As the editors of *PTJ* note, Jefferson's marginal notes on this letter state that he meant the "Alien Law" by "libel on legislation." This likely referred to the Alien Friends Act, which was far more objectionable to Republicans than the Alien Enemies Act.

55. Wood, *Empire of Liberty*, 287; see also 277 for a defense of Jefferson and his legacy. *Democratic Press*, March 27, 1807.

56. Smith, *Freedom's Fetters*, chaps. 11, 14, 15; Wilson, *United Irishmen, United States*, 100–103; Aleine Austin, *Matthew Lyon, "New Man" of the Democratic Revolution* (University Park: Pennsylvania State University Press, 1981); Lyon quote in *AC*, 8th Cong., 1st Sess., 544; Dumas Malone, *The Public Life of Thomas Cooper, 1783–1839* (New Haven, Conn.: Yale University Press, 1926).

57. *Aurora General Advertiser*, December 23, 1806, December 21, 1799, February 6, 1805.

58. William John Duane to Andrew Jackson, July 19, 1833, as cited in Phillips, "William Duane," 621. The letter to Jackson was never sent, but it was reprinted in William John Duane, *Narrative and Correspondence Concerning the Removal of the Deposites, and Occurrences Connected Therewith* (Philadelphia, 1838).

59. *Aurora General Advertiser*, September 12, 15, 18, 1800 (Jefferson quote), September 22, 1800 ("circumspect philosopher"), September 24, 1800 ("emancipation of the blacks"), September 15, 1803.

60. Rushton, *Expostulary Letter*, 7–8.

61. *Aurora General Advertiser*, December 21, 1799 ("twin sister"), February 14, 1800 ("men of genius"), September 6, 1800 (New England's promotion of "monarchy and church establishments"), September 12, 1800 (Connecticut ruled by an "aristocracy"), September 22, 1800 (Virginia as source of gradual emancipation), September 30, 1800 (Adams v. Jefferson); September 15, 1803 (Virginia as source of religious liberty).

62. *Aurora General Advertiser*, January 17 (copying Carey's *Constitutional Diary* of January 16) and January 23, 1800; Henry Adams, *John Randolph* (Boston: Houghton Mifflin, 1882), 40–43. Duane printed the debates on Absalom Jones's petition on January 8, 15, and 16, 1800.

63. The three major accounts of Gabriel's Rebellion are Douglas Egerton, *Gabriel's Rebellion: The Virginia Slave Conspiracies of 1800 and 1802* (Chapel Hill: University of North Carolina Press, 1993); James Sidbury, *Ploughshares into Swords: Race, Rebellion, and Identity in Gabriel's Virginia, 1730–1810* (Cambridge: Cambridge University Press, 1997); and Michael Nicholls, *Whispers of Rebellion: Narrating Gabriel's Conspiracy* (Charlottesville: University of Virginia Press, 2012). Egerton has argued that Gabriel, a skilled blacksmith who lived just outside Richmond, was able to hire his own time in the city, where he formed relationships to white artisans who believed in republicanism and opposed the Federalist merchants of Richmond. The bitter partisanship leading up to the election of 1800 led Gabriel to develop a largely secular opposition to slavery, in which he identified the Federalist elite of Richmond as his primary enemies. Sidbury and Nicholls dispute many of Egerton's claims, especially the argument that Gabriel appropriated a form of "artisan republicanism" to oppose slavery. Sidbury suggests instead that the rebellion was rooted in the development of an Afro-Virginian identity and black Christianity. All accounts do seem to agree that the rebels had some knowledge of the slave revolt in Saint Domingue.

64. On the newspaper war over Gabriel's Rebellion see Michael Nicholls, " 'Holy Insurrection!': Spinning the News of Gabriel's Conspiracy," *JSH* 78, 1 (February 2012): 37–68 and Nicholls, *Whispers of Rebellion*, 115–16.

65. Randolph to Joseph Nicholson, September 26, 1800 (or, as Randolph dated it, "26 Sept. 25 Independence"), Nicholson Papers, LC; *Aurora General Advertiser*, September 24, 1800.

66. On "diffusion," see Adam Rothman, *Slave Country: American Expansion and the Origins of the Deep South* (Cambridge, Mass.: Harvard University Press, 2005), 24–35; Lacy K. Ford, *Deliver Us from Evil: The Slavery Question in the Old South* (New York: Oxford University Press, 2011), 73–75, 106–7; *Aurora General Advertiser*, October 21, 1803; February 18, 1803; for more cotton boosterism, see February 16, August 5, 1803 (reprinting *The National Intelligencer*).

67. *Aurora General Advertiser*, September 24, 1800.

68. The quote is Branagan's, from *Serious Remonstrances*, 78.

69. The 1802 act required that one declare an intent to become a citizen three years prior; it exempted aliens who resided in the United States before January 29, 1795 from that provision and allowed aliens who had resided in the United States between January 29, 1795 and June 18, 1798 to become a citizen within two years of the 1802 act without declaring their intent to do so three years prior. Act of April 14, 1802. Ch. 28, 2 *Stat.* 154

70. *AC*, 7th Cong., 2nd Sess., 465–67, 474–80, 569–81; Smilie quotes at 477 and 573; Act of March 26, 1804. Ch. 47, 2 *Stat.* 292. Kettner, *The Development of American Citizenship*, 246. See also Rogers Smith, *Civic Ideals: Conflicting Visions of Citizenship in U.S. History* (New Haven, Conn.: Yale University Press, 1997), 165–96; Jon Gjerde, "'Here in America There Is Neither King nor Tyrant': European Encounters with Race, 'Freedom,' and Their European Pasts," *JER* 19, 4 (Winter 1999): 673–90; Bradburn, *The Citizenship Revolution*, 260.

71. Act of January 29, 1795. Ch. 20 1 *Stat.* 414. Citizenship Papers of Thomas H. Bradley, Brock Collection, Box 264 #27, HL.

72. *Aurora General Advertiser*, September 24, 1800; see Furstenberg, *In the Name of the Father*, 206–9, on how whites often ascribed slave rebellion to external influence.

73. *Aurora General Advertiser*, August 14, 17, 1801.

74. Duane to J. Barlow and F. Skipwith, January 2, 1801, William Duane Papers, LC. *Aurora General Advertiser*, January 23, 1806; on the Haitian embargo in Congress, see Chapter 3 of this work.

75. *Serious Remonstrances*, 45–46; for reports of the massacres in Haiti, see, e.g., *Aurora General Advertiser* June 5, 1804; *Philadelphia Evening Post*, June 5, 1804; on the influence of Edwards, see Edward Rugemer, *The Problem of Emancipation: The Caribbean Roots of the American Civil War* (Baton Rouge: Louisiana State University Press, 2008).

76. On the 1813 legislation, see Nash, *Forging Freedom*, 181–82; for southern demands for registration of northern blacks, see *AC*, 7th Cong., 1st Sess., 423–25 and Chapter 3 of this book.

77. Hahn, *The Political Worlds of Slavery and Freedom*, 1–54; James J. Gigantino II, "'The Whole North Is Not Abolitionized': Slavery's Slow Death in New Jersey, 1830–1860," *JER* 34, 3 (Fall 2014), 411–37; Gigantino, *The Ragged Road to Abolition: Slavery and Freedom in New Jersey, 1775–1865* (Philadelphia: University of Pennsylvania Press, 2014).

78. For examples of runaway ads, see April 2, 1800 (from Loudon County, Virginia), April 5, 1800 (Queen Anns County, Maryland), August 15, 1800 (Trenton, New Jersey). "People with prices" refers to Walter Johnson's notion of the "chattel principle," in *Soul by Soul: Life Inside the Antebellum Slave Trade* (Cambridge, Mass.: Harvard University Press, 1999). On fugitive advertisements as a manifestation of slaveholder power in the antebellum South, see Johnson, *River of Dark Dreams: Slavery and Empire in the Cotton Kingdom* (Cambridge, Mass.: Harvard University Press, 2013), 224–25. For an alternative reading of fugitive advertisements in Pennsylvania see Richard S. Newman, "Lucky 'Lucky to be born in Pennsylvania': Free Soil, Fugitive Slaves, and the Making of Pennsylvania's Anti-Slavery Borderland," *Slavery & Abolition* 32, 3 (September 2011), 420. Newman argues that the high prices masters offered in runaway advertisements indicate the difficulty they faced in recapturing fugitive slaves in the state. My contention is not that fugitive advertisements made white northerners effective slave catchers, but that they simultaneously solicited a distrust of black people and an accommodation of slaveholder power.

79. Branagan to Jefferson, May 7, 1805, Jefferson Papers, AMLC.

80. Branagan to Jefferson, May 7, 1805; Jefferson to Logan, May 11, 1805; Branagan to Jefferson, November 17, 1805, Jefferson Papers, AMLC; Branagan, *Avenia*, 332.

81. *Avenia*, 313–14; 318; 322,

82. *Aurora General Advertiser*, December 21, 1799.

83. On this point, see especially Robin Blackburn, *The American Crucible: Slavery, Emancipation, and Human Rights* (London: Verso, 2011), 233–34.

Chapter 3. Jeffersonians go to Washington

1. Leonard Richards, *The Slave Power: The Free North and Southern Domination, 1780–1860* (Baton Rouge: Louisiana State University Press, 2000). Congressional data in this chapter are based on Kenneth C. Martis, *The Historical Atlas of Political Parties in the United States Congress, 1789–1989* (New York: Macmillan, 1989) and the Biographical Directory of the United States Congress (bioguide.congress.gov).

2. Roughly another 3,000 people lived in Georgetown and just under 5,000 lived in Alexandria, which at the time was included in the federal district. Eliza Quincy as cited in Robert A. McCaughey, *Josiah Quincy, 1772–1864: The Last Federalist* (Cambridge, Mass.: Harvard University Press, 1974), 46. Josiah Quincy to Jabez Upham, September 17, 1810, Jabez Upham Papers, Houghton Library, Harvard University; Harry M. Tinkcom, ed., "Sir Augustus in Pennsylvania:

279

The Travels and Observations of Sir Augustus J. Foster in Early Nineteenth-Century Pennsylvania," *PMHB* 75, 4 (October 1951): 392 (muddy boots); Stanley Elkins and Eric McKitrick, *The Age of Federalism* (New York: Oxford University Press, 1990), 170; James Sterling Young, *The Washington Community, 1800–1828* (New York: Columbia University Press, 1966).

3. Nahum Mitchell to Nabby Mitchell, December 1, 1804, Nahum Mitchell Papers, MHS; on early Washington society, see Catherine Allgor, *Parlor Politics: In Which the Ladies of Washington Help Build a City and a Government* (Charlottesville: University of Virginia Press, 2000).

4. Don E. Fehrenbacher, *The Slaveholding Republic: An Account of the United States Government's Relations to Slavery* (New York: Oxford University Press, 2001), 59–66; John Witherspoon DuBose as quoted in Harvey Tolliver Cook, *The Life and Legacy of David Rogerson Williams* (Garden City, N.Y.: Country Life Press, 1916), 97.

5. Of course, this was not true for all northerners. A significant minority, including some congressmen, held slaves into the 1800s. But with the adoption of gradual abolition in New York in 1799 and New Jersey in 1804, the largest slaveholding states in the North were now committed to ending slavery as an institution. To be sure, gradual emancipation by no means ensured African American equality (or even mere freedom), as many historians have argued. But the slow decline of northern slavery and intensity of post-abolition racism did not give slaveholders confidence that northern congressmen would prove reliable partners in governing slavery at the national level. Congressional debates suggest they were right to be wary.

6. See David Ericson, *Slavery in the American Republic: Developing the Federal Government, 1791–1861* (Lawrence: University Press of Kansas, 2011), 11.

7. On the 1790 debates, see Howard Ohline, "Slavery, Economics, and Congressional Politics," *Journal of Southern History* 46, 3 (August 1980): 335–60; Gary Nash, *Race and Revolution* (Madison, Wis.: Madison House, 1990); Richard Newman, "Prelude to the Gag Rule: Southern Reaction to Antislavery Petitions in the First Federal Congress," *JER* 16, 4 (Winter 1996): 571–99; Joseph Ellis, *Founding Brothers: The Revolutionary Generation* (New York: Knopf, 2000), 81–119; Randolph in *AC*, 6th Cong., 1st Sess., 233–34.

8. Douglas Bradburn questions prior analysis of the 1790 debates by arguing that Congress reached a settled decision in that conflict that slavery was primarily a problem for the states (a "municipal concern") and that the federal government had "*no power* over slavery without the direct cooperation of slaveholders." Douglas Bradburn, *The Citizenship Revolution: Politics and the Creation of the American Union, 1774–1804* (Charlottesville: University of Virginia Press, 2009), 250. But persistent discord in Congress suggests that any such consensus in 1790 was short-lived at best. Compare Fehrenbacher, *Slaveholding Republic*, 10–13, on the relative inability of the "federal consensus" (that regulation of slavery should be left to the states) to solve or suppress conflict over slavery.

9. The Constitution established that Congress should begin on the first Monday of December, unless legislation were passed otherwise; this was not altered until the 20th amendment of 1933, which set a new start date for Congress of January 3. Special circumstances did lead to different start dates and terms, but a late fall start and early spring end-date were the norm.

10. *Mr. Nicholson's Motion . . . 22nd January 1801* (Washington, D.C., 1801).

11. Fehrenbacher, *Slaveholding Republic*, 211–16; Thomas Morris, *Free Men All: The Personal Liberty Laws of the North, 1780–1861* (Baltimore: Johns Hopkins University Press, 1974), 19–35; Richard S. Newman, *The Transformation of American Abolitionism: Fighting Slavery in the Early Republic* (Chapel Hill: University of North Carolina Press, 2002), 60–85; Newman, "'Lucky to be

Born in Pennsylvania': Free Soil, Fugitive Slaves, and the Making of Pennsylvania's Anti-Slavery Borderland," *Slavery & Abolition* 32, 3 (September 2011): 413–30.

12. *AC*, 6th Cong., 2nd Sess., 916, 940–41, 1054; Henry Adams, *History of the United States of America During the Administrations of Thomas Jefferson* (New York: Library of America, 1986), 204. The 6th Congress had a Federalist majority of 60–46 in the House; the 7th had a Republican majority of 68–38. Southern Republicans held 27 seats in the 6th Congress and 38 in the 7th. Northerners (regardless of party affiliation) had a slight edge in the 7th Congress, 56–50.

13. *AC*, 7th Cong., 1st Sess., 423–25. Philadelphia Republican Michael Leib, a colleague of William Duane, voted with the southerners.

14. *Aurora General Advertiser*, September 15, October 21, 1803; Abraham Bishop, *Oration in Honor of the Election of President Jefferson and the Peaceable Acquisition of Louisiana . . .* (New Haven, Conn.: Sidney's Press, 1804), 6; Jed H. Shugerman, "The Louisiana Purchase and South Carolina's Reopening of the Slave Trade in 1803," *JER* 22 (Summer 2002): 263–90, 272–74 on the South Carolina press.

15. This overview depends on Patrick Brady, "The Slave Trade and Sectionalism in South Carolina," *Journal of Southern History* 38, 4 (November 1972): 601–20; Rachel N. Klein, *Unification of a Slave State: The Rise of the Planter Class in the South Carolina Backcountry, 1760–1808* (Chapel Hill: University of North Carolina Press, 1992); James McMillin, *The Final Victims: Foreign Slave Trade to North America, 1783–1810* (Columbia: University of South Carolina Press, 2004); Adam Rothman, *Slave Country: American Expansion and the Origins of the Deep South* (Cambridge, Mass.: Harvard University Press, 2005); and especially Brian Schoen, *The Fragile Fabric of Union: Cotton, Federal Politics, and the Global Origins of the Civil War* (Baltimore: Johns Hopkins University Press, 2009).

16. Americans often used "Louisiana" to describe either or both parts of the Purchase, a linguistic confusion resolved when the Orleans Territory was admitted to the Union as the state of Louisiana in 1812 and the District of Louisiana was renamed the Missouri Territory. On the problems of incorporating the residents of Louisiana into the Union, see Peter Kastor, *The Nation's Crucible: the Louisiana Purchase and the Creation of America* (New Haven, Conn.: Yale University Press, 2004), 45–52; for Jefferson's influence on the bill for governing the Orleans Territory, see James E. Scanlon, "A Sudden Conceit: Jefferson and the Louisiana Government Bill of 1804," *Louisiana History* 9, 2 (Spring 1968): 139–62.

17. Everett S. Brown, ed., "The Senate Debate on the Breckinridge Bill for the Government of Louisiana, 1804," *AHR* 22, 2 (January 1917): 351. The notes on the debate were recorded by Senator William Plumer of New Hampshire.

18. John Craig Hammond, "'They Are Very Much Interested in Obtaining an Unlimited Slavery': Rethinking the Expansion of Slavery in the Louisiana Purchase Territories, 1803–1805," *JER* 23, 3 (Autumn 2003): 353–80; Hammond, *Slavery, Freedom and Expansion in the Early American West* (Charlottesville: University of Virginia Press, 2007), 30–54.

19. Jefferson apparently agreed. Much of the bill introduced by Breckinridge was based on an earlier draft by Jefferson, who had written: "Insert in some part of the paper of yesterday 'Slaves shall be admitted into the territory of Orleans from such of the United States or of their territories as prohibit their importation from abroad, but from no other state, territory or country'." That language would have condoned domestic trade to Louisiana. Jefferson to Breckinridge, November 25, 1803, Breckinridge Family Papers, LC; Scanlon, "A Sudden Conceit," 152–53.

20. Brown, "The Senate Debate on the Breckinridge Bill," 361, 354. The extent to which Southerners opposed or supported the "bona fide owner" restriction is not entirely clear. The

Senate debates as recorded by Plumer suggest Breckinridge and others wanted to allow the domestic trade to Louisiana. Steven Deyle, arguing on the basis of the Jefferson note to Breckinridge cited above, believes the "Virginians, led by Jefferson, fought to permit any American owned slaves, including those brought there for the purpose of sale, to enter." Deyle, "'An Abominable New Trade': The Closing of the African Slave Trade and the Changing Patterns of U.S. Political Power, 1808–60," *WMQ* 66, 4 (October 2009): 833–50, 838. John Craig Hammond, arguing on the basis of the final vote on Hillhouse's bona fide restriction, contends there was significant southern Republican support to limit the domestic slave trade by supporting the bona fide restriction and significant northern Federalist support to allow the domestic trade (*Slavery, Freedom, and Expansion*, 45). A more detailed reading of the *Annals* and Plumer's record demonstrates that the reality was somewhat more complicated than either Deyle or Hammond suggests. On Tuesday January 31, there was a motion to strike out Hillhouse's original bona fide restriction. This motion led to a debate in which Southerners Breckinridge, Jackson, Nicholas of Virginia, and Samuel Smith of Maryland, along with John Smith of Ohio appeared to speak in favor of the domestic trade, based on a reading of the Plumer record; Venable of Virginia seconded Breckinridge's defense of slavery under the Constitution. All these men were Republicans. The motion to strike out lost, in the most sectional vote in the Hillhouse debates: 9 southern Republicans, 3 northern Republicans, and 1 southern Federalist supported striking out, while 7 northern Republicans, 5 northern Federalists, and 3 southern Republicans voted to maintain the bona fide clause. Federalists John Quincy Adams and Pickering voted to maintain, and Adams rebutted Breckinridge's proslavery constitutionalism: "If I must vote, it will be in favor of liberty. The Constitution does not recognize *slavery*—it contains no such *word*—a great circumlocution of words is used merely to avoid the term *slaves*" (Brown, "The Senate Debate on the Breckinridge Bill," 354). This should temper Hammond's suggestion that Pickering and Adams universally backed slavery expansion in these debates, while southern Republicans proved willing to limit it. At the same time, it is not obvious that the Senators who voted to strike out the bona fide clause wanted to allow the domestic trade, as Deyle implies. They suggested instead a bona fide owner restriction of their own, which had two crucial differences from Hillhouse's: slaves could be willed to residents in the Orleans Territory from "persons or persons deceased in some one of the United States or their territories"; and, most critically, any slave brought in contrary to the bona fide restriction would not be emancipated, but rather "forfeited, and may be recovered by any person who shall sue for the same" (*AC*, 8th Cong., 1st Sess., 243). In other words, there would be no emancipation of illegally imported slaves, a position similar to that which Southerners would later take in debates over interdicting the international slave trade to the United States. This was not a transparent defense of the domestic trade, but it was—as Plumer's record indicates—a strong defense of slaveholder property rights. Only after losing the motion to strike out the bona fide clause did southern Republicans Breckinridge, Cocke, and Samuel Smith accede to a modified version of the clause, limiting importation to bona fide owners who were also citizens of the United States. Strangely, Adams, Pickering, and Republican Ellery of Rhode Island now reversed course and voted against the restriction (244).

21. Brown, "The Senate Debate on the Breckinridge Bill," 355–56, 349. Jackson's ultimate position on Louisiana was not entirely clear, as at other points he argued against the rapid incorporation and settlement of Louisiana, on grounds that the inhabitants of the territory were not prepared for self-government and that settlement would destabilize the Union and lead to a depreciation of land values in the extant western states (356–57).

22. Simeon Baldwin to Timothy Pitkin, February 24, 1804, Papers of Timothy Pitkin, HL.

23. *AC*, 8th Cong., 2nd Sess., 1606; Hammond, *Slavery, Freedom, and Expansion*, 48–50.

24. Phillips and Gardner to Gardner and Dean, November 4, 1806; see also December 9 and 14, 1806, Slavery Collection, NYHS, Box 3, Folder 1. The firm imported slaves until the very end of the legal trade, sending at least 15 ships to Africa in 1807 (McMillin, *The Final Victims*, 106). For estimates of total numbers imported into Charleston, see McMillin, *The Final Victims*, 32 (51,485) and Nicholas Wood, "Considerations of Humanity and Expediency: The Slave Trades and African Colonization in the Early National Antislavery Movement," Ph.D. dissertation, University of Virginia, 2013, 174 n. 21 (46,823, based on the slavevoyages.org database.)

25. Alan Kulikoff, "Uprooted Peoples: Black Migrants in the Age of the American Revolution," *Slavery and Freedom in the Age of the American Revolution*, ed. Ira Berlin and Ronald Hoffman (Charlottesville: University of Virginia Press, 1983), 143–71. On the destinations of Chesapeake slaves, see 147, 151, and 165. See also Michael Tadman, *Speculators and Slaves: Masters, Traders, and Slaves in the Old South* (Madison: University of Wisconsin Press, 1989), 12–21; Steven Deyle, "The Irony of Liberty: Origins of the Domestic Slave Trade" *JER* 12, 1 (Spring 1992): 37–62; Steven Deyle, *Carry Me Back: The Domestic Slave Trade in American Life* (New York: Oxford University Press, 2005), 15–39; Edward Baptist, *The Half Has Never Been Told: Slavery and the Making of American Capitalism* (New York: Basic Books, 2014), 1–37.

26. *AC*, 8th Cong. 1st Sess., 996–97.

27. *AC*, 8th Cong., 1st Sess., 1001, 1009, 1017, 1019.

28. Parker was supported by James Madison and opposed, with characteristic vehemence, by James Jackson of Georgia. See *AC*, 1st Cong., 1st Sess., 349–56.

29. *AC*, 6th Cong., Sess. 1, 686–88, 699–700.

30. *AC*, 8th Cong., 1st Sess., 1028–29 (Eppes) and 1031–32 (Jackson)

31. Plumer in Brown, "The Senate Debate on the Breckinridge Bill," 354. On Virginia's economic interest see Deyle, "'An Abominable New Trade'"; Deyle, "The Irony of Liberty"; Willie Lee Rose, "The Domestication of Domestic Slavery," *Slavery and Freedom*, ed. William Freehling (New York: Oxford University Press, 1982), 18–36; Rothman, *Slave Country*, 20.

32. *AC*, 8th Cong., 1st Sess., 997–98 (Macon); *AC*, 8th Cong., 1st Sess., 1006–7 (Huger). As William Cooper has argued, such claims to slaveholder power unified the South: "No person and no agency outside the South could make any decision regarding slavery. Slavery had been and remained strictly a southern concern." Cooper, *Liberty and Slavery: Southern Politics to 1860* (New York: Knopf, 1983), 99.

33. Steven Hahn, *A Nation Under Our Feet: Black Political Struggles in the Rural South from Slavery to the Great Migration* (Cambridge, Mass.: Harvard University Press, 2003), 16–17; William Plumer, *William Plumer's Memorandum of Proceedings in the United States Senate, 1803–1807*, ed. Everett Somerville Brown (New York: Macmillan, 1923), 250–51.

34. On February 17, 1804, the House voted against postponement 62 (against) to 55 (for). Although one should be wary of reading too much into a procedural vote, to some extent it indicated the nature of sectional division in the House in late 1804—emerging but still undefined. 22 northerners (including 9 Republicans) and 33 southerners (including 29 Republicans) voted for postponement, while 37 northerners (including 29 Republicans) and 25 southerners (including 23 Republicans) voted against postponement. Of those southerners voting against, 18 were from Virginia or Maryland (*AC*, 8th Cong., 1st Sess., 1035–36).

35. For Southard and Varnum see *AC*, 8th Cong., 2nd Sess., 1189–90, 1221–22 respectively.

36. *Aurora General Advertiser*, November 8, 1804, January 8, 1805.

37. *Aurora General Advertiser*, January 7, 1805.

38. See *Aurora General Advertiser*, June 14, November 8, 1804, January 8, 1805.

39. *AC*, 8th Cong., 2nd Sess., 995–96. The 24 northern Republicans who backed Sloan's proposal were just over half their contingent (there were 47 northern Republicans as opposed to 56 southern Republicans) in the House; 16 northern Republicans recorded votes against Sloan's motion. Both Don Fehrenbacher and Sean Wilentz isolate this vote as a key indication of northern Democratic-Republican opposition to slavery. Fehrenbacher, *Slaveholding Republic*, 66; Wilentz, *The Rise of American Democracy: Jefferson to Lincoln* (New York: Norton, 2005), 221.

40. *AC*, 9th Cong., 1st Sess., 364–65.

41. See electoral returns for "New Jersey, 1803 House of Representatives," at "A New Nation Votes: American Electoral Returns 1787–1825" (http://elections.lib.tufts.edu/); Bendler, "James Sloan," 8; Carl E. Prince, *New Jersey's Jeffersonian Republicans: the Genesis of an Early Party Machine, 1789–1817* (Chapel Hill: University of North Carolina Press, 1967).

42. *AC* , 9th Cong., 1st Sess., 364. As North Carolina Republican Nathaniel Macon put it, if the legislature of South Carolina had sinned, "was it not better and more christian like to forgive them?" (362).

43. *AC*, 9th Cong., 1st Sess., 365.

44. Early in *AC*, 9th Cong., 1st Sess., 371; Plumer, *Plumer's Memorandum*, 392.

45. "There was not a State in the Union," said Williams, "which had appropriated so much money for objects of munificence and improvement, for the encouragement of literature, for the maintenance of the poor." *AC*, 9th Cong., 1st Sess., 374, 439. On the importance of personal challenges and conflicts over honor in early national politics, see Joanne Freeman, *Affairs of Honor: National Politics in the New Republic* (New Haven, Conn.: Yale University Press, 2001); on the relationship between personal conflict and slavery politics, see Elizabeth Varon, *Disunion!: The Coming of the American Civil War, 1789–1859* (Chapel Hill: University of North Carolina Press, 2008), 7.

46. Ronald Johnson, *Diplomacy in Black and White: John Adams, Toussaint Louverture, and Their Atlantic World Alliance* (Athens: University of Georgia Press, 2014), 60–61, 139–41 (Gallatin); Arthur Scherr, *Thomas Jefferson's Haitian Policy: Myths and Realities* (Lanham, Md.: Lexington Books, 2011); Scherr, "Arms and Men: The Diplomacy of U.S. Weapons Traffic with Saint-Domingue Under Adams and Jefferson," *International History Review* 35, 3 (2013), 600–648; Laurent DuBois, "The Haitian Revolution and the Sale of Louisiana; or, Thomas Jefferson's (Unpaid) Debt to Jean Jacques Dessalines," in *Empires of the Imagination: Transatlantic Histories of the Louisiana Purchase*, ed. Peter J. Kastor and Francois Weil (Charlottesville: University of Virginia Press, 2009), 93–116. On Jeffersonian hostility toward Haiti, see Donald R. Hickey, "America's Response to the Slave Revolt in Haiti," *JER* 2, 4 (Winter 1982): 361–79; Michael Zuckerman, "The Power of Blackness: Thomas Jefferson and the Revolution in St. Domingue," in Zuckerman, *Almost Chosen People: Oblique Biographies in the American Grain* (Berkeley: University of California Press, 1993), 175–218; Tim Matthewson, *A Proslavery Foreign Policy: Haitian-American Relations During the Early Republic* (Westport, Conn.: Praeger, 2003); Robin Blackburn, "Haiti, Slavery, and the Age of Democratic Revolution," *WMQ* 634 (October 2006); Ashli White, *Encountering Revolution: Haiti and the Making of the Early American Republic* (Baltimore: Johns Hopkins University Press, 2010), 163–65. See also Arthur Scherr's revisionist account in *Thomas Jefferson's Haitian Policy*, which has demonstrated that Jefferson's commercial policy toward Saint-Domingue was more complex than previously allowed. Republican ideological hostility toward an independent Haiti, on the other hand, was fairly straightforward and united northern and southern Jeffersonians in Congress.

47. Jackson in *AC*, 9th Cong., 1st Sess. (Senate), 30–31, 36–38; "pledge the Treasury" came in

a December 1804 debate over restricting America merchants from arming their vessels, a policy intended to limit trade to Haiti. Eppes in Plumer, *Plumer's Memorandum*, 243; a more mild rendering in the *Annals of Congress* has Eppes declaring that "it is the interest of the United States to depress and keep down" a certain "class of people" in the West Indies, "rather than put arms in their hands, to do such extensive mischief as is every day practiced in that island" (*AC*, 8th Cong., 2nd Sess. (House), 813); "fairest portion," *AC*, 9th Cong., 1st Sess. (House), 515.

48. 22 of 31 Federalists in the House voted against the embargo. See *AC*, 9th Cong. 1st Sess., 512; 515–16.

49. On this point see Scherr, *Thomas Jefferson's Haitian Policy*.

50. In effect, there were three votes for postponement. The first, proposed by Randolph on February 4, 1806, lost 42–61. No roll-call was recorded. The second, proposed by Jacob Crowinshield, Republican of Massachusetts on February 5, lost 42–69. 28 southern Republicans voted in favor of postponement, joined by 5 northern Republicans and 9 northern Federalists. They were opposed by 40 northern Republicans, 8 northern Federalists, 20 southern Republicans, and 1 southern Federalist. On February 27, a third vote for postponement lost 42–69. 27 southern Republicans were joined by 10 northern Federalists, 4 northern Republicans, and 1 southern Federalist in favor of postponement. They were opposed by 40 northern Republicans, 8 northern Federalists, 19 southern Republicans and 2 southern Federalists.

51. *AC*, 9th Cong., 1st Sess., 434 (Randolph) 533, 439–40. On February 4, Williams introduced an amendment to the slave trade tax that would prohibit slaves imported to the United States from being sent on to any American territory. On the same day, he asked that the House cease debating Sloan's bill, leading some members to believe that his amendment regarding the South Carolina loophole was a mere ploy to defer consideration of the slave trade tax. In response, Williams reported his amendment as a separate proposal, but Congress did not act on it (442–45, 472–73). Williams may have been sincere about closing the South Carolina loophole, but he was equally sincere Congress should place no limit on the ability of masters to move their slave property from one state to another, a position he defended forcefully in debates over closing the international trade the following winter.

52. Details on Williams's life can be found in Cook, *The Life and Legacy of David R. Williams*. On South Carolina Republicans, see Lacy K. Ford, *Origins of Southern Radicalism: The South Carolina Upcountry, 1800–1860* (New York: Oxford University Press, 1988); Klein, *Unification of a Slave State*.

53. Noble E. Cunningham, *The Jeffersonian Republicans in Power; Party Operations, 1801–1809* (Chapel Hill: University of North Carolina Press, 1963), 95–96; Taggart to John Taylor, February 12, 1804, "Letters of Samuel Taggart, Part One," *Proceedings of the American Antiquarian Society 33*, pt. 1 (April 1923), 133; Plumer, *Plumer's Memorandum*, 123; Randolph in *AC*, 9 Cong., 1st Sess., 434. On Randolph's break with Jefferson, see Norman K. Risjord, *The Old Republicans: Southern Conservatism in the Age of Jefferson* (New York: Columbia University Press, 1965), 44–71; Adams, *History of the United States During the Administrations of Thomas Jefferson*, 704–21.

54. W. E. B. Du Bois argued in 1898 that "the Act of 1807 came very near being a dead letter" and that the enforcement of legislation against the international trade was "criminally lax" (*The Suppression of the Atlantic Slave Trade to the United States of America, 1638–1870* (New York: Longman's, 1896), 109, 129). Most contemporary historians disagree with this assessment and argue that Du Bois's numbers for illegally imported slaves are far too high. The persistence of an illegal trade, contends Don Fehrenbacher, was, like the exodus of fugitive slaves from the South, "politically inflammatory but demographically insignificant. . . . Compared with

twentieth-century efforts to prevent the introduction of alcoholic beverages, drugs, and illegal aliens into the United States, the legislation banning importation of slaves must be regarded as relatively successful" (Fehrenbacher, *Slaveholding Republic*, 149–50). These analogies are not quite apposite, however, since the United States had its own burgeoning and entirely legal domestic supply of slaves. Even if one considers the Act of 1807 a relative success, the Congressional record offers little ground for describing the measure as "vigorously abolitionist" (136). For increased penalties against the international trade over time, see Paul Finkelman, "Regulating the African Slave Trade," *Civil War History* 54, 4 (2008): 379–405. For American weakness in preventing the international slave trade to other nations, see Fehrenbacher, *Slaveholding Republic*, 135–204 and Eliga H. Gould, *Among the Powers of the Earth: The American Revolution and the Making of a New World Empire* (Cambridge, Mass.: Harvard University Press, 2012), 157–77.

55. Steven Deyle, "The Domestic Slave Trade in America: The Lifeblood of the Southern Slave System," in *The Chattel Principle: Internal Slave Trades in the Americas*, ed. Walter Johnson (New Haven, Conn.: Yale University Press, 2005); Walter Johnson, "White Lies: Human Property and Domestic Slavery Aboard the Slave Ship *Creole*," *Atlantic Studies* 5, 2 (August 2008): 237–63.

56. *AC*, 9th Cong., 2nd Sess., 168–75.

57. *AC*, 9th Cong., 2nd Sess., 180–84, 220–28; Bidwell at 221, Quincy at 222–23; Sloan at 226. African colonization was addressed in more detail in the Senate, but in a private session. See Wood, "Considerations of Humanity," 247.

58. *AC*, 9th Cong., 2nd Sess., 265–67. Macon quote from 1806 debates, *AC*, 9th Cong., 1st Sess., 361.

59. *AC*, 9th Cong., 2nd Sess., 270–274

60. *AC*, 9th Cong., 2nd Sess., 238, 236–37, 239–40. Lloyd's argument echoed a longstanding European justification for slavery. See Gould, *Among the Nations of the Earth*, 60–62.

61. *AC*, 9th Cong., 2nd Sess., 241, 184, 242–43.

62. *AC*, 9th Cong., 2nd Sess., 477–78.

63. *AC*, 9th Cong., 2nd Sess., 481; Act of March 2, 1807, Ch. 22, 2 *Stat.*, 428. On the parliamentary maneuvering, see Wood, "Considerations of Humanity," 250–51, citing *United States Gazette* of February 12, 1807.

64. Fehrenbacher, *Slaveholding Republic*, 136. Fehrenbacher recognizes the sectional animosity in the debates of 1806–1807 (144–47), but his summary description emphasizes national unity. In contrast, members of the House acknowledged strong sectional differences on implementing the slave trade ban. Said Connecticut's Benjamin Tallmadge, "I can scarcely recollect an instance in which members seem so generally to agree in the principles of a bill, and yet differ so widely as to its details" (*AC*, 9th Cong., 1st Sess., 232). Southerners later acknowledged that on crucial points the bill would pass "by a bare majority" but claimed that this was not a problem, as "it would receive the unanimous, or nearly unanimous sanction of those among whom it was principally, if not exclusively, to take effect" (ibid., 272). That was a declaration of slaveholder as opposed to national unity.

65. On this point see Matthew Mason, "Slavery Overshadowed: Congress Debates Prohibiting the Atlantic Slave Trade to the United States, 1806–1807," *JER* 20, 1 (Spring 2000): 59–81.

66. *Democratic Press*, April 8, 1807.

67. David Waldstreicher, *In the Midst of Perpetual Fetes: The Making of American Nationalism, 1776–1820* (Chapel Hill: University of North Carolina Press, 1997), 329–47; Paul Polgar, "'To Raise Them to an Equal Participation': Early National Abolitionism, Gradual Emancipation, and the Promise of African American Citizenship," *JER* 31, 2 (Summer 2011): 229–58.

68. Wood, "Considerations of Humanity," 256; Act of March 2, 1807, Ch. 22, 2 *Stat.* 429–430. Wood points out that a similar manifest provision was proposed in a House debate over kidnapping of free blacks in 1796. See *AC* 4th Cong., 2nd Sess., 1730–1737; "Manifest of the Brig Uncas," November 19, 1839, Slavery Collection, Box 5, NYHS. The six-month-old infant was probably the daughter of Celia Ganes, listed above her on the manifest. On Williams, see Deyle, *Carry Me Back*, 120–21.

69. *AC*, 9th Cong., 2nd Sess., 484, 527–28. See also Mason, "Slavery Overshadowed," 70–71 and, for the Senate bill and an alternative reading than that offered here, Wood, "Considerations of Humanity," 257–60. The Senate's fifty-ton proposal can be found in U.S. House, *January 28, 1807 . . . An Act to Prohibit the Importation of Slaves. . . .* (Washington, D.C., s.n., 1807) and U.S. Senate, *January 13, 1807 . . . A Bill (as Amended by the Committee) to Prohibit the Importation of Slaves . . .* (Washington, D.C., s.n., 1807)

70. U.S. Senate, *February 24, 1807 . . . Mr. Bradley, from the Conferrees from the Senate, on the Disagreement Between the Two Houses on the Bill, 'To Prohibit the Importation of Slaves . . .'* (Washington D.C., s.n., 1807), as cited in Wood, "Considerations of Humanity," 259; Act of March 2, 1807, Ch. 22, 2 *Stat.* 429

71. *AC*, 9th Cong., 2nd Sess., 626. The speech was not recorded in the *Annals of Congress*, but was printed in a number of contemporary papers. I rely on the version printed in, among other papers, *New-York Commercial Advertiser*, March 4, 1807, *Poulson's American Daily Advertiser*, March 5, 1807, and *The Precursor* (Montpelier, Vermont), March 30, 1807. For other versions of the speech, see *United States Gazette*, March 3, 1807, *New-York Evening Post*, March 5, 1807 and Mason, "Slavery Overshadowed," 71, n. 31.

72. *AC*, 9th Cong., 2nd Sess., 636–38; *The Precursor*, March 30 1807; Mason, "Slavery Overshadowed," 70. On February 26, the House voted 63–49 to concur with the Senate and uphold the forty-ton limit. 51 northerners (42 Republicans) joined 12 southerners (all Republicans) to support concurring and 11 northerners (6 Republicans) joined 38 southerners (36 Republicans) in opposition. The following day, the House voted 60–49 along similar lines to postpone consideration of Randolph's amendment (*AC*, 9th Cong., 2nd Sess., 627, 637–638). Randolph was prescient: Abolitionists later drew on the forty-ton clause to argue that Congress could shut down the coastal trade in slaves entirely, as part of an effort to outlaw the domestic slave trade. See Deyle, "The Domestic Slave Trade in America," 103.

73. "Mr. R also observed, that he considered it no imputation to be a slaveholder, more than to be born in a particular country. It was a thing with which they had no more to do than with their own procreation" (*AC*, 9th Cong., 2nd Sess., 627). Nicholas Wood, "John Randolph of Roanoke and the Politics of Slavery in the Early Republic," *Virginia Magazine of History and Biography* 120, 2 (Summer 2012): 106–43.

74. *AC*, 10th Cong., 1st Sess., 1531; James Sloan, *Reasons Offered . . . In Favor of Removal of the Seat of Government* (Washington, D.C., s.n., 1808), 4, 6–7.

75. *AC*, 10th Cong., 1st Sess., 1537, 1540, 1567.

76. *AC*, 10th Cong., 1st Sess., 1565, 1558, 1562.

77. *AC*, 10th Cong., 1st Sess., 1590.

Chapter 4. The Idea of a Northern Party

1. Eliga H. Gould, *Among the Powers of the Earth: The American Revolution and the Making of a New World Empire* (Cambridge, Mass.: Harvard University Press, 2012), 142–43; Reginald Horsman, *The Causes of the War of 1812* (Philadelphia: University of Pennsylvania Press, 1962);

J. C. A. Stagg, *Mr. Madison's War: Politics, Diplomacy, and Warfare in the Early American Republic* (Princeton, N.J.: Princeton University Press, 1983); J. C. A. Stagg, *The War of 1812: Conflict for a Continent* (Cambridge: Cambridge University Press, 2012); and Troy Bickham, *The Weight of Vengeance: The United States, the British Empire and the War of 1812* (New York: Oxford University Press, 2012), 20–48.

2. On impressment see Paul Gilje, *Free Trade and Sailors' Rights in the War of 1812* (Cambridge: Cambridge University Press, 2013); on Anglophobia see Lawrence A. Peskin, "Conspiratorial Anglophobia and the War of 1812," *JAH* 98, 3 (December 2011): 647–69; on commemoration of the Revolution, see Sarah J. Purcell, *Sealed with Blood: War, Sacrifice, and Memory in Revolutionary America* (Philadelphia: University of Pennsylvania Press, 2011).

3. *Democratic Press*, July 1, 1807.

4. Thus Spintext in closing: "Hasten, hasten the time, great God of armies, when the power of tyrants shall be broken, slavery banished from the world, freedom triumphant, man learn war no more, and when these insolent turners of the world upside down, shall not have it in their power to come hither also." *Democratic Press*, July 1, 1807.

5. Robert E. Cray, "Remembering the USS *Chesapeake*: The Politics of Maritime Death and Impressment," *JER* 25, 3 (Fall 2005): 445–74; *The Trial of John Wilson, Alias Jenkin Ratford* (Boston: Snelling and Simons, 1807), 17; *Aurora General Advertiser*, September 22, 1807.

6. Burton Spivak, *Jefferson's English Crisis: Commerce, Embargo, and the Republican Revolution* (Charlottesville: University Press of Virginia, 1979); Robert R. Thompson, "John Quincy Adams, Apostate: From 'Outrageous Federalist' to 'Republican Exile,' 1801–1809," *JER* 11, 2 (Summer 1991): 161–83; and John Quincy Adams, *A Letter to Harrison Gray Otis* (Boston: Oliver and Munroe, 1808), 29–30.

7. Bradford Perkins, *Prologue to War: England and the United States, 1805–1812* (Berkeley: University of California Press, 1961), 140–83; Leonard Levy, *Jefferson and Civil Liberties: The Darker Side* (Cambridge, Mass.: Harvard University Press, 1963), 139; Marshall Smelser, *The Democratic Republic, 1801–1815* (New York: Harper, 1968), 151–80; Sloan in *AC*, 10th Cong., 2nd Sess., 926.

8. Among other papers, the letter appeared in the *Alexandria Daily Advertiser*, April 28, 1808; *American Citizen*; April 30, 1808; *Trenton Federalist*, May 2, 1808; *The Balance*, May 3, 1808; *Connecticut Herald*, May 3, 1808; *Republican Watch-Tower*, May 3, 1808; *New-England Palladium*, May 6, 1808. Sloan complained that the caucus had been moved to an earlier date than usual to ensure Madison's nomination. Madisonian supporters had in fact pushed for an early caucus, to fend off a challenge from dissident Virginians led by John Randolph. See Irving Brant, "The Election of 1808," in *History of American Presidential Elections*, vol. 1, ed. Arthur Schlesinger, Jr. (New York: Chelsea, 1971).

9. Samuel L. Mitchill to Catharine Mitchill, January 25, 1808, Samuel L. Mitchill Papers, MCNY.

10. Leonard Richards, *The Slave Power: The Free North and Southern Domination* (Baton Rouge: Louisiana State University Press, 2000), 60–70.

11. Adams to Nahum Parker, December 5, 1808, Adams Papers, MHS.

12. Francis Blake, *An Oration, Pronounced at Worcester, On the Anniversary of American Independence* (Worcester, Mass.: Thomas and Thomas, 1796), 11, 15, 16, 18; "Prospectus of a new Political and Literary Paper to be Published at Worcester Massachusetts, Entitled The National Aegis" (appended to *National Aegis*, December 2, 1801); for Blake's biography see William Lincoln, *History of Worcester, Massachusetts* (Worcester, Mass.: C. Hersey, 1862) 199–200; on the

Aegis, see Jeffrey Pasley, *"The Tyranny of Printers": Newspaper Politics in the Early American Republic* (Charlottesville: University of Virginia Press, 2001), 196–216.

13. For Blake's public spats, see *Boston Democrat*, April 14, November 6, 1804; *National Aegis*, April 25, 1804, March 12, 26, April 2, May 7, 1806 (reprinting the *Aurora*), September 3, 1806; *Massachusetts Spy*, March 26, 1806.

14. Francis Blake to Jabez Upham, April 29, 1804, Jabez Upham Papers, Houghton Library, Harvard University; for Blake's departure from the *Aegis*, see *National Aegis*, April 4, 1804; Pasley, *"Tyranny of Printers"*, 219.

15. Blake to Upham, April 29, 1804, Upham Papers.

16. *Massachusetts Spy*, April 11, 1810.

17. David Hackett Fischer, *The Revolution of American Conservatism: The Federalist Party in the Era of Jeffersonian Democracy* (Chicago: University of Chicago Press, 1965); James M. Banner, *To the Hartford Convention: the Federalists and the Origin of Party Politics in Massachusetts, 1789–1815* (New York: Knopf, 1970); Edward Bangs to Nathaniel Howe, June 14, 1808, Bangs Family Papers, AAS.

18. Richard Buel, *America on the Brink: How the Political Struggle over the War of 1812 Almost Destroyed the Young Republic* (New York: Palgrave Macmillan, 2006); on the increase in Federalist partisanship and thus electoral turnout, see Donald Ratcliffe, "The Right to Vote and the Rise of Democracy," *JER* 33, 2 (Summer 2013): 219–54 and Philip Lampi, "The Federalist Party Resurgence: Evidence from the New Nation Votes Database," ibid., 255–81.

19. David Waldstreicher, *In the Midst of Perpetual Fetes: The Making of American Nationalism, 1776–1820* (Chapel Hill: University of North Carolina Press, 1997), 227.

20. Francis Blake, *An Oration, Pronounced at Worcester, on the Thirty-Sixth Anniversary of American Independence, July 4, 1812* (Worcester, Mass.: Isaac Sturtevant, 1812), 5; "radical defect": *Columbian Centinel*, November 16, 1814, as cited in Matthew Mason, *Slavery and Politics in the Early American Republic* (Chapel Hill: University of North Carolina Press, 2006), 53; for the entirety of this speech see *Columbian Centinel*, October 29, November 9, 1814; "monarchy and all": *Independent Chronicle*, April 4, 1814; on January 28, 1814, the *National Aegis* reported that Blake publicly questioned the treatment of British officers who had been taken as prisoners of war and "outrageously abused the national government in their hearing." See also Matthew Mason, "'Nothing Is Better Calculated to Excite Divisions': Federalist Agitation Against Slave Representation During the War of 1812," *NEQ* 75, 4 (December 2002): 531–61 (537, 542 on Blake).

21. Matthew Carey, *The Olive Branch* (Philadelphia: Matthew Carey, 1814), 17–18.

22. Bangs to Howe, September 27, 1807 and July 9, 1808, Bangs Papers, AAS.

23. Bangs to Howe, December 16, 1811, Bangs Papers, AAS; on the Massachusetts elections see Stagg, *Mr. Madison's War*, 256–57.

24. Buel, *America on the Brink* makes the opposite argument regarding the Clintonian campaign of 1812 (149). During the war itself, Federalist opposition was certainly more dangerous, given that regional leaders openly resisted Madison's war aims and policies, while many Clintonians returned to the Republican mainstream after the election of 1812. But in many ways Clintonianism was an omen of things to come. The future demographic and political strength of the North was in the mid-Atlantic and the emerging states of the Old Northwest, not New England, a fact already obvious by 1812. And while Federalist criticism had repeatedly proved its limited appeal, Republican dissidence suggested the capacity for a widespread movement that could undermine the Jeffersonian alliance. Compare the narrative of Richards, *The Slave Power*, which identifies the Clinton campaign as an early moment in northern sectional politics that would eventuate in the Republican party of the 1850s.

25. *AC*, 10th Cong., 2nd Sess., 919–20; the speech was reprinted as James Sloan, *"Politics for Farmers"* (Salem, Mass.: Cushing and Appleton, 1809); see also Bruce Bendler, "James Sloan: Renegade or True Republican?" *New Jersey History* 125, 1 (2010): 1–19.

26. *AC*, 10th Cong., 2nd Sess., 919–20.

27. On suffrage restrictions in New York, which were extreme in voting for the state senate, see Ratcliffe, "The Right to Vote," 225, 229.

28. A Citizen of New York [Edmond Charles Genet], *Communications on the Next Election for President of the United States, and on the Later Measures of the Federal Administration* (New York, 1808), 4, 11, 20. For Genet in the 1790s, see Stanley Elkins and Eric McKitrick, *The Age of Federalism* (New York: Oxford University Press, 1993), 330–74.

29. Samuel L. Mitchill to Catharine Mitchill, February 24, 1808, Samuel L. Mitchill Papers, MCNY.

30. See *The Columbian*, August 12, 1812, excerpting the pamphlet "Touchstone"; October 16, 1812, copying from *The Pilot*. On the canal, see *The Columbian*, January 8, February 13, 25, 26, 1811. On Charles Holt and *The Columbian*, see Pasley, *"Tyranny of Printers"*, 145.

31. Stagg, *Mr. Madison's War*, 81–83. Pennsylvania Republican Jonathan Roberts recalled that "DeWitt Clinton made a visit to Washington, ostensibly to get a grant of land to aid the New York canal. It seems that he had then determin'd, to be a candidate against Madison. He made overtures to me, but met no encouragement." In Philip S. Klein, ed., "Memoirs of a Senator from Pennsylvania," *PMHB* 62, 2 (April 1938): 227.

32. John Lauritz Larson, *Internal Improvement: National Public Works and the Promise of Popular Government in the Early United States* (Chapel Hill: University of North Carolina Press, 2001), 73–80.

33. Genet, *Communications on the Next Election*, 12, 20–21.

34. See George Clinton to Genet, August 19, 1795, in gratitude "for your letter of the 7th by the Negro Boy Michael. I believe I will buy him. He is now with me a few days on trial. His being a brother to your servant [name unclear]. . . will be a considerable inducement added to this" (Genet Papers, NYHS). In 1805, Genet wrote to a colleague to ask assistance regaining a truant servant, Nancy, who seems to have run away, or refused to travel to upstate New York, to remain with her husband in the city. Said Genet: "If she is willing to return I am willing to forgive her to pay her passage and to employ her husband as one of my hands at L.30 a year. If she refuses, I intend to have her arrested put on board of a sloop and her husband prosecuted for all the damage or to sell her if any body will buy her." Genet to McKesson, May 18, 1805, Genet Papers, NYHS.

35. Shane White, *Somewhat More Independent: the End of Slavery in New York City, 1770–1810* (Athens: University of Georgia Press, 1991); David N. Gellman, *Emancipating New York: The Politics of Slavery and Freedom, 1777–1827* (Baton Rouge: Louisiana State University Press, 2006).

36. On Clinton's shifting course, see Steven E. Siry, *DeWitt Clinton and the American Political Economy: Sectionalism, Politics, and the Republican Ideology, 1787–1828* (New York: Peter Lang, 1990) and Evan Cornog, *The Birth of Empire: DeWitt Clinton and the American Experience, 1769–1828* (New York: Oxford University Press, 1998), 84–103

37. Gaspare J. Saladino, "Gilman, Nicholas" ANB; Nicholas Gilman to Levi Bartlett, March 15, 1806, and unknown recipient, December 8, 1808, Nicholas Gilman Papers, LC; Nicholas Gilman to John Goddard, May 1 and 23, 1812, William Dawes Papers, Box 1, Folder 5, MHS.

38. Gideon Granger to DeWitt Clinton, March 27, 1810, Papers of Gideon and Francis

Granger, LC (microfilm edition). Granger to Clinton, March 27, 1804, Clinton Papers, Columbia University Library, as cited in Siry, *DeWitt Clinton*, 77–78; Richard E. Ellis, *The Jeffersonian Crisis: Courts and Politics in the Young Republic* (New York: Oxford University Press, 1971), 89–90. On Granger and the election of 1812, see Donald R. Hickey, *The War of 1812: A Forgotten Conflict* (Urbana: University of Illinois Press, 1989), 102; Siry, *DeWitt Clinton*, 160.

39. On conflict within the Republican coalition, see Stagg, *Mr. Madison's War*, 48–119

40. Charles R. King, ed., *The Life and Correspondence of Rufus King* (New York: Putnam's, 1896), 5: 277; Samuel Eliot Morrison, ed., *The Life and Letters of Harrison Gray Otis* (Boston: Houghton Mifflin, 1913), 1: 309–12.

41. Edward St. Loe Livermore to Timothy Pitkin, November 7, 1812, Timothy Pitkin Papers, HL.

42. Other historians have been less sanguine. See Fischer, *Revolution of American Conservatism*, 90.

43. *Connecticut Journal*, October 15 and 22, 1812; Boreas [Sereno Edwards Dwight], *Slave Representation* (New Haven, Conn. 1812); Mason, *Slavery and Politics*, 52–59.

44. Perkins, *Prologue to War*, 395.

45. See also Richards, *The Slave Power*, 52–82 on Republican challenges to the three-fifths clause.

46. For the New School/Old School split see Kim Phillips, "William Duane, Revolutionary Editor" (Ph.D. dissertation, University of California, Berkeley, 1968), 101–344; and Andrew Shankman, *Crucible of American Democracy: The Struggle to Fuse Egalitarianism & Capitalism in Jeffersonian Pennsylvania* (Lawrence: University Press of Kansas, 2004).

47. Phillips, "William Duane," 316–37; for Duane's attacks on Gallatin, see, e.g., *Weekly Aurora*, February 4, 1812.

48. "Constitution of Virginia," *Weekly Aurora*, February 19, 1812.

49. James Sloan, *An Address to the Citizens of the United States, But More Particularly to Those of the Middle and Eastern States* (Philadelphia: James Maxwell, 1812), 8, 12–14. The address was also published in *Poulson's American Daily Advertiser*, September 22, 1812.

50. Sloan, *An Address to the Citizens of the United States*, 12.

51. "James Sloan's Mare," *United States Gazette*, December 24, 1807. This article was reprinted throughout the northern press. See, e.g., *Trenton Federalist*, January 4, 1808; *Connecticut Courant*, January 6, 1808; *The Political Atlas*, January 9, 1808; *Portsmouth Oracle* January 9, 1808; *Massachusetts Spy*, January 13, 1808; *Connecticut Herald*, January 19, 1808; *The Tickler*, January 20, 1808.

52. *The Tickler*, October 6, 1812.

53. Bangs to Howe, September 10, 1811, June 15, 1812, Bangs Papers, AAS.

54. Bangs to Howe, June 15, 1812, Bangs Papers, AAS; *National Aegis*, July 8, 1812; Enoch Lincoln, *An Oration Pronounced at Worcester in Commemoration of American Independence* (Worcester, Mass.: Henry Rogers, 1812), 11, 9–10.

55. *Aurora General Advertiser*, September 19, 1807.

56. Act of May 8, 1792, chap. 33, 1 *Stat.* 271; Barbara Welke, *Law and the Borders of Belonging in the Long Nineteenth Century United States* (Cambridge: Cambridge University Press, 2010), 35.

57. John Craig Hammond, *Slavery, Freedom, and Expansion in the Early American West* (Charlottesville: University of Virginia Press, 2007); Stanley Harrold, *Border War: Fighting Over Slavery Before the Civil War* (Chapel Hill: University of North Carolina Press, 2010).

58. On the prevalence of Anglophobia see Peskin, "Conspiratorial Anglophobia and the

War of 1812"; for the antebellum period, see Samuel Haynes, *Unfinished Revolution: The Early American Republic in a British World* (Charlottesville: University of Virginia Press, 2011).

Chapter 5. Republican Nation

1. J. C. A. Stagg, *Mr. Madison's War: Politics, Diplomacy, and Warfare in the Early American Republic* (Princeton, N.J.: Princeton University Press, 1983), 3–47 ; Donald R. Hickey, *The War of 1812: A Forgotten Conflict* (Urbana: University of Illinois Press, 1989), 20–28; J. C. A. Stagg, *The War of 1812: Conflict for a Continent* (Cambridge: Cambridge University Press, 2012), 18–47; Lawrence A. Peskin, "Conspiratorial Anglophobia and the War of 1812," *JAH* 98, 3 (December 2011): 647–669

2. The institutional story of the War of 1812 is best told in Stagg, *Mr. Madison's War*.

3. Hickey, *War of 1812*, 105.

4. Alan Taylor, *The Internal Enemy: Slavery and War in Virginia, 1772–1832* (New York: Norton, 2013); Gene Allen Smith, *The Slaves' Gamble: Choosing Sides in the War of 1812* (New York: Palgrave Macmillan, 2013); Gerald Horne, *Negro Comrades of the Crown: African Americans and the British Empire Fight the U.S. Before Emancipation* (New York: New York University Press, 2012), 29–77; Robert G. Parkinson, "'Manifest Signs of Passion': The First Federal Congress, Antislavery, and Legacies of the Revolutionary War," in *Contesting Slavery: The Politics of Bondage and Freedom in the New American Nation*, ed. John Craig Hammond and Matthew Mason (Charlottesville: University of Virginia Press, 2011), 49–68; Matthew Mason, "'Nothing is Better Calculated to Excite Divisions': Federalist Agitation Against Slave Representation During the War of 1812," *NEQ* 75, 4 (December 2002): 531–61.

5. For earlier links between nationhood, violence, and racial exclusion, see Peter Silver, *Our Savage Neighbors: How Indian War Transformed Early America* (New York: Norton, 2008); Carroll Smith-Rosenberg, *This Violent Empire: The Birth of an American National Identity* (Chapel Hill: University of North Carolina Press, 2010); Gerald Horne, *The Counter-Revolution of 1776: Slave Resistance and the Origins of the United States of America* (New York: New York University Press, 2014).

6. See *Weekly Aurora*, October 1, 1811, reprinting "Wallace" from the *Independent Chronicle*.

7. *Weekly Aurora*, October 27, 1812. See also Stagg, *Mr. Madison's War*, 116–17.

8. Morgan D. Dowd, "Justice Joseph Story and the Politics of Appointment," *American Journal of Legal History* 9, 4 (October 1965): 265–85.

9. Joseph Story to Nathaniel Williams, August 24 1812, William Wetmore Story, ed., *The Life and Letters of Joseph Story* (Boston: Little and Brown, 1851), vol. 1: 228–29.

10. Entry of June 24, 1812, John Gallison Diaries 1807–1820, Journal D, 89, MHS.

11. Story to Williams, October 8, 1812, *Life and Letters* vol. 1: 243.

12. Stagg, *Mr. Madison's War*, 254–58; Richard Buel, *America on the Brink: How the Political Struggle over the War of 1812 Almost Destroyed the Young Republic* (New York: Palgrave Macmillan, 2006), 143–49; Paul Goodman, *The Democratic-Republicans of Massachusetts* (Cambridge, Mass.: Harvard University Press, 1964), 154–81; George Athan Billias, *Elbridge Gerry: Founding Father and Republican Statesman* (New York: McGraw-Hill, 1976), chap. 20

13. Elbridge Gerry, *Speech of His Excellency the Governor . . . January 1812* (Boston: s.n., 1812), 14. See also *Message from His Excellency the Governor, February 27, 1812* (Boston: s.n., 1812), on libels in the Federalist press. In September 1811 Gerry wrote to Henry Dearborn, "if we do not kill them"—meaning the Federalists—"they will kill us" (as quoted in Stagg, *Mr. Madison's War*, 254).

14. Elbridge Gerry to Richard Cutts, June 16, 1812, Gerry to Samuel Dana, June 27 1812, Gerry to Madison, July 13, 1812, Microfilm edition of the Elbridge Gerry Papers, 1706–1895, MHS.

15. Jefferson to Madison, June 29, 1812, Madison Papers, LC; Alan Taylor, *The Civil War of 1812: American Citizens, British Subjects, Irish Rebels, and Indian Allies* (New York: Knopf, 2010), 177; Edward C. Carter, II, "Matthew Carey and 'The Olive Branch,' 1814–1818," *PMHB* 89, 4 (October 1965: 402; Hickey, *The War of 1812*, 52–71; Jeffrey Pasley, *"The Tyranny of Printers": Newspaper Politics in the Early American Republic* (Charlottesville: University of Virginia Press, 2001), 241–48; Paul Gilje, "The Baltimore Riots of 1812 and the Breakdown of the Anglo-American Mob Tradition," *Journal of Social History* 13, 4 (Summer 1980): 547–64.

16. Entry of August 8, 1812, John Gallison Diaries, Journal B, 126–28, MHS; Hickey, *The War of 1812*, 69–70.

17. *AC*, 12th Cong., 1st Sess., 1637. For a sectional breakdown see Reginald Horsman, *The Causes of the War of 1812* (Philadelphia: University of Pennsylvania Press, 1962), 293. On the influence of partisan unity on the vote for war, see Ronald L. Hatzenbuehler, "Party Unity and the Decision for War in the House of Representatives, 1812," *WMQ* 29, 3 (June 1972): 367–90.

18. Jonathan Roberts to Matthew Roberts, January 31, 1813; John Binns to Jonathan Roberts, May 24, 1812, Roberts Papers, HSP; Philip S. Klein, ed., "Memoirs of a Senator from Pennsylvania," *PMHB* 62, 2 (April 1938): 232–33; Richard Rush to Charles J. Ingersoll, February 20, 1812, Ingersoll Papers, HSP. A symbolic victory over Randolph came in December 1811, when Speaker of the House Henry Clay ordered the Virginian to remove his dog from the legislative chamber (Hickey, *War of 1812*, 30). Clay's interdiction was perhaps related to events of the previous session. In January 1811, Willis Alston of North Carolina became tangled up with Randolph's dogs while leaving the House. "He struck the dogs," reported William Duane, "and John Randolph who had a hickory stick beat Alston several times over the head and shoulders." William Duane to Thomas Jefferson, January 25 1811, "Letters of William Duane," ed. Worthington C. Ford, *Proceedings of the Massachusetts Historical Society* 20 (May, 1906): 344.

19. Rush to Ingersoll, December 4, 1812 and August 2, 1812, Ingersoll Papers, HSP. See also Rush to Ingersoll December 1, 1812, where Rush rants, "There is no man half so insolent, half so intolerant, as Quincy; no, certainly not; not even John Randolph!" On Quincy, see Matthew Mason, *Slavery and Politics in the Early American Republic* (Chapel Hill: University of North Carolina Press, 2006), 67–70.

20. Dixon Ryan Fox, *The Decline of Aristocracy in the Politics of New York* (New York: Columbia University Press, 1919), 176.

21. Salman Child to John W. Taylor, December 30, 1813, John W. Taylor Papers, NYHS; Taylor, *Civil War of 1812*, 255.

22. Seth Baldwin et al. to John W. Taylor, December 2, 1812; John W. Taylor to Seth Baldwin et al., December 2, 1812 (draft), Taylor Papers, NYHS.

23. New York held two congressional elections in 1812. The first, in April, was declared invalid because the state had not drawn new districts based on the 1810 census, leading to a second election in December. By that point, Madison had already secured reelection. In December, Taylor defeated Federalist Samuel Stewart, winning 2209 to Stewart's 1974 votes. "New York 1812 Election for Congress District 11," *A New Nation Votes: American Electoral Returns, 1787–1825*, Tufts Digital Library.

24. Thomas Palmer to John Taylor, June 23, 1813; Child to Taylor, December 30, 1813; Barry Fenton to John Taylor, January 13, 1814 and January 15, 1815, Taylor Papers, NYHS.

25. An Oration to be Delivered on the 4th of July, 1803"; Taylor 1810 speech against Jonas Platt, Taylor Papers, "Speeches," NYHS; see also Edward K. Spann, "John W. Taylor, The Reluctant Partisan, 1784–1854," Ph.D. dissertation, New York University, 1957, 25–26. Draft speech on Clinton and Federalists, likely composed sometime in late 1812 or early 1813.

26. Draft speech on War of 1812, Taylor Papers, "Speeches," NYHS. Spann believes this speech was given in January of 1814. It was not recorded in the *Annals*, but there is a note of an hour-long speech by Taylor on January 26, 1814. See *AC*, 13th Cong., 2nd Sess., 1145; Spann, "John Taylor," 80–81. "Men of straw" referred to the refusal of militiamen to cross the Niagara River into Canada at the Battle of Queenston Heights on October 13, 1812.

27. John Taylor to Jane Taylor, November 29, October 15, 1814, Taylor Papers, NYHS.

28. Taylor opposed dueling, and in March 1820 he rejected John Randolph's proposal to commemorate Stephen Decatur, naval hero of the War of 1812, by wearing a crepe armband for the rest of the session. Taylor claimed that Decatur, who had been killed in a duel with James Barron, had "died in the violation of the laws of God and his country." *AC*, 16 Cong., 1st Sess., 1670. For later comments against dueling, see John W. Taylor to Jane Taylor, November 29, 1827, Taylor Papers, NYHS.

29. Stagg, *Mr. Madison's War*, 67; Kim Phillips, "William Duane, Revolutionary Editor," Ph.D. dissertation, University of California, Berkeley, 1968, 373–74, 391–92, 400–404; Hickey, *War of 1812*, 162.

30. John Binns, *Recollections of the Life of John Binns* (Philadelphia: Binns and Parry and M'Millan, 1854), 213–20; Taylor, *The Civil War of 1812*, 358–79.

31. Taylor, *The Civil War of 1812*, 359; Richard Rush to John Binns, July 27, 1813, Gratz Collection, Case 3, Box 18, HSP; *Public Documents Containing Proceedings of the Hartford Convention* . . . (Boston, s.n., 1815), 49; Binns, *Recollections*, 154.

32. Binns, *Recollections*, 220–221; Taylor, *The Internal Enemy*, 186; Benton J. Lossing, *The Pictorial Field Book of the War of 1812* (New York: Harper, 1868), 673–674; *Democratic Press*, May 18, July 10, 1813.

33. Philip S. Klein, ed., "Memoirs of a Senator from Pennsylvania," *PMHB* 62, 1 (January 1938): 83; Raymond W. Champagne, Jr., and Thomas J. Rueter, "Jonathan Roberts and the War Hawk Congress of 1811–1812," *PMHB* 104, 4 (October 1980): 444. Paschal Hollingsworth questioned the causes for war and claimed that a prewar embargo (passed by Congress on April 1, 1812) would hurt millers in Easton, in Roberts's district. Said Rogers: "We care not for a few bawling millers" (Rogers to Roberts, April 20, 1812, Roberts Papers). For more on Rogers, see Jeffrey Pasley, *"Tyranny of Printers"*, 332–47.

34. Rush to Ingersoll, February 1, April 26, 29, 1812, Ingersoll Papers, HSP. On Rush's appointment, see Stagg, *Mr. Madison's War*, 67. On Ingersoll, see Steven Watts, *The Republic Reborn: War and the Making of Liberal America, 1790–1820* (Baltimore: Johns Hopkins University Press, 1987), 93–99. Watts argues that the war allowed Americans to "relieve the social tensions accruing to liberalizing change" and thus ultimately "served as the catalyst in the larger consolidation of American capitalism" (105, 321). While this thesis is often convincing, for Pennsylvania Republicans like Ingersoll and Rush, legitimating capitalist development was secondary to building American nationalism and Republican power. See also Samuel Haynes, *Unfinished Revolution: The Early American Republic in a British World* (Charlottesville: University of Virginia Press, 2011), 25–27.

35. Thomas J. Rogers to Jonathan Roberts, November 17, 1811, Roberts Papers, HSP; Jefferson to William Duane, August 4, 1812, Jefferson Papers, AMLC. Jefferson thought that only Canada "as

far as the neighborhood of Quebec" would be taken by marching; the following year, the United States would take Halifax, Nova Scotia, completing "the final expulsion of England from the American continent."

36. William Stedman to Timothy Pitkin, April 11, 1812, Timothy Pitkin Papers, HL.

37. Rush to Ingersoll, April 29, 1812, Ingersoll Papers, HSP. In the First Punic War, Carthage had a more powerful navy than Rome. Yet as Rush explained, citing Gibbon by volume and page, "in the first Punick war the Romans exerted such diligence that within sixty days after the first stroke of the axe had been given in the forest a fleet of 160 gallies rode at anchor in the sea." Rush used a similar line in an oration on July 4, 1812 in front of Congress, Madison, and members of the administration: "We are also perhaps the only genuine republic which, since the days of the ancients, has taken up arms against a foreign foe in defence of its rights and its liberties. Animating thought! Warmed with the fire of ancient freedom, may we not expect the valor of Thermopylae and Marathon again displayed!" Richard Rush, *An Oration Delivered . . . on the 4th of July* (Washington: s.n., 1812), 42. On Rush's militant defense of the republic, see Roger H. Brown, *The Republic in Peril: 1812* (New York: Columbia University Press, 1964), 83–84.

38. Rush to Ingersoll, April 29, August 28, 2, 29, September 4, 1812, Ingersoll Papers, HSP. Falmouth (which at the time included what would become Portland, Maine) was burned by the British in the fall of 1775, propelling the colonies toward independence.

39. Jefferson to William Duane, August 4, 1812, Jefferson Papers, AMLC.

40. Nicole Eustace, *1812: War and the Passions of Patriotism* (Philadelphia: University of Pennsylvania Press, 2012), 36–75; Madison 70–71. For Rush and Monroe's efforts to frame Hull, rather than the Madison administration, as responsible for the loss of Detroit, see Stagg, *Mr. Madison's War*, 207.

41. John Binns to Jonathan Roberts, May 3, 5, 1812, Roberts Papers, HSP.

42. Thomas J. Rogers to Jonathan Roberts, May 16, 1812, Roberts Papers, HSP. See also John Binns to Jonathan Roberts, June 1, 1812: "We shall strangle them [the Federalists] and forever be clear of a venomous corrupting influence which they have too long and too successfully disseminated." For the weak national consensus in favor of war, see Bradford Perkins, *Prologue to War: England and the United States, 1805–1812* (Berkeley: University of California Press, 1961), 394–95; on partisanship and nationalism in Pennsylvania, see Victor A. Sapio, *Pennsylvania and the War of 1812* (Lexington: University Press of Kentucky, 1970).

43. For this older view, see Brown, *Republic in Peril*, 182–83. In Peter Onuf's reading, Jefferson viewed Federalists in this light during the War of 1812; see *Jefferson's Empire: The Language of American Nationhood* (Charlottesville: University of Virginia Press, 2000), 123–28.

44. For the importance of the war as a political measure see Stagg, *Mr. Madison's War*, 116.

45. Edward Fox to Jonathan Roberts, June 2, 1812; John Binns to Jonathan Roberts, June 22 1812, Roberts Papers, HSP. See also Binns to Ingersoll, July 13 and 21, 1812, Ingersoll Papers, HSP.

46. Stagg, *Mr. Madison's War*, 411–18; Joseph Varnum to Joseph Bradley Varnum, May 9, 1814, Varnum Family Papers I, MHS; Taylor, *The Internal Enemy*, 275–316.

47. Hickey, *War of 1812*, 298–99; Paul Gilje, *Free Trade and Sailor's Rights in the War of 1812* (Cambridge: Cambridge University Press, 2013), 277–87.

48. A "Catholic lieutenant" exhorting Irishmen to enlist in Baltimore, as cited in David Wilson, *United Irishmen, United States: Immigrant Radicals in the Early Republic* (Ithaca, N.Y.: Cornell University Press, 1998), 8.

49. Rush to Ingersoll, August 29, 1812, Ingersoll Papers, HSP; Taylor, *Civil War of 1812*, 205–14; *Aurora General Advertiser*, March 24, 1813, as cited in Taylor, 206.

50. Jefferson to David Bailie Warden, December 29, 1813, *Papers of Thomas Jefferson, Retirement Series* (Princeton, N.J.: Princeton University Press, 2010), vol. 7: 90–93; Ohio Circular as printed in *New York Columbian*, July 13, 1813.

51. Taylor, *Civil War of 1812*, 244–245; R. David Edmunds, *The Shawnee Prophet* (Lincoln: University of Nebraska Press, 1983).

52. Claudio Saunt, *A New Order of Things: Property, Power, and the Transformation of the Creek Indians, 1733–1816* (Cambridge: Cambridge University Press, 1999), chap. 11; Hickey, *War of 1812*, 146–51; Adam Rothman, *Slave Country: American Expansion and the Origins of the Deep South* (Cambridge, Mass.: Harvard University Press, 2005), 119–64.

53. Taylor, *The Internal Enemy*; Smith, *The Slaves' Gamble*, 85–131; Gerald Horne, *Negro Comrades of the Crown*, 29–77; Harvey Amani Whitfield, "'We Can do as We Like Here': An Analysis of Self-Assertion and Agency Among Black Refugees in Halifax, Nova Scotia, 1813–1821," *Acadiensis* 32, 1 (Autumn 2002); Christopher T. George, "Mirage of Freedom: African Americas in the War of 1812," *Maryland Historical Magazine* 91, 4 (Winter 1996): 427–50; Frank. A. Cassell, "Slaves of the Chesapeake Bay Area and the War of 1812," *Journal of Negro History* 57, 2 (April 1972): 144–55. Taylor estimates 3,405 slaves escaped in the Chesapeake region during the War (*The Internal Enemy*, 442).

54. John Taylor to Jane Taylor, July 2, 1813, Taylor Papers, NYHS.

55. Jonathan Roberts to Matthew Roberts, July 4, 1813, Roberts Papers, HSP; *The Columbian*, July 20, 1813. See Nicole Eustace, *1812*, 206–8. The British blamed the outrages at Hampton on French prisoners of war who had joined the British forces (Hickey, *War of 1812*, 154). According to Alan Taylor, the story of rape by slaves "had no basis in evidence from Hampton" (*The Internal Enemy*, 195)

56. "British Barbarities," *Weekly Aurora*, October 12, 1813. A congressional report on Hampton was published under the title *Barbarities of the Enemy* (Eustace, *1812*, 206). See also *AC*, 13th Cong., 2nd Sess., 2330–47.

57. *Democratic Press*, December 20, 1813; Taylor, *The Internal Enemy*, 164.

58. *Democratic Press*, March 15, 1813. Both slaves were presumed to be traveling under "a pass with John Wise's name thereunto, the clerk of the county of Accomack." Kesiah's ad was listed by Robert Jenkins, from Accomack County; Jacob's by Thomas Marshall from Shell Town, Somerset County, Maryland, just north of Accomack County.

59. Taylor, *The Internal Enemy*, 271–73.

60. This formulation is influenced by Orlando Patterson's definition of slavery as natal alienation. Patterson, *Slavery and Social Death: A Comparative Study* (Cambridge, Mass.: Harvard University Press, 1982), 5.

61. For relative dismissal of impressment as a cause of war, see Troy Bickham, *The Weight of Vengeance: The United States, the British Empire, and the War of 1812* (New York: Oxford University Press, 2012), 31, which echoes Perkins, *Prologue to War*, 94–95. Compare Gilje, *Free Trade and Sailor's Rights*, 171–89; Denver Brunsman, "Citizen vs. Subject: Impressment and Identity in the Anglo-American Atlantic," *JER* 30, 4 (Winter 2010): 557–86.

62. Binns, *Recollections*, 157; *Democratic Press*, August 30, 1809; January 2, May 3, June 22, 1810.

63. Robert E. Cray, "Remembering the USS *Chesapeake*: The Politics of Maritime Death and Impressment," *JER* 25, 3 (Fall 2005): 445–74. See especially 466–67, 472, 474; W. Jeffrey Bolster, *Black Jacks: African American Seamen in the Age of Sail* (Cambridge, Mass.: Harvard University Press, 1997), 103. See also Bolster, "Letters by African American Sailors, 1799–1814," *WMQ* 64

(January 2007): 167–82, for letters by African Americans attempting to free themselves from impressment; many openly identify themselves as American citizens.

64. *Weekly Aurora*, May 19, 1812.

65. Matthew Carey, *The Olive Branch* (Philadelphia: Matthew Carey, 1814), 118. For more on these appropriations of slavery, see Matthew Mason, "The Battle of the Slaveholding Liberators: Great Britain, the United States, and Slavery in the Early Nineteenth Century," *WMQ* 59, 3 (July 2002): 665–96; Mason, *Slavery and Politics*, 87–90. Federalists (and some Republicans) criticized these comparisons, as they had never been much moved by the supposed crime of impressment (48–49).

66. Rush, *An Oration Delivered . . . on the 4th of July*, 25; *Message from the President of the United States Transmitting Copies of a Communication from Mr. Russell . . .* (Washington: Roger C. Weightman, 1812) Eustace, *1812*, 174–76.

67. *Democratic Press*, September 15, 1809, copying the *Maryland Republican*; Isaac Anderson to Jonathan Roberts, May 15, 1812, Roberts Papers, HSP; O'Rourke in *Democratic Press*, July 22, 1813. See Taylor, *The Civil War of 1812*, on British desertion (333–35) and Willcocks (passim).

68. The song was first titled "The Defence of Fort M'Henry" after the event in the Battle of Baltimore Key describes. For an early printing, see, e.g., Boston's *Independent Chronicle*, October 3, 1814. Two caveats: Key was a Federalist and had initially opposed the war, but he became embittered with the British after they raided his family tomb in Chaptico, Maryland, in the summer of 1814 (Taylor, *The Internal Enemy* 293, 309). "Hireling and slave" was used prior to "The Star-Spangled Banner" to denote the difference between free, republican militias and armies composed of dependent forces, as in a Fourth of July toast by Philadelphia cavalrymen from 1804: "The militia of the United States—which supersedes the necessity of embodying hirelings and slaves" (*Aurora General Advertiser*, July 6, 1804). But in the context of the Chesapeake war, "hireling and slave" would have implied an obvious referent to many Americans— the French forces who were responsible for the Hampton raid, and the runaway slaves turned colonial marines who enabled the British to wreak havoc up and down the Potomac and Patuxent rivers in 1814, eventually capturing and burning Washington. See Taylor, *The Internal Enemy*, 309–10 and Smith, *The Slaves' Gamble*, 215–16.

69. Bolster, *Black Jacks*, 115; Rothman, *Slave Country*, 144–49; Smith, *The Slave's Gamble*, 131–41, 159–73. On how not enlisting slaves weakened military efforts, see Taylor, *The Internal Enemy*, 323–26.

70. Bolster, *Black Jacks*, 102; Taylor, *Civil War of 1812*, 364–71, 423–25.

71. Untitled Fourth of July Address, n.d. Taylor Papers, "Speeches," NYHS. The first line of the speech is: "National Independence is the first political blessing." Internal evidence, such as the comment on Dartmoor, strongly suggests that the speech was given in 1815. *The Civil War of 1812*, 370–71; Robin F. A. Fabel, "Self-Helf in Dartmoor: Black and White Prisoners in the War of 1812," *JER* 9, 2 (Summer 1989): 165–190.

72. "The Siege of Plattsburgh," Taylor Papers, NYHS. The song is filed in Taylor's incoming correspondence under the letter "P". David Waldstreicher, "Minstrelization and Nationhood: 'Backside Albany,' Backlash, and the Wartime Origins of Blackface Minstrelsy," in Nicole Eustace and Fredika J. Teute, eds., *Warring for America, 1803–1818* (Chapel Hill: University of North Carolina Press, forthcoming); Waldstreicher, *In the Midst of Perpetual Fetes: The Making of American Nationalism, 1776–1820* (Chapel Hill: University of North Carolina Press, 1997), 327–28.

73. Duane to Jefferson, August 11, 1814, "Letters of William Duane," ed. Worthington C. Ford, *Proceedings of the Massachusetts Historical Society* 20 (May 1906): 373–75.

74. Thus Alan Taylor, based on this letter to Jefferson as well as additional letters to

Secretary of War John Armstrong, suggests that Duane and other Irish American advocates of black troops "had not yet adopted the full racial prejudices of the republic" (*The Civil War of 1812*, 327–28). This seems hard to sustain in the case of the 1814 Jefferson letter, but it is possible Duane emphasized black inferiority to convince Jefferson, and through him other Virginians, that black troops would be a safe option for the republic. Arming blacks and potentially slaves did gain some traction toward the end of 1814, but in many ways that was a sign, as Taylor notes in his more recent work, of the desperate state of the republic's forces (*The Internal Enemy*, 323–26).

75. Mason, "The Battle of the Slaveholding Liberators," 677 n.49.

76. *Weekly Aurora*, January 18, 1814; *American Law Journal* 5, ed. John E. Hall (Baltimore: William Fry, 1814), 465–73; Paul Finkelman, *An Imperfect Union: Slavery, Federalism, and Comity* (Chapel Hill: University of North Carolina Press, 1981), 68–69; Robert Cover, *Justice Accused: Antislavery and the Judicial Process* (New Haven, Conn.: Yale University Press, 1975), 64–66; Richard Newman, *Transformation of American Abolitionism: Fighting Slavery in the Early Republic* (Chapel Hill: University of North Carolina Press, 2002), 81–83; on slaves seeking freedom in Pennsylvania, see *Commonwealth ex rel. negro Lewis v. Holloway* 6 Binney 20 (1814); Newman, "'Lucky to Be Born in Pennsylvania': Free Soil, Fugitive Slaves, and the Making of Pennsylvania's Anti-Slavery Borderland," *Slavery & Abolition* 32, 3 (September 2011).

77. Carey, *The Olive Branch*, 5; Matthew Carey, *A Calm Address to the People of the Eastern States* (Boston: Rowe and Hooper, 1814), 14–15.

78. On representation, see *A Calm Address*, 23–43; for the economic argument, see *The Olive Branch*, 193–215. Andrew Shankman, "Neither Infinite Wretchedness nor Positive Good: Matthew Carey and Henry Clay on Political Economy and Slavery During the Long 1820s," in Mason and Hammond, eds., *Contesting Slavery*, 247–66.

79. The slave traders were carrying "12 or 14 negroes"; Rogers and some associates had them brought before a court by a writ of habeas corpus, at which point the judge freed the children, but allowed the traders to keep the adults. Thomas J. Rogers to Jonathan Roberts, December 1, 1811, Roberts Papers, HSP.

80. Thomas J. Rogers to Jonathan Roberts, December 11, 1811; John Binns to Jonathan Roberts, December 19, 1812, Roberts Papers, HSP.

81. Taylor, *Civil War of 1812*, 260; Emil Olbrich, *The Development of the Sentiment on Negro Suffrage to 1860* (Madison: University of Wisconsin Press, 1912), 29–30; Dixon Ryan Fox, "The Negro Vote in Old New York," *Political Science Quarterly* 32 (June 1917): 257; David N. Gellman and David Quigley, *Jim Crow New York: A Documentary History of Race and Citizenship, 1777–1877* (New York: NYU Press, 2004), 64–66; David N. Gellman, *Emancipating New York: The Politics of Slavery and Freedom, 1777–1827* (Baton Rouge: LSU Press, 2006), 202–3; Paul Polgar, "'Whenever They Judge it Expedient': The Politics of Partisanship and Free Black Voting Rights in Early National New York," *American Nineteenth Century History* 12, 1 (April 2011): 10–11. In 1811, an initial law restricting black suffrage had been vetoed by the state's Council of Revision because it was deemed too discriminatory, but a subsequent law requiring "official" certificates of freedom to vote then passed. Certificates could be obtained from "any one of the justices of the supreme court, any mayor, recorder, or judge of any court of common pleas" for a cost of twelve and a half cents; they then had to be recorded with a county or town clerk (for an additional fee); a copy of that record had to be produced in order to vote. The 1814 law required all certificates of freedom in New York city to be issued by the "office of the register in and for the city and county of New-York," and required all black voters to have a record from the register in

order to vote. Presumably, this new law may have required some African Americans to obtain yet another certificate in order to prove free status. See Olbrich, *Negro Suffrage*, 30; *Laws of the State of New York, Passed at the Thirty-Fourth Session of the Legislature . . .* (New York: S. Southwick, 1811), 370–74; *Laws of the State of New York, Passed at the Thirty-Seventh Session of the Legislature* (New York: H.C. Southwick, 1814), 94–95. Examples of these certificates of freedom can be found in "BV-New York City Indentures," Box 2, NYHS.

82. James Forten, "Letters from a Man of Colour," reprinted in *Early American Abolitionists: A Collection of Antislavery Writings*, ed. James G. Basker (New York: Gilder Lehrman, 2005), 312.

Chapter 6. Democracy in Crisis

1. Trumbull had been working on a version of *The Declaration of Independence* since 1786 and used this original version in his proposal to Congress to execute a set of paintings for the capitol. The painting in the Rotunda is a larger version of this first painting, which is at the Yale University Art Gallery. See John Trumbull, *Autobiography, Reminiscences and Letters of John Trumbull* (New Haven, Conn.: B.L. Hamlen, 1841), 261–265; Jules David Prown, "John Trumbull as a History Painter," in Helen A. Cooper, *John Trumbull: The Hand and Spirit of a Painter* (New Haven, Conn.: Yale University Art Gallery), 22–92.

2. *Democratic Press* January 21, 1819.

3. John Binns, *Recollections of the Life of John Binns* (Philadelphia: John Binns and Parry and M'Millan, 1854), 236. For laudatory reviews of the print, see, e.g., *Daily National Intelligencer*, November 25, 1819; New York *Commercial Advertiser*, November 20, 1819; *National Aegis*, January 5, 1820, copying the Richmond, Virginia *Compiler*. Trumbull was not impressed: "Binns is publishing a mere verbal copy of the act itself (which is already in every body's hands,) embellished with flags and state armorial bearings and some heads, for which he gets numerous subscribers at ten dollars. How is it my dear sir, that an Irish emigrant can obtain patronage for such a work, Gothic at best—when an old officer cannot obtain it for a work, which I will proudly say will do honor to the nation in the eyes of the civilized world?" John Trumbull to Joseph Hopkinson, February 18, 1818, Trumbull, *Autobiography*, 360–61. See also Trish Loughran, *The Republic in Print: Print Culture in the Age of U.S. Nation Building, 1770–1870* (New York: Columbia University Press, 2007), 218.

4. The cemetery in the image may or may not have had metaphorical significance for Torrey; its presence, like the scattered objects in the foreground, seems to be a result of the fact that Rider and Lawson based the engraving on an 1814 drawing by George Munger depicting the Capitol shortly after the British attack. Jesse Torrey, *A Portraiture of Domestic Slavery in the United States* (Philadelphia: John Bioren, 1817), 32–34. For a related reading of Torrey's frontispiece, see Nicole Eustace, *1812: War and the Passions of Patriotism* (Philadelphia: University of Pennsylvania Press, 2012), 168–70.

5. In some respects, they could not even agree on the depiction of nationalist triumphalism. In February 1819, as the Declaration painting was on its way to Washington, the House had a brief argument about Trumbull's artistic efforts. New York Republican John Taylor thought the cost of the paintings too high, while his New Hampshire colleague Arthur Livermore was upset that Trumbull had been displaying the Declaration painting for admission fees in northern cities, despite the fact that the public, through Congress, had already contracted to pay for the painting. See *AC*, 15th Cong., 2nd Sess., 1141–46. Taylor voted against commissioning the paintings in the first place. See *AC*, 14th Cong., 2nd Sess., 761–63.

6. Joseph Story to Nathaniel Williams, February 22, 1815, *Life and Letters of Joseph Story*, ed.

William Wetmore Story, vol. 1 (Boston: Little and Brown, 1851), 254; Harlow Sheidley, *Sectional Nationalism: Massachusetts Conservative Leaders and the Transformation of America, 1815–1836* (Boston: Northeastern University Press, 1998).

7. George Dangerfield, *The Awakening of American Nationalism, 1815–1828* (New York: Harper and Row, 1965); Charles Sellers, *The Market Revolution: Jacksonian America, 1815–1846* (New York: Oxford University Press, 1994); Daniel Walker Howe, *What Hath God Wrought: The Transformation of America, 1815–1848* (New York: Oxford University Press, 2009); C. Edward Skeen, "'Vox Populi, Vox Dei': The Compensation Act of 1816 and the Rise of Popular Politics," *Journal of the Early Republic* 6, 3 (Autumn 1986): 253–74; Rosemarie Zagarri, "The Family Factor: Congressmen, Turnover, and the Burden of Public Service in the Early American Republic," *JER* 33, 2 (Summer 2013): 283–316

8. Alan Taylor, *The Internal Enemy: Slavery and War in Virginia, 1772–1832* (New York: Norton, 2013), 340–42; Frank L. Owsley, Jr., and Gene A. Smith, *Filibusters and Expansionists: Jeffersonian Manifest Destiny, 1800–1821* (Tuscaloosa: University of Alabama Press, 1997), 82–102

9. Owsley and Smith, *Filibusters and Expansionists*, 103–17, 141–63; Taylor, *The Internal Enemy*, 347; Claudio Saunt, *A New Order of Things: Property, Power, and the Transformation of the Creek Indians, 1733–1816* (Cambridge: Cambridge University Press, 1999), 233–90.

10. For an overview of the congressional debates, see David S. Heidler and Jeanne T. Heidler, *Old Hickory's War: Andrew Jackson and the Quest for Empire* (Mechanicsburg, Pa.: Stackpole, 1996), 201–21.

11. *AC*, 15th Cong., 2nd Sess., 615, 716, 728–29. Hillis Hadjo, a.k.a. Josiah Francis, did travel to England in 1815 with Major Edward Nicolls, who had established the British base in Florida during the war. Owsley and Smith, *Filibusters and Expansionists*, 114.

12. James Tallmadge, Sr., to James Tallmadge, January 7, 1819, Tallmadge Family Papers, NYHS. David S. Heidler, in "The Politics of National Aggression: Congress and the First Seminole War" *JER* 13, 4 (Winter 1993): 501–30 tabulates the vote in the House as follows: 11–4 in New England and 36–3 in the mid-Atlantic North against resolutions disapproving the execution of Ambrister and Arbuthnot; 14–4 and 34–7 against a similar resolutions disapproving of the seizure of Pensacola. New York was the strongest pro-Jackson state, with no representatives supporting disapproval of the executions and only two supporting the resolution on Pensacola. Southern Republicans, by comparison, were far more divided, voting 26–15 and 26–19 in favor of disapproving the executions and the seizure of Pensacola respectively (520–21). Jonathan Roberts of Pennsylvania was among the northern minority that objected to Jackson's invasion; he would remain opposed to the General for the rest of his career, describing him as "a man who had prov'd himself at all times, where his passions were excited, a lawless Barbarian." Philip S. Klein ed., "Memoirs of a Senator from Pennsylvania," *PMHB* 62, 3 (July 1938): 398–404.

13. Dangerfield, *Awakening of American Nationalism*, 66; Eliga H. Gould, *Among the Powers of the Earth: The American Revolution and the Making of a New World Empire* (Cambridge, Mass.: Harvard University Press, 2012), 210–17; John Quincy Adams, *Memoirs of John Quincy Adams: Comprising Portions of His Diary from 1795 to 1848*, ed. Charles Francis Adams, 12 vols. (Philadelphia: Lippincott, 1874–1877), 4: 438–39.

14. *AC*, 15th Cong., 2nd Sess., 305–12; Suzanne Cooper-Guasco, "'The Deadly Influence of Negro Capitalists': Southern Yeomen and the Resistance to the Expansion of Slavery in Illinois," *Civil War History* 47, 1 (March 2001): 7–29; Suzanne Cooper-Guasco, "'To Put into Complete Practice those Hallowed Principles': Edward Coles and the Crafting of Antislavery Nationalism in Early Nineteenth-Century America," *American Nineteenth-Century History* 11, 1 (March

2010): 17–45; Cooper-Guasco, *Confronting Slavery: Edward Coles and the Rise of Antislavery Politics in Nineteenth Century America* (DeKalb: Northern Illinois University Press, 2013), 71–133.

15. John Craig Hammond, *Slavery, Freedom, and Expansion in the Early American West* (Charlottesville: University of Virginia Press, 2007), 55–75.

16. Matthew Mason, *Slavery and Politics in the Early American Republic* (Chapel Hill: University of North Carolina Press, 2006), 145–48.

17. E.g., James Tallmadge, who argued in February 1819 that "fourteen thousand slaves have been brought into our country this last year," *AC*, 15th Cong., 2nd Sess., 1210. See also *AC*, 16th Cong., Sess. 1, 1207, 1301, 1433–34 for other examples. On new legislation against the international trade, see Don E. Fehrenbacher, *The Slaveholding Republic: An Account of the United States Government's Relations to Slavery* (New York: Oxford University Press, 2001), 150–52; and Paul Finkelman, "Regulating the African Slave Trade," *Civil War History* 54, 4 (2008): 379–405.

18. *AC*, 14 Cong., 1st Sess., 1115–17; Nicholas Wood, "John Randolph of Roanoke and the Politics of Slavery in the Early Republic," *Virginia Magazine of History and Biography* 120, 2 (Summer 2012): 106–43. On Torrey see John L. Brooke, *Columbia Rising: Civil Life on the Upper Hudson from the Revolution to the Age of Jackson* (Chapel Hill: University of Pennsylvania Press 2010), 129–30; 393–96.

19. Torrey, *A Portraiture of Domestic Slavery*, 45.

20. Mason, *Slavery and Politics*, 133–45; Hammond, *Slavery, Freedom, and Expansion*, 153; *AC*, 14th Cong., 1st Sess., 1068; 15th Cong., 1st Sess., 829; 15th Cong., 2nd Sess., 336–37; *Minutes of the Proceedings of the Fifteenth American Convention for Promoting the Abolition of Slavery* (Philadelphia: Merritt, 1817), 6, 13–14, 24, 28, 36.

21. See, e.g., *AC*, 16th Cong. 1, 1214–15, 1400–1401, 1432–33; see also Nicholas Wood, "Considerations of Humanity and Expediency: The Slave Trades and African Colonization in the Early National Antislavery Movement," Ph.D. dissertation, University of Virginia, 2013, 331–34.

22. *AC*, 15th Cong., 2nd Sess., 1210.

23. Darlington Journal, March 2, 19, 1820, William Darlington Papers, NYHS.

24. Taylor, *The Internal Enemy*, 395–98; Gene Allen Smith, *The Slaves' Gamble: Choosing Sides in the War of 1812* (New York: Palgrave Macmillan, 2013), 212–13; Glover Moore, *The Missouri Controversy, 1819–1821* (Lexington: University of Kentucky Press, 1953), 240–43; Robert Pierce Forbes, *The Missouri Compromise and Its Aftermath: Slavery and the Meaning of America* (Chapel Hill: University of North Carolina Press 2007), 64; Richard E. Ellis, *Aggressive Nationalism: McCulloch v. Maryland and the Foundation of Federal Authority in the Young Republic* (New York: Oxford University Press, 2007).

25. Thomas D. Morris, *Free Men All: The Personal Liberty Laws of the North, 1780–1861* (Baltimore: Johns Hopkins University Press, 1974), 35.

26. Morris, *Free Men All*, 36–41; *AC*, 15th Cong., 1st Sess. (House), 446–47, 513, 825–31, 837–40, 1339, 1393, 1716–17; 15 Cong., 1st Sess. (Senate), 161, 165–66, 258–59.

27. Recent work on the ACS has emphasized that many colonizationists, although opposed to increasing the free black population of the United States, had antislavery motivations. See Eric Burin, *Slavery and the Peculiar Solution: A History of the American Colonization Society* (Gainesville: University Press of Florida, 2005); Beverly Tomek, *Colonization and Is Discontents: Emancipation, Emigration, and Antislavery in Antebellum Pennsylvania* (New York: New York University Press, 2011); Wood, "Considerations of Humanity," 274–318. On Torrey and colonization, see *Portraiture of Domestic Slavery*, 29–30, 84–94. Torrey thought that slaves should be emancipated but that they should not be granted full citizenship. He wanted to prohibit

interracial sex, and believed that was a primary reason to end slavery (58–59). On increasing penalties against the international trade, see Finkelman, "Regulating the African Slave Trade."

28. On lower South rejection of the ACS, see Lacy K. Ford, *Deliver Us from Evil: The Slavery Question in the Old South* (New York: Oxford University Press, 2009), 300–301 and Douglas Egerton, "Averting a Crisis: The Proslavery Critique of the American Colonization Society," *Civil War History* 43, 2 (June 1997): 142–56. On the Philadelphia meeting, which was chaired by James Forten, see Gary Nash, *Forging Freedom: The Formation of Philadelphia's Black Community, 1720–1840* (Cambridge, Mass.: Harvard University Press, 1988), 237–38. Torrey, *Portraiture of Domestic Slavery*, 94. The classic story of black opponents of colonization converting white abolitionists is that of William Lloyd Garrison. See, e.g., Paul Goodman, *Of One Blood: Abolitionism and the Origins of Racial Equality* (Berkeley: University of California Press, 1998), 23–44, and Richard S. Newman, *The Transformation of American Abolitionism: Fighting Slavery in the Early Republic* (Chapel Hill: University of North Carolina Press, 2002), 107–16. But as Nicholas Wood argues, this process began much earlier, soon after the formation of the ACS. Wood, "Considerations of Humanity," 313–17; Tomek, *Colonization and Its Discontents*, 149.

29. On the relationship between the politics of colonization and the Missouri Crisis, see especially Wood, "Considerations of Humanity," 319–56.

30. *AC*, 15th Cong., 1st Sess., 1672, 1675–76; Moore, *Missouri Controversy*, 33.

31. *AC*, 14th Cong., 1st Sess., 1115.

32. Anna Tallmadge to Matthias B. Tallmadge, February 3, 1819, Tallmadge Family Papers, NYHS.

33. *AC*, 15th Cong., 2nd Sess., 1170–79, 1177–78.

34. *AC*, 15th Cong., 2nd Sess., 1178; Draft speech on War of 1812, Taylor Papers, "Speeches," NYHS (see also Chapter 5 of this book). John Scott on Taylor: "He did not desire that gentleman, his sons, or his brothers, in that land of brave, noble, and independent freemen" (*AC*, 15th Cong., 2nd Sess., 1202).

35. *AC*, 15th Cong., 2nd Sess., 1170 (Taylor), 1206 (Tallmadge).

36. *AC*, 15th Cong., 2nd Sess., 1180–81 (Fuller), 1211 (Tallmadge on Declaration), 307 (Tallmadge in Illinois debates).

37. On March 2, a motion to agree to the Senate's striking out of the Tallmadge amendment lost by the narrow vote of 76–78; the House then voted to adhere to their opposition to the Senate by the wider margin of 78–66. *AC*, 15th Cong., 2nd Sess., 1214–15, 1433–38; Moore, *The Missouri Controversy*, 53–55.

38. This debate began February 17, the same day the House sent the Missouri bill, Tallmadge amendment intact, to the Senate. John Taylor proposed a similar amendment for the territorial government of Arkansas. Multiple votes indicated a strong commitment to restrict slavery; Taylor's motion to restrict slavery lost 68–80 on February 17, but it was proposed again the following day, and lost by only one vote, 70–71. A connected motion to gradually emancipate the children of Arkansas slaves then passed, 75–73, and a motion for reconsideration failed 77–79. The following day, a motion to recommit the entire bill led to a tie vote of 88–88, broken in the South's favor by Speaker Henry Clay; a motion to strike out the gradual emancipation clause passed, 89–87, and a final attempt to restrict slavery failed, 86–90. *AC*, 15th Cong., 2nd Sess., 1223–40, 1272–83.

39. Robert Pierce Forbes, *The Missouri Compromise and its Aftermath: Slavery and the Meaning of America* (Chapel Hill: University of North Carolina Press 2007), 51–59.

40. Major Wilson, *Space, Time, and Freedom: The Quest for Nationality and the Irrepressible

Conflict, 1815–1861 (Westport, Conn.: Greenwood Press, 1974); Sean Wilentz, "Jeffersonian Democracy and the Origins of Political Antislavery in the United States: The Missouri Crisis Revisited," *Journal of the Historical Society* 4, 3 (September 2004): 375–401.

41. *AC*, 16th Cong., 1st Sess., 1374, 1380–81. For more on Darlington see "Biographical Notes," Darlington Papers, NYHS; Jeffrey Pasley, "*The Tyranny of Printers": Newspaper Politics in the Early American Republic* (Charlottesville: University of Virginia Press, 2001), 320–29, regarding his close friend James J. Wilson. Plumer, Jr., believed the Constitution "was universally considered as leading to the gradual abolition of slavery, even in the old States, and as furnishing no excuse for its extension to the new." *AC*, 16th Cong., 1st Sess., 1437, 1439 ("kingly government"). For elaboration of Plumer's arguments, see Wilentz, "Jeffersonian Democracy."

42. Thomas Jefferson to John Taylor, February 13, 1821, Taylor Papers, NYHS; this letter is reprinted in Ray W. Irwin, "Documents on the Origin of the Phi Beta Kappa Society," *WMQ* 19, 4 (October 1939): 476–78. See also George William Van Cleve, *A Slaveholder's Union: Slavery, Politics, and the Constitution in the Early American Republic* (Chicago: University of Chicago Press, 2010), 265. On Jefferson and Missouri, see Peter S. Onuf, "Thomas Jefferson, Missouri, and the 'Empire of Liberty,'" in *Thomas Jefferson and the Changing West: From Conquest to Conservation*, ed. James P. Ronda (Albuquerque: University of New Mexico Press, 1997), 111–53; and Peter S. Onuf, *Jefferson's Empire: The Language of American Nationhood* (Charlottesville: University of Virginia Press, 2000), 109–46.

43. Holmes in *AC*, 16th Cong., 1st Sess., 988. Glover Moore argued that the Federalists galvanized northern attention to the Missouri debates. See *The Missouri Controversy*, 67, 83, 106–7. This view has been refuted in more recent literature. See Leonard Richards, *The Slave Power: The Free North and Southern Domination, 1780–1860* (Baton Rouge: Louisiana State University Press, 2000), 52–82; Mason, *Slavery and Politics*, 177–212; Hammond, *Slavery, Freedom, and Expansion*, 150–68; Forbes, *Missouri Compromise*; Wilentz, "Jeffersonian Democracy," Wilentz, *The Rise of American Democracy: Jefferson to Lincoln* (New York: Norton, 2005), 218–53.

44. "Resolutions of the Republican Members of the New York Legislature, February 14, 1816" (filed under "Speeches"), V. Birdseye to John W. Taylor, March 13, 1816 ("as a Republican & as a man"), Taylor Papers, NYHS. Caleb Tompkins, a New York congressman and the vice president's brother, was conveniently absent for the final vote on Missouri statehood. Richards, *The Slave Power*, 83–85.

45. Mason, *Slavery and Politics*, 177–79; Adams, Entry of February 20, 1820, *Memoirs*, 4: 529.

46. Story on Virginia patriotism and signing himself a Virginian: Joseph Story to Jacob Crowinshield, January 25, 1805 and January 4, 1806, Crowinshield Papers, Peabody Essex Museum, Salem, Mass., as cited in Gerald T. Dunne, *Justice Joseph Story and the Rise of the Supreme Court* (New York: Simon and Schuster, 1970), 21–22; "southern clime": Story to Nathaniel Williams, *Life and Letters*, 1: 105–6.

47. New York Manumission Society (Cadwallader Colden et al.) to John W. Taylor, February 23, 1819, Taylor Papers, NYHS; *Speech of the Honorable James Tallmadge . . .* (New York: Conrad, 1819); Isaac M. Ely to John W. Taylor, November 30, 1819, and February 22, 1820; Salma Hale to John W. Taylor, December 27, 28, 1819, Taylor Papers, NYHS.

48. "At a Meeting of the Freeholders of the County of Oneida" (filed in correspondence, under "O"), Josiah Goodall to Taylor, August 24, 1819, Taylor Papers, NYHS; *AC*, 16th Cong. 1st Sess., 947.

49. John Hurter to Thomas J. Rogers, January 15, 1820, Dreer Collection, Box 15 Folder 11, HSP; for Rogers's vote, see *AC*, 16th Cong., 1st Sess., 1587. Jeffrey Pasley cites later attacks on

Rogers that accused him of voting against restriction. He did not, but he did later vote for the 1821 compromise that admitted the new state of Missouri despite the proscription of free black migrants in its Constitution; see *"Tyranny of Printers"*, 346 and Forbes, *Missouri Compromise*, 118, 123–24.

50. William Jones to Jonathan Roberts, May 27, 1812, February 3, 1820, Roberts Papers, HSP.

51. Jonathan Roberts to Matthew Roberts, February 16, 1820, commenting on the Jones letter; Eliza Roberts to Jonathan Roberts, January 20, 1820; Jonathan Roberts to Eliza Roberts, January 25, 27, April 4, 1820, Roberts Papers, HSP.

52. *Aurora General Advertiser*, January 4, February 12 ("Political Agriculture"), 1820. Duane began addressing the Missouri debates in 1819. See *Aurora General Advertiser*, March 5, November 23, December 7, 1819, as cited in Kim Phillips, "William Duane, Revolutionary Editor," Ph.D. dissertation, University of California, Berkeley, 1968, 537; see also *Weekly Aurora*, March 15, November 22, 29, December 6, 13, 20, 27, 1819. See also Mason, *Slavery and Politics*, 78–80, 101, 136, 144, for Duane's prior post-War of 1812 attacks on slavery.

53. *Aurora General Advertiser*, February 24, 29, 1820; see also March 2, 1820, for an additional letter to Pennsylvania congressmen.

54. Garnett to John Randolph, February 22, 1820, Randolph-Garnett Letterbook, LC.

55. Darlington in *AC*, 16th Cong., 1st Sess., 1381; Entry of February 8, 1820, William Darlington Journal, NYHS; *Aurora General Advertiser*, January 4, 1820; Entries of November 17, December 2 1819, Journal L, 123, 132, John Gallison Diaries, 1807–1820, MHS; "At a Numerous Meeting of the Citizens of Boston . . . to Consider the Subject of Restraining the Further Extension of Slavery," Box 1819, MHS. Gallison is identified as the author of these resolutions by George Ticknor; see *Proceedings of the Massachusetts Historical Society* 2nd ser. 7 (1891–1892): 119–20. The Boston resolutions were reprinted in *Boston Commercial Gazette*, December 6, 1819; the subsequent memorial drawn up for Congress was printed as *A Memorial to the Congress of the United States, on the Subject of Restraining the Increase of Slavery in New States to be Admitted into the Union* (Boston, 1819).

56. And presumably in the state of Louisiana, where the national government, John Sergeant argued in Congress, made allowance for slavery not because it was inherently right to do so, but on principles of political necessity (*AC*, 16th Cong., 1st Sess., 1194, 1214).

57. *AC*, 16th Cong. 1st Sess., 952, 965–66. See also Mason, *Slavery and Politics*, 189–90; Richards, *The Slave Power*, 77, 80–81.

58. Story to Edward Everett, May 7, 1820, *Life and Letters*, 1: 366–68; Plumer in *AC*, 16th Cong., 1st Sess., 1436–37.

59. Jones to Roberts, February 3, 1820, Roberts Papers, HSP.

60. Fourteen northerners joined the South on March 2 to concur with the Senate in striking out the restriction of slavery in the Missouri bill. The final vote was 90 in favor of concurring, 87 opposed. Four other northern members absented themselves during the vote, notably Caleb Tompkins, older brother of Vice President Daniel D. Tompkins. No southern member voted in favor of restricting slavery in Missouri. The 36°30' line was adopted by a vote of 134–42; 37 of the nay votes came from Southerners and 18 from Virginians. *AC*, 16th Cong., 1st Sess., 1586–1588. For the legislative details, see Moore, *Missouri Controversy*, 84–102.

61. Jefferson to Holmes, April 22, 1820, Jefferson Papers, AMLC. For a detailed analysis of Holmes, see Matthew Mason, "The Maine and Missouri Crisis: Competing Priorities and Northern Slavery Politics in the Early Republic," *JER* 33, 4 (Winter 2013): 675–700.

62. Jonathan Roberts to Eliza Roberts, January 13, 1820 ("Hartford men"); Jonathan Roberts

to Matthew Roberts, February 16, 1820 ("genius of our government"; "baffle the factions"; "spoild child"); February 21, 1820 ("harmony & union"); February 25, 27, 1820 ("ultra federalists"); April 29, 1820.("constitutionally this cannot be made out"). See also Jonathan Roberts to Matthew Roberts, January 23, 27, 1820 on his prior opposition to Pinkney. For a detailed rendition of Roberts's evolution, see Forbes, *Missouri Compromise*, 75–81.

63. Henry Meigs to Josiah Meigs, May 30 1819 ("Aristo Feds"); January 8, 23, 1819 (on his love of Jackson); February 25, 1819 (Clinton's "intrigues with government"); July 24, 1818 (on suffering: "I do most earnestly endeavor, never to forget that all is right, and I do commonly succeed in the preservation of reasonable contentment"); May 2, 1819 ("Governments answer"); October 11, 1819 ("instruments of God"), Meigs Papers, NYHS. Meigs's speech on Missouri is in *AC*, 16th Cong., 1st Sess., 942–47; on Meigs and patronage, see Richards, *The Slave Power*, 83, 123–24.

64. *AC*, 16th Cong., 1st Sess., 1113–14; see also mention of Meigs's plan on 1108. Forbes, *Missouri Compromise*, suggests that Meigs's proposal may have been genuine, especially considering that his father was Commissioner of the Land Office (68, 95, 304 n.15). John Quincy Adams, in contrast, believed it was "an apology to his constituents for voting against the restriction" (Entry of February 5, *Memoirs*, 4: 518). My view is that Meigs took his proposal seriously, but that it was grandiose and improbable, much like his fears of a Federalist aristocracy. In a letter to Joseph D. Hay in February 1820, he wrote the following:

"The Missouri question has put on an aspect which alarms me for our common welfare. And I have on severe reflection arrived at the conclusion that it concerns us all, as soon as possible to agree in some grand national effort to eradicate the whole cause of dissention, slavery. With that view I have introduced the resolution which you have seen.

"My plan is to consecrate to the redemption of slaves & colonizing them comfortably, in Africa, 500 millions of acres, west of the Mississippi. When I first introduced the resolution, not more than 30 or 40 rose in favor. On the next call which I made there arose 66 members in favor. In a day or two I will call it up again & I have reason to believe it has gained friends.

"I wish that instead of quarrelling about an existing evil, we should make at once the most magnificent effort ever recorded, in favor of human liberty—the devotion of 500 millions of acres, worth $100,000,000 to that object alone!

"I have turned an eye towards the River Zaire in Lat. 6° South, on [the] Western Shore of Africa as the best place for colonizing. It is 2000 miles distant from the Arabs, whose ferocious habits would always prove injurious if not destructive to such plantations as should invite to attack by their prosperity!" Henry Meigs to Joseph D. Hay, February 12, 1820, Brock Collection, Box 266 #18, HL. For a detailed assessment of this letter in terms of the politics of colonization, see Wood, "Considerations of Humanity," 340–44.

65. Henry Meigs to Josiah Meigs, July 11, 1820, May 6, July 1, 1821, Meigs Papers, NYHS.

66. Jonathan Russell to Jarvis, January 19, 1822, copy or draft, Jonathan Russell Family papers, 1792–1863, MHS.

67. "The Voice of Freedom," by "Wilberforce," Broadside Collection, NYHS. The broadside was written to support DeWitt Clinton's 1820 gubernatorial campaign. See Van Cleve, *A Slaveholder's Union*, 258–60.

68. Many southerners based their opposition to restriction on federalism, arguing that each state should have the equal right to decide on the question of slavery for itself. Congressional restriction of slavery in Missouri would limit Missouri's rights as a state in comparison to the other states, and thus undermine the federal union. Northerners argued that Missouri could not

be considered an independent state until admitted to the Union by Congress, and that during the process of admission, Congress was justified in restricting slavery there. The truth was somewhere in between. Missouri was not a state in 1820, but the implementation of restriction would happen after it acquired statehood, an ominous threat that Congress might use implied powers drawn from the republican government clause to control slavery in the existing states. See Don E. Fehrenbacher, *The South and Three Sectional Crises* (Baton Rouge: Louisiana State University Press, 1980), 22.

69. *AC*, 15th Cong., 2nd Sess., 1184–91 (Barbour, quotes at 1187, 1188); 1227–35 (McLane, quotes at 1232–33)

70. *AC*, 15th Cong., 2nd Sess., 1188 (Barbour); 1228, 1233–34 (McLane). For the various ethical justifications of slavery expansion in the 16th Congress, see *AC*, 16th Cong., 1st Sess. 1080, 1086 (slaves as family members; love of slaves), 1018 (diffusion will increase chances for emancipation); 1011 (diffusion will lead to better treatment and more food). Barbour had likewise argued that slaves would receive more food in Missouri the previous session, and accused one restrictionist of trying to keep slaves confined east of the Mississsippi, "to prevent their increase, even by shutting them out from food" (*AC*, 15th Cong., 2nd Sess., 1191). Lacy K. Ford argues that the Missouri debates marked the emergence of paternalism as a public defense of slavery (*Deliver Us from Evil*, 202–3). On the weakness of southern ethical defenses of slavery, see Forbes, *Missouri Compromise*, 41. On the contrasting strength of southern political arguments that northerners should not interfere with slavery as an institution, see Fehrenbacher, *The South and Three Sectional Crises*, 23.

71. *AC*, 16th Cong., 1st Sess., 1328, 1014; 15th Cong., 2nd Sess., 1180. William Cooper, *Liberty and Slavery: Southern Politics to 1860* (New York: Knopf, 1983), 99.

72. Entry of January 26, 1820, Adams, *Memoirs*, 4: 532; Entries of February 22, 26, 1820, Darlington Journal, Darlington Papers, NYHS; John W. Taylor to Jane P. Taylor, February 4, 1820, Taylor Papers, NYHS; John Randolph to James Garnett, February 9, 20, 23, 1820, Randolph-Garnett Letterbook, LC. None of Randolph's speeches were recorded in the *Annals*.

73. Entry of January 16, 1820, Adams, *Memoirs*, 4: 506; Story to Stephen White, February 27, 1820, *Life and Letters*, 1: 362–63.

74. This is the classic reading of the referent for "doughface," but see Nicholas Wood, "John Randolph of Roanoke," for a variant reading that argues that Randolph intended to refer to northern restrictionists by the term, as men who masked their true interests (Federalist revival, Clintonianism, northern economic domination) with antislavery arguments. Whatever Randolph did in fact mean, northerners quickly appropriated the term to indict allies of the South. In an 1821 New York congressional race, for example, supporters of Albert H. Tracy composed a pamphlet titled "Beware of 'Dough Faces'" to attack his opponent, Benjamin Ellicott. Describing Ellicott as a southern-born man who admired the South and hated Yankees, the broadside asked, "who can think of the votes of the 'dough-faces' from the north, who introduced slavery beyond the Mississippi, which will now spread over a country of greater extent than the old United States, without horror and shame?" Tracy narrowly won the election. See "Beware of Doughfaces," Broadside Collection, NYHS; "New York 1821 Election for Congress District 22," at "A New Nation Votes: American Electoral Returns, 1787–1825" (elections.lib.tufts.edu). For a version of Randolph's remarks in Congress, see Moore, *Missouri Controversy*, 103–4.

75. *Aurora General Advertiser*, October 26, November 1, 2, 1820. For other examples see *Aurora General Advertiser*, May 8, October 27, 28, 30, 31, November 21, 27, 1820.

76. See Forbes, *Missouri Compromise*, 89, on Duane's grievances against Monroe. Phillips,

"William Duane," identifies Simpson as the author of the Brutus essays, and describes him as "discernibly hypocritical," given "that his true concern was with the sufferings of free labor" (543, 546). Simpson later became a Jacksonian and an early articulator of the idea of the "wage-slave." See his *Workingman's Manual* (Philadelphia: Thomas Bonsal, 1831), 85. See also Wilentz, *The Rise of American Democracy*, 211–13, 245.

77. Not to be confused with longtime Jeffersonian Representative William Findley of Pennsylvania. For examples of antislavery argument on behalf of Hiester, see *Democratic Press*, August 18 and 26, 1820 and *Aurora General Advertiser*, August 26, 29, 1820. Binns had material reasons for opposing Findlay, as he had fallen out of favor with the Governor and lost the state printing contracts. See Philip S. Klein, *Pennsylvania Politics, 1817–1832: A Game Without Rules* (Philadelphia: Historical Society of Pennsylvania, 1940), 100–109.

78. "The Voice of Freedom," by "Wilberforce," Broadside Collection, NYHS; Moore, *The Missouri Controversy*, 182–83; Craig Hanyan with Mary Hanyan, *DeWitt Clinton and the Rise of the People's Men* (Montreal: McGill-Queen's University Press, 1996), 11.

79. See Forbes, *Missouri Compromise*, 123 and Richards, *The Slave Power*, 124.

80. *Democratic Press*, October 20, 1820; see also October 21, 24, November 3, 1803. On the disruption of Duane's meeting, see *Aurora General Advertiser*, October 27, 1820 and *Democratic Press*, November 1, 1820.

81. *Democratic Press*, October 24, 1803

82. John Taylor to Jane Taylor, March 3, 1820; Salma Hale to John Taylor, March 15, November 28, 1820; Isaac Ely to John Taylor, December 23, 1820; Charles G. Haines to John Taylor, November 1820, John Taylor to Jane Taylor, November 11, 1820, Taylor Papers NYHS. For additional comments along these lines, see Moore, *Missouri Controversy*, 139–40. Haines was Clinton's personal secretary. See Craig Hanyan with Mary Hanyan, *DeWitt Clinton and the Rise of the People's Men* (Montreal: McGill-Queen's University Press, 1996), 3.

83. Forbes, *Missouri Compromise*, 125; for southern accolades, see *AC*, 16th Cong. 1st Sess., 1294–95. In a letter to his wife, Taylor noted that even John Randolph was "well satisfied thus far in the manner in the manner in which I have administered the office of Speaker." John W. Taylor to Jane Taylor, December 29, 1820, Taylor Papers, NYHS.

84. John Taylor to Jane Taylor, December 4, 1821; Taylor to [Josiah A.] Harris, December 11, 1845, draft, Taylor Papers, NYHS. This incomplete letter is not signed and refers to Taylor in the third person, but it appears to be in Taylor's hand and demonstrates detailed knowledge of the 1821 Speakership contest as well as Taylor's role in the Missouri Crisis. It is dated from Cleveland, where Taylor was living in 1845, and addressed to "Harris," regarding an article in the "Herald" about the speakership. Josiah A. Harris was editor of the *Cleveland Herald* in 1845.

85. Forbes, *Missouri Compromise*, 125–30; see also Edward K. Spann, "John W. Taylor, The Reluctant Partisan, 1784–1854," Ph.D. dissertation, New York University, 1957; and "The Souring of Good Feelings: John W. Taylor and the Speakership Election of 1821," *New York History* 41 (October 1960): 379–99.

86. Moore, *Missouri Controversy*, 183.

87. Entries of February 20, January 16, 1820, Adams, *Memoirs*, 4: 529, 506.

88. Richard Brown, "The Missouri Crisis, Slavery, and the Politics of Jacksonianism," *South Atlantic Quarterly* 65 (Winter 1966): 55–72.

89. *AC*, 16th Cong., 1st Sess., 1360. Johnson made a similar point in response to John W. Taylor, who had expressed alarm at "this new doctrine—the invasion of State Rights." The doctrine was not at all new, said Johnson, and one had to look no farther than the widespread

protest against the Alien and Sedition Acts for a defense of state prerogative against excessive federal power (1359).

90. According to William Darlington's retrospective account, *Desultory Remarks on the Question of Extending Slavery into Missouri* (Westchester, Pa.: Lewis Marshall, 1856), 24. For the southern argument that the Declaration was not a document of governance, see Wilson, *Space, Time, and Freedom*, 42–43, citing among others Nathaniel Macon of North Carolina, now serving in the Senate. Like Randolph, Macon was a veteran of the early Jeffersonian slavery debates and like Randolph he had always taken a firm stance in defense of slaveholder autonomy. In the midst of imagining the terrors restrictionists would inflict on the South—racial intermixture and black congressmen, if not "the scenes of St. Domingo"—Macon noted that "the words of the Declaration of Independence" formed "no part" of the Constitution, a fact that was "as true as that they are no part of any other book." *AC*, 16th Cong., 1st Sess. (Senate), 227.

91. *AC*, 16th Cong., 1st Sess., 957.

Conclusion. Democracy, Race, Nation

1. See in particular Massachusetts Republican John Bacon's opposition to blanket racial restrictions on American seamen in 1803. *AC*, 7th Cong. 2nd Sess., 467–69

2. *Democratic Press*, November 20, 1820. See also November 14, 1820.

3. See *AC*, 16th Cong., 2nd Sess., 1219–1220; 1223–1224; 1228; 1236–1240. The resolution was proposed by a joint committee of the House and Senate and both Glover Moore and Robert Forbes argue that the resolution was orchestrated if not drafted by Henry Clay, who originally proposed the joint committee and had a hand in its composition. Glover Moore, *The Missouri Controversy, 1819–1821* (Lexington: University of Kentucky Press, 1953), 154–60; Robert Pierce Forbes, *The Missouri Compromise and Its Aftermath: Slavery and the Meaning of America* (Chapel Hill: University of North Carolina Press 2007), 117–18. The vote on the compromise resolution in the House was 87 in favor to 81 opposed. The 81 nays were composed of 1 southerner (John Randolph of Virginia), 18 northern Federalists, and 62 northern Republicans, based on party affiliations from the Congressional Biographical Directory (bioguide.congess.gov), supplemented by "A New Nation Votes: American Electoral Returns, 1787–1825" (elections.lib.tufts.edu)

4. Defenders of black citizenship (with examples of specific arguments cited) included Sergeant (F-Pa.; see *AC*, 16th Cong. 2nd Sess., 530); Storrs (F-N.Y.; 538 on impressment); Strong (F-N.Y.; 574 on military service); Hemphill (F-Pa.; 598, on electing delegates to state ratifying conventions); Mallary (R-Vt., 632–33, citing equality before the law in Vermont, New Hampshire, New York, and Massachusetts); Eustis (R-Mass., 636–37 on military service; "we the white people"); Butler (R-N.H., 988–89 defending black rights in the northern states and the privileges and immunities clause); Cushman (R-Me., 1018, defending black rights abstractly by appeal to the Declaration).

5. William Plumer, Jr., to Margaret Plumer, February 22, 1821, December 1, 1820, Plumer Papers, AHMC, NYHS.

6. See James H. Kettner, *The Development of American Citizenship, 1608–1870* (Chapel Hill: University of North Carolina Press, 1978), 312–13; Rogers M. Smith, *Civic Ideals: Conflicting Visions of Citizenship in U.S. History* (New Haven, Conn.: Yale University Press, 1997), 175–77.

7. *AC*, 16th Cong., 2nd Sess., 616, 617, 620.

8. *AC*, 16th Cong., 2nd Sess., 546–47 (Massachusetts); 625 (Connecticut); 550–51 (Barbour), 557 (Smyth), 993 (Floyd), 1134–35 (Pinckney). All these arguments about black citizenship were

anticipated in the previous session, when McLane of Delaware employed them to undermine the northern claim that the Declaration of Independence intended all men to be equal. See *AC*, 16th Cong. 1st Sess., 1154–55.

9. *AC*, 16th Cong., 2nd Sess., 1136–37; *Democratic Press*, November 25, 1820. On Coxe, see multiple works by Gary Nash: *Forging Freedom: The Formation of Philadelphia's Black Community, 1720–1840* (Cambridge, Mass.: Harvard University Press, 1988); *The Forgotten Fifth: African Americans in the Age of Revolution* (Cambridge, Mass.: Harvard University Press, 2006); "Race and Citizenship in the Early Republic," in *Antislavery and Abolition in Philadelphia: Emancipation and the Long Struggle for Racial Justice in the City of Brotherly Love*, ed. Richard Newman and James Mueller (Baton Rouge: Louisiana State University Press, 2011), 90–117.

10. Nathaniel H. Carter and William L. Stone, *Reports of the Proceedings and Debates of the Convention of 1821, Assembled for the Purpose of Amending the Constitution of the State of New York* (Albany: E. and F. Hosford, 1821), 181, 189–91, 191.

11. Carter and Stone, *Reports on the Proceedings*, 184, 364–65. See also David N. Gellman, *Emancipating New York: The Politics of Slavery and Freedom, 1777–1827* (Baton Rouge: Louisiana State University Press, 2006), 206–13. Tallmadge ran for state senate in New York in the spring of 1819. On April 27, 1819, Theodorous Bailey wrote to Matthias Tallmadge: "Our Election commences this day. There is a prospect of the General's [James Tallmadge's] success—He will get the Quaker votes—the Manumission Society and the People of Color will generally support him" (Tallmadge Family Papers, NYHS). To his credit, Tallmadge did try to persuade the New York Convention to expedite gradual emancipation in the state, but without success (see Gellman, *Emancipating New York*, 212).

12. Pinckney in *AC*, 16th Cong., 2nd Sess., 1143; Jonathan Roberts to Matthew Roberts, November 23, 1820, Roberts Papers, HSP.

13. *AC*, 16th Cong., 2nd Sess., Senate, 351–55, 360–64, 391.

14. Philip S. Klein, ed., "Memoirs of a Senator from Pennsylvania: Jonathan Roberts, 1771–1854," *PMHB* 62, 2 (April 1938): 216; Jonathan Roberts to Eliza Roberts, May 20, 1820, Roberts Papers, HSP.

15. Nicholas Biddle to Charles Jared Ingersoll, Ingersoll Papers, HSP. See also Robert Pierce Forbes, *The Missouri Compromise and Its Aftermath: Slavery and the Meaning of America* (Chapel Hill: University of North Carolina Press, 2007), 118.

16. In the Southard papers at Princeton University are multiple copies of a pamphlet entitled *A Short Statement of Facts Connected with the Conduct of Mr. Southard on what is Usually Called the Missouri Question* (likely 1821, place of publication and publisher unknown). They are still in the original full printed sheet, suggesting Southard had them made to distribute on his behalf (Samuel L. Southard Papers, Princeton University Library).

17. Among many works on the development of white supremacy, see James Brewer Stewart, "The Emergence of Racial Modernity and the Rise of the White North, 1790–1840," *JER* 18, 2 (Summer 1998): 181–17 and Stewart, "Modernizing 'Difference': The Political Meanings of Color in the Free States, 1776–1840" *JER* 19, 4 (Winter 1999): 691–712.

18. *Columbian Centinel*, August 26, 1820, as cited in Moore, *Missouri Controversy*, 288. The *Centinel* drew the quote not from Branagan but from its original source, a stanza in Erasmus Darwin's *The Botanic Garden*, which the *Centinel* slightly revised so that Darwin's lines specifically addressed Missouri. The Randolph reference is to a quote cited in chapter 3 of this book: "Mr. R also observed, that he considered it no imputation to be a slaveholder, more than to be

born in a particular country. It was a thing with which they had no more to do than with their own procreation." *AC*, 9th Cong., 2nd Sess., 627.

19. On this point, see James Oakes, "Conflict vs. Racial Consensus in the History of Antislavery Politics," in *Contesting Slavery: The Politics of Bondage and Freedom in the New Nation*, ed. John Craig Hammond and Matthew Mason (Charlottesville: University of Virginia Press, 2011), 291–303.

20. On the antebellum "decline" of antislavery, see Donald Ratcliffe, "The Decline of Antislavery Politics, 1815–1840," in Hammond and Mason, eds., *Contesting Slavery*, 267–90, and Nicholas Wood, "'A Sacrifice on the Altar of Slavery': Doughface Politics and Black Disenfranchisement in Pennsylvania, 1837–38," *JER* 31 (Spring 2011): 75–106. On the corresponding rise of antislavery politics, I am depending most on James Oakes, *Freedom National: The Destruction of Slavery in the United States, 1861–1865* (New York: Norton, 2012) and Corey M. Brooks, *Liberty Power: Antislavery Third Parties and the Transformation of American Politics* (Chicago: University of Chicago Press, 2016).

21. See, e.g., William Darlington, *Desultory Remarks on the Question of Extending Slavery into Missouri* (Westchester, Pa.: Lewis Marshall, 1856); Joshua Giddings to John Taylor, January 6, 1846 and January 9, 1847, Taylor Papers, NYHS.

22. Frederick Douglass, "The Right to Criticize American Institutions," in *Frederick Douglass: Selected Speeches and Writings*, ed. Philip S. Foner and Yuval Taylor (Chicago: Lawrence Hill, 1999), 81.

23. Frederick Douglass, *My Bondage and My Freedom* (New York: Miller, Orton & Mulligan, 1855), 365, 368; Douglass, "Farewell Speech to the British People," in *Selected Speeches and Writings*, 58.

24. Douglass, "The Right to Criticize American Institutions," 78.

25. David W. Blight, *Race and Reunion: The Civil War in American Memory* (Cambridge, Mass.: Harvard University Press, 2001); Frederick Douglass, "I Denounce the So-Called Emancipation as a Stupendous Fraud," in *Selected Speeches and Writings*, 711–21.

INDEX

ACKNOWLEDGMENTS

I could not have written this book without the aid and support of many people and institutions. First and foremost, I am indebted to a number of teachers and fellow students at the University of California, Berkeley for a remarkable education. I especially want to acknowledge the early and, for me, pivotal influence of Stephen Best, Christopher Nealon, and Kerwin Lee Klein. Robin Einhorn, who was at once mentor, colleague, and example, continues to inspire through her commitment to scholarship and education. I am also deeply obliged to David Henkin, David Hollinger, and Samuel Otter for their help and counsel.

A fellowship from the Massachusetts Historical Society enabled a research trip to Boston that helped me develop this project at an early stage. My deep thanks to Conrad E. Wright. I was fortunate to spend the 2007–2008 academic year working in the archives of the New-York Historical Society and teaching at Eugene Lang College, the New School, thanks to a Bernard and Irene Schwartz fellowship. I am grateful to Nina Nazionale, Ted O'Reilly, Tammy Kiter, Maurita Baldock, Eric Robinson, Joseph Ditta, and Mariam Touba at the N-YHS and David Plotke and Oz Frankel at Eugene Lang College. I completed the penultimate draft of this book during a semester-long fellowship at the Gilder Lehrman Center for the Study of Slavery, Resistance, and Abolition at Yale University, and I would like to thank David Blight, Melissa McGrath, and David Spatz for my time in New Haven.

In addition to the MHS and N-YHS, I am grateful for the many libraries and archives which have made this book possible, especially the libraries of UC Berkeley and Yale University, the Killam Library at Dalhousie University, the Reed College Library, the Library of Congress, the Historical Society of Pennsylvania, the Houghton Library at Harvard University, the Museum of the City of New York, the Rubinstein Library at Duke University, the Huntington Library, and the American Antiquarian Society.

During the years I spent working on this book, I had the privilege to

teach in the History Department at Dalhousie University in Halifax, Nova
Scotia. I am grateful to my colleagues Jerry Bannister, Jack Crowley, and Justin Roberts for their advice and criticism. I thank the administration at Dalhousie for granting me leave in order to write. I thank the students in my
courses for their engagement and their sincere interest in American history.
And I thank my friend and office neighbor Philip Zachernuck for teaching
me how to curl; for me, he remains the heart and soul of the Dalhousie History Department. My greatest intellectual debt in Halifax is to John Munro of
Saint Mary's University, who has helped me think about the concerns of this
book and the historical problem of the United States many times over.

As I developed this manuscript for publication, I benefited from the advice and knowledge of a number of historians. Rachel Hope Cleves, Ariel
Ron, and Christopher Shaw read some version of this book in its entirety and
gave me helpful advice and encouragement. Paul Baines, Paul Polgar,
Gautham Rao, Wendy Wong, and Nicholas Wood generously answered detailed questions or read portions of the manuscript. Every trip I have made to
the Society for Historians of the Early American Republic annual conference
has provoked me to think about this project in new ways. So too have opportunities to present my work at Dalhousie University, Saint Mary's University,
Eugene Lang College, the New-York Historical Society, Princeton University,
and the Gilder Lehrman Center at Yale. I thank James Huston, Andrew
Shankman, Alec Dun, and Jan Ellen Lewis for their formal comments on
conference papers, and too many people to name individually for their challenging questions. I am especially grateful to Corey Brooks, François Furstenberg, John Craig Hammond, Matthew Mason, and Carroll Smith-Rosenberg,
each of whom read the entire manuscript at a late stage and offered detailed
criticism and constructive suggestions for revision. Carroll's engagement
with this project has been so important to me in the last years of writing.

I am deeply obliged to my editors at the University of Pennsylvania Press.
Robert Lockhart was incredibly supportive throughout the editorial process
and I am grateful for his encouragement, patience, and good cheer. Deepak
Patney carefully copyedited the manuscript and Alison Anderson patiently
saw the book through production. The influence of David Waldstreicher's
work will be obvious throughout this book; he also read the entire manuscript twice and offered thoughtful and incisive criticism each time. He has
been a wonderful colleague to me over the last few years.

As I worked on this book I had the support of friends and family, who
helped me intellectually and materially. In particular, I would like to thank

Daniel Geary and his parents, Daniel Riley, Erin Swanson, Georgina Cullman, and Christopher Berry for offering me a place to stay during research trips and providing good company besides. Bibi Obler and Elise Archias have been wonderful friends and colleagues for so many years. Michelle Kuo generously read a draft of this book and shared her own inspiring work. During research and conference travel to Philadelphia, I would often meet with Emily Abendroth, who reminded me of the long-term significance of the problems in this book, and thus of why I needed to write it.

My family have supported this project from the beginning and I would not have been able to complete it without them. I am grateful for my sisters, my brother, and my mother. And I thank my father, Philip Boo Riley, to whom I have dedicated this book; his love of reading and learning has been a constant example to me.

I am so thankful for my partner, colleague, and dearest friend Radhika Natarajan. She has helped me in incalculable ways over the past several years. Her work and her moral intelligence have pushed me to confront the deepest questions in this book. In the difficult times, she always gives me the best advice: "Just write. Just keep writing." And, finally, at the most crucial moment of all: "Stop writing!"